The White Doe of Rylstone

The Cornell Wordsworth

General Editor: Stephen Parrish
Associate Editor: Mark L. Reed
Assistant Editor: James Butler

Advisory Editors: M. H. Abrams, Geoffrey Hartman, Jonathan Wordsworth

An Evening Walk, edited by James Averill
Descriptive Sketches, edited by Eric Birdsall
The Salisbury Plain Poems, edited by Stephen Gill
The Borderers, edited by Robert Osborn
The Ruined Cottage and *The Pedlar,* edited by James Butler
Peter Bell, edited by John E. Jordan
The Prelude, 1798–1799, edited by Stephen Parrish
Home at Grasmere, edited by Beth Darlington
Poems, in Two Volumes, and Other Poems, 1800–1807, edited by Jared Curtis
Benjamin the Waggoner, edited by Paul F. Betz
The White Doe of Rylstone, edited by Kristine Dugas
The Tuft of Primroses, edited by Joseph F. Kishel
The Fourteen-Book *Prelude,* edited by W. J. B. Owen

CENTER FOR
SCHOLARLY EDITIONS
AN APPROVED EDITION
MODERN LANGUAGE
ASSOCIATION OF AMERICA

The White Doe of Rylstone;
or The Fate of the Nortons
by William Wordsworth

Edited by

KRISTINE DUGAS

CORNELL UNIVERSITY PRESS

ITHACA AND LONDON

THIS BOOK HAS BEEN PUBLISHED WITH THE AID OF A GRANT FROM THE
COLLEGE OF THE HUMANITIES OF THE OHIO STATE UNIVERSITY.

PUBLICATION OF THIS BOOK WAS ASSISTED BY A GRANT FROM THE
PUBLICATIONS PROGRAM OF THE NATIONAL ENDOWMENT FOR THE HUMANITIES,
AN INDEPENDENT FEDERAL AGENCY.

First published 1988 by Cornell University Press.

Printed in the United States of America

Library of Congress Cataloging in Publication Data

Wordsworth, William, 1770–1850.
The White doe of Rylstone, or, The fate of the Nortons.

(The Cornell Wordsworth)
I. Dugas, Kristine Ann. II. Title. III. Title: Fate of the Nortons. IV. Series:
Wordsworth, William, 1770–1850. Selections. 1988.
PR5868.A2D84   1988   821'.7   87-9265
ISBN 0-8014-1946-8

The Cornell Wordsworth

The individual volumes of the Cornell Wordsworth series, some devoted to long poems, some to collections of shorter poems, have had two common aims. The first has been to bring the early Wordsworth into view. Wordsworth's practice of leaving his poems unpublished for years after their completion, and his lifelong habit of revision—Ernest de Selincourt called it "obsessive"—have obscured the original, often the best, versions of his work. These original versions are here presented in the form of clean, continuous "reading texts" from which all layers of later revision have been stripped away. In volumes that cover the work of Wordsworth's middle and later years, bringing the "early Wordsworth" into view means simply presenting as "reading texts," wherever possible, the earliest finished versions of the poems, not the latest revised versions.

The second aim of the series is to provide, for the first time, a complete and accurate record of variant readings, from Wordsworth's earliest drafts down to the final lifetime (or first posthumous) publication. The most important manuscripts are shown in full transcription; on pages facing the most complex and interesting transcriptions, photographs of the manuscript pages are also provided. Besides the transcriptions and the photographs, on which draft revisions may be seen, and an *apparatus criticus* in which printed variants are collected, a third device for the study of revisions is adopted: when two versions of a work match sufficiently well, they are arrayed on facing pages so that the steps by which one was converted into the other become visible.

Volumes in the series are unnumbered, but upon publication their titles are inserted into the list of volumes in print in the order in which the works were written. A more detailed introduction to the series may be found in the first volume published, *The Salisbury Plain Poems*, edited by Stephen Gill.

S. M. PARRISH

Ithaca, New York

Contents

viii   Contents

Preface

Just eight or ten months after reading the thirteen-book *Prelude* aloud to Coleridge through the long Coleorton evenings in the winter of 1806–1807, Wordsworth began *The White Doe of Rylstone; or The Fate of the Nortons,* the poem he came to consider "in conception" his "highest work." *The White Doe* thus closes the "great decade" of poetry, 1797–1807, and links earlier explorations of suffering with an emphasis on the imagination as renovative power. A mixture of genres, it can be looked upon as the last lyrical ballad to be written, yet also as a long narrative poem based on popular legend. It was delivered to the printer in 1808, but the response at private readings made Wordsworth pull it back from publication until 1815.

This volume offers for the first time a full account of the seriocomic history of *The White Doe*'s composition, based on the rich legacy left us in the Wordsworth and Coleridge letters, which demystify much of the poem's enigmatic character. The first complete record of verse and prose draftings in the earliest version, MS. 61 at Dove Cottage, is presented, as well as the initial draftings for the prefatory poem, "In trellis'd shed," and the earliest surviving versions of the concluding poem, *The Force of Prayer.* Most important, this volume offers for the first time all surviving portions of the version of *The White Doe* that went to the printer in 1808. About half of the original text, previously thought to be lost, actually survives, and the remainder of the poem can now be reconstructed by analysis of the manuscripts. Readers will thus be able to appraise the character of Wordsworth's original intentions and follow the conflicts that ensued. Full transcriptions of changes made in 1808, when publication was still thought to be imminent, are presented in the context of their composition, which represents an interestingly skewed replay of earlier controversies that Wordsworth and Coleridge had fought out over *Lyrical Ballads.* This textual reconstruction and the history of composition animating it are intended to make the poem more accessible to readers and to illuminate some of the conflicts between intention and execution which lie behind it.

As a third-generation editor of the Cornell "syndicate," I learned many tricks of the trade reading proof on earlier editions, whose editors I here thank. In addition, Mark Reed, James Butler, and Jared Curtis generously shared their knowledge with me. Carol Landon, Karen Green, Beth Darlington, and Robert Osborn, along with Marta Emmitt, treated me to many delightful hours in Grasmere, Keswick, Lancashire, and London. Warmest thanks go to Stephen Parrish, general editor and friend, who introduced the Wordsworth texts and the Lakes to me, with special recognition to Barbara Salazar of Cornell University Press for her expert editorial skill. All of us know them for their years of dedicated work on these texts.

Thanks are also owing to J. C. C. Mays for the verification of some Coleridge handwriting and to Keith Moore, Adela Pinch, and Carol Dole for checking the *apparatus criticus*. I am grateful to Robert Kirkpatrick for sharing some of his early work on *The White Doe*, and later for allowing me to make use of the printer's copy for the second edition, in his possession. A critical edition of printed versions of *The White Doe* by Alice Pattee Comparetti provided many useful annotations. Most regrettably, the lively wit and helpfulness of the late Peter Laver, librarian in Grasmere and resident poet, will be very sadly missed by all of us who work on the Wordsworth texts.

Preparation of this volume was made possible by the Trustees of Dove Cottage, who allowed me access to the Wordsworth Library manuscripts and authorized their publication. Photographs of the main texts appear through the courtesy of Drs. Robert Woof and Terry McCormick of the Grasmere and Wordsworth Museum. Michael Halls and the late Peter Croft of King's College Library in Cambridge; Eleanor Nicholes, formerly in charge of Special Collections in the Wellesley College Library; and the entire staff of the Rare Books Collection of Cornell University Libraries were unfailingly helpful to me. Photographs of the King's College manuscript of *The White Doe* and the citations of its text are published by the courtesy of the Provost and Scholars of King's College; material from the Royal Library at Windsor Castle appears through the gracious permission of Her Majesty Queen Elizabeth II. A subvention and grants from the Ohio State University College of the Humanities and the Publications Program of the National Endowment for the Humanities aided in the publication of this volume. I remain grateful to the National Endowment for the Humanities and the Cornell University Department of English for generously supporting my travel and research. Finally, in the production of this book as in all things, I am indebted to the never-failing humor of my husband, Jeff Yokota, who always knows what to say when.

KRISTINE DUGAS

Ithaca, New York,
and Cleveland, Ohio

Abbreviations

APC	Alice Pattee Comparetti, ed., *The White Doe of Rylstone* (Ithaca, 1940).
Chronology: MY	Mark L. Reed, *Wordsworth: The Chronology of the Middle Years, 1800–1815* (Cambridge, Mass., 1975).
DC MS.	Dove Cottage Manuscript (revised numbering, 1785–1850).
De Q	Thomas De Quincey.
DW	Dorothy Wordsworth.
EY	*Letters of William and Dorothy Wordsworth: The Early Years, 1787–1805*, ed. Ernest de Selincourt (2d ed., rev. Chester L. Shaver; Oxford, 1967).
F.Q.	Edmund Spenser, *The Faerie Queene.*
JC	John Carter, Wordsworth's secretary at Rydal Mount.
Knight	William Knight, ed., *The Poetical Works of William Wordsworth* (11 vols.; Edinburgh, 1882–1889).
LB	*Lyrical Ballads.*
LY, I, II, III	*The Letters of William and Dorothy Wordsworth: The Later Years, 1821–1850*, ed. Ernest de Selincourt (2d ed., rev., arranged, and ed. Alan G. Hill; Oxford, 1978, 1979, 1982).
Marrs	Edwin W. Marrs, Jr., ed. *The Letters of Charles and Mary Anne Lamb* (3 vols.; Ithaca, 1975–).
Memoirs	Christopher Wordsworth, *Memoirs of William Wordsworth* (2 vols.; London, 1851).
MW	Mary Wordsworth.
MY, I, II	*The Letters of William and Dorothy Wordsworth: The Middle Years, 1806–1820*, ed. Ernest de Selincourt (2 vols.; 2d ed.; Part I, 1806–1811, rev. Mary Moorman [Oxford, 1969]; Part II, 1812–1820, rev. Mary Moorman and Alan G. Hill [Oxford, 1970]).
OED	*Oxford English Dictionary.*
PW	*The Poetical Works of William Wordsworth*, ed. Ernest de Selincourt and Helen Darbishire (5 vols.; Oxford, 1940–1949; rev. 1952–1959).
STC	Samuel Taylor Coleridge.
STCL	*Collected Letters of Samuel Taylor Coleridge*, ed. E. L. Griggs (6 vols.; Oxford, 1956–1971).

WD   William Wordsworth, *The White Doe of Rylstone; or The Fate of the Nortons* (London, 1815).

Whitaker   Thomas Dunham Whitaker, *The History and Antiquities of the Deanery of Craven* (London, 1805)

WW   William Wordsworth.

The White Doe of Rylstone

Introduction

I. History of Composition

In a letter dated 19 July 1807, Dorothy Wordsworth told Catherine Clarkson about part of a trip that took the Wordsworths (probably between 6 and 10 July) "to Otley and up the Wharf as far as Bolton Abbey . . . in the most beautiful valley that ever was seen . . . a retired woody winding valley, with steep banks and rocky scars, no manufactories" (*MY*, I, 158). During the months that followed, William conceived "a plan" for a new poem, again revealed by one of Dorothy's letters, this one to Jane Marshall, from Grasmere, 18 October 1807:

I cannot express how much pleasure my Brother has already received from Dr. Whitaker's Books [*The History of the Original Parish of Whalley, and Honour of Clitheroe* (1801) and *The History and Antiquities of the Deanery of Craven* (1805)], though they have been only two days in his possession— Almost the whole time he has been greedily devouring the History of Craven, and, (what is of more importance) he has found all the information which he wanted for the prosecution of his plan. [*MY*, I, 167–168]

That plan would culminate in *The White Doe of Rylstone; or The Fate of the Nortons*, a long ballad of triumph over suffering, in which the heroine's ability to endure loss is set against a headstrong pursuit of symbols superstitiously invested with significance. This pursuit, brought about by her father's confusion of the material with the spiritual world, leads to death and war; while Emily's communings with memories of past love in the form of a white doe, which is both an imaginative symbol and a material presence, lead to a solitary transcendence of permanent loss.

In gratitude for the books, sent to Kendal from New Grange (just southeast of Bolton) by the Marshalls at William's request, Dorothy transcribed an early version of "the story of young Romelli and the Strid," in which "endless sorrow" is eventually softened by the consolations of time. This poem, *The Force of Prayer; or The Founding of Bolton Priory*, which would serve as a companion piece to *The White Doe*, details the origins of the priory eventually used by the Nortons. It was erected as a physical expression of Lady Romilly's grief for the loss of her son, who drowned after his hound checked

3

his leap across the river Strid. Dorothy writes that William, having written the poem "about a month ago, [offers the] short one . . . in the [mean]time" in lieu of the longer, adding, "but that is a foolish phrase for it may be many months before the poem he is now writing is finished, and many more before it is *published*."

Dorothy's gentle irony succinctly anticipates the compositional history of *The White Doe*—a history of revision, hesitancy, and delay. Here she was having fun at William's expense; some six months later she would write to him in exasperation to "pluck up your Courage" and publish the thing. It would be "but a *little trouble*" for him, while financial pressures made it impossible for the Wordsworth women to "go on so another half-year." "Without money," Dorothy implored, "what *can* we do . . . [but] work the flesh *off our poor bones*" (*MY*, I, 207).

If Dorothy's uncompromising rebuke seems out of character, William's response to his friends' criticism of the poem was not. Bruising arguments with Coleridge and Lamb, moral indignation, and self-justifications characterize the history of this outwardly tranquil poem. The controversy struck a chord peculiarly deep, for no other poem has left so rich a legacy of heated detail in the Wordsworths' personal correspondence. Clearly at work was something more formidable than the usual anxieties about publishing and defensiveness in the face of criticism. It is perhaps the disparity between the poem's tranquil surface and the events concerning it that makes this poem unlike any other Wordsworth wrote. The events suggest a partially un-raveled seam that we might pull to reveal what lies at the poem's center. Along with an increasingly hortatory stance and a particularly moral tone to his defense of the imagination, the poem and the events surrounding its reworkings evince Wordsworth's frustration at the difference between the representations of ideas and of actions, the problems of intention and ex-ecution, and the morality of the use of imaginative symbols. It may be that in the contradiction sustained by being utterly "different from any other poem" Wordsworth had written and yet, by his own reckoning, "in concep-tion the highest work" he ever produced, the poem in its largest context is also unexpectedly revealing.

In no other poem did Wordsworth invest so much explication, and per-haps none aroused in him so much frustration. It was one of the few poems he published in quarto, and he did so "to show the world his opinion of it" (*Chronology: MY*, p. 602n). In addition to the prefatory matter, Wordsworth appended extensive notes on his historical and balladic sources. The legend of the doe, the history of the principal characters, and the ballad on which the poem was based deserve consideration for what Wordsworth chose to incorporate, exclude, or invent.

After he had formed a plan for a new poem based on the legend of the white doe, Wordsworth turned to a borrowed copy of Thomas Dunham

Whitaker's *History and Antiquities of the Deanery of Craven*. In his published notes, Wordsworth quotes only a part of what he must have gleaned from the book. For example, he uses Whitaker's account of the hostility between the Nortons and the Cliffords suggested in the poem's first canto. "In particular," Richard Norton "seems to have been a turbulent man, violently addicted to the old religion." Norton tower was said to have been built by him; it remained as "a monument of the old warfare" between the two clans. After the ascension of James I, when Rylstone became a possession of the Cliffords, "the same ground" was "enclosed for a park" and visited by a white doe, which "the aged people of the neighbourhood" used to say made "a weekly pilgrimage from [Rylstone] over the fells" to the churchyard of Bolton Abbey during the service.

Yet Whitaker's most teasing paragraph was one Wordsworth chose not to reproduce in his notes. The tradition of the doe's journey, Whitaker wrote,

awakens the fancy. Shall we say that the soul of one of the Nortons had taken up its abode in that animal, and was condemned to do penance, for his transgressions against "the lords' deere" among their ashes? But for such a spirit the Wild Stag would have been a fitter vehicle. Was it not then some beautiful and injured female, whose name and history are forgotten? Had the milk-white doe performed her mysterious pilgrimage from Ettrick Forest to the precincts of Dryburgh or Melrose, the elegant and ingenious editor of the Border Minstrelsy would have wrought it into a beautiful story.   [Whitaker, 382–383]

It seems to have been Whitaker, then, not Wordsworth or the legend, who explicitly related the Nortons to the doe; who suggested its feminine character and its relation to a single injured female; who contrasted her character with that of a wild stag; and who brought in Walter Scott, the editor of the *Border Minstrelsy*, as a model author.

If Wordsworth found the germ of his poem in Whitaker's fanciful musing, Emily Norton was Wordsworth's own conception. Both Whitaker and the histories Wordsworth consulted state that Norton had nine daughters, some of whom were directly involved in the uprising, none of them Protestant. Several were married to men who had also been fomenters of the rebellion, and the aftermath of that rebellion saw bloody reprisals. But Wordsworth decided not to incorporate this wholesale slaughter in his poem. It would not have gone well with the harmonizing mood of the final canto, and would have detracted from Emily's image as a type of all sufferers, her loss universalized, her figure the exemplar of endurance. The record of actual suffering is thus suppressed in favor of an idealized account. Conversely, Wordsworth fleshed out Richard Norton for his own purposes. Neither Norton's momentary despondency nor his eloquent speeches are found in the sources; he is given a kind of tragic stature in maintaining the spirit of the rebellion which is not historically accurate. And although the histories provide few details of his character, the ballad "The Rising of the North" represents him as a man eager to join the fray—but that eagerness is attributed to fealty to his overlord, Thomas Percy, Earl of Northumberland, not to religious zeal, as Wordsworth has it. Moreover, Norton's dying plea to Francis to safeguard the standard is Wordsworth's own conception, as is the importance of the standard itself. While the historical sources and the ballad mention the Nortons' banner, no account of its origin is given, and it does not play a role in the ensuing conflict. Finally, the old man who was Norton's friend and Emily's erring counselor is also Wordsworth's own, and a felicitous invention, allowing Wordsworth to narrate the material action of the tale at one remove so that he could downplay external events and set them against the actions of the heroine of his tale. Thus in all these adaptations, and despite the many plots and subplots of intrigue available to him, Wordsworth clearly preferred a subtler drama of principles in which the language of religion offered symbols capable of being transformed according to his own vision.

Wordsworth indicates that it was not the history of the insurrection that drew him to the project. Impressed by Bolton Abbey and fascinated by the legend, he developed his tale out of its balladic origins. The long opening exchange in "The Rising of the North" between the insurrectionist Earl of Percy and his "fair leddie" focuses on their love rather than the coming war. The Countess Percy counsels her lord and pledges to ride with him to the court to be "his faithful borrowe." Their intimacy seems to have been the inspiration for the closeness between Francis and Emily, which lies at the heart of Wordsworth's poem. Wordsworth had another source for details of his narrative, though he fails to give it credit. His published note quotes three pages verbatim from Bishop Thomas Percy's note on "The Rising of the North" in his *Reliques of Ancient English Poetry* (see pp. 150–152, below). The historians that Wordsworth seems to say he consulted for these details (Stowe, Speed, Camden, Rapin, and Carte) are listed by Percy, though to them Wordsworth adds William Guthrie (*A General History of England*). But it is only in a collective portrait that the ballad and the histories provide us of Norton's sons, Christopher, Francis, and William, that we find the mold of Wordsworth's Francis. In the histories, it is Norton's son William who repudiates the rebels and refuses their armor, accompanying the band only for his father's sake, while Francis is drawn into battle unwillingly, joining up in response to his father's anger. (William is later accused of collaborating with the rebels, but is eventually acquitted of wrongdoing.) It is only in the ballad that Francis pledges to follow his family "naked and unarmed," a pledge Wordsworth incorporated into his poem. Thus the elaboration of Francis's motives, his pessimism, pacifism, dream vision and fated unconscious flight with the standard are all Wordsworth's conceivings.

Where history contradicted evolving poetry, then, Wordsworth followed his instincts, writing to Francis Wrangham in February 1819, "As to the Nortons the Ballad is my authority, and I require no more. It is much better than Virgil had for his Aeneid" (*MY*, II, 524). As early as mid-1808 he knew that the Nortons had not been executed—that all but one of them had fled safely to Flanders. It was Walter Scott who had, unsolicited, offered this information, which made the "popular tradition . . . totally groundless."[1] Wordsworth replied:

Thank you for the interesting particulars about the Nortons; I shall like much to see them for their own sakes; but so far from being serviceable to my Poem they would stand in the way of it; as I have followed (as I was in duty bound to do) the tradition-ary and common historic records — —. Therefore I shall say in this case, a plague upon your industrious Antiquarianism that has put my fine story to confusion.— [*MY*, I, 237]

As for the uprising itself, Wordsworth follows the common account. Clearly, the heart of Wordsworth's poem was its origin not in fact but in legend, in what people commonly believed. In that belief lay the proof of their imaginative powers. Unlike Scott, Wordsworth was "duty bound" to the imaginations of "the people"; and thus his poem, rather than being "shut up for the studious," demanded harmonizing in accord with a higher standard of truth than material fact. It is this higher standard that helps set off *The White Doe* as the supreme representative of Wordsworth's epitaphic mode.

Dorothy Wordsworth's exasperated letter about the family's need for money was written in late March 1808; the earlier chronology was more placid. By 8 November 1807 William could read "the Introduction" (proba-bly the first canto, as there is no evidence that an introduction as such ever existed) to De Quincey, who was "delighted" by it.[2] By 2 December 1807 William had, according to Dorothy, "written above 500 lines of a new poem. A Tale, very beautiful." From the first, it must have been considered a major undertaking, because in the same letter she wrote that "he has not yet done half of it" (*MY*, I, 179). On the first of December William had left for a month's stay at Stockton-upon-Tees, where, according to one of the notes he dictated to Isabella Fenwick in 1843, he composed the "earlier half" of the poem. By 3 January it had a provisional title and, at more than 1,200 lines, was thought to be nearly finished. Again our authority is Dorothy, this time in a letter to Lady Beaumont:

My Brother has seized upon the Book [Izaak Walton's *Compleat Angler*] for his own reading this night, as he fancies that the imagery and sentiments accord with his own

---

[1]H. J. C. Grierson, ed., *Letters of Sir Walter Scott* (12 vols.; London, 1932–1937), III, 161.

[2]John E. Jordan, *De Quincey to Wordsworth: A Biography of a Relationship* (Berkeley, 1962), pp. 89–90.

train of thought at present, in connection with his poem, which he is just upon the point of finishing . . . ; it is in irregular eight-syllable verse, and will be called *a Tale*. I certainly misled you when I said that it would be a sort of romance, for it has nothing of that character; yet it is very different from any other poem that my Brother has written.   [*MY*, I, 187]

As much as a week before Dorothy's letter, Wordsworth had "fixed upon the day of his finishing" it to write to Sir George Beaumont, "but, as he said, having waited so long, he would now wait till the work was done." It is hardly surprising that Sir George had to wait considerably longer. On the 18th Wordsworth wrote Walter Scott that "with many interruptions" he had "written a narrative Poem of about 1700 lines," having finished it two days before (*MY*, I, 191). Even though it was not until a letter dated the following February that the poem was referred to by its eventual title, plans for publication were already in progress. Dorothy wrote Catherine Clarkson: "William has finished his poem of the White Doe of Rylston or The Fate of the Nortons and it will probably be sent to the press in less than a month." It was to be published in quarto, at 100 guineas for 1,000 copies. And then she added what would prove to be perhaps the single most important factor in Wordsworth's hesitancy and outright recoil—the long delay that led not only to the work's withdrawal from publication but eventually to its transformation into a substantially different poem—"Before he publishes it he intends to send the Manuscript to Coleridge" (*MY*, I, 192).

In the intervening three weeks, the Wordsworths "had such alarming accounts of the state of our poor Friend Coleridge's health that [William] has determined to go up to London to see him, and if he be strong enough, to endeavour to prevail upon him to return with him to this Country." In this harried letter of 23 February to Jane Marshall, Dorothy urgently requested that the manuscript of *The White Doe*, sent to the Marshalls to be sent to Dr. Whitaker, be forwarded instead "immediately by the Coach to London . . . and as Wm will be in London himself he wants to push the printing, and to correct the press himself" (*MY*, I, 198–199). "Forward the Poem," Dorothy entreats, "(if it be yet in your hands, and if more than four days delay is likely to arise from its going to Dr. Whitaker) forward it directed to my Brother at the Courier Office, Strand, London." The mini-odyssey of the manuscript, in view of its subsequent history, here proleptically transforms future agonies into farce. Not only specific instructions but insurance against contingencies had to be orchestrated from a distance, and no one knew who controlled the manuscript: "We have written to Dr. W. to beg him to send the M.S. to London if he has it," the hope being that "tomorrow's post will bring a letter from you with news of the safe arrival of the Poem." Like William's fears that a capitulation to criticism would destroy the integrity of his poem, the fears that *The White Doe* would be battered about half of

England proved to be imaginary: Dorothy sheepishly wrote the next day that Southey had made off with it nearly a week before. And like the pain of conceiving and reconceiving the poem, the pitch of emotions was intense on all sides of the conflict, with twists no one had expected.

In the farcical mini-odyssey, neither Southey's whereabouts nor those of the poem were strictly known. Dorothy continued:

Mr. Southey left Ambleside last Tuesday but one, took the M.S. with him, and intended to take the Coach from Kendal to Leeds. I have this day had a note from Mrs. Coleridge, wherein she says "Southey did not go to Leeds but went by Liverpool"—and not a word from him about the M.S.—and we have had no letter from him. I think he must have taken it with him to London, knowing that my Brother intended to have it printed as soon as Dr. W. had seen it. It is true he may have forwarded it by the Leeds coach from Kendal, and if so, I hope you have received it. I wrote a note to you last night telling you the melancholy cause of my Brother's sudden departure to London; and desiring you to forward the M.S. to him there if it were not already with Dr. W. I *hope* Southey has taken it to London; though I am heartily vexed that you should have so much plague for nothing; however your loss respecting the reading of the poem is not much, for it is much pleasanter to read a printed book than a Manuscript, and my Brother intends to send you a Copy as soon as ever it is printed.   [*MY*, I, 199–200]

Jane Marshall would, like Sir George Beaumont, have to wait a bit longer. As for Thomas Whitaker, who had already received two bogus entreaties about a manuscript he had twice been promised and had still not set eyes on, Dorothy was obliged to send him one more letter, probably containing yet another unfulfilled pledge. Presumably the manuscript found its way to London—whether by post or hand-delivered by Southey we do not know. But the problems were only beginning. Besides the loss of anticipated pleasure by the poem's readers and the persistence of monetary "vexations" articulated less politely, heated reactions and tortured recoil were destined to produce sharp words and unexplainable actions, some of which caused wounds that would not heal for years.

In London the manuscript met with an indifferent reception at best. From the first, Wordsworth read the poem only to those he thought would appreciate it: De Quincey, for instance, who had already heard the "Introduction," now heard "the whole." Against any more public reading Wordsworth was adamant. When he finally did give way under repeated pressure, he was stung by a response even sharper than he had feared. Witness his account to Coleridge, written 19 April 1808, where he was still hotly defensive twelve days after his return from London—some three weeks after the incident itself.

In compliance with frequent entreaties I took the MSS to Lamb's to read it, or part of it, one evening. There unluckily I found Hazlitt and his Beloved; of course, though I had the Poem in my hand I declined, nay absolutely refused, to read it. But as they were very earnest in entreating me, I at last consented to read one Book, and when it was done I simply said that there was a passage which probably must have struck Hazlitt as a *Painter* 'Now doth a delicate shadow fall' etc, and mentioned that Sir G. Beaumont had been greatly pleased with it. We then had a short talk about that part and nothing more took place. As to the reception which the Doe has met with in Mitre Court [home of the Lambs] I am much more sorry on Lamb's account than on my own. I had no wish that they should see the Poem by an act of private courtesy on my part, because as I knew it could not please them, I did not think that I had the right to subject them to the disagreeable feeling of owing to my kindness this sight of a Work which they could not approve of.   [*MY*, I, 221]

It is clear that Wordsworth had already given considerable thought to the kind of audience he would (and would not) appeal to. He was here beginning to give name to the distinction between the vulgar and unimaginative reading public and the people—simple but feeling, sensitive, and reflective—which he would develop explicitly in the *Essay, Supplementary to the Preface*, and which is present in an inchoate form in the 1800 Preface to *Lyrical Ballads*. This distinction first appears explicitly in a letter of February 1808 to Sir George Beaumont:

I am afraid that the sale of Peter [*Peter Bell*] would not carry the expense of the Engraving, and that the Poem in the estimation of the public would be a weight upon the Print. I say not this in modest disparagement of the Poem, but in sorrow for the sickly taste of the Public in verse. The *People* would love the Poem of Peter Bell, but the *Public* (a very different Being) will never love it.

As the letter continues, a nexus of concerns emerges which were apparently not easily separable in Wordsworth's mind. Primarily they link the heart and the people to (his) poetic greatness, the imagination to (his) hortatory function—linkages that eventually struck both Coleridge and Lamb as overtly self-interested. They assumed a formula for art which, given the author's personal investment, was less pure than Wordsworth was willing to admit. Wordsworth continued:

What then shall we say? Why let the Poet first consult his own heart as I have done and leave the rest to posterity; to, I hope, an improving posterity. The fact is, the English *Public* are at this moment in the same state of mind with respect to my Poems, if small things may be compared with great, as the French are in respect to Shakespear; and not the French alone, but almost the whole Continent. In short, in your Friend's Letter, I am condemned for the very thing for which I ought to have been praised; viz., that I have not written down to the level of superficial observers and unthinking minds. — — Every great Poet is a Teacher: I wish either to be considered as a Teacher, or as nothing.   [*MY*, I, 194–195]

The comparison with Shakespeare, here modestly suggested, was apparently less cautiously advanced in other encounters, and probably played a role in the treatment his poem later received from the Lambs, who seem to have been spoiling to deflate their guest. Certainly the openly derisive reception accorded the informal reading of *The White Doe,* along with a less than enthusiastic response to other poems Wordsworth thought highly of—such as the 1807 volumes, *Peter Bell,* and *Benjamin the Waggoner*— confirmed his insistence on the increasingly hortatory, often meditative-religious bent to his poetry evidenced in some of these works, in *The Excursion,* and in many of the later revisions of *The Prelude.* It was as if, goaded by the poor reception of poem after poem, Wordsworth had been pushed toward defining, even limiting, his objectives. He insisted on valuing what he found devalued, even to the exclusion of a range of previous concerns.

In this atmosphere of frustration, the problem of intention was centrally involved. The burning letter to Coleridge continues:

I also told Lamb that I did not think the Poem could ever be popular first because there was nothing in it to excite curiosity, and next, because the main catastrophe was not a material but an intellectual one; I said to him further that it could not be popular because some of the principal objects and agents, such as the Banner and the Doe, produced their influences and effects not by powers naturally inherent in them, but such as they were endued with by the Imagination of the human minds on whom they operated: further, that the principle of action in all the characters, as in the Old Man, and his Sons, and Francis, when he has the prophetic vision of the overthrow of his family, and the fate of his sister, and takes leave of her as he does, was throughout imaginative; and that all action (save the main traditionary tragedy), i.e. all the action proceeding from the will of the chief agents, was fine-spun and inobtrusive, consonant in this to the principle from which it flowed, and in harmony with the shadowy influence of the Doe, by whom the poem is introduced, and in whom it ends.   [*MY,* I, 221–222]

The inner motivations of the main characters terminate in spiritual or intellectual catastrophe as a result first of the misuse and then of the eventual purifying use of imagination. That made *The White Doe* a poem for thinking people, a poem that invited—even demanded—a reflective response from its readers as part of its teaching function. As a poem about the imagination, it stimulated, or was intended to stimulate, the imaginations of readers, who were invited directly into the "action" of the poem, "to finish" the poem, "this picture," for themselves. The mutual exercise of power by poet and people is mirrored in the relations of the doe as living epitaph and the tale as enduring epitaph with the townspeople, whose imaginations continue to evolve the legend's meaning for themselves.

To allow for this mutual exercise of power, Wordsworth felt that he had to suggest motivation unobtrusively. In a lyrical ballad, a genre he had defined for himself, either the voices in the ballad spoke for themselves or the narrative voice implied their action. The result, at least in part implicitly dramatic, was aided by the lyrical compression of the form. But *The White Doe* was yet another blending of genres. As a long, specifically narrative poem, the last lyrical ballad forfeited much of its implicitly dramatic power. And *The White Doe* was an experiment, an attempt to call forth an imaginative response as strongly as it presented the imagination as subject, and in doing so, to share power and sensitivity with "the people." Moreover, Wordsworth's minimizing of a previously successful artistic tactic, as a conscious rejection of the mode of his balladic source and his own earlier experiments in the genre, was part of a movement toward what he considered his poetic maturity.

In his irritation with what he considered Lamb's utter (and perhaps congenital) misunderstanding of these intentions, Wordsworth not only castigated Lamb's failings as a reader but articulated his belief that his own artistic stance was new. It was based on foundations he assumed he shared with Coleridge:

Let Lamb learn to be ashamed of himself in not taking some pleasure in the contemplation of this picture, which supposing it to be even but a sketch, is yet sufficiently made out for any man of true power to finish it for himself— As to the principal characters doing nothing it is false and too ridiculous to be dwelt on for a moment. When it is considered what has already been executed in Poetry, strange that a man cannot perceive, particularly when the present tendencies of society, good and bad, are observed, that this is the time when a man of genius may honourably take a station upon different ground. If he is to be a Dramatist, let him crowd his scene with gross and visible action; but if a narrative Poet, if the Poet is to be predominant over the Dramatist,—then let him see if there are no victories in the world of spirit, no changes, no commotions, no revolutions there, no fluxes and refluxes of the thoughts which may be made interesting by modest combination with the stiller actions of the bodily frame, or with the gentler movements and milder appearances of society and social intercourse, or the still more mild and gentle solicitations of irrational and inanimate nature. But too much of this—of one thing be assured, that Lamb has not a reasoning mind, therefore cannot have a comprehensive mind, and, least of all, has he an imaginative one.   [*MY*, I, 222–223]

The criticism that *The White Doe* lacked action was one that Coleridge would level in a more sophisticated way slightly more than a month later in a sharply ironic reversal of the two poets' differences over *The Ancient Mariner*. For the moment, the irony was gentler, and Wordsworth's was partly self-parodic. Immediately following this heated dismissal of Lamb's mental powers, Wordsworth signed "Farewell, most tenderly yours." That sign-off, however, boded ill, for the passionate tone of his letter indicates that Wordsworth expected intimate accord with Coleridge on matters they had already extensively discussed. In their earlier parting of ways over *The Ancient Mariner*, Coleridge had been the one to require a precipitating "Action" in his poem, and Wordsworth had supplied the poem's principal act—the shooting of the albatross. Clearly Wordsworth felt justified in expecting Coleridge's approbation as he moved toward Coleridge's camp. But Coleridge thought differently, and his response helped to change not just the timetable for publication but the tale itself.

More had happened in London than Wordsworth's letter to Coleridge indicates, and some of it he seemed to want to suppress. In a letter written to Francis Wrangham just the day before he wrote Coleridge, he said of his trip only that his "sole errand to London was to see Coleridge who had been dangerously ill, and is still very poorly" (*MY*, I, 213). But a lengthy letter from Coleridge written on 21 May 1808, recapitulating events and agreements made between the two men in London, makes clear that William had talked with Thomas Norton Longman and had set his terms as Dorothy had originally revealed them, but that he was now wavering, and that Dorothy knew it. Dorothy offers confirmation in her letter of 28 March to Catherine Clarkson:

I wonder whether [William] read his poem to you. I *hope* he did; for I am sure you would be delighted—nay that is too cold a word, *enraptured* with it, and may perhaps have had some influence in persuading him to publish it, which he very much dislikes now that it comes to the point, though he left us fully determined. I can never expect that poem, or any which he may write to be immediately popular, like The Lay of the Last Minstrel; but I think the story will help out those parts which are above the common level of taste and knowledge, and that it will have a better sale than his former works, and perhaps help them off.   [*MY*, I, 203]

Within three days, Dorothy was privy to more distressing information, and she wrote immediately to Coleridge, enclosing a letter for her brother which he did not, however, see until Coleridge's letter to him of 21 May. Part of her letter survives only as Coleridge copied it:

We are exceedingly concerned, to hear that you, William! have given up all thoughts of publishing your Poem. As to the Outcry against you, I would defy it—what matter, if you get your 100 guineas into your pocket? Besides it is like as if they had run you down, when it is known you have a poem ready for publishing, and keep it back. It is our belief, and that of all who have heard it read, that the *Tale* would bear it up—and without money what *can* we do? New House! new furniture! such a large family! two servants and little Sally![3] we *cannot* go on so another half-year; and as Sally will not be

---

[3]The Wordsworth women had taken in Sally Green, one of the children orphaned when George and Sarah Green, bewildered by night mist and snow, fell down a scree while returning from the Langdale valley. See Dorothy Wordsworth, *George and Sarah Green—A Narrative*, ed. Ernest de Selincourt (Oxford, 1936).

fit for another place, we must take her back again into the old one, and dismiss one of the Servants, and work the flesh *off our poor bones*. Do, dearest William! do pluck up your Courage—overcome your disgust to publishing—It is but a *little trouble*, and all will be over, and we shall be wealthy, and at our ease for one year, at least.   [*MY*, I, 207]

Owing to her own literary convictions and to pressing domestic realities, Dorothy had a perspective her preoccupied brother could not share. To her and to the family, on whom the delay weighed heavily, this was no time to languish over poetic sensitivities: economic realities overruled her usual tolerance of William's all-too-characteristic fibrillations of the ego. The delay reflected badly on him, since many people knew the work was completed, and many others had been promised copies. But open defiance was hardly characteristic of William, especially before publication, and sometime before Dorothy's letter arrived, he effected a compromise, at least partly because Sara Hutchinson had become gravely ill. Before he left London, he let Coleridge understand himself to have authority to complete negotiations with Longman and to make necessary corrections in the manuscript. But it was not clear what constituted a necessary correction. The three principals—Dorothy, William, and Coleridge—all had different ideas. About a month later, on the first of May, Dorothy once more wrote to Coleridge. Again, the letter survives only as Coleridge copied it.

We are very anxious that 'the White Doe' should be published *as soon as possible*—if you would simply mention the passages, to which you object, without attempting to alter them, it would be better. . . . Our main reason (I speak in the name of the Females) for wishing that the Poem may be *speedily* published, is that William may get it out of his head; but further we think that it is of the *utmost importance*, that it should come out before the Buz of your Lectures is settled. The alterations, we trust, will not be of a difficult or troublesome kind.   [*MY*, I, 230–231]

If Dorothy did not trust Coleridge, William trusted him even less. Although his letter is no longer extant, William wrote to Longman by 18 May (and possibly before) to prevent publication in a way that implied that Coleridge had been acting without authority. Coleridge's injured letter of 21 May says much. It begins:

At 8 o/clock this evening I received a note from the Longmans' in consequence of one from you to them—I have been hunting for your Sister's Letter, as yet to no purpose; but as I put it up with many others from Grasmere, in some one or other of my repositories, I shall be sure to find it before this can go off to you; & will leave a space for her words concerning the Poem. At present, I can only state how I understood, and what I believe to be the substance of, them.

After stating his major criticisms of the poem, Coleridge offered certain "Accidents" to remedy its defects; they accorded at least in part with Lamb's notions. Coleridge continued: "But after my receipt of your Letter concerning Lamb's censures I felt my courage fail—and that what I deemed a harmonizing would disgust you, as a *materialization* of the Plan, & appear to you like insensibility to the power of the history in the mind." Then, taking great pains so as to appear not to give offense, Coleridge allowed his reasoning to become complexly involuted. Disarmingly, he used the very terms of the poem he was speaking about:

Not that I should have shrunk back from the mere fear of giving transient pain & a temporary offence, from the want of sympathy of feeling & coincidence of opinions—I rather envy than blame that deep interest in a production, which is inevitable perhaps, and certainly not dishonorable to such, as feel poetry their calling and their duty, & which no man would find much fault with if the Object, instead of a Poem, were a large Estate or a Title—it appears to me to become a foible then only, when the Poet denies or is unconscious of, it's existence. But I did not deem myself in such a state of mind, as to entitle me to rely on my opinion when opposed to your's—

Coleridge first cast Wordsworth as an Emily Norton manqué, expected to transcend the momentary pain of well-intended criticism, and then invoked Wordsworth's moral and intellectual dismissal of Lamb, the arch-unsympathetic reader, to imply that this very criticism could be applied to Wordsworth himself if he did not take these mild censures in the right spirit. Coleridge suggested how incongruous Wordsworth's repugnance toward a "materialization" of his poem seemed when his desire to push publication was so obviously motivated by the need for money. And he strongly implied that Wordsworth was so preoccupied with defending his lofty poetic calling and transcendent poetic subject that he was unconscious of his own tortured interestedness as a human subject—so much so that he had become unaware of the ironies this unconsciousness provoked. At one level, the paragraph is a barely disguised rebuke, cold in its manipulation of real events and poetic fictions, powerful because it is so politely self-effacing.

The attack once mounted, in mid-sentence Coleridge launched into a Mad Hatter's digression, singular in its wit, intended first to be amusing and then perhaps to evoke pity. Part of this digression is too entertaining to exclude here:

. . . —from the heat & bustle of these disgusting Lectures, for which I receive whole Hods full of plaister of Paris-flatteries about as pleasant to me as rancid large Spanish Olives—these on the one side—& permanent hatred, and the most cruel public Insults on the other—& all this to cost me at least sixty £, exclusive of Lodgings. . . . —2. the necessity of publishing the substance of my Lecture on national Education in

a very enlarged form, in order to obviate the charge made against me, most un-
provokedly, in a very large Company . . . of 'base cowardice'—& even this was not the
severest sentence of his most solemn & yet most wanton attack. —3. for the sake of
money, I am at the same time employed every spare hour in a complete '*Rifacciamen-
to*', or '*Umarbeitung*', of the *Geist der Zeit*. . . . —I not only add a long Preface, but
throughout by notes or marked Interpolations, joined to softenings, omissions, and
the lowering of the dytherambic style prevalent in the original, make almost a new
work. . . .

Yet we may wonder whether Coleridge's plight is being brought forward to
characterize the troubles endemic to a writer's life, his reactions to his diffi-
culties being exemplary behavior, designed to teach and to instruct. The
servile flattery that is the inverse of just criticism is neither pleasant nor
useful, and Wordsworth could not claim to be alone either in receiving
insults or in being pressed for money. Coleridge implied that Wordsworth
was better off than his long-suffering collaborator, who was (by the way) at
work revising certain of his own texts despite these complications. The
upshot was that Coleridge bore these trials, as Wordsworth should have
done, cheerfully and alone. Yet such humiliations were only the start of his
troubles; he had endured physical disabilities, melancholia, and outright
public betrayal by family and friends:

4. In getting out of a boat at Som[r]set stairs, the little Boy stirred it, & I half turning
round to bid him be still, had the misfortune of falling backward, & struck the back of
my head on the very part, on which I fell at Malta. . . . —This produced the whole
next day such a shuttle-like motion from the part horizontally to my forehead with
such odd confusion, that I was unable to give the Lecture—& it returns every now
and then tho' but for a few seconds, if ever a Thought agitates me or a sudden Sound.
—5. I have been sorely vexed in the failure of my plan of increasing my assurance,
after I had procured all the money necessary. . . . I had set my heart & hope upon it:
and the refusal made me very melancholy. 6. Among other wicked calumnies, & in
addition to my Brother's shameful Usage of me, John Wedgewood & his family have
shamefully abused me. . . . —These have all conspired to prevent sorer anguish from
going to rest, as a slight Breeze will keep up the working of a ground-swell; and a
mere atom of Dirt occasion wounds to rankle—

The climax (and the return to a grammatical sentence) is Coleridge's
protestation of innocence in the most conciliatory, almost obsequious tones:

From most of these causes I was suffering, so as not to allow me any rational confi-
dence in my opinions, when contrary to your's which had been formed in calmness
and on long reflection; then I received your Sister's Letter—stating the wish, that I
would give up the thought of proposing the *means* of correction, and merely point out
the things to be corrected—which as they could be of no great consequence, you
might do in a day or two, & the publication of the Poem, for the immediacy of which

she expressed great anxiety, be no longer retarded—assigning a reason. —Now the merely verbal *alteranda* did appear to *me too* very few, & trifling—from your letter on L[amb] I concluded that you would not, from your own opinion, have the Incidents & Action interfered with—& therefore I sent it off—but soon retracted it, in order to note down the single words & phrases that I disliked in the books after the two first—as there would be time to receive your opinion of them during the printing of the two first, in which I saw nothing amiss except the one passage, we altered together, & the two Lines which I scratched out, because *you* yourself were *doubtful;* & Mrs. Skepper had told me, that *she* had felt them exactly as *I* did—namely, as interrupting the spirit of the continuous tranquil motion of the White Doe—

Coleridge then expressed his anxiety lest the "decaying of genial Hope" and the "recurrence of fears, which had harrassed you at Racedown" should be behind the family's urgency. He went on, somewhat turgidly, about his fears that Dorothy's judgment "should be in danger of *warping,* from money-motives in affairs, which concern—if not your *fame*—yet your thereto introductory *reputation*—& which too by expediting or retarding the steady establishment of your classical Rank would affect, of course, even your average pecuniary Gains—." He offered Wordsworth a "very warm & zealous patronage" from a "fast ripening" plan of his own—what would ultimately turn out to be *The Friend.* Having claimed to have written out the last two hundred lines or so of the third book of *The White Doe,* either "on the mere possibility of a genial mood coming upon me, in which I should either see the whole *conduct* of the Poem in the light, in which you & she see it," or the chance that "such a flash of conviction concerning the excellence of *my own* imagined amendment, as would SETTLE me," Coleridge added that he once more "sent it off, in order that it might be *advertised* as *in* the Press, about the time, when I gave my Lecture on your System & Compositions."[4]

Ostensibly fearing that *The White Doe* would be taken as an imitation of Walter Scott's *Lay of the Last Minstrel,* Coleridge did not, however, send "the little preface, in which my name was, because I know, that the Public are quick-witted in detecting the most hidden thing that can be made a topic of chit-chat Scandal." Reasoning, first, that people mistook the meter of *Christabel* to be the same as that in Scott's poem; second, that Wordsworth had claimed that his meter imitated Coleridge's; and third, that Wordsworth referred to his poem as being in manuscript before the publication of *The Lay of the Last Minstrel,* Coleridge feared that Wordsworth's preface would "appear strange and almost *envious* . . . [if not] *invidious,* and a covert attack on Scott's Originality." Whether these were indeed his motives for holding

---

[4] F. I. Griggs notes that "no such lectures were given" (*STCL,* III, 111n). A search for the 200 original lines of Wordsworth's that Coleridge copied out has failed to turn them up.

back the preface we do not know, but those, pleaded Coleridge, were the sum of his alterations.

Coleridge had one more point to make about the poem's meter, and it, too, touched on tensions between the two men. After first praising *The White Doe* as a poem "so peculiarly your's, and beyond any other *in rhyme* illustrative of your characteristic excellences," he expressed "something like the same suspicion that you entertained concerning Xtabel, how far this would or would not be an obstacle to it's popularity." What Coleridge was driving at remains obscured by the ambiguity of reference. The obstacle referred to seems to have been the "rather dramatic than lyric" meter, "i.e. not such an arrangement of syllables, not such a metre, as acts a priori and with complete self-subsistence . . . but depending for it's beauty always, and often even for it's metrical existence, on the *sense* and *passion*." The "sense" was one "that demands thought in the Reader, & will not leave him to a lax free-will." But was the problem primarily the meter, or was it Wordsworth's more generally entertained "suspicion"? Wordsworth's opposition to *Christabel* applied to *The Ancient Mariner* as well; he felt that the poems were too removed from common humanity. Wordsworth felt that *Christabel* specifically, by Coleridge's account, "was in direct opposition to the very purpose for which the Lyrical Ballads were published—viz—an experiment to see how far those passions, which alone give any value to extraordinary Incidents, were capable of interesting, in & for themselves, in the incidents of common Life" (*STCL*, I, 631).

If Wordsworth's "suspicion" about *Christabel* was different from his opposition, we have no more explicit statement by either poet which might link that opposition to questions of popular acceptance. Coleridge may have been ironically playing off the more lurid elements of his poem (which ought to make it the more popular) against the absence of anything like them in Wordsworth's. Elsewhere he seems to have been responding to Wordsworth's rather crude disparagement of the dramatic in pointing out that the meters of both poems are inherently dramatic, and that the sense and the passion that Wordsworth had always associated with the pleasure that is the poet's means of teaching are also integral parts of *The White Doe*, the author's defense of his new stance notwithstanding. Like Coleridge's earlier maneuver, this one seems designed to bring Wordsworth back to the human realm—to point out that, as it stood, *The White Doe* strayed too far from humanity, or at least Wordsworth's articulation of his intentions did.

At any rate, Coleridge's ambiguous "this," which locates the problem of the poem's popularity, appears to be linked to Lamb's criticism. Immediately after the phrase that contains it, Coleridge writes:

Lamb & Miss Lamb, who evidently read it—he twice thro', he said—with no genial effort, no exertion from sympathy, are for the very reason that disqualifies them as

Judges concerning it's *true merit,* no unfair Specimens of perhaps the majority of readers of Poetry, especially in the perusal of a new Poem, which does not employ the common excitements of lively interest, namely, curiosity, and the terror or pity from unusual external Events & Scenes—convent dungeons &c &c—.

Meter aside, both *Christabel* and *The Ancient Mariner* integrally employ curiosity and pity, and Coleridge juxtaposes Lamb's criticism with his discussion of *Christabel* to evoke both men's past practice in the *Lyrical Ballads* as a tempering gesture. Once again arguing whenever possible from a previous Wordsworthian position, using Wordsworth's own words, Coleridge points to *Salisbury Plain* as well, a poem that also uses lurid incidents to excite its readers, and in *The Ruined Cottage* to the story of Margaret, a woman who suffers without the possibility of an unearthly transcendence. Her suffering unambiguously belongs within the human realm, and the narrative imbues that suffering with dramatic power. Coleridge continues:

I beg to be understood solely as referring to *the Public,* not *the People,* according to your own distinction—and this only for a while—and chiefly influenced by the wish, that two publications should not succeed each other, both failing in their *first general* Impression—& perhaps in some measure, by comparing it's *chances* of immediate Sale with the almost *certainty* of the great popularity of either Peter Bell, or Margaret, or even the Salisbury Plain—

Whatever their theoretical differences, Coleridge was plainly trying to return Wordsworth to the sources of his previous power, and to temper some of the rigidity in his response to his critics. Although at another level Coleridge was also justifying his own actions, and could never wholly free himself of their rivalry, he was trying not only to mediate between Wordsworth and his critics but to save Wordsworth from himself, to prevent him from languishing unread in a moralistic empyrean he had increasingly identified with the people, the heart, and the imagination, and had invested with unconscious egotism.

But that was on a larger scale. More immediately, Coleridge hoped to introduce a saving materiality to what appeared to be a flawed poem. He attempted a further healing gesture, lest he had offended both his friends, and once again pointed Wordsworth back to what he felt was Wordsworth's own more flexible past, a time when poetic intention and execution were guided as much by what was as by what ought to be:

God forbid, your Sister should ever cease to use her own Eyes and heart, and only her own, in order to know how a Poem *ought* to affect mankind; but we must learn to see with the Eyes of others in order to guess luckily how it *will* affect them— Neither do I *wish* her to learn this; but then I would have her learn to entertain neither warm Hopes or confident Expectations concerning Events dependent on minds & hearts

BELOW the distinct Ken of her Sympathies. Let her only reflect that (even *excluding* the effect of Routs & continued personal gossip, &c &c, yet) the great majority of the modern Buyers of new Poems read at least so whole *Novels* of 2, 3, 4, 5 Volumes each, for ONE poem   You have slightly mentioned this in the Preface to the L.B.—but it deserves to be dwelt on at length—.

And so Coleridge concludes:

In fine, I did it for the best—the extracts on the next leaf will shew what grounds I had for taking it as granted, that the speedy Publication of the White Doe had been decided on at Grasmere—the first extract shews your Sister's opinion & feeling, for and from herself—and as the next [the letter of 1 May] was written since your return, & expresses the same opinion, and as I had not received any letter to the contrary from you—nor had any reason to expect one—I coincided with her, that the speedier the better, & for her reasons—I was concerned, not at her opinion, but at the anxiety that seemed to have influenced it, from the very beginning.   [*STCL*, III, 107–113]

By his reckoning, Coleridge stood not as an obstacle to publication but as a facilitator—rebuffed. Whether or not Wordsworth felt him to be disloyal in the struggle against such scoffers as Lamb, it is likely that the possibility of tamperings he could not control unnerved him, while the need for changes he alone could make was becoming increasingly clear. We also should not underestimate the resentment that must have colored Wordsworth's responses to Coleridge during this period. He had anxiously raced to London fully expecting Coleridge to be near death, and instead found him less than seriously ill and often drunk. Given the highly charged atmosphere of the London visit, Wordsworth must have reasoned from the relative cool of Grasmere that the best thing to do was to pull the poem back completely, regain his self-confidence, and make crucial judgments concerning it at a more judicious ease.

But whatever Coleridge's increasingly tense relationship with Wordsworth contributed to the disaster, he does seem to have been caught in a cross fire that should have been exchanged directly between William and Dorothy, in a situation exacerbated by the bemused reaction of the Lambs, which, more than any other evidence we have, appears to have been responsible for William's recoil. The vehemence of his response suggests that their incomprehension touched something deep within him. It is hard to believe that their criticisms did not rankle, given the intensity with which he expressed his morally indignant scorn some three weeks after the exchange. It is not as though he were unprepared for a cool reception: he anticipated that the poem "could not please them." However, the manner in which they expressed their dissatisfaction may have burned more deeply than its substance. The Lambs later treated the production as an occasion for wit-play; that superciliousness must have erupted at the time rather more unpleasantly. Charles Lamb's letter of 28 April 1815 to Wordsworth—complete with tellingly conciliatory strokes and an elaborate *mea culpa*—jestingly recalls the earlier disagreement. The occasion was the 1815 publication of Wordsworth's *Poems,* in which *The Force of Prayer* appeared (publication of the revised *White Doe* would soon follow). Here is Lamb:

Young Romilly is divine, the reasons of his mothers grief being remediless—I never saw parental love carried up so high, towering above the other **Loves—.** Shakspeare had done something for the filial in Cordelia, & by implication for the fatherly too in Lears resentment—he left it for you to explore the depths of the maternal heart—. I get stupid, and flat & flattering—whats the use of telling you what good things you have written, or—I hope I may add—that I know them to be good—. Apropos—when I first opened upon the just mentioned poem, in a careless tone I said to Mary as if putting a riddle "What is good for a "bootless bean"?" to which with infinite presence of mind (as the jest book has it) she answered a "**shooless pea.**"— It was the first joke she ever made.   [Marrs, III, 147–148]

Here, perfectly deadpan, Lamb miniaturizes the previous controversy, jokingly pitting his risible materiality against Wordsworth's solemn answer to the "riddle" of *The Force of Prayer.* It was not exactly flattery to compare *The Force of Prayer,* an insignificant seventy-odd-line poem, with Shakespeare's tragedy. We may wonder whether this was a private parody of an earlier opinion, dating from that first February reading of *The White Doe.* On 26 February 1808 Lamb had written Thomas Manning this quip: "Wordsworth the great poet is coming to town. He is to have apartments in the Mansion House. He says he does not see much difficulty in writing like Shakspeare, if he had a mind to try it. It is clear then nothing is wanting but the mind. Even Coleridge a little checked at this hardihood of assertion" (Marrs, II, 274–275).

Wordsworth's testiness toward the dramatic as a genre and as a literary mode seems to stem in part from needling he must have received about his pretensions to write as well as Shakespeare, dramatist and poet of the popular imagination. Was *The White Doe* an attempt to do in narrative, in Wordsworth's poetic maturity, the kind of thing he had tried to do in drama with a possibly more searching mind in *The Borderers?* Eventually, in 1836, he annexed these famous lines from *The Borderers* for his narrative experiment, prefixing them to the poem as a way to introduce it.

> Action is transitory—a step, a blow,
> The motion of a muscle—this way or that—
> 'Tis done; and in the after-vacancy
> We wonder at ourselves like men betrayed:
> Suffering is permanent, obscure and dark,
> And has the nature of infinity. . . .

At any rate, the poem is a work of his maturity, with only *The Waggoner* coming between its composition and that of the 1805 *Prelude,* which he had read night after night to Coleridge just a few months before conceiving *The White Doe*. This last lyrical ballad is unique in its conjunction of the problem of suffering, fictional and real, with the post *Prelude* emphasis on imagination. In reworking his ideas of suffering to accord not just with an outcome diametrically opposed to those of *The Ruined Cottage* and his early Shakespearean play but to his now more sophisticated handling of the imagination, Wordsworth needed tactics appropriate to this stand upon different ground. With such tactics he may have hoped to rival Shakespeare as he had rivaled Milton just months before.

In any case Lamb, charmingly dextrous, was by that very dexterity slippery. What did his pirouettes do to a single, apparently flat statement of conviction but undercut a capacity to take it straight? His letter of April 1815 continues:

Joke the 2d I make—you distinguish well in your old preface between the verses of Dr. Johnson of the man in the Strand, and that from the babes of the wood.[5] I was thinking whether taking your own glorious lines—

> And for the **love** was in her **soul**
> For the youthful **Romilly**—

which, by the love I bear my own soul, I think have no parallel in any of the best old Balads, and just altering it to

> And from the great respect she felt
> For Sir Samuel **Romilly**—

would not have explained the boundaries of prose expression & poetic feeling nearly as well. Excuse my levity on such an occasion. I never felt deeply in my life if that

---

[5]Lamb here refers to that part of the Preface to *Lyrical Ballads* (1800) where Wordsworth contrasts Johnson's "superlatively contemptible" parody of a stanza in "The Hermit of Warkworth, A Northumberland Ballad" (found in Thomas Percy's *Reliques of Ancient English Poetry* [4th ed., 1794]) with one of the "most justly admired" stanzas from "Babes in the Wood." Wordsworth countered these lines of Johnson's:

> I put my hat upon my head
> And walked into the Strand,
> And there I met another man
> Whose hat was in his hand,

with the following from "Babes in the Wood":

> These pretty Babes with hand in hand
> Went wandering up and down;
> But never more they saw the Man
> Approaching from the Town.
>   [Marrs, III, 150–151n]

poem did not make me both lately and when I read it in MS. No alderman ever longed after a haunch of buck venison more than I for a Spiritual taste of that white **Doe** you promise. I am sure it is superlative, or will be when *drest,* i.e. printed—. **All** things read **raw** to me in **MS.**—to compare magna parvis, I cannot endure my own writings in that state.[6] The only one which I think would not very much win upon me in print is Peter Bell. But I am not certain. You ask me about your preface. I like both that & the Supplement without exception.[7] The account of what you mean by Imagination is very valuable to me. It will help me to like some things in poetry better, **which is a little humiliating in me to confess.** I thought I could not be instructed in that science (I mean the critical).   [Marrs, III, 148]

Each compliment is double-edged, either ironically by itself (as in "I never felt deeply") or wedged between playful putdowns; the general effect is of a belated general, but not specific, approbation. Again he mixes the material with the spiritual, giving the latter a particularly appetitive flavor. For all his breast-beating and dumb flattery, Lamb has his sport. Seven years earlier the reality of the "great poet" Wordsworth intoning his etherial production must have been provoking. It appealed to the disruptive element in Lamb, as evidenced in this letter of the same year to Southey:

I am going to stand Godfather, I dont like the business, I cannot muster up decorum for these occasions. I shall certainly disgrace the font. I was at Hazlitts marriage & had like to have been turned out several times during the ceremony. Any thing awful makes me laugh. I misbehaved once at a funeral. Yet I can read about these ceremonies with pious & proper feelings—. The realities of life only seem the mockeries.   [Marrs, III, 181]

If we can believe Lamb when he says that his opinion of the poem did improve, it must have been Wordsworth's solemnity that made the occasion of the poem's declamation too "awful" to resist, and so vividly rememberable seven years later. Only with hindsight could Lamb respond properly—or, as his but half-repentant letter to Wordsworth illustrates, properly for Lamb.

A glance at the letters exchanged between the two families reveals that their rapprochement was slow in coming. It is almost three years before we have evidence that Lamb wrote to Wordsworth, in a letter praising *The Essays upon Epitaphs* (Marrs, III, 57–58). The only earlier message we know of, sent more than a year after the London reading, is one ostensibly transmitted through Coleridge, in which Lamb sent the Wordsworths "kind love" and God's blessings. He hoped Wordsworth would send him a copy of *The Con-*

---

[6]Lamb would write some five years later, "There is something to me repugnant, at any time, in written hand. The text never seems determinate. Print settles it" (Marrs, III, 151n).

[7]Lamb refers to the preface to the edition of 1815 and the *Essay, Supplementary to the Preface* (Marrs, III, 151n).

vention of Cintra and asked to "hear from some of you, for I am desolate" (Marrs, III, 12–14). A spate of letters from the Lambs to Dorothy after her visit to them in late October 1810 indicates reconciliation and a growing thaw (Marrs, III, 60–66). But it was not until August 1814, another three years later, that the correspondence from Lamb became regular, almost monthly, after Wordsworth sent him a copy of *The Excursion*, which Lamb praised considerably, as he did the 1815 *Poems* (Marrs, III, 95–97, 111–113, 124–126, 139–141). In his letter of early January 1815 concerning an unsigned review of *The Excursion* which he wrote for the *Quarterly*, he wrote: "I hoped it would make more than atonement" (Marrs, III, 128–130).[8]

No letters from either Dorothy or William to the Lambs from this period survive, so it is impossible to gauge the degree of intimacy they reciprocated.[9] There is only this letter from Lamb on 9 August 1815:

> We acknowledge with pride the receit of both your handwritings. . . . Mary and I felt quite queer after your taking leave. . . . We wishd we had seen more of you, but felt we had scarce been sufficiently acknowledging for the share we had enjoyed of your company. We felt as if we had been not enough *expressive* of our pleasure. . . . We want presence of mind and presence of heart. What we feel comes too late like an after thought impromptu. But perhaps you observed nothing of that which we have been painfully conscious of and are every day in our intercourse with those we stand affected to through all the degrees of love.   [Marrs, III, 173–175]

The language here—careful, conciliatory—seems to mimic the language of *The White Doe,* a poem concerned with the course of chaste love between people of sensitivity, and substantiates (even as it reverses) William's earlier denunciation of their lack of feeling. The rift the poem exposed was not merely between kinds of poetic taste.

If the break with Lamb, more easily mended than the 1810 quarrel with Coleridge, also came more swiftly, Coleridge's influence at the same time was harder to dismiss, especially since he had control of the negotiations for publication. In his aggrieved letter of 21 May 1808, Coleridge's "extracts" that "shew what grounds I had for taking it as granted, that the speedy Publication of the White Doe had been decided on at Grasmere" include Dorothy's letters of 31 March and 1 May as well as Coleridge's own narrative account of his dealings with Longman, part of which reports the agreements

---

[8]The review had, however, been modified beyond recognition by William Gifford (Marrs, III, 128n).

[9]The only exception no longer exists. On 10 December 1808 Mary Lamb wrote to Catherine Clarkson that when Coleridge was "in town" she had received "two letters from Miss Wordsworth which I never answered because I would not complain to her of our old friend." It is possible, however, that Dorothy wrote them before the fireworks at Mitre Court. In any case, Mary Lamb "never . . . explained" her silence to Dorothy (Marrs, II, 289).

the poets had made with Wordsworth's publishers. Having been "assuredly . . . commissioned" by Wordsworth "to retalk" the matter with them, Coleridge did; they "finally agreed to your own terms." Coleridge then promised to send the manuscript "as soon as I had revised it in order to be aware of any little verbal inaccuracies." One reason for Wordsworth's wavering becomes clear: Longman had wanted him to allow his poem to be appraised by "any set of Critics, he chose to appoint." Coleridge hoped to meet the difference halfway, reasoning that while Wordsworth was "quite right" in not acceding to this plan, "on the other hand, that as the question was not the intrinsic merit, but the immediate saleability of the article (for remember, it was not for a Copy-right, but an Edition of 1000) that he had a right to have some clue to guide his calculation."

The solution was one Wordsworth agreed to, and later revoked without Coleridge's knowledge. It was this "solution" that now prompted Coleridge's letter: "I proposed, that you should leave it with me, & leave me plenipotentiary—[which] you did." In executing this power, Coleridge had read aloud nearly a third of the poem, and "explained the *sort* & conduct of the whole" to Longman's partner, Owen Rees, mutually agreed upon by Wordsworth and Longman as arbiter and judge. In response, Longman "acceded to your Terms. . . . I wrote—you exprest no dissatisfaction." Here Coleridge feels obliged yet again to reiterate his decision not to interfere with the body of the tale:

I found the Poem in diction exceedingly correct; but feared concerning the flow of the Interest ab extra—from your letter concerning L. [Lamb], I, tho' agreeing with you fundamentally, in the general principle, yet deduced that you had made up your mind as to the essentiality of the *Business* bearing this, & no other proportion to the internal Action—from many of the circumstances, annumerated in this Letter, I conscientiously did not dare rely on my own persuasions in my so disturbed state of mind—therefore receiving from Dorothy in a letter written May the first, the following . . .

At this point Coleridge inserted his transcription of Dorothy's letter in which she asked that the poem be published as soon as possible and that no alterations be made. But characteristically, Coleridge did not finish the sentence. He concluded lucidly, exasperated and wounded:

Now having promised Mr. Longman, that I would take the trouble of correcting every Sheet—having found so few & so trifling corrigenda or melioranda, in the language, and submitting my own Judgement to your's, as to the general conduct of the Story, I am at a loss to know—in what way the having sent it to the Press, under the conviction, that any trifling *verbal* defects which might remain after *my* revisal, & which would have been removed by your's, could bear no proportion to the pecuniary advantage of having the poem published before the King's Birth-day—how this can deserve that not to me (let that be as nothing; but) not to Montague, or your Brothers, but to the Booksellers you should write to inform them, that I had proceeded without authority—& so much so, that the poem itself was no longer to be intrusted. . . .   [*STCL*, III, 114–115]

The rest of the manuscript does not survive. After eight oversize pages of tightly written script, Coleridge at last expressed his deep sense of personal injury, which seems on the face of it to have been justified; and it may be that William or Dorothy found the pages that followed too painful or too enraging to retain. In any case, these events set the stage for the building of tensions between the two men, which ultimately led to their lasting rift of October 1810, just twenty-nine months away.

Coleridge also had to reply to the letter he received from Longman, by which he learned of Wordsworth's humiliating action. Two days after writing Wordsworth, Coleridge informed the publisher that he was "painfully surprised" by the extract from the letter Wordsworth had sent Longman, which Longman had evidently included in his letter to Coleridge. He recounted his actions to Longman in an "appeal to you, & to common Sense, whether my transmission of the Poem can be deemed a 'misinterpretation' of the above? or whether after having been authorized to negociate, after the result had been confirmed (not to say, received with thanks) and after I had been thus spurred on, it is exactly agreeable with common English to speak of 'Mr. Coleridge's having sent A Mss poem of MINE to you—A!'" (*STCL*, III, 115–116). Closing with a resounding "God bless you, my dear Sir," Coleridge, affecting solidarity with Longman, added this postscript: "'Tis a strange World, Mr Longman!—especially with those, who have to do with Authors!—."

Although we know roughly which of the principals knew what when, the exact date on which Wordsworth wrote to subvert Coleridge's authority is in doubt, his letter to Longman not having survived. But it must have been sometime between 12 and 18 May. Dorothy wrote on 20 April to Lady Beaumont and again on the 22d to Catherine Clarkson that "the Poem is to be published. Longman has consented . . . according to [William's] Demand" [*MY*, I, 225, 228). This agreement was ostensibly an arrangement achieved through Coleridge (although Dorothy does not say so), who on 5 May wrote to his wife, Sara, "having besides all this to prepare William's Poem for the Press" (*STCL*, III, 98). In early May Coleridge wrote to Longman that he would "take upon [himself] the correction of the [proof] Sheets of 'the White Doe'" (*STCL*, III, 99), at which point the arrangement seems still to have been on, since Longman did not respond to the contrary. On 10 May, Dorothy included an oral message from William to Clarkson warning her not to be "in such a bustle of expectation about the poem, he is sure it will not sell, nor be admired more than the [?poems] he has already published"

(*MY*, I, 234). Finally, a letter of Dorothy's written the next day to Jane Marshall perhaps best chronicles the psychological change in William's view of *The White Doe*, his resignation to his readers' attitudes toward it, his growing conviction that certain major changes were necessary if it were to command their interest, and finally his need to learn from a range of readers which portions most provoked criticism:

My Brother was very much pleased with your frankness in telling us that you did not perfectly like his Poem. He wishes to know, what your feelings were—whether the *tale* itself did not interest you—or whether you could not enter into the conception of Emily's Character, or take delight in that visionary communion which is supposed to have existed between her and the Doe. Do not fear to give him pain. He is far too much accustomed to be abused to receive pain from it.

It is interesting here, but perhaps not surprising, that behind Wordsworth's questions are the criticisms and reactions of Lamb and Coleridge. He seems to have taken his critics' responses, however painfully received, to heart, and come round to the inevitability of their reappearance in a wider audience, one composed of "the people" as well as "the public." Although for the moment publication—now mainly "for the sake of the money" only—was still on, it would be off within the week, as it had been for a short time at the end of March. In March, as now, the principal opponent of holding the poem back was Dorothy, whose letter continues:

My reason for asking you these questions is, that some of our Friends who are equal admirers of the "White Doe" and of my Brother's published poems, think that *this* Poem will sell, on account of the Story; that is, that the Story will bear up those parts which are above the level of the publick taste; whereas in the two last volumes, which except by a few solitary individuals, who are passionately devoted to my Brother's works are abused by wholesale.

Dorothy here refers to the very mixed reaction to the recently published *Poems, in Two Volumes* in April 1807. The Wordsworths now felt they were taking a real chance with *The White Doe*, William more than the others, but Dorothy and Mary would not yet allow him his way:

Now as his sole object for publishing this poem at present would be for the sake of the money—he would not publish it if he did not think from the several judgments of his Friends that it would be likely to have a Sale. He has no pleasure in publishing—he even detests it—and if it were not that he is *not* over wealthy, he would leave all his works to be published after his Death. William himself is sure that the *White Doe* will not sell or be admired except by a very few at first; therefore though he once was inclined to publish it, he is very averse to it now and only yields to Mary's entreaties and mine. We are determined, however, if we are deceived this time to let him have his own way in future. [*MY*, I, 236]

He would, however, have his way within the week.

We can now understand just why Wordsworth stopped publication of *The White Doe*. It seems clear that it was not Coleridge's handling of the arrangements with Longman, which were inoffensive by Coleridge's accounting and seem to have amounted to an arbitrative coup. Certainly the details had been approved at least once by Wordsworth himself. Instead, as he became convinced that he ought to revise the poem, and turned from being wounded by criticism to recognizing his need to hear its advocates out, Wordsworth became convinced that publication "as soon as possible" would not be in the poem's or his own best interest. Convinced that he alone could make extensive changes, whether in the tale itself, in Emily's character, or in her spiritual communion with the doe, Wordsworth decided he had to remove Coleridge as "plenipotentiary."

The most charitable reading of Wordsworth's actions is that by alleging that Coleridge had acted without authority, Wordsworth had found a way out of what may already have been a binding contract. At any rate, multiplying tensions between the two men determined subsequent events. In the drafts of a letter to Coleridge written in the same month as the one above (but perhaps never sent), Wordsworth proposed to read calmly rather than "harshly" certain "pernicious" accusations leveled against him. Coleridge's claim that Wordsworth possessed a more than brotherly interest in Sara Hutchinson could have originated only in "a man in a lamentably insane state of mine" whose "habit" it was to give "by voice and pen" an "external existence" to "your most lawless thoughts, and to your wildest fancies" (*MY*, I, 239–245). It is possible that the torn-off portion of the letter of 21 May contained these allegations. In any case, Coleridge rather than Wordsworth was forced to lose face with Longman.

On 17 April 1808 Wordsworth wrote Francis Wrangham that he would send *The White Doe* to him "if I publish it" (*MY*, I, 212), and by the end of May he had decided to pull the poem back. Exactly what timetable did he have in mind? The only other news of *The White Doe* in 1808 is this single line from a letter of Dorothy's to Catherine Clarkson on 5 June: "The poem is not to be published till next winter" (*MY*, I, 253).

It is clear that by the following April, nearly a year later and two years after he had begun the poem, revision was progressing. Sara Hutchinson wrote on the 19th that "William came in to me just now to read some of his additions to the *White Doe* with which he is at present busy."[10] Some delay in commencing revision may have resulted from Wordsworth's difficulty in retrieving the manuscript from London. Between February 20 and sometime in March 1809, De Quincey was asked to get a poem, probably *The*

---

[10]Kathleen Coburn, *The Letters of Sara Hutchinson from 1800 to 1835* (London, 1954), p. 20.

White Doe, from Mary Monkhouse, but it arrived in Grasmere by some other means by 26 March (*Chronology: MY,* p. 409). By the first of May, Dorothy could write to De Quincey:

My Brother has begun to correct and add to the poem of the White Doe, and has been tolerably successful. He intends to finish it before he begins any other work, and has made up his mind, if he can satisfy himself in the alterations he intends to make, to publish it next winter, and to follow the publication by that of Peter Bell and the Waggoner.[11] . . . William read the White Doe; and Coleridge's Christabel to [John Wilson], with both of which he was much delighted.   [*MY,* I, 325–326]

But it was another eight months before Dorothy, still hopeful, reported any progress, and this time the report was mixed. On 28 December 1809 she wrote Lady Beaumont, "You will be glad to hear that [William] is going to finish the Poem of the White Doe, and is resolved to publish it, when he has finished it to his satisfaction" (*MY,* I, 379). But he turned instead to Coleridge's *Friend,* wrote the *Reply to Mathetes,* and composed *The Essays upon Epitaphs*—both of which explore issues raised by *The White Doe.* Exactly two months after the December letter to Lady Beaumont, Dorothy wrote again that William was "deeply engaged in" *The Recluse,* and hoped to complete *The White Doe* only after he had finished what would turn out to be a much longer project (*MY,* I, 392). We do not hear of *The White Doe* again until 24 April 1814, over four years later.

It may be useful here to set down a rough timetable of the events of 1807–1810.

1807

C. July 6–10	The Wordsworths explore Bolton Abbey.
C. September 18	WW writes *The Force of Prayer.*
Between mid-July and mid-October	WW conceives "a plan" for a new poem.
October 16	WW "devours" Whitaker's histories.
November 8	WW reads what is probably *WD* Canto I (then called Part I) to De Q.
December 1–24	WW at Stockton-upon-Tees, where probably ll. 500–1200 were composed.
December 2	WW has completed some 500 lines.

1808

January 3	Above 1,200 lines of "a Tale" completed.
January 16	*WD* finished, over 1,700 lines.

---

[11]*Peter Bell* and *The Waggoner* were not published until 1819.

February 5	WD has proper title; asking terms for publication set. WW decides to send MS to STC before publishing.
February 24	WW leaves for London to see to STC's health, push WD's printing, and correct proofs.
February 26	Lamb hears WW is coming to London.
C. February 26	WW dines with Longman.
Between February 27 and March 26	WW talks with Longman, sets terms for publication, refuses to show MS.
C. February 28	WW reads Canto I to the Lambs and Hazlitt; reads entire poem to De Q.
C. March 1	WW reads entire poem at Mitre Court.
March 1–28	WW and STC work on WD together, alter one passage, and talk about doubtful lines.
C. March 28	DW learns that WW's resolve to publish is wavering, then that he won't publish WD; writes letter urging action.
C. March 28–April 2	STC left "plenipotentiary" with Longman.
April 3	WW leaves STC and London upon news of Sara Hutchinson's illness.
Between April 4 and 17	STC reads Rees one-third of WD, solidifies agreements with Longman, and writes WW, who expresses "no dissatisfaction."
C. April 4 and 18 May	The Lambs read WD and communicate their criticisms to STC, who also reads MS to the Beaumonts.
C. April 4 and early May	STC sends MS to Longman, retracts all but the first two books, and sends back the third without the "little preface."
April 7	WW returns to Grasmere.
April 19	WW writes STC about Lamb's response to WD.
May 1	DW urges STC not to alter passages so that WD can be published "as soon as possible."
May 11	WW interested in Jane Marshall's criticism; is convinced the poem "won't sell."
May 12–18	WW sends letter to Longman, subverting STC and preventing publication.
May 21	STC sends aggrieved letter to WW about WW's letter to Longman.
June 5	WD publication put off until winter.
June 29	WD to be published when "sufficiently corrected."

1809

March 26	WD retrieved from London.
May 1	De Q hears WW is revising and correcting WD.

December 28   DW believes *WD* will appear next winter if WW satis-
fies himself with his revisions. WW writes *Reply to
Mathetes* and begins *The Essays upon Epitaphs.*

1810

February 28   DW writes that WW will return to *WD* only after he
finishes *The Recluse.*

II. Manuscripts and Wordsworth's Revisions

What did the early *White Doe,* the version that entertained the Lambs and
caused Coleridge such grief in London, look like? Ernest de Selincourt
believed it to be no longer extant, and other scholars and critics have accept-
ed his opinion. Two manuscripts of *The White Doe* survive. The first, DC MS.
61, contains fair copy through most of the third canto, draftings for what is
now Canto VII as well as for the prose "Advertizement" that was never
published, and fair copy with revisions of most of *The Force of Prayer.* The
second manuscript is DC MS. 62. Later taken apart, its pages scrambled or
discarded, it was partially reassembled into a notebook in which Wordsworth
transcribed fair copy of *Vaudracour and Julia* onto some of the blank versos.
Twenty leaves and four stubs give us twenty pages containing two closely
related stages of the original text, in addition to two pieces of verse drafting
and three pages of fair-copy verse revision toward the poem that was finally
published in 1815. The twenty pages of original text are scattered, with pages
numbered 25 and 26 corresponding to lines 540 to 586 of the 1815 version;
pages 28, 29, 30, 31, 32, 33, 34, 35, 36, 36 (misnumbered by the copyist), 40,
41, and the first third of 42 corresponding to lines 599 to 939 of the 1815 text;
page 56 corresponding to lines 1362 to 1379 of the 1815 text; and pages 67,
68, and 69 corresponding to lines 1588 to 1654 of the 1815 text. The last two-
thirds of page 42 and all of 43 correspond to nothing that is in the 1815 text;
rather, they contain thirty-seven lines of the original tale which featured,
according to Coleridge, Francis delivering up the Norton family. These pages
have been supplanted on facing versos and one recto by a fresh sequence of
pages numbered 42, 43, and 44 (referred to hereafter as 42a, 43a, and 44a)
which represent material revised after the manuscript was returned to
Wordsworth—that is, following the May 1808 decision not to publish.

These pages of MS. 62 can now be identified as pieces of the version
intended for publication by Longman in 1808, and from them we can recon-
struct a good deal of the original Longman text. This first version had not
seven but only six cantos, in about 1,700 rather than over 1,900 lines; hero-
ine Emily Norton appeared less frequently throughout the poem; and quite
unexpectedly Francis, rather than passively observing his family's misplaced
heroism, delivered them up. The first two cantos and much of the third

were almost identical to those of the later version, but the original poem's third canto was longer than that of the later version by at least thirty-seven lines and possibly by another few pages, which are, however, no longer extant. The fifth and sixth cantos of the original poem correspond to the sixth and seventh cantos of the 1815 text. Thus the major differences between the two versions begin at the end of the third canto and continue through the fourth canto of 1808, which becomes the fourth and fifth cantos of 1815.

Why can MS. 62 be considered part of the 1808 text? First, its pages, which are numbered, contain carefully prepared fair copy in Mary Wordsworth's hand, exactly of the sort to go to the printer, with neat erasures and almost no overwritings. Second, Coleridge penciled a note on the original page 43, which he expanded on the facing verso *before* that verso was used for fair-copy revision, as can be seen by the ink lines that slant away from his penciling in order to preserve it (see pp. 328–329, below). The presence in this fair copy of Coleridge's hand, which appears in only three or four other places in Wordsworth's manuscripts, establishes it as the version of the poem that was in Coleridge's possession while he was preparing it for publication by Longman. (It is hard to believe that Wordsworth would have allowed Coleridge to tamper with the manuscript after having relieved him as "plenipotentiary," or that Coleridge, after his ignominious dismissal, would have been interested in working further on it.) The fair-copy revision itself, because it signals the end of the original longer third canto and the insertion of a new fourth canto, represents work done after the first plans for publication were broken off, and thus serves to date Coleridge's penciling more exactly.

The evidence for an original six-canto *White Doe* begins with the April 1809 letter of Sara Hutchinson's: "William came in to me just now to read some of his additions to the *White Doe* with which he is at present busy— there is to be another canto added to it." We also know the original poem to have contained about 1,700 lines, while the 1815 version has exactly 1,929 lines. Matching the difference, a likely canto length, with Sara Hutchinson's information gives us the single most compelling evidence we have.

But there is more. Coleridge's letter of 21 May contains this criticism:

In my re-perusals of the Poem it seemed always to strike on my feeling as well as judgement, that if there were any serious defect, it consisted in a disproportion of the Accidents to the spiritual Incidents, and closely connected with this, if it be not indeed the same,—that Emily is indeed talked of, and once appears; but neither speaks nor acts in all the first 3 fourths of the Poem: and as the outward Interest of the Poem is in favor of the old man's religious feelings, and the filial Heroism of his band of Sons, it seemed to require something in order to place the two Protestant Malcontents of the Family in a light, that made them *beautiful*, as well as virtuous—In short . . . that 3/4ths of the Work is every thing rather *than* Emily; *then*, the last almost a separate (& doubtless most exquisite Poem) wholly *of* Emily.   [*STCL*, III, 107–108]

Three-fourths of 1,700 lines put us at the end of the original Canto IV. And it is the 1815 Canto IV that Wordsworth began to transcribe as fair copy to supplant the ending of his original third canto. He did so following the verse that ends the 1815 third canto; at some point, he also drew a line under that verse and scribbled the words "end of the 3 Canto." What follows in the original text is the only fair-copy verse that has no correspondence with anything in the 1815 text. But the end of the original fourth canto is word for word the same as the end of the 1815 fifth canto. Thus it seems clear that Wordsworth, responding to the criticism of Coleridge and others, opened up a space after the original Canto III, which he shortened, for a new fourth canto that focuses primarily on Emily. That is, the 1815 Canto IV consists of material written more than fifteen months later than the beginning of the poem, roughly in April 1809, but probably not completed to the poet's satisfaction just then.

Internal evidence within MS. 62 also gives us clues to the poem's original structure. The extant pages average twenty-two lines a page; page 28 clearly marks the beginning of the 1808 Canto III, with page 43 marking the end of as much of the original third canto as we have, and page 56 the end of a canto that we can reconstruct as the original fourth. The 1815 Canto III ends one-third of the way down page 42, while the new sequence 42a, 43a, and 44a marks the beginning of a version of the 1815 Canto IV. In addition, Wordsworth penciled in line numbers on pages 67, 68, and 69; these numbers indicate that the last canto must have begun on page 66 (no longer extant). His penciled numbers also appear on pages 29, 30, 32, 33, and 34 as well as on pages 40, 41, 42, and 43 but not on pages 42a, 43a, and 44a—indicating, first, that the line numbers were entered before the revising of Canto IV, and second, that Canto III was originally a book of considerable length which told a story different from that of the published version. The 1808 *White Doe* that Longman saw, then, was an eighty-page poem in six cantos, about 1,700 lines long (see Table 1).

Table 1. Approximate number of pages and lines in *The White Doe,* 1808, by canto

Canto	MS. pages	Number of pages	Number of lines
I	1–(?)14	14	300
II	15(?)–27	13	240
III	28–(?)44	17	350
IV	45(?)–56	12	290
V	57–65	9	190
VI	66–(?)80	15	330
All cantos		80	1,700

Canto by canto, what was in this early version of *The White Doe*? As already noted, the first three cantos were much the same as the later version. Canto I begins at the ruin of Bolton Priory, the physical wreck of the Nortons' faith, where all that remains is the tower and a small chapel. As people approach the church, we are introduced to the legend of the white doe through the animal's regular, perplexing appearance. The scene is a meeting of opposites and contrasts: the communion of the churchgoers, old with young; the stern ruin against the meek creature; its apparent pride against the doe's humble pilgrimage; the doe's ethereal nature against her obviously material presence; and finally the sense, within the fiction, of the past meeting the present, and then outside the fiction, of the poem's antiquity. Within the tale, explanations for the mystery of the doe abound. Against the inquiring awe of a child are the "fancies" of a number of the assembled crowd, each with her or his own self-interested interpretation. After these explanations are disposed of, the narrative voice invokes a harp "to chaunt" the truth, described as "a tale of tears, a mortal story."

In the second canto, the harp responds with the tale of the uprising in the north after delineating the dutiful but inwardly resisting part played by Emily Norton in designing the religious banner that would revive the rebel cause at key moments. Later, it would unjustly betray her brother Francis's involvement in the plot as well. This eldest, pacifist son confronts their militant father to no avail and, convinced by a sudden vision of the inevitability of the family's destruction, Francis forbids his sister to hope that their fate may be averted. He points to the white doe, playmate of their youth, as his emblem of their loss, claiming that even she will return to the wilderness she knew "ere she had learn'd to love us all." As much a projection of his own pessimism as an act of love, his prophecy is intended to prepare Emily to bear her sorrow alone.

The third canto follows the story of the rebellion, emphasizes the importance of the standard, symbol of the rightness of the cause, in inspiring the rebel followers, and records their advance. The distinction between old Norton's religious zeal and the purely materialistic ends motivating the leading earls is made clear. When the royal army unexpectedly meets them, the leaders quail, and Norton alone resists. Meeting the old man in his despondency, Francis makes a second and ultimately only provoking appeal to his father to abandon the cause. Revitalized, the old man again spiritedly rejects him.

It is at this point that the texts diverge. In the 1815 text, the fourth canto begins here, but in the original version, Canto III continues. Because of the haste of both sides' advance, the rebels' allies are unable, and then unwilling, to join the fray; those assembled scatter. Some of them seem intent on regrouping, Norton among them, and with his family he makes for the Scottish border in the woods. In lines potent with foreboding, given the family's betrayal as reported by Coleridge, Francis observes their retreat to a forest lodge (ll. 882–888 of the numbered transcription text; see below, p. 331):

> And yet Another, and the best,
> Is near them in this time of rest,
> A guard of whom they do not know,
> 'Tis Francis!—much he longs to entreat
> (For he hath cause of dread this night)
> That they would urge their weary feet
> To yet a further, further flight, . . .

Here MS. 62 breaks off, and we must be content with conjectures. Whether these lines are merely another instance of Francis's inspired foreknowing or the first suspicion of his act of betrayal is hard to say, though one may favor the latter conjecture on the strength of Coleridge's criticism.

Of the contents of the original Canto IV, we know only that they concerned Francis and the Nortons in their flight rather than Emily, and that the last eighteen lines are almost exactly the same as those of Canto V in 1815. Here an old friend of Emily's father (and a sort of Archimago figure, naturalized by Wordsworth) concludes his narration of the Nortons' fate in battle, encouraging Emily to look forward to the return of her eldest brother. He thus tempts her to hope against the prophecy she was counseled by.

Of the 1808 Canto V nothing survives. The correspondent canto of 1815, Canto VI, is primarily the story of Francis's flight with the standard, his attempt at self-defense, and his summary execution by soldiers in the wood near Bolton. When the villagers bring his body to the priory for hasty burial, Emily divines the coffin's contents and collapses in grief. The eighty-odd lines still extant of the sixth and final canto of 1808, which correspond to the opening lines of Canto VII of 1815, show only slight differences from the later text. Thus almost a thousand lines of the original 1808 text survive in MSS. 61 and 62.

Although it is not possible to say with precision what those portions of the original text which have disappeared in fact contained, something more can be said. The schematic comparison of the two versions shown in Table 2 may be offered as a starting point.

Since Canto III up to the very end is nearly the same in both the manuscripts and the 1815 text, it is helpful to look at Cantos IV and V of the later version to get an idea of what Wordsworth had to draft when he was adding "another canto." Because he needed to cut the lines that described the Nortons' flight into the woods and Francis's betrayal of the family, more than 40 lines are usable for revisions past the point where the texts diverge. But this is close to the number of lines he added, after 1808, through the

Table 2. Approximate number of lines in 1808 and 1815 texts of *The White Doe,* by canto

1808 text in MSS 61 and 62			1815 text		
Canto	Number of lines		Canto	Number of lines	
I	300		I	340	
II	240		II	260	
		540			600
III	350		III	340	
IV	290		IV	230	
		640	V	210	
					780
V	190		VI	190	
VI	330		VII	360	
		520			550
All cantos	1,700			1,930	

third canto before this point of divergence. The total difference between the two texts is almost 230 lines, as Table 2 indicates. Since we know the difference between the first two cantos of the 1808 text and those of the 1815 text to be about 60 lines, and are fairly certain that the difference between the last two cantos of these two versions is about 30 lines, we are left with some 140 lines of expansion, in addition to some 300 existing lines that consist of the difference between Canto III of the 1808 and 1815 texts added to the original Canto IV, much of which needed heavy revision.

A closer look at the text of the 1815 Cantos IV and V allows us an even greater measure of precision. They are broken down in Table 3.

Clearly the first 140 lines of Canto IV are new. The next 40 may, but need not, be new. The final 50 were probably altered somewhat to accord with the new story line. In Canto V, the first 60 lines are probably also close to their originals; the next 150, in which the Nortons' fate is decided, obviously required substantial changes, but the two versions end similarly, with the old man yet again encouraging Emily to wait and hope, this time for Francis's return.

In sum, we can say that the revisions Wordsworth made after retrieving the poem from Longman in 1808 and before its publication in 1815 were directed primarily toward Canto I (some 40 lines added); Canto III (some 50 lines added, some deleted, a final 40 or more lines canceled and the canto thus shortened); a new Canto IV (some 140 lines added to some 50 to 90 altered lines); and finally, the old Canto IV renumbered Canto V (with some 150 lines extensively rewritten). Additional changes were undertaken in Canto II (some 20 lines added) and in Canto VI, renumbered Canto VII (some 30 lines added).

Table 3. Burden of Cantos IV and V, 1815 text

Approximate number of lines	Burden
Canto IV	
60	"Lyrical precipitation" at Barden Castle and Bolton Abbey
80	Emily's first meditation, in the presence of the white doe, whom she ignores
40	The old man's successful temptation of Emily, who hopes Francis has the power to intervene in events
50	Francis's hope of averting disaster; a brief "precipitation" of the Nortons' impending fate follows
Canto V	
60	Character and history of Norton Tower, followed by Emily's second fight against the resignation she must embrace
150	The old man relates the Nortons' fate, then again tempts Emily to hope

The controversial letter of 21 May 1808 from Coleridge to Wordsworth also gives us more precise information about the early version. Responding to Coleridge's criticisms in that letter, Wordsworth completely altered a crucial part of the action of his tale, the behavior of Francis, whom he transformed from betrayer to pacifist. In this revision Wordsworth followed Coleridge, even as to the placement of the change, which gives further support to the form of the original poem as reconstructed here. Coleridge wrote:

The whole of the Rout and the delivering up of the Family by Francis I never ceased to find not only *comparatively* very heavy, but to me quite obscure, as to Francis's motives. And on the few, to whom within my acquaintance the Poem has been read either by yourself or me (I have, I believe, read it only at the Beaumonts') it produced the same effect.—Now I had conceived two little Incidents, the introduction of which joined to a little abridgement, and lyrical precipitation of the last Half of the third [canto], I had thought, would have removed this defect—so seeming to me—and bring to a finer Balance the *Business* with the *Action* of the Tale. [*STCL*, III, 108]

Did one of Coleridge's "Incidents" have the Nortons contrive to raise their standard within the enemy's camp, an action that allowed Coleridge to put the character of the "Protestant malcontent" Francis in a more complex and sympathetic light? No longer a man who actually betrays his family, he becomes someone who only apparently betrays his country, and in doing so is inadvertently caught between feelings for his family and his pacifist principles. This incident also reinforces the distinction between internal and external action central to Wordsworth's intentions. If this was Coleridge's contri-

bution, he was returning the favor Wordsworth had managed for him some
years back in suggesting the shooting of an albatross as the precipitating
action for the supernatural events of *The Ancient Mariner*. Compare the
language Coleridge used to describe *The White Doe's* defects in the letter of
21 May with this note to *The Ancient Mariner*, which Wordsworth wrote and
published in the 1800 edition of *Lyrical Ballads*. It is worth quoting in full.

I cannot refuse myself the gratification of informing such Readers as may have been
pleased with this Poem, or with any part of it, that they owe their pleasure in some
sort to me; as the Author was himself very desirous that it should be suppressed. This
wish had arisen from a *consciousness of the defects* of the Poem, and from a knowledge
that *many persons had been much displeased* with it. The Poem of my Friend has indeed
great defects; first, that *the principal person has no distinct character*, either in his profes-
sion of Mariner, or as a human being who having been long under the controul of
supernatural impressions might be supposed himself *to partake of something super-
natural:* secondly, that *he does not act, but is continually acted upon:* thirdly, that *the events
having no necessary connection do not produce each other;* and lastly, that the imagery is
somewhat too laboriously accumulated. Yet the Poem contains many delicate touches
of passion, and indeed the passion is every where true to nature; a great number of
the stanzas present beautiful images, and are expressed with unusual felicity of
language; and the versification, though *the metre is itself unfit for long poems*, is harmo-
nious and artfully varied, exhibiting the utmost powers of that metre, and every
variety of which it is capable. It therefore appeared to me that these several merits
(the first of which, namely that of the passion, is of the highest kind,) gave to the
Poem a value which is not often possessed by better Poems. On this account I re-
quested of my Friend to permit me to republish it.   [*LB*, 1800; my italics]

What is interesting here is not so much the way Coleridge's poem was
condescendingly allowed to appear, or even that Wordsworth was oblivious
of the injury his public criticism inflicted on Coleridge's poetic reputation,
let alone his self-confidence. Directly relevant to *The White Doe*, so openly
imitative of *Christabel's* meter, was the way Coleridge later echoed Words-
worth's criticisms of Coleridge's poem years earlier. These criticisms touch
on the problems of audience; of obscurity in the connectedness of events; of
defects in the characterization of the principal person, who for "three-
fourths" of the poem neither speaks nor acts, and of the consequent diffi-
culty of understanding Emily's partaking of the spiritual or supernatural; of
"heaviness" in certain aspects of the poem's plot; of meter; of balancing
emphasis on harmony and passion; and of a need within the main characters
for beauty, a quality that Wordsworth granted Coleridge's poem but that
Coleridge declined to grant without reservation to Wordsworth's. Coleridge
was scrupulous to praise the rhyme as unsurpassed in Wordsworthian excel-
lences, but his action mimicked Wordsworth's own backhanded compliment
to his versification, and both poets praised or criticized most where they

wished to dissociate their own style and their own poetic convictions from the corpse they were dissecting. Coleridge's criticism was, however, not just a matter of *quid pro quo*. Because in some respects the poems shared intentions, they also shared peculiar problems in execution.

In another appraisal of *The Ancient Mariner,* Wordsworth wrote to Joseph Cottle in 1799: "it seems that The Ancyent Mariner has upon the whole been an injury to the volume, . . . the old words and the strangeness of it have deterred readers from going on. If the volume should come to a second Edition I would put in its place some little things which would be more likely to suit the common taste" (*EY,* p. 264).

It is tempting to apply these very criticisms to *The White Doe.* The strangeness of the subject, the necessity of modernizing the old words and spellings (a persistent feature of Wordsworth's revisions of his poem), the problem of whether to resist or to meet the common taste—these multiple ironies alert us to matters more troubling than tantalizing personal relations between the poets. The congruences and the disagreements that marked the evolution and publication of *Lyrical Ballads* are being replayed with twists and differences here. Coleridge plays old Wordsworth against new Wordsworth, with both new and old Coleridge thrown in. The old axis of disparate critical thinking between the two men is here convoluted with borrowings and apparent reversals. With the last lyrical ballad uncompleted, the past was still unresolved, and the controversies of the past were being reopened and reevaluated. In being made to accord with newer concerns, fundamental questions about the form were once again subjects of experimentation and dispute.

If we turn to the differences between the texts of *The White Doe,* we see these concerns, and others previously mentioned, appearing in drafts and revisions. These concerns include the choice of dramatic or narrative mode, the problems of a suggestive intention as opposed to its actual execution, and the controversies over meter and audience. Most of the differences between MS. 61 and MS. 62 are minimal. MS. 61 contains fair copy with revisions of both the first three sections of *The White Doe* and most of *The Force of Prayer.* The sections are not called cantos as they are in MS. 62; instead, they are referred to as parts. The break between the first and second "parts" is denoted only by an inked number 20 added as many lines later, probably in conjunction with revision on that page. "Part Third" begins, neatly headed, on its own page.

The most interesting elements of MS. 61 are its verse and prose draftings. The verse drafting is primarily work toward the last canto, and ranges between lines 1778 and 1891 (and possibly between 1617 and 1684) of the 1815 *White Doe.* While some of this material is very close to the 1815 version, other lines were never incorporated, and still others seem to reappear with their sense directly reversed. Drafting on 12^v, 14^v, and 15^v gives evidence of both a dialogue and a spoken monologue—the first between Emily Norton and the old man, the second articulated by Emily alone. In both instances this material was incorporated in an altered form in Canto VII of 1815. In the first case, dialogue becomes narrative because the old man's appearance is restricted to the fourth and fifth cantos. The lines of comfort he speaks to Emily here obviously had to be dropped. While the second set of drafts may include a few lines of Emily's part of that dialogue, most of these lines are monologue. They, too, have been converted to narrative, and the drafting of the lines that follow "Then [she] stands thus saying [?alone]" was never undertaken. Hence it is likely that in an early version of the last canto Emily's transformation was represented in an initially more dramatic form, a combination of monologue and dialogue.

The draft text on other versos was altered by the time the 1815 Canto VII was published. On 16ᵛ, 17ᵛ, 18ᵛ, 19ᵛ, and finally 20ᵛ the doe follows "At distance ... for through fear / ... / Through fear & through confusion strange / At some unexampled change / Love or notice she found none / The Lady's natural looks were gone" (Wordsworth's hasty miswritings are silently corrected). Compare this description of Emily with lines 1617–1625 of the 1815 Canto VII:

> The like authority, with grace
> Of awfulness, is in her face,—
> There hath she fixed it; yet it seems
> To o'ershadow by no native right
> That face, which cannot lose the gleams,
> Lose utterly the tender gleams
> Of gentleness and meek delight
> And loving-kindness ever bright:
> Such is her sovereign mien;—

And compare the moment of Emily's reunion with the doe in lines 1658–1684 of the 1815 text:

> When, with a noise like distant thunder,
> A troop of Deer came sweeping by;
> And, suddenly, behold a wonder!
> For, of that band of rushing Deer,
> A single One in mid career
> Hath stopped, and fixed its large full eye
> Upon the Lady Emily,
> A Doe most beautiful, clear-white,
> A radiant Creature, silver-bright!
>
> Thus checked, a little while it stayed;
> A little thoughtful pause it made;

And then advanced with stealth-like pace,
Drew softly near her—and more near,
Stopped once again;—but, as no trace
Was found of any thing to fear,
Even to her feet the Creature came,
And laid its head upon her knee,
And looked into the Lady's face,
A look of pure benignity,
And fond unclouded memory.
It is, thought Emily, the same,
The very Doe of other years!
The pleading look the Lady viewed,
And, by her gushing thoughts subdued,
She melted into tears—
A flood of tears, that flowed apace
Upon the happy Creature's face.

In the draft version, the doe was initially so discouraged as to leave Emily with the old man as her only company (again Wordsworth's miswritings are mended):

And now the Doe is wholly check'd
Or hath yielded to neglect
I see her not this rueful day
Elsewhere she is at feed or play
An old Man only do I see
Near the Lady Emily.

In revision, Wordsworth emphasizes inner, spiritual change over mere physical alterations in a way that accords with his heroine's achievement of a thoughtful serenity. She retains her capacity for love, which prevents her experience from completely isolating her. The omission of the doe's hesitancy of fear and "confusion strange" toward Emily's "unexampled" change eliminates any suggestion of madness or flirtation with the Coleridgean supernatural. Finally, Wordsworth transforms the pair's gradual movement toward reunion into a single moment of instant recognition, so that reunion and recognition are one in a celebratory "high communion." This communion, ultimately suggestive of a spot of time, rejoins the sufferer to the sources of restorative power, to the past of seminal pain as well as pleasure:

Oh, moment ever blest! O Pair!
Beloved of heaven, heaven's choicest care!
This was for you a precious greeting,—
For both a bounteous, fruitful meeting.
Joined are they, and the sylvan Doe

Can she depart? can she forego
The Lady, once her playful Peer,
And now her sainted Mistress dear?
And will not Emily receive
This lovely Chronicler of things
Long past, delights and sorrowings?
Lone Sufferer! will not she believe
The promise in that speaking face,
And take this gift of Heaven with grace?
[Ll. 1685–1698]

In this Wordsworthian appropriation of Catholicism's central rite, the speaking presence of nature stands as much for nature itself as for the imaginative associations of the past which the human mind projects upon it. In accepting the doe here, Emily accepts the power of the meditative imagination as well as the limitations the world imposes and the consolations it offers. In this act of communion, the sufferer offers herself up to the reality of the past; by accepting its beauty and its pain, she is reconciled to the sources of both. Thus an "irrational and inanimate" nature can be restorative by its own powers and yet produce, in Wordsworth's words, "influences and effects not by power naturally inherent in it but such as it was endued with by the Imagination of the human minds on whom it operated." Clearly in *The White Doe* Wordsworth reaches for a mode that goes beyond symbolism and approaches something like the dual power of Catholic transubstantiation, in which a thing both is and stands for a spiritual reality.

The fact that the only other verse drafts in MS. 61 are lines from part of the final canto raises an interesting possibility. Was *The White Doe*, either at this stage or at one time only in Wordsworth's mind, a poem just four cantos long? (Coleridge, we may remember, had spoken twice of the first "3/4ths" of the poem.) This possibility would account for the presence of the old man in these draftings and for the hesitant steps of the doe, who makes tentative moves toward Emily in the fourth canto of the published version. Such a final canto might have focused on Emily's rejection of the old man in favor of the doe. In view of the fact that many of these lines were dialogue, at one time the last canto would not have celebrated an already achieved serenity of transcendence; it may instead have more fully dramatized the process by which that transcendence was attained. But since narrative, not dialogue, survived, these early draftings show how deliberately Wordsworth was taking "a station upon different ground" in moving away from the dramatic. Not only did he convert to narrative what he drafted as monologue and dialogue, but he deemphasized the very process of transformation, making it less palpable and more celebratory, and thus more suggestive as well.

In the prose drafts of MS. 61 is an early version of the Preface, which de

Selincourt notes as canceled and now lost. Titled "Advertizement," it in-
cludes a form of Wordsworth's diminutive published advertisement (a one-
line acknowledgment of his trip to Bolton Abbey) but goes well beyond it in
beginning to provide a justification for his poem and its meter. In fact, these
draftings seem to be a forerunner to the *Essay, Supplementary to the Preface*, of
1815. Having expressed his gratitude to Thomas Percy for his *Reliques of
Ancient English Poetry*, Wordsworth was "strongly tempted" to launch into
the history of English poetry he would later produce, but after many false
starts he recognized that "this is not the place" (see the transcription below,
p. 191, for what is an almost comic representation of his inner struggle).

   If Wordsworth was able to stop himself in this drafting, we do not know
what form his demurral took in the preface that Coleridge successfully
urged him to suppress. The drafts that follow in MS. 61 do not represent a
continous stream of composition. Rather, they form the basis of work to-
ward several different subjects, most of it in Wordsworth's hand, but some
of it dictated to Mary. In the first sequence, 32ᵛ, 33ᵛ, 34ᵛ, and the top of 35ᵛ,
Wordsworth works his way toward a statement of poetic justification
through personal reflection. Moving from the accident of his visit to Bolton
Priory and his engagement from his earliest childhood with some of its
history, he writes that recollection along with "high delight" justifies the
verse. He writes for his own "benefit" and for those "who think & feel as I
do" (the words in brackets are crossed out or replaced):

Happening in the course of last summer to be on a visit to some Friends in Yorkshire
I was by them conducted to Bolton Priory . . . and from the impression of that day
the foregoing owes its birth. The beautiful Ruin the delicious Vale . . . the River
which flows by it . . . [with its] accompanying traditions . . . had interested me from
my earliest childhood, upon all those objects I looked with that [delight] high delight
which [in] it is natural to man [to express in Verse] when I look back . . . to which
when it was afterwards [remembered] recollected in tranquillity, I felt to be worthy of
being recorded in Verse; [for the benefit of my] my own affections prompted me;
and [for] of those who think & feel as I do.

   Wordsworth tries to orient his readers' approach to this new poem by
grounding his explanation of his impulse to write *The White Doe* in his
description of the origin of poetry from the 1800 preface to *Lyrical Ballads*.
This section of drafting also reveals that he takes his own affections as
paradigmatic in their capacity for giving pleasure, to be followed by a second
impulse: "I have mentioned a [high moral] strong with a high [moral object
with] purpose & in [? reg] regard to this also I have the same confidence, as
that I shall please those whose affections are pure & whose imagination is
vigourous."
   And for those whose imaginations are not so vigorous, Wordsworth seems

to invite a comparison between himself and a select cadre of worthies, pre-
dictable in their selection, who, if read, would allow him to be appreciated or
would at least strengthen and purify his readers' taste:

I [?] refer to the best models among the antient Greeks to the Latin writers before the
Augustan age, to Chaucer, Spenser, Shakespear & Milton, & lastly though of at least
importance considered as a Composition to the bibble, and when they have studied
thes Beyond this I have no wish and little wish even for that [except] . . . as with an
earnest that what I write will live & continue to . . . [exert] a beneficient influence
[when I am nothing more than] purify the affections and to strengthen the Imagina-
tions of my fellow beings.

This combination of humility and hubris is a distinctive manifestation of
this time; another version of it appears in a letter William sent to Coleridge
on 19 April 1808, which included this note from Mary:

If you do not object to the following Motto on the score of its seeming to take too
much notice of Persons utterly unworthy of notice, (for it is not intended for them,
but for respectable People who cannot conceive that a Man can write verses, at least
many & publish them, or long Poems from any other impulse but a love of praise)—
(N.B. I, Mary, am guiltless of the sin of this cumbrous sentence) W. would prefix it to
the White Doe.

> "And for my part, if only one allow
> The care my labouring spir'ts take in this;
> He is to me a theatre large enow,
> And his applause only sufficient is:
> All my respect is bent but to his brow:
>
> That is my all, and all I am is his.
>
> And if some worthy spir'ts be pleased too,
> It shall more comfort breed, but not more will.
> But what if none? it cannot yet undo
> The love I bear unto this holy skill.
> This is the thing that I was born to do:
> This is my scene; this part I must fulfil."
>   [*MY*, I, 223–224, but quoted from DC MS]

The motto is taken from Samuel Daniel's *Musophilus: containing a General
Defense of Learning* (1599). Whether or not Daniel's sensibility contributed to
the dedicatory poem to Mary, *Musophilus* was one of the first pieces of
prefatory matter Wordsworth hoped would create the taste by which *The
White Doe* was to be enjoyed. The 1815 version had four such forerunners—
the "Advertizement," the sonnet "Weak is the will of Man," part of Bacon's

essay *Of Atheism*, and the dedicatory poem itself—as well as an apparatus of notes giving the history of the legend and the uprising, the ballad source, and a host of miscellaneous details about the Bolton valley.[12] Apart from the inappropriate controlling metaphor of the theatre, Samuel Daniel's motto does not directly bear on the argument of *The White Doe*. For this reason, perhaps, and because, in retrospect, it would have seemed little more than an elaborate self-justification, it was never used. On the other hand, the sonnet "Weak is the will of Man" expressly relates the imagination to suffering. Rather than trace the growth of imagination (as he had recently done in *The Prelude*), Wordsworth focused in *The White Doe* on the imagination as generated out of what he thought of as specifically feminine experience— restricted in action but harrowing nonetheless. If this valuation of inner strength other than that which "as Milton sings / Hath terror in it" is less successful, its failure may be due in part to Wordsworth's unfamiliarity with this mode, which did not arise from the main sources of his creative power.

Although the prose drafting thus far gives us some clues as to how the poem is to be read, not all of it is so revealing. The lines dictated to Mary on 35ᵛ are merely a draft for the conclusion to the notes. On 36ᵛ we are back to Wordsworth's hand; the drafts here are observations "as to the feeling of time within" anapestic and trochaic verse, which we may assume is work toward the explanation of *The White Doe*'s meter. On 37ᵛ there are more justifications of the poem, this time referring to its style. The drafts thus suggest that the "little preface" might have been reasonably comprehensive. Though Wordsworth rather dismissively refers readers more curious about his style to the preface he wrote for *Lyrical Ballads*, he does try to elaborate on the problem of audience. He composes the somewhat self-serving tautology that the only readers he wishes to please are those "whose affections are representative of the affections of human nature," and struggles with such qualifiers as "clear," "pure," "healthy," and "independent" to describe more fully the qualities of this ideal audience.

Between the texts of the two manuscript poems there are few important differences: aside from extensive but routine changes in punctuation and paragraphing, only two passages of significance vary. One of these passages, on 42ʳ of MS. 61 and pages 34–35 of MS. 62, is minor, but it makes more

---

[12]The long quotation from Thomas Whitaker which Wordsworth entered in his notes after the ballad describes the landscape surrounding the priory; it seems to be a natural equivalent to the notes that explain the history of the rebellion. In this way we share Emily's landscape of meditation. Like the landscape of human life, the river sometimes reposes and sometimes "resumes its native character, lively, irregular, and impetuous." But Wordsworth's final recommendation, that "all lovers of beautiful scenery" should visit the area, seems an odd way to end a quarto volume with such pretensions to the nonmaterial. It is perhaps a sign of the materiality that could not be repressed.

explicit the contrast between Emily and Francis as opposed to old Norton. Compare MS. 61 (I quote the revised version):

> To guard the Standard which he bore
> They guarding him he round them shed
> While firm he held his dear hearts boast,
> Gods proof of love unmerited,
> A light of glory dimm'd with dread
> Such mixture as his Countenance bred
> Yet still the glory uppermost

with these lines from MS. 62, which replace them (reported in the *apparatus criticus* to ll. 673–678 of the fair-copy transcriptions, below, p. 309):

> To guard the Standard which he bore,
> —With feet that firmly pressed the ground
> They stood, and girt their Father round;
> Such was his choice;—no Steed will he
> Henceforth bestride,—triumphantly
> He stood upon the verdant sod,
> Trusting himself to the earth, and God.

The distinction here is between Norton's pride and his sons' humility, between his confidence in God to act in the material world (based as it is on his trust in an authority he personally appropriates) and their tempered attitude of mixed despair and hope. The one might be more characteristic of Wordsworth in the *Elegiac Stanzas* on Peele Castle before his brother's death; the other, of his painfully slow coming to terms with that loss.

The only other substantive changes between the two texts involve Wordsworth's mini-portraits of old Norton and his eldest son. Compare the description of Francis on 44^r of MS. 61 (again I quote the revised version):

> Nor doth his faithful eye forego
> The pageant glancing to & fro
> For hope is with him thence to learn
> Which way the tide is doom'd to flow
> A knowledge which he soon shall earn.

with that on pages 35 and 36 of MS. 62 (reported in the *apparatus criticus* to ll. 707–711 of the fair-copy transcriptions, below, p. 315):

> —Bold is his aspect; but his eye
> Is pregnant with anxiety,
> While, like a Tutelary Power,
> He there stands fixed, from hour to hour.

Yet sometimes, in more humble guise,
Stretched out upon the ground he lies,
As if it were his only task
Like Herdsman in the sun to bask,
Or by his Mantle's help to find
A shelter from the nipping wind;
And thus with short oblivion blest
His weary Spirits gather rest.
Again he lifts his eyes; and lo!
The pageant glancing to and fro;
And hope is wakened by the sight
That he thence may learn, ere fall of night,
Which way the tide is doomed to flow.

The lines that precede these in both texts establish Francis's link to Emily
as a solitary, a sort of wanderer who, though he forbids his sister to act,
anxiously intervenes himself, as if he possessed something of the super-
natural ability of a "Tutelary Power." Thus he is made to stand more clearly
between Emily and old Norton in the continuum of characters who believe
they can intervene against their fate.

Of changes within MS. 62 little need be said. On page 68 a phrase that
describes Emily's clothing is altered to imply conscious intent ("doth more
express" becomes "fashioned to express"), allowing her deliberately to ap-
pear like the wanderer she is. On page 69 Wordsworth changes the word
"wilfully" to "awfully" to describe the impenetrability of her changed soul,
and to suggest its power:

The mighty sorrow hath been borne
And she is thoroughly forlorn:
Her soul doth in itself stand fast
Sustained by memory of the past
And strength of Reason; held above
The infirmities of mortal love,
Undaunted lofty, calm, and stable,
And [wilfully] awfully impenetrable.
                [Ll. 1640–1647]

In this case, that she seems deliberate is unimportant; Wordsworth needs to
eliminate the sense of resisting caprice that "wilfully" otherwise suggests in
order to revalorize this feminine experience of the restorative imagination,
which can no longer be harmed by the caprice of the world.

A comparison of what amounts to three stages of revision in the drafting for
the new Canto IV with the first published version is more revealing. Here we

can trace a persistent impulse in Wordsworth which signifies Coleridge's waning influence. The first stage is the original fair copy in Mary Wordsworth's hand; the second, the revision and deletion in Wordsworth's; and the third, the 1815 version. Each opens with a "lyrical precipitation," almost certainly suggested by Coleridge, which begins (in MS. 62, p. 42a) with these lines:

> From cloudless ether looking down
> The Moon this tranquil evening sees
> A Camp and a beleaguered Town
> And Castle like a stately Crown
> On the steep rocks of winding Tees.

A castle, moonlight, a besieged town, those steep rocks rising above a twisting river: we may wonder what direction this half-Coleridgean, half-Wordsworthian lyricism may take, given the conflicts of the recent and the distant past—the controversies over supernatural versus commonplace passion, the need for outward interest versus the defense of the mild and the spiritual. How far will Wordsworth bend to his critics or yield to the influence of Coleridge's inventions? How committed is Wordsworth to the meditative imagination as embodied by a calmly resilient feminine character?

In the first version of the new Canto IV, one feels the presence of Coleridge as well as Wordsworth's reversion to the Gothic of his past. After a mere fourteen lines of "rural quietness," Wordsworth introduces these disquieting and discordant elements:

> But list the Dog, the household Guard
> Repeats a faint uneasy howl
> And from the distant crags are heard
> The houtings of the riotous Owl.

These lines and those below which immediately follow them (in MS. 62, p. 43a) do not stray far from their probable model—the opening of *Christabel*.

> [All else is still] The courts are hush'd for timely sleep
> The Greyhounds to their kennels creep
> The Peacock in the broad ash tree
> Aloft is roosted for the night
>
> . . .
>
> And higher still above the bower
> Where he is perch'd, from yon lone Tower
> The Hall-clock in the clear moonshine
> With glittering finger points at nine.

Consider the way *Christabel* begins:

> 'Tis the middle of the night by the castle clock,
> And the owls have awakened the crowing cock;
> Tu—whit!——Tu—whoo!
> Sir Leoline, the Baron rich,
> Hath a toothless mastiff bitch;
> From her kennel beneath the rock
> She maketh answer to the clock.

Almost immediately after these lines, we see Christabel in the moonlight, with the bitch's moan recurring throughout the poem like a refrain. And in Wordsworth's poem we also suddenly come upon Emily:

> [Not by the hour serene and fair
> Not by the freshness of the air]
> Is Emily called forth to seek
> The place she cannot find within
> By restlessness or blank despair
> Impelled she wanders here and there
> And if no comfort she may win
> No truce yet still the cool night air
> Breathes freshly on her feverish cheek.

The suggestion of madness or distraction in a lone virginal female is of course a standard element of the Gothic. There is the muted suggestion of sexual tension as well, a tension prominent in Coleridge's *Christabel*, which certainly plays with the suggestiveness it creates. The same is true of the supernatural element, and both stories turn in part on a motherless heroine's relation to her father. Return to Wordsworth's fair copy of the rewritten Canto IV (pp. 43a–44a, MS. 62):

> She through the Garden takes her way
> Where round a Pool soft breezes play
> And lift, and lift the willows hoary
> That screen a small secluded Pile
> Right in the centre of an isle
> Her Father's secret Oratory
> There stands the Holy-water Stone
> From which he crossed his wrinkled brows
> Entering here to pray alone
> And offer up his private vows
> There to with reverential dread
> The Banner was deposited
> And thence did come that fatal morn
> When forth in triumph it was borne.

Feverish and distracted, Emily comes to the very center of imaginative transgression: the source of her father's inspiration. In these passages, very neatly copied into the manuscript as if MS. 62 were still going to be sent to the printer, the poem seems about to escalate into a potently supernatural mode.

But this version of the altered MS. 62 was never sent to the printer. Many of the lines were canceled in the second stage of revision; still more were dropped in the 1815 published version. Some of the first lines to go were those about the howling dog and hooting owl. And Wordsworth drafted some lines that delay the appearance of Emily, probably to replace the lines above, where Emily wandered, "driven by her thoughts from place to place" (I quote the revised versions on p. 42a):

> Ah who would think that sadness here
> Had any sway or pain or fear?
> A soft and lulling sound is heard
> Of streams inaudible by day
> The garden pool's dark surface—stirred
> By the night Insects in their play
> Breaks into Dimples small & bright
> A thousand thousand rings of light
> That shape themselves and disappear
> Almost as soon as seen—and Lo
> Not distant far the milkwhite Doe

At the second stage of revision, then, Canto IV begins with the opening lines of the "cloudless ether" passage. It no longer contains the howling dog and hooting owl, but retains the lines about the "silver smoke" and the roosting peacock, up to and including the hall clock, whose "glittering finger points at nine." There the new insertion takes over, followed by a long passage that describes the doe. How far this passage ran we do not know, because the pages that followed it are no longer extant. But the force of this second "lyrical precipitation" is directed toward establishing a contrast between the tranquil evening, where everything blends into a lulling softness of "streams inaudible by day," and the disembodied idea of "sadness . . . pain or fear." The eeriness and the discord of the evening, in which Emily is made to partake, are eliminated in favor of a ministrant nature and a particularized condition of the soul. Thus Wordsworth first indulges in the Gothic and then eliminates it as a mode of the imagination, as he modifies Coleridge's inventions along the lines of his original design.

The 1815 version continues in the direction of these revisions, for there, too, description is carefully harmonized to emphasize the doe's oneness with the surrounding moonlight, and she appears as an emblem of what will be

Emily's action, "feeding in tranquillity." This description, occupying a sub-
stantial block of verse, shifts emphasis away from the heroine, whose pres-
ence has so far only been intimated by the lines about pain. Eventually we
see Emily "Emerging from the cedar shade / To open moonshine" in an-
swer to the interrogative "But where at this still hour is she?" Here Words-
worth describes Emily not as "feverish" or wandering but as "consecrated," a
change that eliminates any suggestion of distraction or titillating sexuality
and replaces it with a specifically spiritual form of the supernatural. Descrip-
tion again turns to the white doe as a "lonely relic," a symbol of death and
lingering impermanence with the promise of vernal life. Only then do we
discover Emily's mental state, unhappily "thought-bewildered" but com-
posed. The description is offered only to explain why she earlier slighted the
doe's ministrations. In addition to downplaying the Gothic, then, Words-
worth deemphasizes Emily in order to point to the spiritual significance of
her relation to nature, memory, and suffering.

Sometime between the writing of the original fair copy of this opening to
Canto IV and publication in 1815, Wordsworth incorporated another major
change. In the original fair copy, a distracted Emily wanders to her father's
"secret Oratory," from which sprang the inspiration that led to "that fatal
morn," and which also reminds us that she contributed to the rebel cause.
But by 1815, encouraged by the night's "viewless breeze," "fraught with
acceptable feeling, / And instantaneous sympathies / Into the Sufferer's
bosom stealing," the scene had changed.

> Ere she hath reached yon rustic Shed
> Hung with late-flowering woodbine spread
> Along the walls and overhead,
> The fragrance of the breathing flowers
> Revives a memory of those hours
> When here, in this remote Alcove,
> (While from the pendant woodbine came
> Like odours, sweet as if the same)
> A fondly anxious Mother strove
> To teach her salutary fears
> And mysteries above her years.
> [Ll. 1025–1035]

Here the emphasis shifts in revision from distracted, because purely pain-
ful, recollection to memories of an earlier experience of communion and
accommodated loss. The revised version illustrates the potency of human
memory when it is supported by receptivity to the suggestive influences in
nature. The action of this passage may thus be said to reverse the movement
of the spots of time in *The Prelude*, where the boy feels he is stealing from

nature: here it is nature that steals its way into the young woman's feelings. Where he was disturbed, she is "soothed":

> —an Image faint—
> And yet not faint—a presence bright
> Returns to her;—'tis that bless'd Saint
> Who with mild looks and language mild
> Instructed here her darling Child,
> While yet a prattler on the knee,
> To worship in simplicity
> The invisible God, and take for guide
> The faith reformed and purified.
> [Ll. 1036–1044]

We have in the faintness of the image a sense of the abidingness of her loss, and we should recall the dedicatory stanzas, set within their own "rustic Shed," where the Wordsworths themselves read fictions of grief. There, as here, the memory and its sweetness beguile as well as soothe:

> 'Tis flown—the Vision, and the sense
> Of that beguiling influence!
> "But oh! thou Angel from above,
> Thou Spirit of maternal love,
> That stood'st before my eyes, more clear
> Than Ghosts are fabled to appear
> Sent upon embassies of fear;
> As thou thy presence hast to me
> Vouchsafed—in radiant ministry
> Descend on Francis:—through the air
> Of this sad earth to him repair,
> Speak to him with a voice, and say,
> "That he must cast despair away!"
> [Ll. 1045–1057]

These lines implicitly dismiss the Gothic while they suggest how heterodox Wordsworth's position toward even the Protestant religion is. Emily's Protestant mother represents a belief in the power of prayer and the unquestioned generosity of hope which Wordsworth could not find in his own experience of loss, and the poem does not fully embrace her vision. Emily eventually recognizes the wisdom of part of Francis's injunction

> That interdicted all debate,
> All prayer for this cause or for that;
> All efforts that would turn aside
> The headstrong current of their fate;

Her duty is to stand and wait;
In resignation to abide
The shock, and finally secure
O'er pain and grief a triumph pure.
                    [Ll. 1066–1073]

Only then does she find herself fortified and achieve a sort of peace: "—She knows, she feels it, and is cheared; / At least her present pangs are checked" (ll. 1074–1075).

What, therefore, we may inquire, is the "religious hope" offered in *The White Doe*? In a letter of 1808 to Francis Wrangham, Wordsworth indicates that he finds all religions insufficient, and suggests a sort of spiritual alternative:

I will allow with you that Religion is the eye of the Soul, but if we would have successful Soul-oculists, not merely that organ, but the general anatomy and constitution of the intellectual frame must be studied: farther, the powers of that eye are affected by the general state of the system. My meaning is, that piety and religion will be best understood by him who takes the most comprehensive view of the human mind, and that for the most part, they will strengthen with the general strength of the mind; and that this is best promoted by a due mixture of indirect nourishment and discipline.   [*MY*, I, 249]

The interrelation of religion and imaginative vision appears in other revisions as well. At the same time, many of the changes between Cantos II and III in MS. 61 and in the 1815 version of *The White Doe* seem to have arisen out of the desire to meet Coleridge's criticisms. On 22^r, for example, lines 384–385 of MS. 61 have been altered presumably to accord with Coleridge's urging that the "Protestant malcontents" of the family be put in a better light. The corresponding lines in the 1815 text, lines 424–426, give a sense of sudden lucidity, akin to possession, before Francis's experience of the phantasm convinces him of his family's fate. These lines replace the loose, dreamy first version, which make Francis seem limp in comparison.

A few passages later, on 24^r, Wordsworth alters the meeting between Francis and Emily to reveal Francis's inner motivations. In MS. 61 (l. 410), he turns straight toward Emily immediately upon seeing her; in the 1815 text (ll. 451–454), he first sees her from afar as she sits with her head upon her lap, "concealing / In solitude her bitter feeling." The narrative of both texts has already prepared us to expect that Francis will be unable to sustain the "fortitude" "cleansed from the despair / And sorrow of his fruitless prayer" he had achieved after meditating on the landscape. But in the second version, Wordsworth underlines Francis's failure by incorporating it in his reaction to the sight of his troubled sister with the lines "How could he chuse but shrink or sigh? / He shrunk, and muttered inwardly." Francis also keeps to himself the thought "Might ever son *command* a sire, / The act were justified to-day," a gesture toward the rebellion to which Emily will eventually be tempted in her battle with her brother's vision of unremitting despair.

In Canto III, certain other changes also accord with Coleridgean criticisms. This time the alterations give old Norton less justification for his pride and less reason for rebelling, so that his two Protestant children command more of our sympathy. On 33ʳ of MS. 61 (ll. 547–551), the arrival of the Nortons upon the rebel scene is the event that rallies the wavering leaders, then amid "tremblings and perplexity," to advance. By 1815 (in ll. 605–608), the Nortons' role as the determining pledge has been revoked: they simply join the forces like any other group. And in lines 804–815 of the 1815 text, when the decision for a judicious retreat is given, rumor of it merely filters down to Norton: he does not have the access to his leaders that he does in the corresponding lines (727/728) on 45ʳ of MS. 61. On 37ʳ (ll. 601–604), when Norton explains the reasons for his rebellion, he cites "redress of wrongs / In what to high or low belongs" and an heirless crown in addition to the religious cause. These lines do not appear in the 1815 text.

Finally, in two other changes, old Norton's susceptibility to superstitious reasoning is given full vent. In a long passage in the 1815 text (ll. 818–856) which was absent from the correspondent lines in MS. 61 (45ʳ, ll. 729/730), Wordsworth includes in Norton's tirade against retreat a vitriolic account of other battles in which faith in Catholic relics won the day, though the victorious forces were badly outnumbered: Norton clearly expects God to be materially with "us, who war against the Untrue." Although momentarily swayed, the leaders retreat anyway. The physical sight of the banner thereafter becomes a scourge to Norton's pride. In lines 887–892 of the 1815 text, Norton becomes superstitious about the reasons for the retreat. As he casts his mind back to Emily's reluctant fashioning of the banner, he blames first her, then her brother, and finally her "other Parent," who "from reason's earliest dawn beguiled" his "unsuspecting" daughter. We are startled less by the ludicrousness of his superstitions than by the coldness of his feelings toward his dead wife and children. These changes deflect considerably the "outward Interest of the Poem" away from the "old man's religious feelings, and the filial Heroism of his band of Sons." Norton's zealotry seems in part a mask for absent warmth, and overwhelms fundamental paternal feelings. Moreover, it not only deemphasizes the filial feeling of his faceless sons but implicates religious passion in inhumane acts.

If changes in the second and third cantos seem prompted primarily by Coleridge, those in the first canto are the kind a writer is likely to make, once the structure of a work is complete. Lines 193–219, 220–226, and 272–280 of the 1815 text represent a considerably sharpened version of lines 194–205 on 10ʳ and lines 247–248 on 13ʳ of MS. 61. Wordsworth elaborates on the responses of a young boy whose mother has shown him the white doe in the churchyard as well as those of an old man and a young scholar, each of whom has his own explanation for the doe. Their explanations arise out of their preexisting contexts: the old man, who "brought home the scars / Gathered in long and distant wars," relates the doe to the history that he is "studious to expound"; the young scholar, perhaps a type of early Wordsworth, prefers to believe that the doe is the fairy woman who taught his legendary hero the "song of Nature's hidden powers." She is a beneficent Geraldine figure who can "all shapes" wear "in semblance of a lady fair." Revision entered in MS. 61 on 10ʳ about the old man and on 12ʳ about another doe watcher, a well-to-do female church visitant, is evidence of an earlier attempt to elaborate the message that each person's explanation of the doe is the projection of his or her own desire rather than a reflection of any objective truth. The young boy's awe thus stands for the conflict over the meaning of the white doe, with history (the supposed factual record of external events) set against internal significance. As the explanations of the old man, the scholar, and the haughty churchgoer demonstrate, "the facts" have been determined by "strange delusions" and fanciful "conjectures." Thus each conception of the doe arises from a history whose lineaments reflect the colors of the mind that has produced it.

The conceptions, whether productions of superstition, fancy, self-interest, or sweet sublimity, cannot be separated from the sensibilities that produce them, and it is this relativity that produces the call for the harp at the end of the canto, which, like these passages, underwent elaboration between MS. 61 and publication in 1815. Wordsworth's solution to the relativity to which the harp "with no reluctant strings" has "attuned" its "murmurings" links poetic inspiration, religious being, and the people's "command." Compare 16ʳ of MS. 61, lines 292–297—

> Harp sound the truth upon thy strings
> For a Spirit with angel wings
> Is near us, & a Spirit's hand;
> A Voice is with thee, a command
> To chaunt in strains of heavenly glory
> A tale of tears, a mortal story—

with the 1815 version, lines 325–337:

> Harp! we have been full long beguiled
> By busy dreams, and fancies wild;
> To which, with no reluctant strings,
> Thou has attuned thy murmurings;
> And now before this Pile we stand
> In solitude, and utter peace:

But, harp! thy murmurs may not cease,—
Thou has breeze-like visitings;
For a Spirit with angel wings
Hath touched thee, and a Spirit's hand:
A voice is with us—a command
To chaunt, in strains of heavenly glory,
A tale of tears, a mortal story!
                    [Ll. 325–337]

The elaboration of the diverse conceptions in the earlier version required in this passage an elaboration in kind; thus we have the new lines 325–328. The "peace" of line 330—a tranquillity that in other Wordsworthian contexts produces poetry—is a necessary but insufficient condition for release from the foregoing subjectivities. Line 331 offers the standard tropes for poetic inspiration—a harp and "breeze-like" visitings—joined by "a Spirit with angel wings." Together spiritual and poetic authority join with the decapitalized "voice," which belongs to the communal "we" whose desire is not so much for truth as for a meaningful fiction, "a tale of tears, a mortal story." Thus the combined inspiration and desire of poet, spirit, and assembled readers generate the poem and its reading upon the site of the ruined church in this epitaphic moment.

III. Publication and Critical Reception

On 24 April 1814 Dorothy Wordsworth wrote that *The White Doe* was to be published shortly after the following winter; in November, publication was expected for the spring (*MY*, III, 140, 165). Sir George Beaumont and Christopher Wordsworth seem to have taken the completed poem to London around 8 February 1815, and about two weeks later proof sheets began to arrive (*MY*, III, 202, 207; *Chronology: MY*, p. 592). On 16 March the Wordsworths had received no more than three sheets, but by 8 April they had "nothing to complain of" after the initial delay in Edinburgh, where James Ballantyne was printing the poem. On the 11th, Dorothy wrote that they hoped *The White Doe* would "be out in two or three weeks" (*MY*, III, 222, 226, 230). By 10 May, William wrote Longman to say that Ballantyne was correcting the press of the prose parts, "the poetry [having] been printed off," and a week and a half later he told Coleridge to expect the poem in a few days. Much to Wordsworth's regret, "some prefatory" lines "found their way into the Courier" and were "printed with vile incorrectness" (*MY*, III, 236, 238–239). But finally, on 28 June, *The White Doe* "arrived at last" (*MY*, III, 243). It did not, however, sell well, and Dorothy wrote Catherine Clarkson on 15 August: "I now perceive clearly that till my dear Brother is laid in his grave his writings will not produce any profit. This I now care no more about and *shall* never *more* trouble my head concerning the sale of them. I once thought *The White Doe* might have helped off the other [poems], but I now perceive it can hardly help itself." She regrets that it was printed in "so expensive a form," which deprived many people "of the pleasure of reading it," but felt that "however cheap his poems might be I am sure it will be very long before they have an extensive sale—nay it will not be while he is alive to know it" (*MY*, III, 247).

Wordsworth had anticipated this problem, of course, and had tried to orient readers to the poem by prefacing the manuscript sent to the printer for the first edition of 1815 with the quotation from Bacon and the sonnet "Weak is the will of Man." Sometime before publication, however, he decided they did not sufficiently introduce his poem. We may ask why they did not. The lines from Bacon suggest that Emily's relation to the doe will be a sign of the human relationship to the divine, while the sonnet "Weak is the will of Man" indicates that the new ballad will be about the way the mind responds to suffering. Both prefatory sonnet and Bacon's prose direct readers beyond the material plot. Their inclusion was Wordsworth's first attempt to raise "the distinct ken" of his readers' sympathies.

Yet neither passage fully indicates the way in which the poem was to be read. In 1808 Wordsworth had to counter expectations that his work would be like something by Walter Scott and to bridge the gap between the new work and his earlier experiments with the ballad form. But by 1814 the terms had shifted from those of the discarded "little preface." He had to circumvent the kind of response Lamb had exhibited before readers approached the main text. This was the purpose of the "dedicatory epistle," which first appears as drafting now bound in at the back of the 1815 printer's copy. Deliberately written to precede the ballad, "In trellis'd shed" provides the link with Spenser which tells Wordsworth's readers how to read *The White Doe*—to read it as they would read Spenser's *Faerie Queene*, as an allegory of human life, but also as a self-conscious fiction of a peculiarly Romantic sort.

Wordsworth had his own sense of self-conscious allegory. In the terms set by "In trellis'd shed," he was interested both in the way the tale's symbols were invested with significance by his characters and, more fundamentally, in the human response to fictions themselves. As it prepares readers for the "action" of *The White Doe*, "In trellis'd shed" shows how every symbolic action, whether in the world or as a response to a fictional representation, requires an extended exercise of suspended disbelief. Belief is at the heart of both poems: it makes possible both aesthetic pleasure and restorations from pain. In this sense we can understand Wordsworth's fervid valuation of his poem, whose sophistications were rendered so (apparently) artlessly that the poem was by his reckoning, "in conception, the highest work he had ever produced" (*Memoirs*, II, 313). Hence the following, one of Words-

worth's many elaborations on this theme, in a January 1816 note to Francis
Wrangham:

> Of the White Doe I have little to say, but that I hope it will be acceptable to the
> intelligent, for whom alone it is written.—It starts from a high point of imagination,
> and comes round through various wanderings of that faculty to a still higher; nothing
> less than the Apotheosis of the Animal, who gives the first of the two titles to the
> Poem. And as the Poem thus begins and ends, with pure and lofty Imagination, every
> motive and impulse that actuates the persons introduced is from the same source, a
> kindred spirit pervades, and is intended to harmonize, the whole. Throughout, ob-
> jects (the Banner, for instance) derive their influence not from properties inherent in
> them, not from what they are actually in themselves, but from such as are bestowed
> upon them by the minds of those who are conversant with or affected by those
> objects. Thus the Poetry, if there be any in the work, proceeds whence it ought to do
> from the soul of Man, communicating its creative energies to the images of the
> external world.   [*MY*, II, 276]

Whether "the people," for whom the poem was written, fully appreciated
Wordsworth's conception was less important than that they could take plea-
sure in a tale of suffering endured, and benefit in distress by their sympathetic
interchange with the tale. Yet it was *The White Doe*'s apparent artlessness that
made "In trellis'd shed" necessary. For more sophisticated readers, the highly
wrought language of its stanzas implies that the fictional representation of
pain is invariably artificial. The drowning of John Wordsworth and the deaths
of William and Mary's children (that "lamentable change" in "the bosom of
our rustic Cell") had fundamentally altered the Wordsworths' previously
vicarious response to fictional sorrow. Matching the artifice in Spenser's *Faerie
Queene* with an artifice of their own, they found that response to be narrowly
aesthetic, self-gratifying, and only superficially "fraught" with "sacred
wisdom." At the height of their pain, they even lost the ability to take pleasure
in fictions, finding that "For us the stream of fiction ceased to flow, / For us
the voice of melody was mute." It was some time before they could again take
pleasure in fictive suffering, and by then they were very aware that those
fictions "beguiled" as well as "soothed."

But artifice in itself (whether the poet's or the reader's) did not invalidate
the "truth" of such a work, which lay in its ability to help people deal with
loss. By acknowledging the varying dynamics of his response as a reader,
then, Wordsworth emphasizes that whether the fiction is heard or resisted
depends on what the reader brings to the text as much as it depends on the
craft of the author. And, because one can never wholly lose an inner anguish
"strange as dreams of restless sleep" after a devastating loss, fictions of
distress, however soothing, inevitably remain fictions. Thus they do not
"fail" by the poet's execution alone: in the real world their soothing power is
always limited.

By bringing in Spenser to illustrate his own failed response, Wordsworth shows potential critics first that he is self-consciously factitious, and second, that he is aware of what his artifice can and cannot do. Readers must be prepared to yield to his fictiveness, with its inevitable limitation, in the same way that they yield to the fictiveness of Spenser. If readers can delight in Spenser's representation of tenacious innocence, then they should also find solace in his poem—without accusing either poet of worshiping nature, of being sentimental, or of lacking sophistication. Thus by focusing on every reader's artifice in responding to fictions, Wordsworth directs questions of his readers' incredulity away from the legend, which was an actual product of people's imaginations, to the difficulty of reconstructing spiritual serenity after great personal loss, a theme that may explain why the Victorians favored the poem after a largely dismissive Romantic response.

A key feature of Wordsworth's adaptation of his primary source is pertinent here. The narrative voice that begins the ballad is not explicitly heard again; instead, the poem ends with the community's participation in a loss that we assume is not vicarious. The balladeer, so enthusiastic about the plucky responses of his characters to their adventure, ends with these muted stanzas, in which the border between narrative involvement and historical fact most clearly breaks down:

> But the dun bulle is fled and gone,
>   And the halfe moone vanished away:
> The Erles, though they were brave and bold,
>   Against soe many could not stay.
>
> Thee Norton, wi' thine eight good sonnes,
>   They doomed to dye, alas! for ruth!
> Thy reverend lockes thee could not save,
>   Nor them their faire and blooming youthe.
>
> Wi' them full many a gallant wight
>   They cruellye bereav'd of life:
> And many a child made fatherless,
>   And widowed many a tender wife.

In a sense, the "catastrophe" of Wordsworth's poem picks up where the ballad leaves off, at the point of irremediable loss. But *The White Doe* invites a different dénouement, one Wordsworth calls attention to by the narrative frame that Canto I establishes and that the self-consciousness of "In trellis'd shed" was designed to arouse. Instead of following the ballad's tactic of exhausting the narrative in a sudden inward turning to pain, Wordsworth leaves us in a state of repose, gazing at an emblem whose historical meaning has been revealed by that narrative. Yet the mystery remains, for the emblem signifies the power of the mind to survive by relying on imaginative fictions, the higher realities of things no longer seen. The power of the epitaphic mode is ephemeral and yet enduring, an oral history inscribed in both "the people's" hearts and blocks of stone.

No critic who had given "In trellis'd shed" an attentive reading should have faulted Wordsworth for being obscure or unsophisticated. But it appears that few read it with care. Reviewing *The White Doe* for the *Edinburgh Review* of October 1815, Francis Jeffrey thought Wordsworth to be "in a state of low and maudlin imbecility," and claimed the poem had "the merit of being the very worst poem we ever saw imprinted in a quarto volume." W. R. Lyall, the reviewer for the *Quarterly Review* for the same month, called it an "out-of-the-way" production whose narrative was told "in scraps" so that "the circumstances which connect [the principal scenes were] left pretty much to the reader's imagination"—ironically a response Wordsworth was probably aiming at. The "broken" narrative was a traditional technique, one Spenser had used to present his tale of Una and the Red Crosse Knight in the first book of the *Faerie Queene*, a work the dedicatory poem had identified as an analogue.

The *Quarterly* went on to charge that Wordsworth's "great simplicity of language [had been] purchased at the expense of perspicuity," for too many of the words were "absolutely devoid of meaning." Instead of a dénouement, "we have merely the explanation of a certain strange phenomenon which had puzzled rather than interested our curiosity." Critics generally attributed these imprecisions to Wordsworth's "metaphysical sensibility," for which they had little sympathy.

The Eclectic's reviewer, Josiah Condor, wrote in this vein in the issue of January 1816:

Faults . . . such as Mr. Wordsworth chooses to commit are not easily overlooked by the intolerance of taste. His bold and determined nonconformity to the creeds and rules of established usages mark him out as a poetical schismatic. For our own parts, we contend, even in the world of taste, for an enlarged toleration. If a poet like Mr. Wordsworth chooses to narrow out for himself a path on the confines of mysticism, inaccessible to common minds . . . let him fondle flowers, and like Ariel, lie sheltered in a cowslip's bell . . . then, half-resuming humanity, let him delight to indue the nobler life of animal consciousness with reflex intelligence, and realize the fables of the Pythagorean; the same propensity which led the grosser imaginations of the old heathens to carry their uninformed sympathy with inferior and even inanimate nature into idolatry. Through all these changes, we may recognize the poet's power, but we cannot accompany him; and we would gladly, when the Proteus again becomes man, fix him in that shape for ever.

Reviewers generally found the poem irritating because it was both too long and annoyingly unintelligible. Despite Wordsworth's nod to Spenser, they repeatedly turned to the example of Scott, arguing that instead of being gratified, as *The Eclectic*'s reviewer put it, by "some busy narrative of lofty adventure, such as Walter Scott's Tales led us to associate with the metre," the reader was "forced to stand in Rylstone Churchyard and look all the while at a White Doe, and listen all the while to a rhapsody, the import of which he is not led to perceive, upon its whiteness, and brightness, and famousness, and holiness." Instead of "the mysterious interest which the mute heroine might have been made to awaken we follow her without curiosity, and resent her after-intrusion, as that of an impertinent spectre." Once again, it was the beauty, not the substance, of the prefatory poem that struck the reviewers' eyes, so that although one might find the tradition referred to in the poem "highly pleasing, . . . the circumstance itself, unconnected with the interest it receives from having been the subject of belief and credulous wonder in former days, strikes us as puerile, and as unworthy of the labor bestowed in drawing the reader's attention to it."

The Monthly for November 1815 was equally dismissive. But the *Gentleman's Magazine* and the July 1818 issue of *Blackwood's Edinburgh Magazine* praised Wordsworth for his pathos and his consummate skill in kindling "emotions congenial with his own." Tellingly, John Wilson, in *Blackwood's*, focused on the autobiographical referents in the dedicatory poem, here able to produce an appreciation for the tale to follow. "No verses" could be found that were "more simply yet profoundly affecting"; the reviewer was "sure" the lines would "dispose every feeling mind to come to the perusal of the poem itself with the most kindly and sympathetic emotions." Those readers who could not appreciate the poem were at fault, not the poet: the imperious demand for "strong passion and violent excitement" was a sign of "defects" in their imaginations which rendered them insensible to the poem's power.

Despite this delayed praise, the response to *The White Doe* was pretty much as Wordsworth's worst fears had supposed it would be: his efforts to win a different response to his poem had failed. Josiah Conder, in *The Eclectic*, willfully mistook Wordsworth's quotation from Bacon, using it as the basis of parody; like the others, he ignored the announced link to Spenser and pursued the inappropriately invoked Sir Walter Scott instead. In general, reviewers seemed to resent the identification they were supposed to feel between themselves and the credulous churchgoers. On the one hand, they peevishly charged Wordsworth with a mysticism that made him "inaccessible to common minds." Yet at the same time, they were irritated by the poem's simplicity of diction, which reminded them that the poem was written for readers less sophisticated than they. Hence, for example, Jeffrey's parting shot in the *Edinburgh Review*: "that the old Priory itself takes [the doe] for a daughter of the Eternal Prime . . . we have no doubt is a very great compliment, though we have not the good luck to understand what it means."

Years later, in 1843, Wordsworth responded to some of these attacks in a note he dictated to Isabella Fenwick. The opening paragraphs of the note turn back to the poem's origin and touch rather plaintively on some of the homelier problems of poetic composition.

The earlier half of this Poem was composed at Stockton-upon-Tees, when Mary and I were on a visit to her eldest Brother, Mr. Hutchinson, at the close of the year 1807. The country is flat, and the weather was rough. I was accustomed every day to walk to and fro under the shelter of a row of stacks in a field at a small distance from the town, and there poured forth my verses aloud as freely as they would come. Mary reminds me that her brother stood upon the punctilio of not sitting down to dinner till I joined the party; and it frequently happened that I did not make any appearance till too late, so that she was made uncomfortable. I here beg her pardon for this and similar transgressions during the whole course of our wedded life. To my beloved Sister the same apology is due.

When, from the visit just mentioned, we returned to Town-end, Grasmere, I proceeded with the Poem; it may be worth while to note, as a caution to others who may cast their eye on these memoranda, that the skin having been rubbed off my heel by my wearing too tight a shoe, though I desisted from walking I found that the irritation of the wounded part was kept up by the act of composition, to a degree that made it necessary to give my constitution a holiday. A rapid cure was the consequence. Poetic excitement, when accompanied by protracted labour in composition, has throughout my life brought on more or less bodily derangement. Nevertheless, I am, at the close of my seventy-third year, in what may be called excellent health; so that intellectual labour is not necessarily unfavourable to longevity. But perhaps I ought here to add that mine has been generally carried on out of doors.

These humble observations are followed by an important retrospective summary of the poet's intention:

Let me here say a few words of this Poem in the way of criticism. The subject being taken from feudal times has led to its being compared to some of Walter Scott's poems that belong to the same age and state of society. The comparison is inconsiderate. Sir Walter pursued the customary and very natural course of conducting an action, presenting various turns of fortune, to some outstanding point on which the mind might rest as a termination or catastrophe. The course I attempted to pursue is entirely different. Everything that is attempted by the principal personages in 'The White Doe' fails, so far as its object is external and substantial. So far as it is moral and spiritual it succeeds. The heroine of the Poem knows that her duty is not to interfere with the current of events, either to forward or delay them, but

> to abide
> The shock, and finally secure
> O'er pain and grief a triumph pure.

This she does in obedience to her brother's injunction, as most suitable to a mind and character that, under previous trials, had been proved to accord with his. She achieves this not without aid from the communication with the inferior Creature, which often leads her thoughts to revolve upon the past with a tender and humanizing influence that exalts rather than depresses her. The anticipated beatification, if I may so say, of her mind, and the apotheosis of the companion of her solitude, are the points at which the Poem aims, and constitute its legitimate catastrophe, far too spiritual a one for instant or widely-spread sympathy, but not therefore the less fitted to make a deep and permanent impression upon that class of minds who think and feel more independently, than the many do, of the surfaces of things and interests transitory because belonging more to the outward and social forms of life than to its internal spirit. How insignificant a thing, for example, does personal prowess appear compared with the fortitude of patience and heroic martyrdom; in other words, with struggles for the sake of principle, in preference to victory gloried in for its own sake.   [PW, III, 542–543, but quoted from DC MS. 153]

Communication with "inferior" creation, whether natural or human, was at the heart of Wordsworth's poetic project; that this idea lay somewhere between condescension and radical poetic vision was part of the mystery of its power. The Fenwick note above can be compared with Wordsworth's first defense of the poem some thirty-five years earlier, in the April 1808 letter to Coleridge which castigated Charles Lamb. The letter covers much the same ground as the later defense, but magnifies the importance of communion in the poem and its role in Emily's ability to endure:

It suffices that everything tends to account for the weekly pilgrimage of the Doe, which is made interesting by its connection with a human being, a Woman, who is intended to be honoured and loved for what she *endures,* and the manner in which she endures it; accomplishing a conquest over her own sorrows (which is the true subject of the Poem) by means, partly, of the native strength of her character, and partly by the persons and things with whom and which she is connected; and finally, after having exhibited the 'fortitude of patience and heroic martyrdom', ascending to pure etherial spirituality, and forwarded in that ascent of love by communion with a creature not of her own species, but spotless, beautiful, innocent and loving, in that temper of earthly love to which alone she can conform, without violation to the majesty of her losses, or degradation from those heights of heavenly serenity to which she has been raised.   [MY, I, 222]

Spiritual transformation ultimately depends more on the communal recognition of the doe's mysterious qualities and connection with the human past than on anything inherent in the animal. Rather than prescribing a Christian orthodoxy or a neo-pagan nature worship, the sanctified doe is the Wordsworthian emblem that replaces the "five dear wounds." It signifies a contemplative endurance achieved by the mind in communion with the memory of "old loves" inspired by nature. The end result is an emblem of suffering become saintlike—a result more important, at least to the human community that remains, than Emily's passage into a thing "wholly of the spirit." Thus, as Christopher Wordsworth, Jr., remembered, the "true action of the poem was spiritual — the subduing of the will, and all inferior passions, to the perfect purifying and spiritualizing of the intellectual nature; while the Doe, by connection with Emily, is raised as it were from its mere animal nature into something mysterious and saint-like" (*Memoirs*, II, 313).

The Catholic mystery of communion, which Wordsworth secularized even in this explicitly religious poem, refers here to the healing interchange between human beings as well as to the relation between the mind and nature. Emily's interchange with Francis, not merely with the doe, makes possible her secular sanctification, as Wordsworth explained in 1816 in a letter to Southey:

Now, the name Emily occurs just fifteen times in the poem; and out of these fifteen the epithet [consecrated] is attached to it *once*, and that for the express purpose of recalling the scene in which she had been consecrated by her brother's solemn adjuration that she would fulfil her destiny, and become

> A soul, by force of sorrows high,
> Uplifted to the purest sky
> Of undisturbed humanity!   [*MY*, II, 325]

He argued that "the point upon which the whole moral interest of the piece hinges, when that speech is closed," occurs when Francis kisses his sister. Thus Catholicism's central religious rite of transcendence and remembrance is here humanized to form the "hinge" on which the moral interest of the entire poem rests.

His defense notwithstanding, Wordsworth did recognize that *The White Doe* could be improved. Major revisions were introduced for the 1836 edition of *Poetical Works;* they can be followed in the *apparatus criticus* to the reading text (at each previous printing changes had been introduced, mostly in punctuation, but Wordsworth modernized spellings and decapitalized common nouns as well). Work toward the 1836 edition shows many transpositions in line or word order which appear to have been introduced purely for poetic effect. We find numerous omissions of awkward phrases and vigorous compressions of language, as in Canto VI, 1381–1383, 1520–1521, and 1551–1552. More substantial changes center on the representations of Francis, Emily, and old Norton. Most often these alterations are clarifications along the lines of Wordsworth's written explications of the poem. Some invoke important details at key moments (for example, Canto IV, 978/979), while others emphasize internal motivations (III, 896–898) or enliven the narrative with more dynamic language (VI, 1437–1444; and in 1827, VI, 1407–1408). The reiteration of key phrases appears most often (for example, III, 931–932; IV, 1056–1057, 1074–1080, 1149–1150; VI,

1533–1535; and the opening epigraph to Canto VII). Lines 1500–1535 of Canto VI are a case in point: lines 1501–1507 of the 1815 text are omitted, and with them much of the savagery of Francis's death; lines 1509–1517 are similarly softened in revision. The change reinvokes Francis's symbolic act of intervention in emphasizing the banner in his hand, and his death becomes an imitation of Christ's. (Revision in 1845 brings the work full circle, with the inclusion of Emily's role in designing the banner as well.) The diction of lines 1520–1527 is compressed, and lines 1533–1535 emphasize the weight of the pain Emily is about to endure.

Nevertheless, after these revisions Wordsworth admitted to Justice John Taylor Coleridge in October 1836 that "he should devote much labour to perfecting the execution of it in the mere business parts, in which, from anxiety to 'get on' with the more important parts, he was sensible that imperfections had crept in, which gave the style a feebleness of character" (*Memoirs*, II, 313). He touched here on a failing he was never able to remedy. The following year he wrote to Edward Quillinan, who had provided him with "too little of the benefit" of his "help and judgement," and asked him to take the trouble of "comparing the corrections in my last edition [of 1836] with the text in the preceding one [of 1832]" to see if anything struck him "as being altered for the worse" (*LY*, VI, 465). But nothing else about *The White Doe* appears in the Wordsworths' personal correspondence, and no further verbal revisions of the poem were ever made. The long history of Wordsworth's last lyrical ballad had come to a close.

We are left with a poem whose principal end of "pure etherial spirituality" rested on Wordsworth's most unobtrusive rendering of the internal workings of the imagination, and for this reason its ideas lay beyond full representation, frustrating even their creator. Thus the poem that had begun as an experiment remained uniquely dependent on its varied series of "forerunners" and notes, quoted or composed—in prose, in epigraphs, in verse. Finally, in 1836, as if convinced at last that only an enigma, expressed in poetry alone, might both explain and represent his "highest work," Wordsworth prefaced the final canto of *The White Doe* with these lines from his *Address to Kilchurn Castle:*

> Powers there are
> That touch each other to the quick—in modes
> Which the gross world no sense hath to perceive,
> No soul to dream of.

Editorial Procedure

Like other volumes in this series, this edition provides two kinds of text: (1) "reading texts," from which all complexities and variant readings are cleared away, and (2) transcriptions of manuscripts, usually with facing photographs. Editorial procedures have been adapted to the different aims of these two styles of presentation.

The reading texts here are reproduced from the first edition of *The White Doe* (London, 1815), a volume that contained not only the title poem but a prose Advertisement, a prefatory sonnet ("Weak is the will of Man"), a prefatory prose passage from Bacon's essay *Of Atheism,* a dedicatory poem ("In trellis'd shed"), and, following *The White Doe,* Wordsworth's ballad-poem *The Force of Prayer* as well as his notes, which run to twenty-two pages in the 1815 edition and contain a 152-line ballad of Thomas Percy's about the Nortons. Beneath these reading texts runs an *apparatus criticus* that shows verbal variants; nonverbal variants are presented separately (pp. 165–181). Two of the texts that appeared with *The White Doe* in 1815—the prefatory sonnet and *The Force of Prayer*—had been published some weeks earlier in 1815 in Wordsworth's collected *Poems,* and their association with the *Doe* was brief: by 1820 *The Force of Prayer* was detached and by 1827 the sonnet reverted to its original identity as one of the "Miscellaneous Sonnets" in Wordsworth's four-volume *Miscellaneous Poems.* Variants for these two texts are therefore reported only where they remained attached to the *Doe;* complete variants for all other reading texts are reported through all authorized lifetime English editions and in pertinent manuscripts. Further particulars are given in the headnote to the reading texts, below (pp. 71–73).

The other main form of text is transcription of a manuscript. Here the aim is to show with reasonable typographical accuracy everything in the manuscript which could be helpful to a study of the poem's growth and development. Even false starts and corrected letters can reveal the writer's intention, and they are here recorded, though reinforced letters and random marks are normally not. Wordsworth's hand in the manuscripts is discriminated by the use of Roman type; the work of all other copyists (here, Dorothy, Mary, and Coleridge) is presented in italic type, with the writer identified in footnotes. Where revision has taken place on a printed text (as when Wordsworth marked up a copy of his 1832 *Poetical Works*), the transcription renders the print in boldface type. As in other volumes in this series, revisions are shown in type of reduced size, and an effort is made to arrange spacing and other physical features so that they resemble those of the manuscript, though minor adjustments have occasionally been made in the interest of clarity. To avoid cluttering and obscuring the transcriptions, which are intended to provide easy reading of the manuscripts, large deletion strokes, X's, and other such devices visible in the facing photographs have been omitted. The transcriptions do, however, show horizontal cross-out lines and slashes run through individual words and letters, since they frequently help the reader to follow the process of revision.

The various materials in the manuscripts fall into discrete units, and transcriptions of them are for convenience presented in the order of materials in the published volume of 1815: drafts for the prose "Advertizement" in DC MS. 61 are followed by texts of the dedicatory poem in DC MS. 80 and MS. 1815, then by fair-copy portions of *The White Doe* proper in DC MSS. 61 and 62. Finally come the verse drafts in DC MS. 61 (and in one piece of MS. 1832/36) and texts of *The Force of Prayer*. A distinctive feature of this edition is that it presents about half of the pre-London, pre-Coleridge *White Doe*, hitherto thought to be lost, in the fair-copy portions of MSS. 61 and 62, which are linked together by sequential line numbering. Fuller information may be found in the headnotes to transcriptions of MSS. 61 and 62.

In the numbering of leaves in these and other manuscripts, stubs are counted, but not pasted-down endpapers. In the *apparatus criticus,* citations from manuscript are given uniformly in roman type, to avoid confusion and unnecessary elaboration.

The following symbols and abbreviations are used, variously, in the reading texts, notes, transcriptions, and collations:

[ ]	Gap or blank.
[?delight]	Conjectural reading.
[? ?]	Illegible passage, each question mark representing one word.
[- - - ?- - -]	Illegible passage, deleted.
d ⎫ has ⎭	An overwriting: the writer converted "has" to "had" by writing the "d" on top of the "s."
delight	Written over an illegible erasure.
beauty ⎫ delight ⎭	Word written over an erasure that can still be read.
alt	Alternate.

del	Deleted or deletion.
del to	Reading changed to another reading; the original is deleted.
erus	Erased or erasure.
illeg	Illegible.
punct	Punctuation.
rev	Revised or revision.

Reading Texts, with Verbal Variants in an *Apparatus Criticus*

Advertisement
"Weak is the will of Man"
Epigraph from Bacon
Dedicatory Poem: "In trellis'd shed"
The White Doe of Rylstone; or The Fate of the Nortons
The Force of Prayer
Wordsworth's Notes

Reading Texts

The texts that follow are based on the first edition of *The White Doe*, published by Longman in 1815. Line numbers in the margin are added editorially. Although the printer's manuscript survives (in Mary Wordsworth's hand, with scattered corrections and revisions in William's), the proof sheets do not, save for a half-sheet without any markings, now cut into three pieces and bound with the manuscript. Discrepancies between manuscript and first edition can thus result either from the printer's alteration of copy or from Wordsworth's alterations on proof. In the absence of further evidence, it must be assumed that Wordsworth read his proofs with care, and that the first edition gives a truer picture of his intentions in 1815 than the printer's manuscript; accidentals, in particular, almost certainly stand in the first edition as Wordsworth wanted them, within the constraints of Longman's house style. In any event, all variant readings in the manuscript are recorded in the *apparatus criticus*.

The *apparatus criticus* is divided into two parts: substantives, or verbal variants, are shown at the foot of the page, while accidentals, or nonverbal variants, are listed separately, beginning on page 165, below. (Changes involving only the ampersand are omitted.) Each *apparatus* records variant readings of *The White Doe* and excerpts from the poem that appeared in authorized English editions during Wordsworth's lifetime. Titles of these editions are abbreviated as follows: (the place of publication is London):

1820 *The Miscellaneous Poems of William Wordsworth* (4 vols.; 1820).
1827 *The Poetical Works of William Wordsworth* (5 vols.; 1827).
1831 *Selections from the Poems of William Wordsworth, Esq.*, ed. Joseph Hine (1831).
1832 *The Poetical Works of William Wordsworth* (4 vols.; 1832).
1834 *Selections from the Poems of William Wordsworth, Esq.*, ed. Joseph Hine (1834).
1836 *The Poetical Works of William Wordsworth* (6 vols.; 1836–1837).
1840 *The Poetical Works of William Wordsworth* (6 vols.; 1840). A stereotyped reissue of the volumes of 1836–1837, with various alterations; again reissued, with a few alterations, in 1841 and 1843.
1845 *The Poems of William Wordsworth* (1 vol.; 1845). Reissued in stereotype in 1847 and 1849.
1846 *The Poetical Works of William Wordsworth* (7 vols.; 1846). Another stereotyped reissue of the six volumes of 1836, with further alterations, including an additional volume consisting mainly of works published in *Poems, Chiefly of Early and Late Years* (1842); reissued, again with a few alterations, in 1849.
1850 *The Poetical Works of William Wordsworth* (6 vols.; 1849–1850).

In the *apparatus,* a citation of each volume in the list above implies stereo-typed reissues as well, unless otherwise noted, as follows:

1840   implies the reissues of 1841 and 1843.
1841   implies the 1843 reissue of *1840.*
1845   implies the reissues of 1847 and 1849.
1846   implies the reissue of 1849.
1847   implies the 1849 reissue of *1845.*

The year of an edition followed by a short dash indicates that subsequent editions repeat the reading.

Other variants cited in the *apparatus* are taken from the manuscript that served as printer's copy for the first edition of 1815 and from three surviving copies of *The White Doe* which were used to prepare later editions of the poem. These sources are abbreviated as follows:

MS. 1815   Printer's copy for the first edition of *The White Doe,* now at King's College Library, Cambridge. A full description may be found below, p. 215.

MS. 1815/20 WD   A copy of the first edition of *The White Doe* marked up to serve as printer's copy for the second edition, in *Miscellaneous Poems* of 1820; now in the possession of Robert Kirkpatrick of Chapel Hill, North Carolina.

MS. 1832/36   A copy of *Poetical Works* (1832) used in preparation of the 1836 edition of *Poetical Works;* now in the English Poetry Collection, Wellesley College Library.

MS. 1836/45   A copy of *Poetical Works* (1836) used in preparation of the 1840 *Poetical Works* and the 1845 *Poems;* now in The Royal Library, Windsor Castle.

The epigraphs and the dedicatory poem in the first edition of *The White Doe,* along with the material added at the end of the volume—*The Force of Prayer* and the notes—are treated in different ways. The following pieces remained attached to *The White Doe* through its lifetime printings, and variants are thus listed routinely in the *apparatus* below: the full title; the prose Advertisement; the prose epigraph, by Lord Bacon; the dedicatory poem, "In trellis'd shed"; and the notes (from which Percy's ballad "The Rising of the North" was dropped in 1820). From 1836 onward, and in MS. 1832/36, a quotation from *The Borderers* was prefaced to the poem, and its variants have been treated in the same way.

Two pieces that were included in the original *White Doe* volume, however, were shortly detached. Both had made their *first* appearance in the 1815 two-volume *Poems,* published five or six weeks before *The White Doe.* The first of these pieces was the dedicatory sonnet, serving as a verse epigraph, "Weak is the will of Man," which was placed among "Miscellaneous Sonnets" in volume 2 of the 1815 *Poems.* In 1820 it remained attached to the *Doe* (in vol. 3), but from 1827 onward it reverted to its original identity as one of the miscellaneous sonnets. Only the 1820 print variants are therefore shown here, along with variants in the 1815 printer's manuscript of *The White Doe;* later variants are included in the volume edited by Carl Ketcham for this series, *Shorter Poems: 1807–1820,* which presents the first printing (in *Poems,* 1815) as the base text.

The second piece to be detached, *The Force of Prayer,* included in both the printer's manuscript and the first edition of *The White Doe,* appeared in the 1815 *Poems* among "Poems of Sentiment and Reflection," where it remained through 1850. Only its prepublication variants are therefore given here: one of the early texts, in DC MS. 61, is presented in full transcription below (pp. 385–389) facing the other early text, Dorothy Wordsworth's letter to Jane Marshall of 18 October 1807. Nonverbal variants in the printer's manuscript (MS. 1815)—there are no verbal variants—are shown separately. All *printed* variants are collected in Carl Ketcham's edition, which presents the version in *Poems* of 1815 as the base text.

In the *apparatus* of variants in Wordsworth's notes to *The White Doe,* changes in citation of page and line numbers required as the pagination changed from edition to edition are not recorded. In citations from MS. 1832/36, the hand may be understood to be Mary Wordsworth's, unless otherwise specified.

An engraving by J.C. Bromley of Sir George Beaumont's painting of the white doe

THE

WHITE DOE

OF

RYLSTONE;

OR   5

THE FATE OF THE NORTONS.

A POEM.

BY

WILLIAM WORDSWORTH.

LONDON: 10

PRINTED FOR
LONGMAN, HURST, REES, ORME, AND BROWN,
PATERNOSTER-ROW,
BY JAMES BALLANTYNE AND CO., EDINBURGH.

1815.

title page   _inscribed_ W. Wordsworth Esqr / Rydal Mount / Kendal / Proofs by / Post. *MS. 1815*
7–13   *omitted 1820–*
11–13   Printed for Longman H. R. O & B / Paternoster Row. *MS. 1815*
14–15   *omitted MS. 1815, 1820–*

ADVERTISEMENT.

DURING *the summer of* 1807, *the Author visited, for the
first time, the beautiful Scenery that surrounds Bolton Priory,
in Yorkshire; and the Poem of* THE WHITE DOE, *founded
upon a Tradition connected with the place, was composed at
the close of the same year.*   5

"Weak is the will of Man, his judgement blind;
"Remembrance persecutes, and Hope betrays;
"Heavy is woe;—and joy, for human kind,
"A mournful thing, so transient is the blaze!"—
Thus might he paint our lot of mortal days   5
Who wants the glorious faculty, assigned
To elevate the more-than-reasoning Mind,
And colour life's dark cloud with orient rays.
Imagination is that sacred power,
Imagination lofty and refined: 10
'Tis her's to pluck the amaranthine Flower
Of Faith, and round the Sufferer's temples bind
Wreaths that endure affliction's heaviest shower,
And do not shrink from sorrow's keenest wind.

---

advertisement   added by WW on verso of leaves containing "In trellis'd shed" *and headed* And the
following brief advertisement to be prefixed to the Poem.— *MS. 1815*
  1 *omitted 1820*
  2 During *rev from* In the *del MS. 1815*   the Author *rev from* the author, *MS. 1815* I
1845–
  2–3 visited, for the first time, *rev from* for the first time, visited *MS. 1815*
  3 Scenery] scenery *1827–1832* country *1836–*
  4 Poem of THE WHITE DOE] following Poem *MS. 1815*
  5 the] that *1836–*
  6 year. *rev from* year, with the [?verse] *del MS. 1815*

---

verse epigraph   follows prose epigraph 1820; omitted 1827–
title inserted   Sonnet.— *MS. 1815 (WW)*
  1/2 [?Glaring] the [?faults], the [? ? ?find;] *entire line del MS. 1815*
  5 Thus *rev from* So *MS. 1815*

"They that deny a God, destroy Man's nobility: for certainly Man is of kinn to the Beasts by his Body; and if he be not of kinn to God by his Spirit, he is a base ignoble Creature. It destroys likewise Magnanimity, and the raising of humane Nature: for take an example of a Dogg, and mark what a generosity and courage he will put on, when he finds himself maintained by a Man, who to him is instead of a God, or Melior Natura. Which courage is manifestly such, as that Creature without that confidence of a better Nature than his own, could never attain. So Man, when he resteth and assureth himself upon Divine protection and favour, gathereth a force and faith which human Nature in itself could not obtain."

5

10

LORD BACON.

---

prose epigraph   entered in MW's hand MS. 1815; transferred by marginal note, MS. 1815/20 WD (MW): This *extract* to come before the sonnet which now precedes it. And [it is submitted to the Printer whether the effect would not be better if they were printed on separate pages *del*] print one on each side of the leaf— *precedes verse epigraph 1820, omitted 1827, follows dedicatory poem 1832, followed by 13 lines from* The Borderers *in MW's hand MS. 1832/36, with notes in MW's and JC's hands:* These two mottoes to be printed in such small type as to prevent the page being crowded— & leaving a requisite space between *then all del to* This *prose* motto to be transferred to the next page—the Poem to begin lower down. *then note extended by JC and enclosed in parens:* The other motto to be placed in the middle of this page. *transferred as directed 1836– but placed following* Borderers *extract 1845–*
   2   Beasts] Beast *1845, 1850*   to God *rev from* of God MS. *1815*
   8   resteth *inserted with caret MS. 1815*
Borderers *extract inserted following Bacon quotation MS. 1832/36 (MW), then preceding Bacon quotation 1836*
            'Action is transitory—a step, a blow,
            The motion of a muscle—this way or that—
            Tis' done; & in the after-vacancy
            We wonder at ourselves like men betrayed:
            Suffering is permanent obscure & dark,   [5]
            And has the nature of infinity.
            Yet through that darkness (infinite [as *del by JC to*] though it seem
            And irremoveable) gracious openings lie
            By which the soul—with patient steps of thought
            Now toiling, wafted now on wings of prayer—   [10]
            May pass in hope, &, tho' from mortal bonds
            Yet undelivered, rise with sure ascent
            Even to the fountain-head of peace divine'.
                                    M. S.
adopted as revised 1836– but [3] Tis' . . . &] 'Tis . . . and   [5] permanent . . .&] permanent, . . . and   [8] lie] lie,   [11] &, tho'] and, though   [13] divine'.] divine.'   [14] M.S. *omitted 1845, 1850*

From Francis Bacon's *Of Atheism*. APC notes divergences from Bacon's text: "base ignoble" for "base and noble" and "humane" for "human." After 1815 "beasts" becomes "beast."

77

In trellis'd shed with clustering roses gay,
And, MARY! oft beside our blazing fire,
When years of wedded life were as a day
Whose current answers to the heart's desire,
Did we together read in Spenser's Lay   5
How Una, sad of soul—in sad attire,
The gentle Una, born of heavenly birth,
To seek her Knight went wandering o'er the earth.

Ah, then, Beloved! pleasing was the smart,
And the tear precious in compassion shed   10
For Her, who, pierced by sorrow's thrilling dart,
Did meekly bear the pang unmerited;
Meek as that emblem of her lowly heart
The milk-white Lamb which in a line she led,—
And faithful, loyal in her innocence,   15
Like the brave Lion slain in her defence.

Notes could we hear as of a faery shell
Attuned to words with sacred wisdom fraught;
Free Fancy prized each specious miracle,
And all its finer inspiration caught;   20
'Till, in the bosom of our rustic Cell,
We by a lamentable change were taught

---

dedicatory poem   for readings of MS. 1815, see full transcription, pp. 217–223, below
7   born of heavenly] of celestial *MS. 1832/36 (JC)–*

The poem is written out in Wordsworth's hand on the back of two scraps of proof sheets of *The White Doe*, one containing text at the end of Canto IV, the other text from Canto V. They are directed to "Mr. James Ballantyne, Printer, Edinburgh," and stamped with a date: "Apr 8 1815." Above the text Wordsworth wrote: "The following is to be prefixed to the Poem." All corrections and revisions are in his hand. The sheets are now bound in at the back of the King's College manuscript of *The White Doe* (MS. 1815).
   1   APC follows Knight in identifying the shed as the one at the top of the orchard behind Dove Cottage.
   5   Spenser, *Faerie Queene* (APC).
   7   *F.Q.*, I.iii.28.9 (APC).
10–12   *F.Q.*, I.iii.1.2–3 (APC).
11   *F.Q.*, I.vii.25.2 (APC).
14   *F.Q.*, I.i.iv.9. In *Personal Talk*, ll. 40–42 (1807), WW claims "heavenly Una with her milk-white Lamb" as among the "personal themes" he held "pre-eminently dear" (APC).
16   *F.Q.*, I.iii (APC).

That "bliss with mortal Man may not abide:"—
How nearly joy and sorrow are allied!

For us the stream of fiction ceased to flow,   25
For us the voice of melody was mute.
—But, as soft gales dissolve the dreary snow
And give the timid herbage leave to shoot,
Heaven's breathing influence failed not to bestow
A timely promise of unlooked-for fruit,   30
Fair fruit of pleasure and serene content
From blossoms wild of fancies innocent.

It soothed us—it beguiled us—then, to hear
Once more of troubles wrought by magic spell;
And griefs whose aery motion comes not near   35
The pangs that tempt the Spirit to rebel;
Then, with mild Una in her sober chear,
High over hill and low adown the dell
Again we wandered, willing to partake
All that she suffered for her dear Lord's sake.   40

Then, too, this Song *of mine* once more could please,
Where, anguish, strange as dreams of restless sleep,
Is tempered and allayed by sympathies
Aloft ascending, and descending deep,
Even to the inferior Kinds; whom forest trees   45
Protect from heating sunbeams, and the sweep
Of the sharp winds;—fair Creatures!—to whom Heaven
A calm and sinless life, with love, hath given.

This tragic Story cheared us; for it speaks
Of female patience winning firm repose;   50
And of the recompense which conscience seeks
A bright, encouraging example shows;
Needful when o'er wide realms the tempest breaks,

---

51   which] that *1836*–

---

23   *F.Q.*, I.viii.44.9. WW refers to the deaths of his brother John in 1805 and his children
Catharine and Thomas in 1812 (APC).
    38–39   *F.Q.*, I.vii.28.8–9 (APC).
    44   *Prospectus to the Recluse*, l. 29.
    44–45   *The Excursion*, IV, 352–358 (de Selincourt).

Needful amid life's ordinary woes;—
Hence, not for them unfitted who would bless   55
A happy hour with holier happiness.

He serves the Muses erringly and ill,
Whose aim is pleasure light and fugitive:
O, that my mind were equal to fulfill
The comprehensive mandate which they give—   60
Vain aspiration of an earnest will!
Yet in this moral Strain a power may live,
Beloved Wife! such solace to impart
As it hath yielded to thy tender heart.

    RYDAL MOUNT, WESTMORELAND, }   65
        April 20, 1815.   }

THE

WHITE DOE OF RYLSTONE.

CANTO FIRST.

FROM Bolton's old monastic tower
The bells ring loud with gladsome power;
The sun is bright; the fields are gay
With people in their best array
Of stole and doublet, hood and scarf,   5
Along the banks of the crystal Wharf,
Through the Vale retired and lowly,
Trooping to that summons holy.
And, up among the moorlands, see
What sprinklings of blithe company!   10
Of lasses and of shepherd grooms,
That down the steep hills force their way,
Like cattle through the budded brooms;
Path, or no path, what care they?
And thus in joyous mood they hie   15
To Bolton's mouldering Priory.

  What would they there?—Full fifty years
That sumptuous Pile, with all its peers,
Too harshly hath been doomed to taste
The bitterness of wrong and waste: 20
Its courts are ravaged; but the tower
Is standing with a voice of power,

---

3   is] shines *MS. 1832/36 (WW)*—
6   of the] of *MS. 1815/20 WD*

Title   See WW's extensive note on the sources of his poem, which includes the popular legend of the doe taken from Whitaker, the history of the rising of the north collected from various sources, the ballad from Percy's collection, and a description of the priory and the surrounding landscape.
    1   See WW's note.
    11–13   Spenser, *The Shepheardes Calendar*, February, ll. 35–36, suggested by J. C. Maxwell, *Notes and Queries*, n.s. 17 (October 1970), 380.

81

That ancient voice which wont to call
To mass or some high festival;
And in the shattered fabric's heart   25
Remaineth one protected part;
A rural Chapel, neatly drest,
In covert like a little nest;
And thither young and old repair,
This Sabbath-day, for praise and prayer.   30

   Fast the church-yard fills;—anon
Look again, and they all are gone;
The cluster round the porch, and the folk
Who sate in the shade of the Prior's Oak!
And scarcely have they disappeared   35
Ere the prelusive hymn is heard:—
With one consent the people rejoice,
Filling the church with a lofty voice!
They sing a service which they feel:
For 'tis the sun-rise now of zeal,   40
And faith and hope are in their prime,
In great Eliza's golden time.

   A moment ends the fervent din,
And all is hushed, without and within;
For, though the priest more tranquilly   45
Recites the holy liturgy,
The only voice which you can hear
Is the river murmuring near.
—When soft!—the dusky trees between,
And down the path through the open green,   50
Where is no living thing to be seen;
And through yon gateway, where is found,
Beneath the arch with ivy bound,
Free entrance to the church-yard ground;
And right across the verdant sod   55

  27–28 A Chapel, like a wild-bird's nest,
          Closely embowered & timely drest; *MS. 1832/36 (WW)— but &*] and *1836—*
  41 Of a pure faith the vernal prime; *MS. 1832/36 (WW)— but* prime;] prime— *1836—*
  55 Across the smooth & even sod *then line del MS. 1832/36 (WW), omitted 1836—*

---

  27 See WW's note.
  34 See WW's note.

Towards the very house of God;
—Comes gliding in with lovely gleam,
Comes gliding in serene and slow,
Soft and silent as a dream,
A solitary Doe!   60
White she is as lily of June,
And beauteous as the silver moon
When out of sight the clouds are driven,
And she is left alone in heaven;
Or like a ship some gentle day   65
In sunshine sailing far away,
A glittering ship, that hath the plain
Of ocean for her own domain.

   Lie silent in your graves ye dead!
Lie quiet in your church-yard bed!   70
Ye living tend your holy cares,
Ye multitude pursue your prayers,
And blame not me if my heart and sight
Are occupied with one delight!
'Tis a work for sabbath hours   75
If I with this bright Creature go;
Whether she be of forest bowers,
From the bowers of earth below;
Or a Spirit, for one day given,
A gift of grace from purest heaven.   80

   What harmonious pensive changes
Wait upon her as she ranges
Round and through this Pile of state,
Overthrown and desolate!
Now a step or two her way   85
Is through space of open day,
Where the enamoured sunny light
Brightens her that was so bright;
Now doth a delicate shadow fall,
Falls upon her like a breath,   90
From some lofty arch or wall,

---

  56 Towards *del to* Right towards *then line del MS. 1832/36 (WW), omitted 1836–*
  72 multitudes *with* s *eras MS. 1815*
  80 gift] pledge *MS. 1832/36 (WW)–*
  86 Is] Leads *MS. 1832/36 (WW)–*

As she passes underneath:
Now some gloomy nook partakes
Of the glory that she makes,—
High-ribbed vault of stone, or cell   95
With perfect cunning framed as well
Of stone, and ivy, and the spread
Of the elder's bushy head;
Some jealous and forbidding cell,
That doth the living stars repel,   100
And where no flower hath leave to dwell.

   The presence of this wandering Doe
Fills many a damp obscure recess
With lustre of a saintly show;
And, re-appearing, she no less   105
To the open day gives blessedness.
But say, among these holy places,
Which thus assiduously she paces,
Comes she with a votary's task,
Rite to perform, or boon to ask?   110
Fair Pilgrim! harbours she a sense
Of sorrow, or of reverence?
Can she be grieved for quire or shrine,
Crushed as if by wrath divine?
For what survives of house where God   115
Was worshipped, or where Man abode;
For old magnificence undone;
Or for the gentler work begun
By Nature, softening and concealing,
And busy with a hand of healing,—   120
The altar, whence the cross was rent,
Now rich with mossy ornament,—

---

106 Sheds on the flowers that round her blow
     A more than sunny liveliness: *MS. 1832/36– but* liveliness. *1836–*
108 assiduously *del to* habitually *MS. 1832/36*
111–112 *del and entered at 120/121, then reinstated with* Stet *in original position, MS. 1832/36*
117 For old *rev from* Old *MS. 1815*
118 Or for] Or *MS. 1815*
120 a] the *del to* a *MS. 1815*
121 The] For *1827–1832; rev to* Or *MS. 1832/36–*

The dormitory's length laid bare,
Where the wild-rose blossoms fair;
And sapling ash, whose place of birth   125
Is that lordly chamber's hearth?
—She sees a warrior carved in stone
Among the thick weeds stretched alone;
A warrior, with his shield of pride
Cleaving humbly to his side,   130
And hands in resignation prest,
Palm to palm, on his tranquil breast:
Methinks she passeth by the sight,
As a common creature might:
If she be doomed to inward care,   135
Or service, it must lie elsewhere.
—But hers are eyes serenely bright,
And on she moves, with pace how light!
Nor spares to stoop her head, and taste
The dewy turf with flowers bestrown;   140
And in this way she fares, till at last
Beside the ridge of a grassy grave
In quietness she lays her down;
Gently as a weary wave
Sinks, when the summer breeze hath died,   145
Against an anchored vessel's side;
Even so, without distress, doth she
Lie down in peace, and lovingly.

---

123   Thc] Or *1827–1832*
123–126   *del MS. 1832/36, then rev to*
        Mourns she to see the chamber's hearth
        That to the sapling ash gives birth
        Or dormitory's & *then restarted on facing verso for insertion before l. 121:*

                 ⎧ for lordly ⎫
        Mourns she ⎨ to see the ⎬ chamber's hearth
                 ⎩   ⎭
        That to the sapling ash gives birth
        F⎫
         ⎬Or dormitory's length laid bare
            ⎧ere
        Wh⎨i[?] the wild-rose blossoms fair;
        Or altar, & —
1836– as MS. 1832/36 rev but birth] birth; *and* wild-rose] wild rose
    127   sees *del, then reinstated MS. 1832/36*
    133   Methinks she passeth by] But she as little heeds *MS. 1832/36* As little she regards *1836–*
    141   in this way . . . till] thus . . . until *1827–*

---

    127   Knight notes that the headstone is WW's invention.

The day is placid in its going,
To a lingering motion bound,   150
Like the river in its flowing;
Can there be a softer sound?
So the balmy minutes pass,
While this radiant Creature lies
Couched upon the dewy grass,   155
Pensively with downcast eyes.
—When now again the people rear
A voice of praise, with awful chear!
It is the last, the parting song;
And from the temple forth they throng—   160
And quickly spread themselves abroad—
While each pursues his several road.
But some, a variegated band
Of middle-aged, and old, and young,
And little children by the hand   165
Upon their leading mothers hung,
Turn, with obeisance gladly paid,
Towards the spot, where, full in view,
The lovely Doe of whitest hue,
Her sabbath couch has made.   170

It was a solitary mound;
Which two spears' length of level ground
Did from all other graves divide:
As if in some respect of pride;
Or melancholy's sickly mood,   175
Still shy of human neighbourhood;
Or guilt, that humbly would express
A penitential loneliness.

"Look, there she is, my Child! draw near;
She fears not, wherefore should we fear?   180

---

152   softer] gentler *del to* softer *MS. 1815 (?WW)*
151–152   Like the crystal stream now flowing
             With its softest summer sound: *MS. 1832/36 (JC)*–
157   —When . . . rear] —But . . . raise *MS. 1832/36*–
158   With awful cheer a voice of praise; *MS. 1832/36*–
167   Turn, with] With mute *MS. 1832/36*–
168   Towards] Turn towards *MS. 1832/36*–   the *rev from* a *MS. 1815*
169   The White Doe, to *her* service true, *MS. 1832/36*– *but no italics 1836*–
170   has] hath *del to* has *MS. 1815 (?WW)*

She means no harm;"—but still the Boy,
To whom the words were softly said,
Hung back, and smiled and blushed for joy,
A shame-faced blush of glowing red!
Again the Mother whispered low,   185
"Now you have seen the famous Doe;
From Rylstone she hath found her way
Over the hills this sabbath-day;
Her work, whate'er it be, is done,
And she will depart when we are gone;   190
Thus doth she keep, from year to year,
Her sabbath morning, foul or fair."

   This whisper soft repeats what he
Had known from early infancy.
Bright is the Creature—as in dreams   195
The Boy had seen her—yea more bright—
But is she truly what she seems?—
He asks with insecure delight,
Asks of himself—and doubts—and still
The doubt returns against his will: 200
Though he, and all the standers-by,
Could tell a tragic history
Of facts divulged, wherein appear
Substantial motive, reason clear,
Why thus the milk-white Doe is found   205
Couchant beside that lonely mound;
And why she duly loves to pace
The circuit of this hallowed place.
Nor to the Child's enquiring mind
Is such perplexity confined: 210
For, 'spite of sober truth, that sees
A world of fixed remembrances
Which to this mystery belong,
If, undeceived, my skill can trace
The characters of every face,   215
There lack not strange delusion here,

193–194   *del MS. 1832/36*
195   is] was *MS. 1832/36–*
206   Couchant] Couch[?ed] *rev to* Couchant *MS. 1815 (WW)*
210   such *rev from* [?this] *MS. 1815(WW)*
216   lack] lacks *MS. 1815*

Conjecture vague, and idle fear,
And superstitious fancies strong,
Which do the gentle Creature wrong.

That bearded, staff-supported Sire,   220
(Who in his youth had often fed
Full cheerily on convent-bread,
And heard old tales by the convent-fire,
And lately hath brought home the scars
Gathered in long and distant wars)   225
That Old Man—studious to expound
The spectacle—hath mounted high
To days of dim antiquity;
When Lady Aäliza mourned
Her Son, and felt in her despair,   230
The pang of unavailing prayer;
Her Son in Wharf's abysses drowned,
The noble Boy of Egremound.
From which affliction, when God's grace
At length had in her heart found place,   235
A pious structure, fair to see,
Rose up—this stately Priory!
The Lady's work,—but now laid low;
To the grief of her soul that doth come and go,
In the beautiful form of this innocent Doe: 240
Which, though seemingly doomed in its breast to sustain
A softened remembrance of sorrow and pain,
Is spotless, and holy, and gentle, and bright,—
And glides o'er the earth like an angel of light.

Pass, pass who will, yon chantry door;   245
And, through the chink in the fractured floor
Look down, and see a griesly sight;

---

221   youth had] youth hath *1827–1832* boyhood *MS. 1832/36–*
223   convent-fire] kitchen-fire *MS. 1815*
224   the] his *MS. 1832/36*   And to his grave will go with scars, *1836–*
225   Gathered in] Relics of *MS. 1832/36 (JC)–*
227   hath mounted] is mounting *MS. 1832/36–*
234   God's] the *MS. 1832/36–*
235   At length] Of God *MS. 1832/36–*
240   beautiful *rev from* innocent *MS. 1815*

---

229   See WW's note.
245   See WW's note.

A vault where the bodies are buried upright!
There face by face, and hand by hand,
The Claphams and Mauleverers stand;   250
And, in his place, among son and sire,
Is John de Clapham, that fierce Esquire,—
A valiant man, and a name of dread,
In the ruthless wars of the White and Red;—
Who dragged Earl Pembroke from Banbury church,   255
And smote off his head on the stones of the porch!
Look down among them, if you dare;
Oft does the White Doe loiter there,
Prying into the darksome rent;
Nor can it be with good intent:—   260
So thinks that Dame of haughty air,
Who hath a Page her book to hold,
And wears a frontlet edged with gold.
Well may her thoughts be harsh; for she
Numbers among her ancestry   265
Earl Pembroke, slain so impiously!

  That slender Youth, a scholar pale,
From Oxford come to his native vale,
He also hath his own conceit:
It is, thinks he, the gracious Fairy,   270
Who loved the Shepherd Lord to meet
In his wanderings solitary;
Wild notes she in his hearing sang,
A song of Nature's hidden powers;
That whistled like the wind, and rang   275
Among the rocks and holly bowers.
'Twas said that she all shapes could wear;

---

258 Oft does the White Doe *rev from* The White Doe oft doth *MS. 1815 (WW)*
260 Nor can it *rev from* Nor it *MS. 1815 (WW)*
264 Harsh thoughts with her high mood agree *MS. 1832/36– but* agree] agree— *1836–*
265 Numbers] She counts *MS. 1832/36* Who counts *1836–*
273 sang *rev from* sung *MS. 1815 (WW)*
275 rang *rev from* rung *MS. 1815 (?WW)*

---

  254 WW's readers would have recognized this allusion to the wars between the rebel Lancastrians and the royalists from York, of whom the Earl of Pembroke was an illustrious member. APC notes that WW follows Whitaker, who says that John Clapham "is said to have beheaded with his own hands the Earl of Pembroke, in the church porch of Banbury."
  271 See WW's note.

And oftentimes before him stood,
Amid the trees of some thick wood,
In semblance of a lady fair,   280
And taught him signs, and shewed him sights,
In Craven's dens, on Cumbria's heights;
When under cloud of fear he lay,
A shepherd clad in homely grey,
Nor left him at his later day.   285
And hence, when he, with spear and shield,
Rode full of years to Flodden field,
His eye could see the hidden spring,
And how the current was to flow;
The fatal end of Scotland's King,   290
And all that hopeless overthrow.
But not in wars did he delight,
This Clifford wished for worthier might;
Nor in broad pomp, or courtly state;
Him his own thoughts did elevate,—   295
Most happy in the shy recess
Of Barden's humble quietness.
And choice of studious friends had he
Of Bolton's dear fraternity;
Who, standing on this old church tower,   300
In many a calm propitious hour,
Perused, with him, the starry sky;—
Or in their cells with him did pry
For other lore,—through strong desire
Searching the earth with chemic fire: 305
But they and their good works are fled—

---

282 Cumbria's] Cumbrian *1827–*
285/286 *illeg pencil alt MS. 1832/36–*
296 the *rev from* his *MS. 1815 (WW)*
297 Of *rev from* In *MS. 1815 (WW)*   humble] lowly *MS. 1832/36–*
304 other *del to* humble *then reinstated MS. 1832/36*   through strong] by keen *MS.*
1832/36–
305 Searching the earth] Urged to close toil *MS. 1832/36–*
305/306 In quest belike of transmutations
          Rich as the mine's most bright creations *MS. 1832/36, pencil (WW) and ink (JC), but*
creations] creations. *1836–*

---

284 Flodden, a ridge of the Cheviot Hills, was the site of the battle between James IV of
Scotland and Henry VIII in 1513 (APC).
290 James IV, 1473–1513 (APC).

And all is now disquieted—
And peace is none, for living or dead!

   Ah, pensive Scholar! think not so,
But look again at the radiant Doe!   310
What quiet watch she seems to keep,
Alone, beside that grassy heap!

   Why mention other thoughts unmeet
For vision so composed and sweet?
While stand the people in a ring,   315
Gazing, doubting, questioning;
Yea, many overcome in spite
Of recollections clear and bright;
Which yet do unto some impart
An undisturbed repose of heart.   320
And all the assembly own a law
Of orderly respect and awe;
But see—they vanish, one by one,
And last, the Doe herself is gone.

   Harp! we have been full long beguiled   325
By busy dreams, and fancies wild;
To which, with no reluctant strings,
Thou hast attuned thy murmurings;
And now before this Pile we stand
In solitude, and utter peace: 330
But, harp! thy murmurs may not cease,—
Thou hast breeze-like visitings;
For a Spirit with angel wings
Hath touched thee, and a Spirit's hand:
A voice is with us—a command   335
To chaunt, in strains of heavenly glory,
A tale of tears, a mortal story!

END OF CANTO FIRST.

---

326 busy dreams, and] vague thoughts, lured by *MS. 1832/36*
332–333 A Spirit, with angelic wings,
       In soft and breeze-like visitings, *1836–* but with] with his *MS. 1836/45, 1840–*
334 Hath] has *1836–*   Has touched thee] has reached us *alt del MS. 1836/45 (WW)*
335 us *rev from* thee *MS. 1815*

THE

WHITE DOE OF RYLSTONE.

CANTO SECOND.

THE Harp in lowliness obeyed:
And first we sang of the green-wood shade,
And a solitary Maid;   340
Beginning, where the song must end,
With her, and with her sylvan Friend;
The friend who stood before her sight,
Her only unextinguished light,—
Her last companion in a dearth   345
Of love, upon a hopeless earth.

    For She it was,—'twas She who wrought
Meekly, with foreboding thought,
In vermeil colours and in gold
An unblessed work; which, standing by,   350
Her Father did with joy behold,—
Exulting in the imagery;
A Banner, one that did fulfil
Too perfectly his headstrong will:
For on this Banner had her hand   355
Embroidered (such was the command)
The Sacred Cross; and figured there
The five dear wounds our Lord did bear;
Full soon to be uplifted high,
And float in rueful company!   360

---

339   sang *rev from* sung MS. *1815* (WW)
347   was, — 'twas She] was—this Maid, *1827*–
351   with *rev from* in MS. *1815*
352   the] its MS. *1832/36*–
353   one that did] fashioned to MS. *1832/36* (JC)–
356   was the] her Sire's MS. *1832/36*–

---

340   *F.Q.*, I.iii.3.2 (APC). Elsewhere Emily, like Una, is described as "meek," "mild," "inno-cent," and "forlorn." She is characterized by her "female patience," her steadfastness, and her wandering.
358   "The Rising of the North," l. 108 (APC).

It was the time when England's Queen
Twelve years had reigned, a sovereign dread;
Nor yet the restless crown had been
Disturbed upon her virgin head;
But now the inly-working North   365
Was ripe to send its thousands forth,
A potent vassalage, to fight
In Percy's and in Neville's right,—
Two earls fast leagued in discontent,
Who gave their wishes open vent;   370
And boldly urged a general plea,
The rites of ancient piety
To be by force of arms renewed;
Glad prospect for the multitude!
And that same Banner, on whose breast   375
The blameless Lady had exprest,
Memorials chosen to give life,
And sunshine to a dangerous strife;
This Banner, waiting for the call,
Stood quietly in Rylstone Hall.   380

It came,—and Francis Norton said,
"O Father! rise not in this fray—
The hairs are white upon your head;
Dear Father, hear me when I say
It is for you too late a day!   385
Bethink you of your own good name;
A just and gracious queen have we,
A pure religion, and the claim
Of peace on our humanity.
'Tis meet that I endure your scorn,—   390
I am your son, your eldest born;
But not for lordship or for land,
My Father, do I clasp your knees—
The Banner touch not, stay your hand,—
This multitude of men disband,   395

373–374   To be triumphantly restored;
         By the dread justice of the sword! *MS. 1815/20 WD– but* restored;] restored,
1827– and dread] stern *1845–*
   379   This] That *1827–*

382–383   "The Rising of the North," ll. 81–84 (APC).

And live at home in blissful ease;
For these my brethren's sake, for me,
And, most of all, for Emily!"

Loud noise was in the crowded hall,
And scarcely could the Father hear   400
That name—which had a dying fall,
The name of his only Daughter dear,—
And on the banner which stood near
He glanced a look of holy pride,
And his wet eyes were glorified;   405
Then seized the staff, and thus did say:
"Thou, Richard, bear'st thy father's name,
Keep thou this ensign till the day
When I of thee require the same:
Thy place be on my better hand;—   410
And seven as true as thou, I see,
Will cleave to this good cause and me."
He spake, and eight brave sons straightway
All followed him, a gallant band!

Forth when Sire and Sons appeared   415
A gratulating shout was reared,
With din of arms and minstrelsy,
From all his warlike tenantry,
All horsed and harnessed with him to ride;
—A shout to which the hills replied!   420

But Francis, in the vacant hall,
Stood silent under dreary weight,—

---

396   blissful] blameless *1827–*
399   noise was in *rev to* noises filled *then line rev to* Tumultous noises filled the hall, (*indented as para*) *MS. 1832/36– but* hall,] hall; *1836–*
401   which had] pronounced with *MS. 1832/36 (pencil and ink)–*
403   And] As *1836–*
405   wet] moist *MS. 1815/20 WD–*
406   Then did he seize the staff, and say: *MS. 1832/36– but* say:] say; *1850*
415–416   Thus, with his sons, when forth he came
            The sight was hailed with loud acclaim (*marked for new para*) *MS. 1832/36–*
417   With] And *MS. 1832/36–*
420   shout] voice *MS. 1832/36–*

---

401   APC follows Knight in suggesting Shakespeare, *Twelfth Night*, I.i.4.

A phantasm, in which roof and wall
Shook—tottered—swam before his sight,
A phantasm like a dream of night.   425
Thus overwhelmed, and desolate,
He found his way to a postern-gate;
And, when he waked at length, his eye
Was on the calm and silent sky;
With air about him breathing sweet,   430
And earth's green grass beneath his feet;
Nor did he fail ere long to hear
A sound of military chear,
Faint—but it reached that sheltered spot;
He heard, and it disturbed him not.   435

    There stood he, leaning on a lance
Which he had grasped unknowingly,—
Had blindly grasped in that strong trance,
That dimness of heart agony;
There stood he, cleansed from the despair   440
And sorrow of his fruitless prayer.
The past he calmly hath reviewed:
But where will be the fortitude
Of this brave Man, when he shall see
That Form beneath the spreading tree,   445
And know that it is Emily?
Oh! hide them from each other, hide,
Kind Heaven, this pair severely tried!

    He saw her where in open view
She sate beneath the spreading yew,—   450
Her head upon her lap, concealing
In solitude her bitter feeling:
How could he chuse but shrink or sigh?
He shrunk, and muttered inwardly,
"Might ever son *command* a sire,   455
The act were justified to-day."
This to himself—and to the Maid,

---

428 waked at length, his] waked, his languid *MS. 1832/36–*
437 grasped *rev from* gra[?]ed *MS. 1815*
447–448 *del MS. 1832/36–*
451 upon *rev from* within *MS. 1815 (?WW)*
453–454 *del MS. 1832/36–*

Whom now he had approached, he said,
—"Gone are they,—they have their desire;
And I with thee one hour will stay,   460
To give thee comfort if I may."

   He paused, her silence to partake,
And long it was before he spake:
Then, all at once, his thoughts turned round,
And fervent words a passage found.   465

   "Gone are they, bravely, though misled,
With a dear Father at their head!
The Sons obey a natural lord;
The Father had given solemn word
To noble Percy,—and a force   470
Still stronger bends him to his course.
This said, our tears to-day may fall
As at an innocent funeral.
In deep and awful channel runs
This sympathy of Sire and Sons;   475
Untried our Brothers were beloved,
And now their faithfulness is proved;
For faithful we must call them, bearing
That soul of conscientious daring.
—There were they all in circle—there   480
Stood Richard, Ambrose, Christopher,
John with a sword that will not fail,
And Marmaduke in fearless mail,
And those bright Twins were side by side;
And there, by fresh hopes beautified,   485
Was He, whose arm yet lacks the power
Of man, our youngest, fairest flower!
I, in the right of eldest born,
And in a second father's place,

---

    463 he *rev from* she *MS. 1815*
    462–463 She heard, but looked not up, nor spake;
             And sorrow moved him to partake, (*marked for para*) *MS. 1832/36–* but partake,]
partake *1836–*
    464 Then, all at once,] Her silence; then *MS. 1832/36–*
    476 were beloved,] have been loved *1836–*
    476/477 With heart by simple nature moved, *1836–* but moved,] moved; *1845–*
    486 Was] Stood *1827–*
    488 in] by *1820–*

Presumed to stand against their scorn,   490
And meet their pity face to face;
Yea, trusting in God's holy aid,
I to my Father knelt and prayed;
And one, the pensive Marmaduke,
Methought, was yielding inwardly,   495
And would have laid his purpose by,
But for a glance of his Father's eye,
Which I myself could scarcely brook.

    Then be we, each, and all, forgiven!
Thee, chiefly thee, my Sister dear,   500
Whose pangs are registered in heaven,—
The stifled sigh, the hidden tear,
And smiles, that dared to take their place,
Meek filial smiles, upon thy face,
As that unhallowed Banner grew   505
Beneath a loving old man's view.
Thy part is done—thy painful part;
Be thou then satisfied in heart!
A further, though far easier task
Than thine hath been, my duties ask;   510
With their's my efforts cannot blend,
I cannot for such cause contend;
Their aims I utterly forswear;
But I in body will be there.
Unarmed and naked will I go,   515
Be at their side, come weal or woe.
On kind occasions I may wait,
See, hear, obstruct, or mitigate.
Bare breast I take and an empty hand."—
Therewith he threw away the lance   520
Which he had grasped in that strong trance,
Spurned it—like something that would stand
Between him and the pure intent
Of love on which his soul was bent.

---

490   stand against] grapple with *1827–*
500   Thee . . . thee] Thou . . . thou *MS. 1832/36–*
510   hath *over illeg eras MS. 1813*
519n   See the Old Ballad,— "The Rising of the North." *1827–*

---

515   "The Rising of the North," ll. 89–90 (APC).

"For thee, for thee, is left the sense   525
Of trial past without offence
To God or Man;—such innocence,
Such consolation, and the excess
Of an unmerited distress;
In that thy very strength must lie.   530
—O Sister, I could prophesy!
The time is come that rings the knell
Of all we loved, and loved so well;—
Hope nothing, if I thus may speak
To thee a woman, and thence weak;   535
Hope nothing, I repeat; for we
Are doomed to perish utterly:
'Tis meet that thou with me divide
The thought while I am by thy side,
Acknowledging a grace in this,   540
A comfort in the dark abyss:
But look not for me when I am gone,
And be no farther wrought upon.
Farewell all wishes, all debate,
All prayers for this cause, or for that!   545
Weep, if that aid thee; but depend
Upon no help of outward friend;
Espouse thy doom at once, and cleave
To fortitude without reprieve.
For we must fall, both we and ours,—   550
This Mansion and these pleasant bowers;
Walks, pools, and arbours, homestead, hall,
Our fate is theirs, will reach them all;
The young Horse must forsake his manger,
And learn to glory in a Stranger;   555
The Hawk forget his perch,—the Hound
Be parted from his ancient ground:
The blast will sweep us all away,
One desolation, one decay!
And even this Creature!" which words saying   560
He pointed to a lovely Doe,
A few steps distant, feeding, straying;
Fair Creature, and more white than snow!
"Even she will to her peaceful woods

---

556   perch *over illeg eras MS. 1815*

Return, and to her murmuring floods,   565
And be in heart and soul the same
She was before she hither came,—
Ere she had learned to love us all,
Herself beloved in Rylstone Hall.
—But thou, my Sister, doomed to be   570
The last leaf which by heaven's decree
Must hang upon a blasted tree;
If not in vain we have breathed the breath
Together of a purer faith—
If hand in hand we have been led   575
And thou, (O happy thought this day!)
Not seldom foremost in the way—
If on one thought our minds have fed,
And we have in one meaning read—
If, when at home our private weal   580
Hath suffered from the shock of zeal,
Together we have learned to prize
Forebearance, and self-sacrifice—
If we like combatants have fared,
And for this issue been prepared—   585
If thou art beautiful, and youth
And thought endue thee with all truth—
Be strong;—be worthy of the grace
Of God, and fill thy destined place:
A soul, by force of sorrows high,   590
Uplifted to the purest sky
Of undisturbed humanity!"

    He ended,—or she heard no more:
He led her from the Yew-tree shade,
And at the Mansion's silent door,   595
He kissed the consecrated Maid;
And down the Valley he pursued,
Alone, the armed Multitude.

                    END OF CANTO SECOND.

571–572   *conflated to* The last leaf on a blasted tree; *MS. 1832/36–*
573   have *omitted 1827–*
597   Valley he] valley then *MS. 1832/36 (pencil and ink)–*

---

593   Milton, *Paradise Lost,* VIII, 452 (APC).

THE

WHITE DOE OF RYLSTONE.

CANTO THIRD.

Now joy for you and sudden chear,
Ye Watchmen upon Brancepeth Towers;   600
Looking forth in doubt and fear,
Telling melancholy hours!
Proclaim it, let your Masters hear
That Norton with his Band is near!
The Watchmen from their station high   605
Pronounced the word,—and the Earls descry
Forthwith the armed Company
Marching down the banks of Were.

   Said fearless Norton to the Pair
Gone forth to hail him on the Plain—   610
"This meeting, noble Lords! looks fair,
I bring with me a goodly train;
Their hearts are with you:—hill and dale
Have helped us:—Ure we crossed, and Swale,
And horse and harness followed—see   615
The best part of their Yeomanry!
—Stand forth, my Sons!—these eight are mine,
Whom to this service I commend;
Which way soe'er our fate incline
These will be faithful to the end;   620
They are my all"—voice failed him here,
"My all save one, a Daughter dear!
Whom I have left, the mildest birth,
The meekest Child on this blessed earth.
I had—but these are by my side   625
These eight, and this is a day of pride!

599–601 *conflated to:*
      Now joy for you who from the Towers
      Of Brancepeth look in doubt and fear, *MS. 1832/36– but* towers *1836–*
602 *omitted, then inserted MS. 1815*
607 Forthwith] Well-pleased, *MS. 1832/36–*
610 hail] greet *MS. 1832/36–*
623 the] Love's *1832/36–*

---

600   See WW's note.

The time is ripe—with festive din
Lo! how the People are flocking in,—
Like hungry Fowl to the Feeder's hand
When snow lies heavy upon the land."   630

  He spake bare truth; for far and near
From every side came noisy swarms
Of Peasants in their homely gear;
And, mixed with these, to Brancepeth came
Grave Gentry of estate and name,   635
And Captains known for worth in arms;
And prayed the Earls in self-defence
To rise, and prove their innocence.—
"Rise, noble Earls, put forth your might
For holy Church, and the People's right!"   640

  The Norton fixed, at this demand,
His eye upon Northumberland,
And said, "The minds of Men will own
No loyal rest while England's Crown
Remains without an Heir, the bait   645
Of strife and factions desperate;
Who, paying deadly hate in kind
Through all things else, in this can find
A mutual hope, a common mind;
And plot, and pant to overwhelm   650
All ancient honour in the realm.
—Brave Earls! to whose heroic veins
Our noblest blood is given in trust,
To you a suffering State complains,
And ye must raise her from the dust.   655
With wishes of still bolder scope
On you we look, with dearest hope,
Even for our Altars,—for the prize
In Heaven, of life that never dies;
For the old and holy Church we mourn,   660
And must in joy to her return.
Behold!"—and from his Son whose stand
Was on his right, from that guardian hand
He took the Banner, and unfurled
The precious folds—"behold," said he,   665

---

657   you *rev from* me MS. *1815*

"The ransom of a sinful world;
Let this your preservation be,—
The wounds of hands and feet and side,
And the sacred Cross on which Jesus died!
—This bring I from an ancient hearth,   670
These Records wrought in pledge of love
By hands of no ignoble birth,
A Maid o'er whom the blessed Dove
Vouchsafed in gentleness to brood
While she the holy work pursued."   675
"Uplift the Standard!" was the cry
From all the Listeners that stood round,
"Plant it,—by this we live or die"—
The Norton ceased not for that sound,
But said, "The prayer which ye have heard,   680
Much injured Earls! by these preferred,
Is offered to the Saints, the sigh
Of tens of thousands, secretly."—
"Uplift it," cried once more the Band,
And then a thoughtful pause ensued.   685
"Uplift it!" said Northumberland—
Whereat, from all the multitude,
Who saw the Banner reared on high
In all its dread emblazonry,
With tumult and indignant rout   690
A voice of uttermost joy brake out:
The transport was rolled down the river of Were,
And Durham, the time-honoured Durham, did hear,
And the Towers of Saint Cuthbert were stirred by the shout!

    Now was the North in arms:—they shine   695
In warlike trim from Tweed to Tyne,
At Percy's voice: and Neville sees
His Followers gathering in from Tees,

---

681   these *rev from* this *MS. 1815*
690   *del MS. 1832/36—*

---

    693   Durham Cathedral was "half church of God, half castle against the Scots" (APC, quot-
ing an unidentified source). It dates from 1093.
    694   The cathedral was dedicated to the Catholic saint Cuthbert (APC).
    696–698   Percy ruled from Tweed to Tyne; Neville, from Tyne to Tees (APC).

From Were, and all the little Rills
Concealed among the forked Hills.—   700
Seven hundred Knights, Retainers all
Of Neville, at their Master's call
Had sate together in Raby Hall!
Such strength that Earldom held of yore;
Nor wanted at this time rich store   705
Of well-appointed Chivalry.
—Not loth the sleepy lance to wield,
And greet the old paternal shield,
They heard the summons;—and, furthermore,
Came Foot and Horse-men of each degree,   710
Unbound by pledge of fealty;
Appeared, with free and open hate
Of novelties in Church and State;
Knight, Burgher, Yeoman, and Esquire;
And the Romish Priest, in Priest's attire.   715
And thus, in arms, a zealous Band
Proceeding under joint command,
To Durham first their course they bear;
And in Saint Cuthbert's ancient seat
Sang Mass,—and tore the book of Prayer,—   720
And trod the Bible beneath their feet.

   Thence marching southward smooth and free,
"They mustered their Host at Wetherby,
Full sixteen thousand fair to see;"
The choicest Warriors of the North!   725
But none for undisputed worth

---

703   in *rev from* at *MS. 1815*
705   this *rev from* that *MS. 1815*
710   Came Foot and Horse-men] Horsemen and Foot *1827–*
713   in] of *rev to* in *MS. 1815*
715   And the] And *1827–*
720   Sang *rev from* Sung *MS. 1815*
724n   From the old Ballad *added MS. 1815/20 WD, adopted 1820– with period*
726   undisputed] beauty and for *1827–*

---

703   Raby Castle, in Durham, belonged to the Nevilles (APC).
719   St. Cuthbert's shrine, destroyed in the Dissolution, was replaced by a blue marble slab (APC).
723   Wetherby, in the West Riding of Yorkshire, sits on a bend of the river Wharfe (APC).
723–724   "The Rising of the North," ll. 99–100 (APC).

Like those eight Sons; who in a ring,
Each with a lance—erect and tall,
A falchion, and a buckler small,
Stood by their Sire, on Clifford-moor,   730
In youthful beauty flourishing,
To guard the Standard which he bore.
—With feet that firmly pressed the ground
They stood, and girt their Father round;
Such was his choice,—no Steed will he   735
Henceforth bestride;—triumphantly
He stood upon the verdant sod,
Trusting himself to the earth, and God.
Rare sight to embolden and inspire!
Proud was the field of Sons and Sire,   740
Of him the most; and, sooth to say,
No shape of Man in all the array
So graced the sunshine of that day:
The monumental pomp of age
Was with this goodly Personage;   745
A stature undepressed in size,
Unbent, which rather seemed to rise,
In open victory o'er the weight
Of seventy years, to higher height;
Magnific limbs of withered state,—   750
A face to fear and venerate,—
Eyes dark and strong, and on his head
Rich locks of silver hair, thick-spread,

727–728   Like those eight Sons—embosoming
          Determined thoughts—who, in a ring *1827–1832 rev to:*
          Like those eight Sons—(who, in a ring
          Ripe men, or blooming in life's spring) *MS. 1832/36– but* ring] ring, *1836–*
731   *omitted 1827–*
733–735   *rev to:*
          On foot they girt their Father round;
          And so will keep the appointed ground
          Where'er their march: no steed will he *MS. 1832/36–*
737   stood] stands *1845–*   verdant] grassy *MS. 1815/20 WD, 1820–*
749   higher] loftier *MS. 1832/36–*
753   Rich] Bright *1827–*

---

729   falchion: a "broad sword more or less curved with the edge on the convex side";
buckler: a small round shield used "'not so much for a shield as for a warder to catch the blow of
an adversary' (Fairhold)" (*OED*).

Which a brown morion half-concealed,
Light as a hunter's of the field;   755
And thus, with girdle round his waist,
Whereon the Banner-staff might rest
At need, he stood, advancing high
The glittering, floating Pageantry.

   Who sees him?—many see, and One   760
With unparticipated gaze;
Who 'mong these thousands Friend hath none,
And treads in solitary ways.
He, following wheresoe'er he might,
Hath watched the Banner from afar,   765
As Shepherds watch a lonely star,
Or Mariners the distant light
That guides them on a stormy night.
And now, upon a chosen plot
Of rising ground, yon heathy spot!   770
He takes this day his far-off stand,
With breast unmailed, unweaponed hand.
—Bold is his aspect; but his eye
Is pregnant with anxiety,
While, like a tutelary Power,   775
He there stands fixed, from hour to hour.
Yet sometimes, in more humble guise,
Stretched out upon the ground he lies,—
As if it were his only task
Like Herdsman in the sun to bask,   780

---

760   many] thousands *MS. 1832/36–*
762   These] Those *MS. 1832/36 (pencil and ink)–*
768   on] through *MS. 1832/36 (pencil and ink)–*
771   this day] alone *MS. 1832/36–*
776–777   *rev to:*
    He on that height, from hour to hour:
    Stands fixed, yet sometimes he in guise *then original restored with stet MS. 1832/36*
778–780   *rev to:*
    More humble on the green sward lies
    Stretched herdsman like, as if to bask
    In sunshine *then recopied at page foot:*
    Upon the turf-clad height he lies
    Stretched, herdsman-like, as if to bask
    In sunshine were his only task, *MS. 1832/36; adopted 1836*

---

754   morion: a "kind of helmet, without beaver or visor, worn in the 16th and 17th c."
(*OED*).

Or by his mantle's help to find
A shelter from the nipping wind:
And thus, with short oblivion blest,
His weary spirits gather rest.
Again he lifts his eyes; and lo!   785
The pageant glancing to and fro;
And hope is wakened by the sight
That he thence may learn, ere fall of night,
Which way the tide is doomed to flow.

    To London were the Chieftains bent;   790
But what avails the bold intent?
A Royal army is gone forth
To quell the Rising of the North;
They march with Dudley at their head,
And in seven days' space, will to York be led!   795
Can such a mighty Host be raised
Thus suddenly, and brought so near?
The Earls upon each other gazed;
And Neville was opprest with fear;
For, though he bore a valiant name,   800
His heart was of a timid frame,
And bold if both had been, yet they
"Against so many may not stay."
And therefore will retreat to seize
A strong Hold on the banks of Tees;   805
There wait a favourable hour,
Until Lord Dacre with his power

---

781   del, *then restored with* stet *MS. 1832/36*
785   eyes *rev from* head *MS. 1815*
788   That he] He *MS. 1815/20 WD, 1820–*
799–801   *rev to:*
      And Neville's cheek grew pale with fear;
      For, with a high and valiant name,
      He bore a heart of timid frame; *MS. 1832/36–*
803n   From the old Ballad *added MS. 1815/20 WD, adopted 1820– with period*
804–809   *inserted, partly over ll. 810–811, eras MS. 1815*
804   Back therefore will they hie to seize *MS. 1832/36–*

---

803   "The Rising of the North," l. 144 (APC).
807–808   Leonard Dacre, plotting with Mary, Queen of Scots, went to Elizabeth's court to assure her of his aid, all the while intending to join the rebels. He fortified Naworth Castle, about twelve miles northeast of Carlisle (APC).

From Naworth comes; and Howard's aid
Be with them—openly displayed.

While through the Host, from man to man,   810
A rumour of this purpose ran,
The Standard giving to the care
Of him who heretofore did bear
That charge, impatient Norton sought
The Chieftains to unfold his thought,   815
And thus abruptly spake,—"We yield
(And can it be?) an unfought field!
—How often hath the strength of heaven
To few triumphantly been given!
Still do our very children boast   820
Of mitred Thurston, what a Host
He conquered!—Saw we not the Plain,
(And flying shall behold again)
Where faith was proved?—while to battle moved
The Standard on the sacred wain,   825
On which the grey-haired Barons stood,
And the infant Heir of Mowbray's blood,
Beneath the saintly Ensigns three,

---

808   comes] come *MS. 1832/36 (pencil and ink)—*
810–811   *inserted, after being erased at ll. 803/804, MS. 1815*
812   giving] trusting *MS. 1832/36 (pencil and ink)—*
818   —How often hath] How oft has strength, *MS. 1832/36—*
820   Still] Yet *MS. 1815*
824   to *rev from* the *MS. 1815*
826–828   *expanded to:*
      That bore it, compassed round by a bold
      Fraternity of Barons old;
      And with the grey-haired champions stood,
      Under the saintly ensigns three,
      The infant Heir of Mowbray's blood— *MS. 1832/36, adopted 1836— but* with the]
with those
828   saintly *rev from* sacred *MS. 1815*

---

808   Howard, Duke of Norfolk, contrived to marry the Queen of Scots, and was imprisoned in the Tower of London (APC).
821   See WW's note.
825   In the Battle of the Standard (1138), Archbishop Thurstan gave the dispirited barons of northern England a sacred standard, which is said to have inspired their men to repel the Scottish invasion when they were at the point of defeat (APC).
827   Roger de Mowbray, a boy about fifteen years old, helped inspire the barons' men along with the archbishop's priests (APC).

Their confidence and victory!
Shall Percy blush, then, for his Name?   830
Must Westmoreland be asked with shame
Whose were the numbers, where the loss,
In that other day of Neville's Cross?
When, as the Vision gave command,
The Prior of Durham with holy hand   835
Saint Cuthbert's Relic did uprear
Upon the point of a lofty spear,
And God descended in his power,
While the Monks prayed in Maiden's Bower.
Less would not at our need be due   840
To us, who war against the Untrue;—
The delegates of Heaven we rise,
Convoked the impious to chastise;
We, we the sanctities of old
Would re-establish and uphold."—   845
—The Chiefs were by his zeal confounded,
But word was given—and the trumpet sounded;
Back through the melancholy Host
Went Norton, and resumed his post.
Alas! thought he, and have I borne   850
This Banner raised so joyfully,
This hope of all posterity,
Thus to become at once the scorn
Of babbling winds as they go by,
A spot of shame to the sun's bright eye,   855

---

829   Their confidence and] stood confident of *MS. 1815/20 WD, 1820–1832* All confident
of *MS. 1832/36–*
    834–839   *rev to:*
        When the Prior of Durham with holy hand
        Raised, as the Vision gave command,
        Saint Cuthbert's Relic—far and near
        Kenned on the point of a lofty spear;
        While the Monks prayed in Maiden's Bower
        To God descending in his power. *MS. 1832/36–*
    846   Be warned. "—His zeal the Chiefs confounded, *1836–* but warned."—] warned"— *MS.
1836/45, adopted 1840–*
    851   so joyfully,] with joyful pride, *MS. 1832/36–*
    852/853   By these dread symbols sanctified; *MS. 1832/36– but* these] those *1836–*

---

833   See WW's note.
839   The Maiden's Bower was "a small mound in a deep narrow valley" west of Durham
(APC).

To the frail clouds a mockery!
—"Even these poor eight of mine would stem,"
Half to himself, and half to them
He spake, "would stem, or quell a force
Ten times their number, man and horse;   860
This by their own unaided might,
Without their Father in their sight,
Without the Cause for which they fight;
A Cause, which on a needful day
Would breed us thousands brave as they."   865
—So speaking, he upraised his head
Towards that Imagery once more;
But the familiar prospect shed
Despondency unfelt before:
A shock of intimations vain,   870
Blank fear, and superstitious pain,
Fell on him, with the sudden thought
Of her by whom the work was wrought:—
Oh wherefore was her countenance bright
With love divine and gentle light?   875
She did in passiveness obey,
But her Faith leaned another way.
Ill tears she wept,—I saw them fall,
I overheard her as she spake
Sad words to that mute Animal,   880
The White Doe, in the hawthorn brake;
She steeped, but not for Jesu's sake,
This Cross in tears:—by her, and One
Unworthier far, we are undone—
Her Brother was it who assailed   885
Her tender spirit and prevailed.
Her other Parent, too, whose head
In the cold grave hath long been laid,

---

856   frail] light *MS. 1832/36–*
866   upraised his] his reverend *1827–*
867   Towards] Raised towards *1827–*
871   Blank fear] Dismay *1827–*
876   She would not, could not, disobey, *MS. 1832/36–*
885–887   *rev to:*
    Her recreant Brother—he prevailed
    Over that tender spirit—assailed
    Too oft, alas, by her whose head *MS. 1832/36– but* oft, alas] oft alas! *1836–*   spirit]
Spirit *1845–*

From reason's earliest dawn beguiled
The docile, unsuspecting Child: 890
Far back—far back my mind must go
To reach the well-spring of this woe!—
While thus he brooded, music sweet
Was played to chear them in retreat;
But Norton lingered in the rear: 895
Thought followed thought—and ere the last
Of that unhappy train was past,
Before him Francis did appear.

   "Now when 'tis not your aim to oppose,"
Said he, "in open field your Foes;   900
Now that from this decisive day
Your multitude must melt away,
An unarmed Man may come unblamed;
To ask a grace, that was not claimed
Long as your hopes were high, he now   905
May hither bring a fearless brow;
When his discountenance can do
No injury,—may come to you.
Though in your cause no part I bear,
Your indignation I can share;   910
Am grieved this backward march to see,

---

889   She first, in reason's dawn, beguiled *MS. 1832/36– but* dawn,] dawn *1845, 1849*
890   The] Her *MS. 1832/36–*
894   *expanded to:*

                            e⎫
       Of border tunes was played to chea⎰r
       The footsteps of a quick retreat; *MS. 1832/36, adopted as rev, 1836–*
896–898   *rev to:*
            Stung with sharp thoughts; and ere the last
            From his distracted brain was cast,
            Before his Father Francis stood,
            And spake in firm & earnest mood. *MS. 1832/36, adopted 1836– followed by line*
   space but &] and   Father] Father, *1845–*
899–914   *rev to:*
            Though here I bend a suppliant
            ~~Unarmed [?   ] [? I bend] this~~ ∧knee
                             ⎰ce, and unarmed,
            In reveren⎱t ~~love, yet do~~ I bear
            In your indignant thoughts my share,
            Am grieved this backward march to see
            So careless and disorderly.
            I scorn your Chiefs—men who would lead
            And yet want courage at their need: *MS. 1832/36, adopted as rev 1836– but* Though]
   "Though   share,] share;   lead] lead,

How careless and disorderly!
I scorn your Chieftains, Men who lead,
And yet want courage at their need;
Then look at them with open eyes!   915
Deserve they further sacrifice?
My Father! I would help to find
A place of shelter, till the rage
Of cruel men do like the wind
Exhaust itself and sink to rest;   920
Be Brother now to Brother joined!
Admit me in the equipage
Of your misfortunes, that at least,
Whatever fate remains behind,
I may bear witness in my breast   925
To your nobility of mind!"

"Thou Enemy, my bane and blight!
Oh! bold to fight the Coward's fight
Against all good"—but why declare,
At length, the issue of this prayer?   930
Or how, from his depression raised,
The Father on his Son had gazed;
Suffice it that the Son gave way,
Nor strove that passion to allay,

916/917 If when they shrink, nor dare oppose
        In open field their gathering foes,
        And fast, from this decisive day,   [3]
        Yon multitude must melt away;
        If now I ask a grace not claimed
        While ground was left for hope; unblamed   [6]
        Be an endeavour that can do
        No injury to them or you. *MS. 1832/36, adopted 1836– but*
[1] If] If— *1845–*   [3] And] (And *1845–*   [5] away;] away;) *1845–*
  924 remains] remain *1836–*
  926 To *rev from* Of *MS. 1815 (WW)*
  930 this *rev from* that *MS. 1815* a *MS. 1832/36–*
  931–932 *del to:*
        Uttered in love that had given scope
        Too free to one bright moments hope? *MS. 1832/36 (WW), then del and recopied*
with moments] moment's *and* hope?] hope
        Which love had prompted, yielding scope
        Too free to one bright moment's hope. *1836– but* hope.] hope? *MS. 1836/45 (JC),*
adopted 1840–
  933 Son gave way,] Son, who strove *1845–*
  934 *expanded to:*
        With fruitless effort to allay
        That passion, prudently gave way; *1845–*

Nor did he turn aside to prove   935
His Brothers' wisdom or their love—
But calmly from the spot withdrew;
The like endeavours to renew,
Should e'er a kindlier time ensue.

END OF CANTO THIRD.

THE

WHITE DOE OF RYLSTONE.

CANTO FOURTH.

FROM cloudless ether looking down,   940
The Moon, this tranquil evening, sees
A Camp, and a beleaguered Town,
And Castle like a stately crown
On the steep rocks of winding Tees;—
And, southward far, with moors between,   945
Hill-tops, and floods, and forests green,
The bright Moon sees that valley small
Where Rylstone's old sequestered Hall
A venerable image yields
Of quiet to the neighbouring fields;   950
While from one pillared chimney breathes
The silver smoke, and mounts in wreaths.
—The courts are hushed;—for timely sleep
The Grey-hounds to their kennel creep;

---

938   The like] His best *MS. 1832/36–*
940–941   *rev to:*
    'Tis night: in silence looking down
    The Moon, from cloudless ether, sees *MS. 1832/36– but* down] down, *1845–*   ether,
sees] ether sees. *1850*
945   moors] moor *MS. 1832/36 (pencil and ink)–*
946   Hill-tops . . . floods . . . forests] Hill-top . . . flood . . . forest *MS. 1832/36 (pencil and ink)–*
952   and *alt* [?now] *MS. 1815 (WW, pencil)*   The smoke, and mounts in silver wreaths. *1827–*

---

942   The town is Barnard Castle, to which the rebels were laying siege (APC). It was held by Sir George Bowes for the Queen (Knight).

The Peacock in the broad ash-tree   955
Aloft is roosted for the night,
He who in proud prosperity
Of colours manifold and bright
Walked round, affronting the day-light;
And higher still, above the bower   960
Where he is perched, from yon lone Tower
The Hall-clock in the clear moon-shine
With glittering finger points at nine.
—Ah! who could think that sadness here
Had any sway? or pain, or fear?   965
A soft and lulling sound is heard
Of streams inaudible by day;
The garden pool's dark surface—stirred
By the night insects in their play—
Breaks into dimples small and bright;   970
A thousand, thousand rings of light
That shape themselves and disappear
Almost as soon as seen:—and, lo!
Not distant far, the milk-white Doe:
The same fair Creature which was nigh   975
Feeding in tranquillity,
When Francis uttered to the Maid
His last words in the yew-tree shade;—
The same fair Creature, who hath found
Her way into forbidden ground;   980

959/960 alt Hushed *in top margin, pencil, MS. 1832/36 (WW)*
965 Had] Hath *1827–*
968 garden pool's *rev from* garden's pools *MS. 1815 (WW)*
971 rays of light *over* small and bright; *eras then* rays *rev to* rings *MS. 1815*
975 which] who *MS. 1815/20 WD, 1820–1834*
975–976 The same who quietly was feeding
    On the green herb and nothing heeding, *MS. 1832/36– but* herb] herb, *1836–*
977 Francis uttered] Francis, uttering *MS. 1832/36–*
978/979 Involved whate'er by love was brought
    Out of his heart, or crossed his thought,
    Or chance presented to his eye,
    In one sad sweep of destiny— *MS. 1832/36 (ink over illeg pencil)–*

973–1003 WW is indebted to his sister's work (see *The Journals of Dorothy Wordsworth,* ed. Ernest de Selincourt [2 vols.; Oxford, 1959], I, 415) for this description: "Mrs. Luff's large white dog lay in the moonshine upon the round knoll under the old yew-tree, a beautiful and romantic image—the dark tree with its dark shadow, and the elegant creature as fair as a Spirit." The passage comes from DW's "Excursion on the Banks of Ullswater, November 1805" (APC suggests the reference, de Selincourt the line numbers).

Where now, within this spacious plot
For pleasure made, a goodly spot,
With lawns, and beds of flowers, and shades
Of trellis-work in long arcades,
And cirque and crescent framed by wall   985
Of close-clipt foliage green and tall,
Converging walks, and fountains gay,
And terraces in trim array,—
Beneath yon cypress spiring high,
With pine and cedar spreading wide   990
Their darksome boughs on either side,
In open moonlight doth she lie;
Happy as others of her kind,
That, far from human neighbourhood,
Range—unrestricted as the wind—   995
Through park, or chase, or savage wood.

    But where at this still hour is she,
The consecrated Emily?
Even while I speak, behold the Maid
Emerging from the cedar shade   1000
To open moonshine, where the Doe
Beneath the cypress-spire is laid;
Like a patch of April snow,
Upon a bed of herbage green,
Lingering in a woody glade,   1005
Or behind a rocky screen;
Lonely relic! which, if seen
By the Shepherd, is passed by
With an inattentive eye.
—Nor more regard doth she bestow   1010
Upon the uncomplaining Doe!

---

992   doth] does *1834*
993   *inserted by WW, MS. 1815*
997–998   *del MS. 1832/36, omitted 1836–*
999   But see the consecrated Maid MS. *1832/36 (pencil and ink, WW) indented–*
1000   the] a MS. *1832/36–*
1002   the *del to* that *then restored, MS. 1836/45 (WW)*

---

996   chase: a "tract of unenclosed land reserved for breeding and hunting wild animals" (*OED*).

Yet the meek Creature was not free,
Erewhile, from some perplexity:
For thrice hath she approached, this day,
The thought-bewildered Emily;   1015
Endeavouring, in her gentle way,
Some smile or look of love to gain,—
Encouragement to sport or play;
Attempts which by the unhappy Maid
Have all been slighted or gainsaid.   1020
—O welcome to the viewless breeze!
'Tis fraught with acceptable feeling,
And instantaneous sympathies
Into the Sufferer's bosom stealing;—
Ere she hath reached yon rustic Shed   1025
Hung with late-flowering woodbine spread
Along the walls and overhead,
The fragrance of the breathing flowers
Revives a memory of those hours
When here, in this remote Alcove,   1030
(While from the pendant woodbine came
Like odours, sweet as if the same)
A fondly anxious Mother strove
To teach her salutary fears
And mysteries above her years.   1035

1012   meek *rev from* mild *MS. 1815 (WW)*
1012–1017   *rev, with no indentation, to:*
      Now couched at ease, though oft this day
      Not unperplexed nor free from pain,
      When she had tried, & tried in vain,
      Approaching in her gentle way,
      To win some look of love, or gain *MS. 1832/36, adopted as rev 1836– but* &] and
1019–1020   *rev to:*
      Attempts which still the heart-sick Maid
      Rejected, or with slight repaid. *MS. 1832/36–*
1021–1024   *conflated to:*
      Yet is she soothed: the viewless breeze
      Comes fraught with kindlier sympathies: *1827–1832, rev to:*

      Yet Emily is soothed {;— the breeze
      Came fraught with kindly sympathies. *MS. 1832/36; adopted as rev 1836– indented,*
below line space
1022   Tis fraught *rev from* Fraught *MS. 1815 (WW)*
1025   hath] had *1832, then line rev to* As she approached yon rustic Shed *1836–*
1029   Revives] Revived *1836–*

1025–1035   "In trellis'd shed," ll. 1–8, 17–22.

—Yes, she is soothed:—an Image faint—
And yet not faint—a presence bright
Returns to her;—'tis that bless'd Saint
Who with mild looks and language mild
Instructed here her darling Child,   1040
While yet a prattler on the knee,
To worship in simplicity
The invisible God, and take for guide
The faith reformed and purified.

　　'Tis flown—the Vision, and the sense   1045
Of that beguiling influence!
"But oh! thou Angel from above,
Thou Spirit of maternal love,
That stood'st before my eyes, more clear
Than Ghosts are fabled to appear   1050
Sent upon embassies of fear;
As thou thy presence hast to me
Vouchsafed—in radiant ministry
Descend on Francis:—through the air
Of this sad earth to him repair,   1055
Speak to him with a voice, and say,
"That he must cast despair away!"

　　Then from within the embowered retreat
Where she had found a grateful seat
Perturbed she issues.—She will go;   1060
Herself will follow to the war,

　　1038 'tis that] that *MS. 1832/36—*   bless'd] blessed *1820* blest *1827–1832; del to illeg word,*
del to blessèd *MS. 1832/36, adopted 1836—*
　　1048 Thou] Mute *MS. 1832/36—*
　　1050 fabled *rev from* [?fated] *MS. 1815 (WW)*
　　1054 Descend on Francis; nor forbear *MS. 1832/36—*
　　1055 *del to* Greeting him with a voice, [?to] say *with comma in pencil, then* Greeting *del to* To
greet *and* [?to] say *rev to* & say;— *MS. 1832/36* To greet him with a voice, and say;— *1836—*
　　1056—1057 *rev to:*
　　　　　　　　'If hope be a rejected stay,
　　　　　　　　'Do thou, my christian Son, beware
　　　　　　　　'The self-reliance of despair! *then last line del and expanded to:*
　　　　　　　　'Of that most lamentable snare,
　　　　　　　　'The self-reliance of despair!'" *MS. 1832/36, adopted as rev 1836—*

　　1036 "In trellis'd shed," l. 33.
　　1046 "In trellis'd shed," ll. 29, 33.

And clasp her Father's knees;—ah, no!
She meets the insuperable bar,
The injunction by her Brother laid;
His parting charge—but ill obeyed!   1065
That interdicted all debate,
All prayer for this cause or for that;
All efforts that would turn aside
The headstrong current of their fate;
Her duty is to stand and wait;   1070
In resignation to abide
The shock, and finally secure
O'er pain and grief a triumph pure.
—She knows, she feels it, and is cheared;
At least her present pangs are checked.   1075
—And now an ancient Man appeared,
Approaching her with grave respect.
Down the smooth walk which then she trod
He paced along the silent sod,
And greeting her thus gently spake,   1080
"An old Man's privilege I take;
Dark is the time—a woeful day!
Dear daughter of affliction, say
How can I serve you? point the way."

"Rights have you, and may well be bold: 1085
You with my Father have grown old
In friendship;—go—from him—from me—
Strive to avert this misery.

1068   efforts *rev from* effort *MS. 1815*
1073   O'er *rev from* Over *MS. 1815*
1074–1080   *rev to:*
      —She feels it, and her pangs are checked.
      But now, as silently she paced
      The turf, & thought by thought was chaced,
      Came One w ho, with sedate respect,
      Approached, & greeting her thus spake; *MS. 1832/36, adopted 1836– but* &]
and   chaced] chased   & greeting her] and, greeting her,
                                          {for
1087   *rev to* In friendship;—go—but on my mind *then rev to* In friendship—strive—{go his
sake go— *MS. 1832/36 (JC), adopted as rev 1836–*
1088   this *rev from* our *MS. 1815*   line *rev to* Turn from us all the coming woe: *MS. 1832/36*
(JC)–

1070   Milton, *On His Blindness* (APC).
1071–1073   De Selincourt suggests Milton, the close of *Samson Agonistes*.

This would I beg; but on my mind
A passive stillness is enjoined.   1090
—If prudence offer help or aid,
On *you* is no restriction laid;
You not forbidden to recline
With hope upon the Will Divine."

    "Hope," said the Sufferer's zealous Friend,   1095
"Must not forsake us till the end.—
In Craven's wilds is many a den,
To shelter persecuted Men:
Far underground is many a cave,
Where they might lie as in the grave,   1100
Until this storm hath ceased to rave;
Or let them cross the River Tweed,
And be at once from peril freed!"

    —"Ah tempt me not!" she faintly sighed;
"I will not counsel nor exhort,—   1105
With my condition satisfied;
But you, at least, may make report
Of what befalls;—be this your task—
This may be done;—'tis all I ask!"

    She spake—and from the Lady's sight   1110
The Sire, unconscious of his age,
Departed promptly as a Page
Bound on some errand of delight.
—The noble Francis—wise as brave,
Thought he, may have the skill to save: 1115

1089 beg; *rev from* say *MS. 1815 (WW)*   *line del, then rewritten by JC, MS. 1832/36*
1091 *rev in stages MS. 1832/36:*
    (*a*)—If *eras to* If *and* help *or del to* mortal (*WW's pencil and ink*)
    (*b*) If prudence offer *del to* If room be left for
    (*c*) be left *del to* on you
    (*d*) *line entered in margin* (*JC*): On you, if room for mortal aid *adopted 1836–*
1092 On *you rev from* On you *MS. 1815* Be left, *MS. 1832/36—*   restriction *rev from* [?in-
struction] *MS. 1815*
1093 recline *rev from* intrude *MS. 1815*
1095–1096 *rev to:*
                   { M
      "Hope," said the old { man, "must abide
     With all of us, whate'er betide *MS. 1832/36, adopted as rev 1836–*
1115 have the] want not *MS. 1832/36–*

With hopes in tenderness concealed,
Unarmed he followed to the field.
Him will I seek: the insurgent Powers
Are now besieging Barnard's Towers,—
"Grant that the Moon which shines this night   1120
May guide them in a prudent flight!"

But quick the turns of chance and change,
And knowledge has a narrow range;
Whence idle fears, and needless pain,
And wishes blind, and efforts vain.—   1125
Their flight the fair Moon may not see;
For, from mid-heaven, already she
Hath witnessed their captivity.
She saw the desperate assault
Upon that hostile Castle made;—   1130
But dark and dismal is the Vault
Where Norton and his Sons are laid!
Disastrous issue!—He had said
"This night yon haughty Towers must yield,
Or we for ever quit the field.   1135
—Neville is utterly dismayed,
For promise fails of Howard's aid;
And Dacre to our call replies
That he is unprepared to rise.
My heart is sick;—this weary pause   1140
Must needs be fatal to the cause.
The breach is open—on the Wall,
This night, the Banner shall be planted!"
—'Twas done:—his Sons were with him—all;—
They belt him round with hearts undaunted;   1145
And others follow—Sire and Son
Leap down into the court—"'Tis won"—

1126–1127   *rev to:*
      The Moon may shine, but cannot be
      Their guide in flight—already she *MS. 1832/36– but* already] for already *then* for
canceled MS. 1836/45
  1134   haughty] faithless *MS. 1832/36–*
  1140   pause *rev from* pain *MS. 1815*
  1141   the *rev from* our *MS. 1815 (WW)* our *MS. 1832/36 (pencil and ink)–*
  1144   —'Twas *rev from* — 'T[?] *MS. 1815 (WW)*

They shout aloud—but Heaven decreed
    Another close
      To that brave deed   1150
Which struck with terror friends and foes!
The friend shrinks back—the foe recoils
From Norton and his filial band;
But they, now caught within the toils,
Against a thousand cannot stand;—   1155
The foe from numbers courage drew,
And overpowered that gallant few.
"A rescue for the Standard!" cried
The Father from within the walls;
But, see, the sacred Standard falls!—   1160
Confusion through the Camp spreads wide:
Some fled—and some their fears detained;
But ere the Moon had sunk to rest
In her pale chambers of the West,
Of that rash levy nought remained.   1165

END OF CANTO FOURTH.

THE

WHITE DOE OF RYLSTONE.

CANTO FIFTH.

HIGH on a point of rugged ground,
Among the wastes of Rylstone Fell,
Above the loftiest ridge or mound
Where Foresters or Shepherds dwell,

    1148   shout *rev from* cried *MS. 1815*
    1149–1150   *inscribed as a single line, then broken into two lines, with comma after* deed *MS. 1815*
(WW); *rev to:*
                     { their
        That with { the   joyful shout should close
        The triumph of a desperate deed *MS. 1832/36 with alt in pencil:* That with this
very shout should [? ?] *adopted as rev 1836–*
    1151   friends *rev from* friend *MS. 1815*
    1152   shrinks *rev from* shrunk *MS. 1815*
    1157   that] a *eras to* the *rev to* that *MS. 1815 (WW)*
    1161   spreads] spread *1820–*
    1165   nought *rev from* none *MS. 1815*

An Edifice of warlike frame   1170
Stands single (Norton Tower its name,)
It fronts all quarters, and looks round
O'er path and road, and plain and dell,
Dark moor, and gleam of pool and stream,
Upon a prospect without bound.   1175

   The summit of this bold ascent,
Though bleak and bare, and as seldom free
As Pendle-hill or Pennygent
From wind, or frost, or vapours wet,
Had often heard the sound of glee   1180
When there the youthful Nortons met,
To practise games and archery:
How proud and happy they! the crowd
Of Lookers-on how pleased and proud!
And from the heat of the noon-tide sun,   1185
From showers, or when the prize was won,
They to the Watch-tower did repair,
Commodious Pleasure-house! and there
Would mirth run round, with generous fare;
And the stern old Lord of Rylstone-hall,   1190
He was the proudest of them all!

   But now, his Child, with anguish pale,
Upon the height walks to and fro;
'Tis well that she hath heard the tale,—
Received the bitterness of woe: 1195
Dead are they, they were doomed to die;
The Sons and Father all are dead,
All dead save One; and Emily
No more shall seek this Watch-tower high,

1177   and as] as *1820–*
1185   heat of the] scorching *1820–*
1187–1188 *reduced to:* They to the Tower withdrew, & there *MS. 1832/36– but* &] and *1836–*
1189   Would] Did *MS. 1815*
1191   He was the proudest] Was proudest, happiest *alt in pencil MS. 1832/36* Was happiest, proudest, *1836–*
1193   the] this *MS. 1815*
1196–1202 *omitted 1820–*

1170–1171 See WW's note.
1178 *Ballad of Flodden Field,* V, 9–12 (APC).

To look far forth with anxious eye,—   1200
She is relieved from hope and dread,
Though suffering in extremity.

   For she had hoped, had hoped and feared,
Such rights did feeble nature claim;
And oft her steps had hither steered,   1205
Though not unconscious of self-blame;
For she her Brother's charge revered,
His farewell words; and by the same,
Yea by her Brother's very name,
Had, in her solitude, been cheared.   1210

   She turned to him, who with his eye
Was watching her while on the height
She sate, or wandered restlessly,
O'erburdened by her sorrow's weight;
To him who this dire news had told,   1215
And now beside the Mourner stood;
(That grey-haired Man of gentle blood,
Who with her Father had grown old
In friendship, rival Hunters they,
And fellow Warriors in their day)   1220
To Rylstone he the tidings brought;
Then on this place the Maid had sought:
And told, as gently as could be,
The end of that sad Tragedy,
Which it had been his lot to see.   1225

   To him the Lady turned; "You said
That Francis lives, *he* is not dead?"

   "Your noble Brother hath been spared,
To take his life they have not dared.
On him and on his high endeavour   1230

1205   hither *rev from* thither *MS. 1815*
1211   his *rev from* her *MS. 1815*
1211–1215   *del MS. 1832/36–*
1216   Beside [that *del to*] the lonely watch-tower stood *MS. 1832/36, marked for paragraph indentation; adopted as rev 1836–*
1222   place] height *MS. 1832/36–*
1223   And, gently as he could, had told *MS. 1832/36 (with commas in pencil)–*
1224   that *rev from* this *MS. 1815*   sad] dire *MS. 1832/36–*

The light of praise shall shine for ever!
Nor did he (such heaven's will) in vain
His solitary course maintain;
Not vainly struggled in the might
Of duty seeing with clear sight;   1235
He was their comfort to the last,
Their joy till every pang was past.

"I witnessed when to York they came—
What, Lady, if their feet were tied!
They might deserve a good Man's blame;   1240
But, marks of infamy and shame,
These were their triumph, these their pride.
"Lo Francis comes," the people cried,
"A Prisoner once, but now set free!
"'Tis well, for he the worst defied   1245
"For the sake of natural Piety;
"He rose not in this quarrel, he
"His Father and his Brothers wooed,
"Both for their own and Country's good,
"To rest in peace—he did divide,   1250
"He parted from them; but at their side
"Now walks in unanimity—
"Then peace to cruelty and scorn,
"While to the prison they are borne,
"Peace, peace to all indignity!"   1255

"And so in Prison were they laid—
Oh hear me, hear me, gentle Maid!
For I am come with power to bless,
To scatter gleams through your distress

1237 till *rev from* when *MS. 1815*
1242/1243 Nor wanted 'mid the pressing crowd
              Deep feeling, that found utterance loud, *1827–*
1243 the people] There were who *1827–*
1246 For sake] Through force *1836–*
1248–1250 *rev in stages to:*
              For concord's sake and England's good,
              Suit to his Brothers often made
              With tears, and of his Father prayed—
              [But *rev to*] And when he had in vain withstood
              Their purpose—then did he divide, *MS. 1832/36, adopted as rev 1836–*
1254 the *rev from* their *MS. 1815*
1256 were they *rev from* they were *MS. 1815*
1259 To scatter gleams] By scattering gleams, *1820–*

Of a redeeming happiness.   1260
Me did a reverend pity move
And privilege of ancient love,
But most, compassion for your fate,
Lady! for your forlorn estate,
Me did these move, and I made bold,   1265
And entrance gained to that strong-hold.

    "Your Father gave me cordial greeting;
But to his purposes, that burned
Within him, instantly returned—
He was commanding and entreating,   1270
And said, "We need not stop, my Son!
"But I will end what is begun;
" 'Tis matter which I do not fear
"To entrust to any living ear."
And so to Francis he renewed   1275
His words, more calmly thus pursued.

    "Might this our enterprize have sped,
"Change wide and deep the Land had seen,
"A renovation from the dead,
"A spring-tide of immortal green: 1280
"The darksome Altars would have blazed
"Like stars when clouds are rolled away;
"Salvation to all eyes that gazed,
"Once more the Rood had been upraised
"To spread its arms, and stand for aye.   1285
"Then, then, had I survived to see
"New life in Bolton Priory;
"The voice restored, the eye of truth
"Re-opened that inspired my youth;
"Had seen her in her pomp arrayed;   1290
"This Banner (for such vow I made)
"Should on the consecrated breast

    1263–1264 *omitted 1820–*
    1265 Me did these move, and] And, in your service, *1820–*   I made bold,] I made bold—
1820–1832 restored to I made bold, *MS. 1832/36* making bold, *1836–*
    1266 And entrance] Entrance I *1836–*
    1272–1274 *reduced to* Thoughts press, & time is hurrying on'— *MS. 1832/36– but &] and
1836–*
    1275 *del then marked stet MS. 1832/36 (JC)*
    1290 Had seen] To see *1820–*

"Of that same Temple have found rest:
"I would myself have hung it high,
"Glad offering of glad victory!   1295

  "A shadow of such thought remains
"To chear this sad and pensive time;
"A solemn fancy yet sustains
"One feeble Being—bids me climb
"Even to the last—one effort more   1300
"To attest my Faith, if not restore.

  "Hear then," said he, "while I impart,
"My Son, the last wish of my heart.
—"The Banner strive thou to regain;
"And, if the endeavour be not vain,   1305
"Bear it—to whom if not to thee
"Shall I this lonely thought consign?—
"Bear it to Bolton Priory,
"And lay it on Saint Mary's shrine,—
"To wither in the sun and breeze   1310
"Mid those decaying Sanctities.
"There let at least the gift be laid,
"The testimony there displayed;
"Bold proof that with no selfish aim,
"But for lost Faith and Christ's dear name,   1315
"I helmeted a brow though white,
"And took a place in all men's sight;
"Yea offered up this beauteous Brood,
"This fair unrivalled Brotherhood,
"And turned away from thee, my Son!   1320
"And left—but be the rest unsaid,
"The name untouched, the tear unshed,—
"My wish is known and I have done:
"Now promise, grant this one request,
"This dying prayer, and be thou blest!"   1325

1295 Glad] Fit *MS. 1832/36–*
1305 be] prove *MS. 1832/36 (pencil and ink)–*
1318 beauteous] noble *MS. 1832/36–*
1319 Unity *pencil alt in margin, MS. 1832/36 (WW)*

1309 The priory was dedicated to St. Mary (APC).

"Then Francis answered fervently,
"If God so will, the same shall be."

"Immediately, this solemn word
Thus scarcely given, a noise was heard,
And Officers appeared in state   1330
To lead the Prisoners to their fate.
They rose, oh! wherefore should I fear
To tell, or, Lady, you to hear?
They rose—embraces none were given—
They stood like trees when earth and heaven   1335
Are calm; they knew each other's worth,
And reverently the Band went forth.
They met, when they had reached the door,
The Banner which a Soldier bore,
One marshalled thus with base intent   1340
That he in scorn might go before,
And, holding up this monument,
Conduct them to their punishment;
So cruel Sussex, unrestrained
By human feeling, had ordained: 1345
The unhappy Banner Francis saw,
And, with a look of calm command
Inspiring universal awe,
He took it from the Soldier's hand;
And all the People that were round   1350
Confirmed the deed in peace profound.
—High transport did the Father shed
Upon his Son—and they were led,

1326–1327   Then Francis answered—'[trust *rev to*] Trust thy Son,
       For, with God's will, it shall be done!'— *MS. 1832/36, adopted as rev 1836–*
1328   "Immediately, this] The pledge obtained, the *MS. 1832/36–*
1332–1333   *inserted in ink, MS. 1815*
1339–1342   One with prophane and harsh intent
       Placed there—that he might go before
       And, with that rueful Banner borne
       Aloft, in sign of taunting scorn, *MS. 1832/36–*
1347   calm command *rev from* calmer pride *MS. 1815*
1348–1349   He took it from the Soldier's hand,
       A look of universal awe, *rev to*
       Inspiring universal awe;
       He took it from the Soldier's hand, *MS. 1815*
1350   were] stood *1836–*

Led on, and yielded up their breath,
Together died, a happy death!   1355
But Francis, soon as he had braved
This insult, and the Banner saved,
That moment, from among the tide
Of the spectators occupied
In admiration or dismay,   1360
Bore unobserved his Charge away."

  These things, which thus had in the sight
And hearing passed of Him who stood
With Emily, on the Watch-tower height,
In Rylstone's woeful neighbourhood,   1365
He told; and oftentimes with voice
Of power to encourage or rejoice;
For deepest sorrows that aspire,
Go high, no transport ever higher.
"Yet, yet in this affliction," said   1370
The Old Man to the silent Maid,
"Yet, Lady! heaven is good—the night
Shews yet a Star which is most bright;
Your Brother lives—he lives—is come
Perhaps already to his home;   1375
Then let us leave this dreary place."
She yielded, and with gentle pace,
Though without one uplifted look,
To Rylstone-hall her way she took.—

END OF CANTO FIFTH.

1357 This] That *MS. 1832/36–*
1358 Athwart the unresisting tide *MS. 1832/36 (pencil and ink)–*
1361 unobserved] speedily *pencil alt (WW)* instantly *MS. 1832/36–*
1367 encourage] comfort *1820–*
1370 "Yes—God is rich in mercy," said *MS. 1832/36–*
1372 1373 "Yet, Lady! shines, through this black, night
        One star of aspect heavenly bright; *MS. 1832/36–* but black,] black *1836–*
night] night, *MS. 1836/45, 1840–*
1379/ *one line illeg pencil in margin, MS. 1832/36 (WW)*

THE

WHITE DOE OF RYLSTONE.

CANTO SIXTH.

WHY comes not Francis?—Joyful chear   1380
In that parental gratulation,
And glow of righteous indignation,
Went with him from the doleful City:—
He fled—yet in his flight could hear
The death-sound of the Minster-bell;   1385
That sullen stroke pronounced farewell
To Marmaduke, cut off from pity!
To Ambrose that! and then a knell
For him, the sweet half-opened Flower!
For all—all dying in one hour!   1390
—Why comes not Francis? Thoughts of love
Should bear him to his Sister dear
With motion fleet as winged Dove;
Yea, like a heavenly Messenger,
An Angel-guest, should he appear.   1395
Why comes he not?—for westward fast
Along the plain of York he past;
The Banner-staff was in his hand,
The Imagery concealed from sight,
And cross the expanse, in open flight,   1400
Reckless of what impels or leads,
Unchecked he hurries on;—nor heeds
The sorrow of the Villages;
From the triumphant cruelties

1380   Joyful chear] From the doleful City *MS. 1832/36 (WW)*–
1381–1383   *del MS. 1832/36*–
1383   the *rev from* that *MS. 1815*
1384   yet] and *MS. 1832/36 (WW)*, *1836* and, *1845*–
1385   death-sound] death-sounds *MS. 1832/36*–
1393   winged] a wingèd *1832 then line rev to* With the fleet motion of a dove; *1836*–
1394   heavenly *rev from* winged *MS. 1815*
1395   An Angel-guest] Of speediest wing *1836*–
1398   his *rev from* her *MS. 1815*
1398–1400   *omitted 1836*–
1400   in *rev from* of *MS. 1815*
1401   Reckless of *rev from* Not knowing *MS. 1815 (WW)*
1403   of] through *1832*–
1404   From the] Spread by *1827*–

Of vengeful military force,   1405
And punishment without remorse,
Unchecked he journies—under law
Of inward occupation strong;
And the first object which he saw,
With conscious sight, as he swept along,—   1410
It was the Banner in his hand!
He felt, and made a sudden stand.

   He looked about like one betrayed:
What hath he done? what promise made?
Oh weak, weak moment! to what end   1415
Can such a vain oblation tend,
And he the Bearer?—Can he go
Carrying this Instrument of woe,
And find, find any where, a right
To excuse him in his Country's sight?   1420
No, will not all Men deem the change
A downward course, perverse and strange?
Here is it,—but how, when? must she,
The unoffending Emily,
Again this piteous object see?   1425

   Such conflict long did he maintain
Within himself, and found no rest;
Calm liberty he could not gain;
And yet the service was unblest.
His own life into danger brought   1430
By this sad burden—even that thought
Raised self-suspicion which was strong,
Swaying the brave Man to his wrong:
And how, unless it were the sense

1406/1407   But both the [? ? ?]
        And [? ?] *MS. 1832/36 (WW's pencil in margin)*
1407–1408   *expanded to:*
    He marked not, heard not as he fled;
    All but the suffering heart was dead
    For him abandoned to blank awe,
      To vacancy, and horror strong; *1827   but* heard not] heard not, *1843*   suffering]
sad *pencil alt MS. 1832/36*   strong;] strong: *1832–*
1410   sight, *rev from* mind *MS. 1815*
1427–1429   *reduced to* Nor liberty nor rest could gain: *MS. 1832/36 (WW)* –
1432   Exciting self-suspicion strong, *MS. 1815/20 WD, 1820– but* strong,] strong *1840–*
1433   Swaying] Swayed *MS. 1815/20 WD, 1820–*

Of all-disposing Providence,   1435
Its will intelligibly shewn,
Finds he the Banner in his hand,
Without a thought to such intent,
Or conscious effort of his own?
And no obstruction to prevent   1440
His Father's wish and last command!
And, thus beset, he heaved a sigh;
Remembering his own prophecy
Of utter desolation, made
To Emily in the yew-tree shade: 1445
He sighed, submitting to the power,
The might of that prophetic hour.
"No choice is left, the deed is mine—
Dead are they, dead!—and I will go,
And, for their sakes, come weal or woe,   1450
Will lay the Relic on the shrine."

    So forward with a steady will
He went, and traversed plain and hill;
And up the vale of Wharf his way
Pursued;—and, on the second day,   1455

1436   intelligibly] unquestionably *MS. 1832/36–*
1437–1444   How has the Banner clung so fast
         ~~To the cold hand to which it passed~~
         To a palsied, an unconscious, hand;
         Clung to the hand to which it passed
                        ?⎫ ⎧A
         Without impediment ⎭ ⎩and why
         But that Heaven's purpose might be known   [5]
         Doth now no hinderance meet his eye,
         No intervention, to withstand
         Fulfilment of a Father's prayer
         ⎰ Breathed
         ⎱ When   to a Son forgiven—and blest
                        s⎫
         When all resentment ⎭ were at rest,   [10]
         And life in death laid the heart bare?—
         Then, like a spectre sweeping by,
                   ⎰through
         Rushed ⎱[? on]   his mind the prophesy
         Of utter desolation made *MS. 1832/36; adopted as rev 1836– but* [2] an] *and 1845–*
unconscious,] unconscious *1836–*   [6] hinderance] hindrance *1845–*   [9] forgiven—] for-
given, *1836–*   prophesy] prophecy *1836–*   [14] desolation] desolation, *1836–*
    1438   to *rev from* of *MS. 1815*
    1441   command! *rev from* intent? *MS. 1815*
    1446   submitting . . . power, *del to* [?   ?] in *then marked* stet *which was in turn del and entire line
rewritten (JC):* He sighed, submitting will & power *MS. 1832/36, adopted 1836– with* &] *and*
    1447   To the stern [?] *del to* embrace of that grasping hour. *MS. 1832/36 (JC); adopted as rev
1836–*
    1455   on the second] ere the dawn of *MS. 1832/36* at the dawn of *1836–*

He reached a summit whence his eyes
Could see the Tower of Bolton rise.
There Francis for a moment's space
Made halt—but hark! a noise behind
Of Horsemen at an eager pace!   1460
He heard and with misgiving mind.
—'Tis Sir George Bowes who leads the Band:
They come, by cruel Sussex sent;
Who, when the Nortons from the hand
Of Death had drunk their punishment,   1465
Bethought him, angry and ashamed,
How Francis had the Banner claimed,
And with that charge had disappeared;
By all the Standers-by revered.
His whole bold carriage (which had quelled   1470
Thus far the Opposer, and repelled
All censure,—enterprise so bright
That even bad Men had vainly striven
Against that overcoming light)
Was then reviewed, and prompt word given,   1475
That to what place soever fled
He should be seized, alive or dead.

   The troop of horse have gained the height
Where Francis stood in open sight.
They hem him round—"Behold the proof,   1480
Behold the Ensign in his hand!
He did not arm, he walked aloof!
For why?—to save his Father's Land;—
Worst Traitor of them all is he,
A Traitor dark and cowardly!"   1485

   "I am no Traitor," Francis said,
"Though this unhappy freight I bear;
It weakens me, my heart hath bled
Till it is weak—but you beware,

1456   He reached] Had reached *MS. 1832/36* Attained *1836–*
1467–1468   How Francis, with the Banner claimed
            As his own charge, had disappeared, *MS. 1832/36–*
1480   "Behold] Beheld *1820* Behold *1827*
1481   Behold the] They cried, "the *MS. 1832/36 (WW)–*
1488–1489   And must not part with. But beware
            Lest ye by hasty zeal misled *MS. 1832/36 (WW)*, then *l. 1489 rewritten with* Lest ye
del to Err not, *and comma after* misled *(JC); adopted as rev 1836– but* beware] beware;—

Nor do a suffering Spirit wrong,   1490
Whose self-reproaches are too strong!"
At this he from the beaten road
Retreated towards a brake of thorn,
Which like a place of 'vantage shewed;
And there stood bravely, though forlorn.   1495
In self-defence with a Warrior's brow
He stood,—nor weaponless was now;
He from a Soldier's hand had snatched
A spear,—and with his eyes he watched
Their motions, turning round and round:—   1500
His weaker hand the Banner held;
And straight by savage zeal impelled
Forth rushed a Pikeman, as if he,
Not without harsh indignity,
Would seize the same:—instinctively—   1505
To smite the Offender—with his lance
Did Francis from the brake advance;
But, from behind, a treacherous wound
Unfeeling, brought him to the ground,

1490   Nor *del to* Would *restored to* Nor MS. *1832/36*
1494   Which] That MS. *1832/36–*
1496   a Warrior's] warlike MS. *1815/20* WD, *1820–*
1499   and with his eyes he] and, so protected, MS. *1832/36 (WW)–*
1500–1533   *for readings of MS. 1832/36, rev in stages toward 1836, see transcriptions and photos below, pp. 374–379*
1500   Their motions] The Assailants *1836–*
1501–1507   *omitted 1836–*
1508   a treacherous *over illeg eras* MS. *1815*   behind, a] behind with *1836–*
1509–1517   A Spearman brought him to the ground.
                   The guardian lance, as Francis fell,
                   Dropped from him; but his other hand
                   The Banner clenched; till, from out the Band,
                   One, the most eager for the prize,   [5]
                   Rushed in; and—while, O grief to tell!
                   A glimmering sense still left, with eyes
                   Unclosed the noble Francis lay—
                   Seized it, as hunters seize their prey;
                   But not before the warm life-blood   [10]
                   Had tinged with searching overflow,
                   More deeply tinged the embroidered show
                   Of His whose side was pierced upon the Rood!
                      Proudly the Horsemen bore away
                   The Standard; and where Francis lay
                   There was he left alone, unwept,
                   And for two days unnoticed slept. *1836– but* [2] *marked for paragraph indentation*
MS. *1836/45, then* [11] *rev to:*
                   Had tinged more deeply, as it flowed,
                   The wounds the broidered Banner showed,
                   Thy fatal work, O Maiden, innocent as good! *1845–*

A mortal stroke:—oh, grief to tell!   1510
Thus, thus, the noble Francis fell:
There did he lie of breath forsaken;
The Banner from his grasp was taken,
And borne exultingly away;
And the Body was left on the ground where it lay.   1515

   Two days, as many nights, he slept
Alone, unnoticed, and unwept;
For at that time distress and fear
Possessed the Country far and near;
The third day, One, who chanced to pass,   1520
Beheld him stretched upon the grass.
A gentle Forester was he,
And of the Norton Tenantry;
And he had heard that by a Train
Of Horsemen Francis had been slain.   1525
Much was he troubled—for the Man
Hath recognized his pallid face;
And to the nearest Huts he ran,
And called the People to the place.
—How desolate is Rylstone-hall!   1530
Such was the instant thought of all;
And if the lonely Lady there
Should be, this sight she cannot bear!
Such thought the Forester express'd,
And all were swayed, and deemed it best   1535
That, if the Priest should yield assent
And join himself to their intent,
Then, they, for Christian pity's sake,
In holy ground a grave would make;
That straightway buried he should be   1540
In the Church-yard of the Priory.

1518 distress and] bewildering *1836–*
1520–1527 But, on the third day, passing by
            One of the Norton Tenantry
            Espied the uncovered Corse; the Man
            Shrunk as he recognised the face, *1836–*
1528 Huts he] homesteads *1836–*
1531 Such] This *1836–*   thought *rev from* wish *MS. 1815*
1532–1533 Should be; to her they cannot bear
            This weight of anguish and despair. *1836–*
1534–1535 So, when upon sad thoughts had prest
            Thoughts sadder still, they deemed it best *on paste-over MS. 1832/36–*
1537 And no one hinder their intent, *MS. 1832/36 (WW)–*
1540 That] And *MS. 1832/36 (WW)–*

Apart, some little space, was made
The grave where Francis must be laid.
In no confusion or neglect
This did they,—but in pure respect   1545
That he was born of gentle Blood;
And that there was no neighbourhood
Of kindred for him in that ground:
So to the Church-yard they are bound,
Bearing the Body on a bier   1550
In decency and humble chear;
And psalms are sung with holy sound.

  But Emily hath raised her head,
And is again disquieted;
She must behold!—so many gone,   1555
Where is the solitary One?
And forth from Rylstone-hall stepped she,—
To seek her Brother forth she went
And tremblingly her course she bent
Tow'rds Bolton's ruined Priory.   1560
She comes, and in the Vale hath heard
The Funeral dirge;—she sees the Knot
Of people, sees them in one spot—
And darting like a wounded Bird
She reached the grave, and with her breast   1565
Upon the ground received the rest,—
The consummation, the whole ruth
And sorrow of this final truth!

END OF CANTO SIXTH.

THE

WHITE DOE OF RYLSTONE.

CANTO SEVENTH.

1544   In *rev from* This *MS. 1815*
1551–1552   And psalms they sung a holy sound,
            That hill and vale with sadness hear. *MS. 1832/36– but* sung] sung— *1836* sing—
MS. 1836/45 (JC), 1840–   sound,] sound *1836–*
    1553   raised *partially over illeg eras MS. 1815*
    1557   Rylstone-hall *rev from* Rylstone's hall *MS. 1815*
    1559   bent *rev from* went *MS. 1815*
    1560   Tow'rds *rev from* Towards *MS. 1815* Toward *MS. 1832/36–*

THOU Spirit, whose angelic hand
Was to the Harp a strong command,   1570
Called the submissive strings to wake
In glory for this Maiden's sake,
Say, Spirit! whither hath she fled
To hide her poor afflicted head?
What mighty forest in its gloom   1575
Enfolds her?—is a rifted tomb
Within the wilderness her seat?
Some island which the wild waves beat,
Is that the Sufferer's last retreat?
Or some aspiring rock, that shrouds   1580
Its perilous front in mists and clouds?
High-climbing rock—deep sunless dale—
Sea—desart—what do these avail?
Oh take her anguish and her fears
Into a calm recess of years!   1585

'Tis done;—despoil and desolation
O'er Rylstone's fair domain have blown;
The walks and pools neglect hath sown
With weeds, the bowers are overthrown,
Or have given way to slow mutation,   1590
While, in their ancient habitation
The Norton name hath been unknown:
The lordly Mansion of its pride
Is stripped; the ravage hath spread wide
Through park and field, a perishing   1595

---

epigraph   'Powers there are
            That touch each other to the quick—in modes
            Which the gross world no sense hath to perccive
                No soul to dream of.' *MS. 1832/36, recopied in margin with single quotes and with*
        perceive] perceive, *then adopted as rev 1836–*
    1570   the] his *MS. 1815*
    1575   in its *rev from* is h[?] *MS. 1815*
    1582   deep] low *MS. 1815/20 WD, 1820–*
    1585   calm] deep *MS. 1815/20 WD, 1820–*
    1588   *rev from* The untended walks and pools are sown *MS. 1815 (WW)* Pools, terraces, and
    walks are sown *1845–*

    1568/1569   After 1837, these lines from the *Address to Kilchurn Castle* (ll. 6–9) appeared with
The White Doe.
    1586–1587   See WW's note.
    1589   *As You Like It,* II.v.4, suggested by J. C. Maxwell, *Notes and Queries,* n.s. 16 (February
1969), 49.

That mocks the gladness of the Spring!
And with this silent gloom agreeing
There is a joyless human Being,
Of aspect such as if the waste
Were under her dominion placed: 1600
Upon a primrose bank, her throne
Of quietness, she sits alone;
There seated, may this Maid be seen,
Among the ruins of a wood,
Erewhile a covert bright and green,   1605
And where full many a brave Tree stood;
That used to spread its boughs, and ring
With the sweet Bird's carolling.
Behold her, like a Virgin Queen,
Neglecting in imperial state   1610
These outward images of fate,
And carrying inward a serene
And perfect sway, through many a thought
Of chance and change, that hath been brought
To the subjection of a holy,   1615
Though stern and rigorous, melancholy!

1597   this *rev from the MS. 1815*
1598   There is] Appears *MS. 1832/36–*
1599   Of aspect *del, then restored with* stet *MS. 1832/36 (JC)*
1603   *del MS. 1832/36–*

1615–1616   The rhyme occurs in *Il Penseroso* ("But hail thee Goddess, sage and holy, / Hail divinest Melancholy"), but was used more recently by Mary Lamb, who wrote the following lines to DW on 7 May 1805, expressing her sympathy on John Wordsworth's death:

> Why is he wandering o'er the sea?
> Coleridge should now with Wordsworth be.
> By slow degrees he'd steal away
> Their woe, and gently bring a ray
> (So happily he'd time relief)
> Of comfort from their very grief.—
> He'd tell them that their brother dead
> When years have passed o'er their head,
> Will be remember'd with such holy,
> True, & perfect melancholy,
> That ever this lost brother John
> Will be their hearts companion.
> His voice they'll always hear, his face they'll always see,
> There's nought in life so sweet as such a memory.
>   [Marrs, II, 166]

WW also uses the metaphor of wandering, and the language of ll. 3–6 and 12–14 elsewhere in his poem.

The like authority, with grace
Of awfulness, is in her face,—
There hath she fixed it; yet it seems
To o'ershadow by no native right   1620
That face, which cannot lose the gleams,
Lose utterly the tender gleams
Of gentleness and meek delight
And loving-kindness ever bright:
Such is her sovereign mien;—her dress   1625
(A vest, with woollen cincture tied,
A hood of mountain-wool undyed)
Is homely,—fashioned to express
A wandering Pilgrim's humbleness.

And she *hath* wandered, long and far,   1630
Beneath the light of sun and star;
Hath roamed in trouble and in grief,
Driven forward like a withered leaf,
Yea like a Ship at random blown
To distant places and unknown.   1635
But now she dares to seek a haven
Among her native wilds of Craven;
Hath seen again her Father's Roof,
And put her fortitude to proof;
The mighty sorrow has been borne,   1640
And she is thoroughly forlorn:
Her soul doth in itself stand fast,
Sustained by memory of the past
And strength of Reason; held above
The infirmities of mortal love;   1645
Undaunted, lofty, calm, and stable,
And awfully impenetrable.

And so—beneath a mouldered tree,
A self-surviving leafless Oak,

1623   omitted MS. *1815*
1629   humbleness *rev from* [?low]liness *MS. 1815*
1634   blown *rev from illeg eras MS. 1815*
1636   But *rev from* And *MS. 1815*
1640   has] hath *1827–*

1631   *As You Like It,* II.iii.42, suggested by J. C. Maxwell, *Notes and Queries,* n.s. 16 (February 1969), 49.

By unregarded age from stroke   1650
Of ravage saved—sate Emily.
There did she rest, with head reclined,
Herself most like a stately Flower,
(Such have I seen) whom chance of birth
Hath separated from its kind,   1655
To live and die in a shady bower,
Single on the gladsome earth.

    When, with a noise like distant thunder,
A troop of Deer came sweeping by;
And, suddenly, behold a wonder!   1660
For, of that band of rushing Deer,
A single One in mid career
Hath stopped, and fixed its large full eye
Upon the Lady Emily,
A Doe most beautiful, clear-white,   1665
A radiant Creature, silver-bright!

    Thus checked, a little while it stayed;
A little thoughtful pause it made;
And then advanced with stealth-like pace,
Drew softly near her—and more near,   1670
Stopped once again;—but, as no trace
Was found of any thing to fear,
Even to her feet the Creature came,
And laid its head upon her knee,
And looked into the Lady's face,   1675
A look of pure benignity,
And fond unclouded memory.
It is, thought Emily, the same,
The very Doe of other years!
The pleading look the Lady viewed,   1680
And, by her gushing thoughts subdued,
She melted into tears—
A flood of tears, that flowed apace

1657 the *rev from* this *MS. 1815*
1661 For One, among those rushing deer, *1836–*
1663 its] his *1832* her *MS. 1832/36 (WW)* –
1671–1672 Looked round—but saw no cause for fear; *MS. 1832/36 (WW)– but* fear;] fear] *1850*
1673 Even] So *MS. 1832/36 (WW)–*
1680 pleading *rev from* pleasing *MS. 1815 (WW)*
1681 gushing *over illeg eras MS. 1815*

Upon the happy Creature's face.

Oh, moment ever blest! O Pair!   1685
Beloved of heaven, heaven's choicest care!
This was for you a precious greeting,—
For both a bounteous, fruitful meeting.
Joined are they, and the sylvan Doe
Can she depart? can she forego   1690
The Lady, once her playful Peer,
And now her sainted Mistress dear?
And will not Emily receive
This lovely Chronicler of things
Long past, delights and sorrowings?   1695
Lone Sufferer! will not she believe
The promise in that speaking face,
And take this gift of Heaven with grace?

That day, the first of a re-union
Which was to teem with high communion   1700
That day of balmy April weather,
They tarried in the wood together.
And when, ere fall of evening-dew
She from this sylvan haunt withdrew,
The White Doe tracked with faithful pace   1705
The Lady to her Dwelling-place;
That nook where, on paternal ground,
A habitation she had found,
The Master of whose humble board
Once owned her Father for his Lord;   1710
A Hut, by tufted Trees defended,
Where Rylstone Brook with Wharf is blended.

When Emily by morning light
Went forth, the Doe was there in sight.

1686 choicest] chosen *MS. 1832/36–*
1688 And may it prove a fruitful meeting! *MS. 1832/36 (WW)–*
1696 Lone] Long *1850*
1698 And welcome, as a gift of grace,
      The saddest thought the Creature brings? *MS. 1832/36–*
1702 wood *rev from* woods *MS. 1815*
1704 this] her *MS. 1832/36–*
1708 had *rev from* hath *MS. 1815 (WW)*
1711 tufted *rev from* tufts of *MS. 1815 (WW)*
1714 was] stood *MS. 1832/36 (WW)–*

She shrunk:—with one frail shock of pain,   1715
Received and followed by a prayer,
Did she behold—saw once again;
Shun will she not, she feels, will bear;—
But wheresoever she looked round
All now was trouble-haunted ground.   1720
So doth the Sufferer deem it good
Even once again this neighbourhood
To leave.—Unwooed, yet unforbidden,
The White Doe followed up the Vale,
Up to another Cottage—hidden   1725
In the deep fork of Amerdale;
And there may Emily restore
Herself, in spots unseen before.—
Why tell of mossy rock, or tree,
By lurking Dernbrook's pathless side,   1730
Haunts of a strengthening amity
That calmed her, cheared, and fortified?
For she hath ventured now to read
Of time, and place, and thought, and deed,
Endless history that lies   1735
In her silent Follower's eyes!
Who with a power like human Reason
Discerns the favourable season,
Skilled to approach or to retire,—
From looks conceiving her desire,   1740

1715   She shrunk:—with *rev from* Why speak of *MS. 1815 (WW)*
1717   Did she behold—saw] When she beheld, [?see] *rev to* Did she behold, saw *MS. 1815*
(WW) She saw the creature *MS. 1832/36 (pencil and ink)*– *but* creature] Creature *1836*–
1721–1722   And therefore now she deems it good
            Once more this restless neighbourhood *MS. 1832/36 (WW)*–
1728–1729   The lingering song full willingly *MS. 1815, del*
1729   Why *rev from* Could *MS. 1815* —Why *1836*–
1730   pathless side *rev from* side *MS. 1815*
1736   her *over illeg eras, MS. 1815*
1738   the *rev from* a *MS. 1815*   season *over illeg eras MS. 1815*
1739   retire,— *rev from* retire, *with first two letters over illeg eras MS. 1815*
1740   *line inserted by WW, MS. 1815*

1715–1728   APC notes that the lines suggest "a comparable state of mind" in the Words-
worths after John's death. The same could be said of their 1813 move to Rydal Mount after the
children's deaths.
1726   See WW's note.
1730   APC, following Knight, notes that Dernbrook is "a small lateral valley" running south-
west from the Linton valley, which makes a "'deep fork' in the hills."

From look, deportment, voice or mien,
That vary to the heart within.
If she too passionately writhed
Her arms, or over-deeply breathed,
Walked quick or slowly, every mood   1745
In its degree was understood;
Then well may their accord be true,
And kindly intercourse ensue.
—Oh! surely 'twas a gentle rouzing
When she by sudden glimpse espied   1750
The White Doe on the mountain browzing,
Or in the meadow wandered wide!
How pleased, when down the Straggler sank
Beside her, on some sunny bank!
How soothed, when in thick bower enclosed,   1755
They like a nested Pair reposed!
Fair Vision! when it crossed the Maid
Within some rocky cavern laid,
The dark cave's portal gliding by,
White as the whitest cloud on high,   1760
Floating through the azure sky.
—What now is left for pain or fear?
That Presence, dearer and more dear,
Did now a very gladness yield
At morning to the dewy field,   1765
While they side by side were straying,
And the Shepherd's pipe was playing;
And with a deeper peace endued
The hour of moonlight solitude.

1741   looks *rev from* look *MS. 1815*   or *rev from* and *MS. 1815*
1743   writhed] wreathed *1827–*
1748   kindly] kindliest *MS. 1832/36 (WW)–*
1753   sank *rev from* sunk *MS. 1815*
1759   portal *rev from* portals *MS. 1815*
1760   the *rev to* a *del to* the *MS. 1815; omitted 1827–*   whitest *rev from* white *MS. 1815*   on
high, *rev from* in the sky. *MS. 1815*
1761   *line inserted MS. 1815*   the] an *1827–1832*
1764–1765   *del and inserted at 1767/1768, 1836–*
1767/1768   *ll. 1764–1765 inserted 1836–*
1768   endued *rev from* ensued *MS. 1815*
1769   moonlight *rev from* deepest *MS. 1815*

1740   *F.Q.,* I.iii.9.9 (APC).

With her Companion, in such frame   1770
Of mind, to Rylstone back she came,—
And, wandering through the wasted groves,
Received the memory of old Loves,
Undisturbed and undistrest,
Into a soul which now was blest   1775
With a soft spring-day of holy,
Mild, delicious melancholy:
Not sunless gloom or unenlightened,
But by tender fancies brightened.

When the Bells of Rylstone played   1780
Their Sabbath music—"𝖌𝖔𝖉 𝖚𝖘 𝖆𝖞𝖉𝖊!"
That was the sound they seemed to speak;
Inscriptive legend, which I ween
May on those holy Bells be seen,
That legend and her Grandsire's name;   1785
And oftentimes the Lady meek
Had in her Childhood read the same,
Words which she slighted at that day;
But now, when such sad change was wrought,
And of that lonely name she thought,   1790
The Bells of Rylstone seemed to say,
While she sate listening in the shade,
With vocal music, "𝖌𝖔𝖉 𝖚𝖘 𝖆𝖞𝖉𝖊!"
And all the Hills were glad to bear
Their part in this effectual prayer.   1795

Nor lacked she Reason's firmest power;
But with the White Doe at her side
Up doth she climb to Norton Tower,

1772   wandering] ranging *MS. 1832/36 (WW, pencil and ink)*–
1773   Loves *rev from* times *MS. 1815* loves *1836*–
1775   now *over illeg eras MS. 1815*
1777   delicious] delicious, *MS. 1815/20 WD, 1820–1836* and grateful *1845*–
1785   her *rev from* his *MS. 1815*
1790   lonely *rev from* lowly *MS. 1815*
1796   firmest *rev from* firmer *MS. 1815*
1798   doth] would *MS. 1832/36 (WW)* –

1781   See WW's note.
1789   "In trellis'd shed," l. 22.

And thence looks round her far and wide.
Her fate there measures,—all is stilled,—   1800
The feeble hath subdued her heart;
Behold the prophecy fulfilled,
Fulfilled, and she sustains her part!
But here her Brother's words have failed,—
Here hath a milder doom prevailed;   1805
That she, of him and all bereft,
Hath yet this faithful Partner left,—
This single Creature that disproves
His words, remains for her, and loves.
If tears are shed, they do not fall   1810
For loss of him, for one or all;
Yet, sometimes, sometimes doth she weep
Moved gently in her soul's soft sleep;
A few tears down her cheek descend
For this her last and living Friend.   1815

   Bless, tender Hearts, their mutual lot,
And bless for both this savage spot!
Which Emily doth sacred hold
For reasons dear and manifold—
Here hath she, here before her sight,   1820
Close to the summit of this height,
The grassy rock-encircled Pound
In which the Creature first was found.
So beautiful the spotless Thrall,
(A lovely Youngling white as foam,)   1825
That it was brought to Rylstone-hall;

1799   looks] look *1836–*
1800   measures,—] measuring;— *1836–*
1801   feeble] Feeble *1832* weak One MS. *1832/36 (WW)–*
1808   single Creature] one associate MS. *1832/36 (WW)– but* one Associate *1845–*
1811   or *rev from* and MS. *1815*
1817   this *rev from* the MS. *1815*
1819   For *rev from* From MS. *1815 (WW)*
1820   Here hath she, here *rev from* For here hath she MS. *1815 (WW)*
1824   spotless] timid MS. *1832/36–*
1825   lovely] spotless MS. *1832/36–*
1826   *del MS. 1832/36–*

1822   See WW's note. After explaining the Pound, WW appends a final recommendation of the beauty of Bolton Abbey, kept up by the interchange of art and nature.

Her youngest Brother led it home,
The youngest, then a lusty Boy,
Brought home the prize—and with what joy!

But most to Bolton's sacred Pile,   1830
On favouring nights, she loved to go:
There ranged through cloister, court, and aisle,
Attended by the soft-paced Doe;
Nor did she fear in the still moonshine
To look upon Saint Mary's shrine;   1835
Nor on the lonely turf that showed
Where Francis slept in his last abode.
For that she came; there oft and long
She sate in meditation strong:
And, when she from the abyss returned   1840
Of thought, she neither shrunk nor mourned;
Was happy that she lived to greet
Her mute Companion as it lay
In love and pity at her feet;
How happy in her turn to meet   1845
That recognition! the mild glance
Beamed from that gracious countenance;—
Communication, like the ray
Of a new morning, to the nature
And prospects of the inferior Creature!   1850

A mortal Song we frame, by dower
Encouraged of celestial power;
Power which the viewless Spirit shed
By whom we were first visited;
Whose voice we heard, whose hand and wings   1855

1827   led *rev to* bore *then to* led *MS. 1815 (WW)* brought *MS. 1832/36 (pencil and ink)*–
1829   Bore it, or led to Rylstone-hall
        With heart brim-ful of pride and joy! *MS. 1832/36, adopted 1836*– *but* led] led, *and*
brim-ful] brimful
    1834   did she fear] feared she *1827*–   in the *rev from* by the *MS. 1815* in *MS. 1815/20 WD,*
1820
    1838   and long] she sate *1836*–
    1839   She sate dejected, but not disconsolate: *del to* She sate forlorn, but not disconsolate: *MS.*
1832/36 (JC) Forlorn, but not disconsolate: *1836*–
    1843   it *rev from* she *MS. 1815*
    1845   her] its *MS. 1815/20 WD, 1820*–
    1846   That] The *MS. 1832/36*–
    1851   frame] sing *MS. 1832/36*–
    1852/1853   *three lines of illeg pencil in margin MS. 1832/36 (WW)*

Swept like a breeze the conscious strings,
When, left in solitude, erewhile
We stood before this ruined Pile,
And, quitting unsubstantial dreams,
Sang in this Presence kindred themes;   1860
Distress and desolation spread
Through human hearts, and pleasure dead,—
Dead—but to live again on Earth,
A second and yet nobler birth;
Dire overthrow, and yet how high   1865
The re-ascent in sanctity!
From fair to fairer; day by day
A more divine and loftier way!
Even such this blessed Pilgrim trod,
By sorrow lifted tow'rds her God;   1870
Uplifted to the purest sky
Of undisturbed mortality.
Her own thoughts loved she; and could bend
A dear look to her lowly Friend,—
There stopped;—her thirst was satisfied   1875
With what this innocent spring supplied—
Her sanction inwardly she bore,
And stood apart from human cares:
But to the world returned no more,
Although with no unwilling mind   1880
Help did she give at need, and joined
The Wharfdale Peasants in their prayers.
At length, thus faintly, faintly tied
To earth, she was set free, and died.
Thy soul, exalted Emily,   1885
Maid of the blasted Family,
Rose to the God from whom it came!
—In Rylstone Church her mortal frame
Was buried by her Mother's side.

Most glorious sunset!—and a ray   1890
Survives—the twilight of this day;
In that fair Creature whom the fields
Support, and whom the forest shields;
Who, having filled a holy place,

1864   nobler *rev from* glorious *MS. 1815*
1877–1878   *transposed to 1879–1880 MS. 1815*
1888   Rylstone *rev from* Rylstones *MS. 1815*

Partakes in her degree heaven's grace;   1895
And bears a memory and a mind
Raised far above the law of kind;
Haunting the spots with lonely chear
Which her dear Mistress once held dear:
Loves most what Emily loved most—   1900
The enclosure of this Church-yard ground;
Here wanders like a gliding Ghost,
And every Sabbath here is found;
Comes with the People when the Bells
Are heard among the moorland dells,   1905
Finds entrance through yon arch, where way
Lies open on the Sabbath-day;
Here walks amid the mournful waste
Of prostrate altars, shrines defaced,
And floors encumbered with rich show   1910
Of fret-work imagery laid low;
Paces softly, or makes halt,
By fractured cell, or tomb, or vault,
By plate of monumental brass
Dim-gleaming among weeds and grass,   1915
And sculptured Forms of Warriors brave;
But chiefly by that single grave,
That one sequestered hillock green,
The pensive Visitant is seen.
There doth the gentle Creature lie   1920
With those adversities unmoved;
Calm Spectacle, by earth and sky
In their benignity approved!
And aye, methinks, this hoary Pile,
Subdued by outrage and decay,   1925
Looks down upon her with a smile,
A gracious smile, that seems to say,
"Thou, thou art not a Child of Time,
But Daughter of the Eternal Prime!"

END OF THE WHITE DOE.

1895   her degree *rev from* heaven's *MS. 1815*
1904   with *rev from* [?when] *MS. 1815*
1906   where *rev from* whose *MS. 1815*
1907   Lies *rev from* Lie *MS. 1815*
1917   single *rev from* honoured *MS. 1815*
1923   benignity *rev from* indignity *MS. 1815 (WW)*
1924   this *rev from* that *MS. 1815 (WW)*
1927   seems *rev from* seemed *MS. 1815 (WW)*

THE

FORCE OF PRAYER;

OR

THE FOUNDING OF BOLTON PRIORY.

A TRADITION.

𝖂𝖍𝖆𝖙 𝖎𝖘 𝖌𝖔𝖔𝖉 𝖋𝖔𝖗 𝖆 𝖇𝖔𝖔𝖙𝖑𝖊𝖘𝖘 𝖇𝖊𝖓𝖊?
With these dark words begins my Tale,
And their meaning is, whence can comfort spring
When prayer is of no avail?   4

Isabella Fenwick transcribed the following note to the poem: "An Appendage to *The White Doe*. My friend, Mr. Rodgers, has also written on the subject. The story is preserved in Dr. Whitaker's 'History of Craven'—a topographical writer of first-rate merit in all that concerns the past; but such was his aversion from the modern spirit, as shown in the spread of manufactures in those districts of which he treats, that his readers are left entirely ignorant both of the progress of these arts and their real bearing upon the comfort, virtues, and happiness of the inhabitants. While wandering on foot through the fertile valleys and over the moorlands of the Apennine that divides Yorkshire from Lancashire, I used to be delighted with observing the number of substantial cottages that had sprung up on every side, each having its little plot of fertile ground won from the surrounding waste. A bright and warm fire, if needed, was always to be found in these dwellings. The father was at his loom; the children looked healthy and happy. Is it not to be feared that the increase of mechanic power has done away with many of these blessings, and substituted many evils? Alas! if these evils grow, how are they to be checked, and where is the remedy to be found? Political economy will not supply it; that is certain, we must look to something deeper, purer, and higher." This expressly political look (disclaimer notwithstanding) at the question of irremediable sorrow which opens his poem suggests that Wordsworth subscribes to a rather fluid assignation of meaning in poems about universal suffering.

Wordsworth must have seen a copy of Whitaker's *History of Craven* before he composed this poem. Whitaker writes that a priory dedicated to St. Mary and St. Cuthbert was founded at Embsay. The founders' daughter, who took her mother's name, Romillè, married William Fitz Duncan, and her son, "commonly called the Boy of Egremond," was "the last hope of the family." He met his death in the woods between Bolton and Barden, where the Wharf "suddenly contracts itself to a rocky channel little more than four feet wide, and pours through the tremendous fissure with a rapidity proportioned to its confinement." The place is called the Strid, "from a feat often exercised by persons of more agility than prudence, who stride from brink to brink, regardless of the destruction which awaits a faltering step." Tradition has it that such "was the fate of young Romillè, who inconsiderately bounding over the chasm with a greyhound in his leash, the animal hung back, and drew his unfortunate master into the torrent." A forester who had accompanied him "returned to the Lady Aaliza, and, with despair in his countenance, enquired, 'What is good for a bootless Bene?' To which the mother, apprehending that some great calamity had befallen her son, instantly replied, 'Endless sorrow.'" Whitaker believed the "almost unintelligible" language of the question proved the antiquity of the story, for "'bootless Bene' is unavailing prayer; and the meaning, though imperfectly ex-

147

𝔚𝔥𝔞𝔱 𝔦𝔰 𝔤𝔬𝔬𝔡 𝔣𝔬𝔯 𝔞 𝔟𝔬𝔬𝔱𝔩𝔢𝔰𝔰 𝔟𝔢𝔫𝔢?
The Falconer to the Lady said;
And she made answer, "ENDLESS SORROW:"
For she knew that her Son was dead.   8

She knew it from the Falconer's words,
And from the look of the Falconer's eye,
And from the love which was in her soul
For her youthful Romilly.   12

—Young Romilly through Barden Woods
Is ranging high and low;
And holds a Greyhound in a leash
To let slip upon buck or doe;   16

And the Pair have reached that fearful chasm,
How tempting to bestride!
For lordly Wharf is there pent in
With rocks on either side.   20

This Striding-place is called THE STRID,
A name which it took of yore:
A thousand years hath it borne that name,
And shall—a thousand more.   24

And hither is young Romilly come,
And what may now forbid
That he, perhaps for the hundredth time,
Shall bound across THE STRID?   28

He sprang in glee,—for what cared he
That the River was strong and the rocks were steep!
But the Greyhound in the leash hung back,
And checked him in his leap.   32

---

pressed, seems to have been 'What remains when prayer is useless?'" The misfortune "is said to have occasioned the translation of the priory from Embsay to Bolton," the site closest to the accident [Whitaker, 324].

12   APC annotates the ballad with the following quotation from Francis James Child's *English and Scottish Ballads*, III, 403: "The Countess of Northumberland would have been the last person to give such advice as is attributed to her. 'His wife, being the stouter of the two, doth encourage him to persevere, and rideth up and down with the army, so as the grey mare is the better horse.' Hunsdon to Cecil, November twenty-sixth, MS. cited by Froude."

The Boy is in the arms of Wharf,
And strangled with a merciless force;
For never more was young Romilly seen
Till he rose a lifeless Corse!   36

Now is there stillness in the Vale,
And long unspeaking sorrow:—
Wharf shall be to pitying hearts
A name more sad than Yarrow.   40

If for a Lover the Lady wept,
A solace she might borrow
From death, and from the passion of death;—
Old Wharf might heal her sorrow.   44

She weeps not for the Wedding-day
Which was to be to-morrow:
Her hope was a farther-looking hope,
And her's is a Mother's sorrow.   48

He was a Tree that stood alone,
And proudly did its branches wave;
And the Root of this delightful Tree
Was in her Husband's grave!   52

Long, long in darkness did she sit,
And her first words were, "Let there be
In Bolton, on the field of Wharf,
A stately Priory."   56

The stately Priory was reared,
And Wharf, as he moved along,
To Matins joined a mournful voice,
Nor failed at Even-song.   60

And the Lady prayed in heaviness
That looked not for relief:
But slowly did her succour come,
And a patience to her grief.   64

Oh! there is never sorrow of heart
That shall lack a timely end,
If but to God we turn, and ask
Of Him to be our Friend!   68

NOTES.

THE Poem of the White Doe of Rylstone is founded on a local tradition, and on the Ballad in Percy's Collection, entitled "The Rising of the North." The tradition is as follows: "About this time," not long after the Dissolution, "a White Doe, say the aged people of the neighbourhood, long continued to make a weekly pilgrimage from Rylstone 5 over the fells of Bolton, and was constantly found in the Abbey Church-yard during divine service; after the close of which she returned home as regularly as the rest of the congregation."—DR WHITAKER'S *History of the Deanery of Craven.*—Rylstone was the property and residence of the Nortons, distinguished in that ill-advised and 10 unfortunate Insurrection, which led me to connect with this tradition the principal circumstances of their fate, as recorded in the Ballad which I have thought it proper to annex.

The Rising in the North.

The subject of this ballad is the great Northern Insurrection in the 12th year of Elizabeth, 1569, which proved so fatal to Thomas Percy, 15 the seventh Earl of Northumberland.

There had not long before been a secret negociation entered into between some of the Scottish and English nobility, to bring about a marriage between Mary Q. of Scots, at that time a prisoner in England, and the Duke of Norfolk, a nobleman of excellent character. This 20

---

1 a local *inserted MS. 1815*

2–3 The Rising of the North *rev from* The Rising the North *MS. 1815*   About] At *MS. 1815*

8–9 —Dr. Whitaker's . . . Craven.— *inserted MS. 1815*

10–11 distinguished . . . Insurrection, *inserted MS. 1815*

11–12 with . . . of *inserted MS. 1815*   the principal *rev from* the main *MS. 1815*

12–13 Ballad . . . annex.] I have thought proper to annex the Ballad on which the preceding Poem is partly founded, with the substance of Dr. Percy's prefatory account. (N.B. to be printed in small type) *inserted by WW, then del MS. 1815* Ballad. "Bolton Priory" says Dr Whitaker in his excellent Book, the History and Antiquities of the Deanery of Craven, stands upon a beautiful curvature of the Wharf, on a level sufficiently *MS. 1815/20 WD (MW)*

13–75 *(including entire ballad) omitted 1820–*

14–33 *all del and apparently rev on separate sheet now missing MS. 1815/20 WD*

18–19 to bring about a marriage *over illeg eras MS. 1815*

20 and firmly attached to the Protestant religion *entered following* character. *then del MS. 1815*

14–75 Taken verbatim from Bishop Percy's notes, in *Reliques of Ancient English Poetry,* 3 vols. (London, 1765), I, 248–250. Wordsworth's acknowledgment of the borrowing was never printed.

match was proposed to all the most considerable of the English no-
bility, and among the rest to the Earls of Northumberland and West-
moreland, two noblemen very powerful in the North. As it seemed to
promise a speedy and safe conclusion of the troubles in Scotland, with
many advantages to the crown of England, they all consented to it,   25
provided it should prove agreeable to Queen Elizabeth. The Earl of
Leicester (Elizabeth's favourite) undertook to break the matter to her,
but before he could find an opportunity, the affair had come to her
ears by other hands, and she was thrown into a violent flame. The
Duke of Norfolk, with several of his friends, was committed to the   30
Tower, and summons were sent to the Northern Earls instantly to
make their appearance at court. It is said that the Earl of Northum-
berland, who was a man of a mild and gentle nature,* was deliberating
with himself whether he should not obey the message, and rely upon
the Queen's candour and clemency, when he was forced into desperate   35
measures by a sudden report at midnight, Nov. 14, that a party of his
enemies were come to seize his person. The Earl was then at his house
at Topcliffe in Yorkshire. When, rising hastily out of bed, he withdrew
to the Earl of Westmoreland at Brancepeth, where the country came in
to them, and pressed them to take up arms in their own defence. They   40
accordingly set up their standards, declaring their intent was to restore
the ancient Religion, to get the succession of the crown firmly settled,
and to prevent the destruction of the ancient nobility, &c. Their com-
mon banner (on which was displayed the cross, together with the five
wounds of Christ) was borne by an ancient gentleman, Richard Nor-   45
ton, Esquire, who, with his sons, (among whom, Christopher, Mar-
maduke, and Thomas, are expressly named by Camden,) dis-
tinguished himself on this occasion. Having entered Durham, they
tore the Bible, &c. and caused mass to be said there; they then
marched on to Clifford-moor near Wetherby, where they mustered   50
their men. * * * * * * *
The two Earls, who spent their large estates in hospitality, and were
extremely beloved on that account, were masters of little ready money;
the E. of Northumberland bringing with him only 8000 crowns, and
the E. of Westmoreland nothing at all, for the subsistence of their

---

* Camden expressly says that he was violently attached to the Catholic Religion.

---

43   ancient *rev from* Catholic MS. *1815*
49   there *rev from* then MS. *1815*
50/51   Their intention was to have preceeded on to York, but, altering their minds, they fell
upon Barnard's castle, which Sir George would hold out against them for eleven days. *del MS.*
1815
51   The asterisks signify Wordsworth's omission of one sentence from Percy's account.

forces, they were not able to march to London, as they had at first   55
intended. In these circumstances, Westmoreland began so visibly to
despond, that many of his men slunk away, though Northumberland
still kept up his resolution, and was master of the field till December
13, when the Earl of Sussex, accompanied with Lord Hunsden and
others, having marched out of York at the head of a large body of   60
forces, and being followed by a still larger army under the command
of Ambrose Dudley, Earl of Warwick, the insurgents retreated north-
ward towards the borders, and there dismissing their followers, made
their escape into Scotland. Though this insurrection had been sup-
pressed with so little bloodshed, the Earl of Sussex and Sir George   65
Bowes, marshal of the army, put vast numbers to death by martial law,
without any regular trial. The former of these caused at Durham sixty-
three constables to be hanged at once. And the latter made his boast,
that for sixty miles in length, and forty in breadth, betwixt Newcastle
and Wetherby, there was hardly a town or village wherein he had not   70
executed some of the inhabitants. This exceeds the cruelties practised
in the West after Monmouth's rebellion.

Such is the account collected from Stow, Speed, Camden, Guthrie,
Carte, and Rapin; it agrees, in most particulars, with the following
Ballad, apparently the production of some northern minstrel.—   75

LISTEN, lively lordings all,
  Lithe and listen unto mee,
And I will sing of a noble earle,
  The noblest earle in the north countrie.   4

Earle Percy is into his garden gone,
  And after him walks his fair leddie:
I heard a bird sing in mine ear,
  That I must either fight, or flee.   8

Now heaven forefend, my dearest lord,
  That ever such harm should hap to thee:
But goe to London to the court,
  And fair fall truth and honestie.   12

---

62   the insurgents *partially over illeg eras* MS. *1815*
63   followers *partially over illeg eras* MS. *1815*
72   but that was not the age of tenderness and humanity *del following* rebellion MS. *1815*
73   Speed *over illeg eras* MS. *1815*
74   Carte *rev from* Carne MS. *1815*
75   Ballad . . . minstrel *rev from several canceled lines:* ballad, which was apparently the pro-
duction of some northern minstrel, who was well [?]ted the two noblemen. It is here printed
from two M. S. copies, one of them in the editor's folio collection. They contained considerable
variations, out of which some readings were chosen as seemed most poetical and consonant to his
story. MS. *1815*

Now nay, now nay, my ladye gay,
   Alas! thy counsell suits not mee;
Mine enemies prevail so fast,
   That at the court I may not bee.   16

O goe to the court yet, good my lord,
   And take thy gallant men with thee;
If any dare to do you wrong,
   Then your warrant they may bee.   20

Now nay, now nay, thou ladye faire,
   The court is full of subtiltie:
And if I goe to the court, ladye,
   Never more I may thee see.   24

Yet goe to the court, my lord, she sayes,
   And I myselfe will ryde wi' thee:
At court then for my dearest lord,
   His faithful borrowe I will bee.   28

Now nay, now nay, my ladye deare;
   Far lever had I lose my life,
Than leave among my cruell foes
   My love in jeopardy and strife.   32

But come thou hither, my little foot-page,
   Come thou hither unto mee,
To Maister Norton thou must goe
   In all the haste that ever may bee.   36

Commend me to that gentleman,
   And beare this letter here fro mee;
And say that earnestly I praye,
   He will ryde in my companie.   40

One while the little foot-page went,
   And another while he ran;
Untill he came to his journey's end,
   The little foot-page never blan.   44

When to that gentleman he came,
   Down he kneeled on his knee;
And took the letter betwixt his hands,
   And lett the gentleman it see.   48

---

38   here *inserted MS. 1815*

And when the letter it was redd,
　　Affore that goodlye companie,
I wis if you the truthe wold know,
　　There was many a weeping eye.　　　　　　　　　52

He sayd, Come thither, Christopher Norton,
　　A gallant youth thou seem'st to bee;
What dost thou counsell me, mý sonne,
　　Now that good earle's in jeopardy?　　　　　　　56

Father, my counselle's fair and free;
　　That erle he is a noble lord,
And whatsoever to him you hight,
　　I would not have you breake your word.　　　　　60

Gramercy, Christopher, my sonne,
　　Thy counsell well it liketh mee,
And if we speed and 'scape with life,
　　Well advanced shalt thou bee.　　　　　　　　　64

Come you hither, my nine good sonnes,
　　Gallant men I trowe you bee:
How many of you, my children deare,
　　Will stand by that good erle and mee?　　　　　68

Eight of them did answer make,
　　Eight of them spake hastilie,
O Father, till the day we dye
　　We'll stand by that good erle and thee.　　　　　72

Gramercy, now, my children deare,
　　You shew yourselves right bold and brave,
And whethersoe'er I live or dye,
　　A father's blessing you shall have.　　　　　　　76

But what say'st thou, O Francis Norton,
　　Thou art mine eldest sonne and heire:
Somewhat lies brooding in thy breast;
　　Whatever it bee, to mee declare.　　　　　　　　80

Father, you are an aged man,
　　Your head is white, your beard is gray;
It were a shame at these your years
　　For you to ryse in such a fray.　　　　　　　　　84

59　light *over illeg eras MS. 1815*
70　spake *over illeg eras MS. 1815*

Now fye upon thee, coward Francis,
  Thou never learned'st this of mee;
When thou wert young and tender of age,
  Why did I make soe much of thee?   88

But, father, I will wend with you,
  Unarm'd and naked will I bee;
And he that strikes against the crowne,
  Ever an ill death may he dee.   92

Then rose that reverend gentleman,
  And with him came a goodlye band
To join with the brave Earle Percy,
  And all the flower o' Northumberland.   96

With them the noble Nevill came,
  The erle of Westmoreland was hee;
At Wetherbye they mustered their host,
  Thirteen thousand fair to see.   100

Lord Westmorland his ancyent raisde,
  The Dun Bull he rays'd on hye,
And three Dogs with golden collars
  Were there set out most royallye.   104

Erle Percy there his ancyent spread,
  The Halfe Moone shining all soe faire;
The Nortons ancyent had the Crosse,
  And the five wounds our Lord did beare.   108

Then Sir George Bowes he straitwaye rose,
  After them some spoile to make:
Those noble erles turned back againe,
  And aye they vowed that knight to take.   112

That baron he to his castle fled,
  To Barnard castle then fled hee.
The uttermost walles were eathe to win,
  The earles have wonne them presentlie.   116

The uttermost walles were lime and bricke;
  But though they won them soon anone,
Long ere they wan their innermost walles,
  For they were cut in rocke and stone.   120

---

92   dee *over illeg eras MS. 1815*

Then news unto leeve London came
  In all the speed that ever might bee,
And word is brought to our royall queene
  Of the rysing in the North countrie.   124

Her grace she turned her round about,
  And like a royall queene shee swore,
I will ordayne them such a breakfast,
  As never was in the North before.   128

Shee caused thirty thousand men be rays'd,
  With horse and harneis faire to see;
She caused thirty thousand men be raised
  To take the earles i' th' North countrie.   132

Wi' them the false Erle Warwicke went,
  The Erle Sussex and the Lord Hunsden,
Untill they to York castle came
  I wiss they never stint ne blan.   136

Now spred thy ancyent, Westmoreland,
  Thy dun Bull faine would we spye:
And thou, the Erle of Northumberland,
  Now rayse thy Halfe Moone on hye.   140

But the dun bulle is fled and gone,
  And the halfe moone vanished away:
The Erles, though they were brave and bold,
  Against soe many could not stay.   144

Thee, Norton, wi' thine eight good sonnes,
  They doomed to dye, alas! for ruth!
Thy reverend lockes thee could not save,
  Nor them their faire and blooming youthe.   148

Wi' them full many a gallant wight
  They cruellye bereav'd of life:
And many a child made fatherlesse,
  And widowed many a tender wife.   152

---

126   shee swore *rev by eras from* swore shee *MS. 1815*
129   thousand *rev from* thirty *MS. 1815*
131   thirty *rev from* thou *MS. 1815*
136   ne *rev from* nor *MS. 1815*
140   hye *rev from* bye *MS. 1815*

"Bolton Priory," Says Dr Whitaker in his excellent book, the History
and Antiquities of the Deanry of Craven, "stands upon a beautiful
curvature of the Wharf, on a level sufficiently elevated to protect it
from inundations, and low enough for every purpose of picturesque
effect.   80
   "Opposite to the East window of the Priory Church, the river washes
the foot of a rock nearly perpendicular, and of the richest purple,
where several of the mineral beds, which break out, instead of main-
taining their usual inclination to the horizon, are twisted by some
inconceivable process, into undulating and spiral lines. To the South   85
all is soft and delicious; the eye reposes upon a few rich pastures, a
moderate reach of the river, sufficiently tranquil to form a mirror to
the sun, and the bounding hills beyond, neither too near nor too lofty
to exclude, even in winter, any portion of his rays.
   "But, after all, the glories of Bolton are on the North. Whatever the   90
most fastidious taste could require to constitute a perfect landscape is
not only found here, but in its proper place. In front, and immediately
under the eye, is a smooth expanse of park-like enclosure, spotted with
native elm, ash, &c. of the finest growth: on the right a skirting oak
wood, with jutting points of grey rock; on the left a rising copse. Still   95
forward are seen the aged groves of Bolton Park, the growth of cen-
turies; and farther yet, the barren and rocky distances of Simon-seat
and Barden Fell contrasted with the warmth, fertility, and luxuriant
foliage of the valley below.
   "About half a mile above Bolton the Valley closes, and either side of   100
the Wharf is overhung by solemn woods, from which huge perpen-
dicular masses of grey rock jut out at intervals.
   "This sequestered scene was almost inaccessible till of late, that rid-
ings have been cut on both sides of the River, and the most interesting
points laid open by judicious thinnings in the woods. Here a tributary   105
stream rushes from a waterfall, and bursts through a woody glen to
mingle its waters with the Wharf: there the Wharf itself is nearly lost in
a deep cleft in the rock, and next becomes a horned flood enclosing a
woody island—sometimes it reposes for a moment, and then resumes
its native character, lively, irregular, and impetuous.   110
   "The cleft mentioned above is the tremendous STRID. This chasm,
being incapable of receiving the winter floods, has formed, on either
side, a broad strand of naked gritstone full of rock-basons, or 'pots of
the Linn,' which bear witness to the restless impetuosity of so many
Northern torrents. But, if here Wharf is lost to the eye, it amply repays   115

94–95   skirting . . . rock *inserted MS. 1815 (WW)*
115   here *eras from* there *MS. 1815*

another sense by its deep and solemn roar, like 'the Voice of the angry
Spirit of the Waters,' heard far above and beneath, amidst the silence
of the surrounding woods.

"The terminating object of the landscape is the remains of Barden
Tower, interesting from their form and situation, and still more so   120
from the recollections which they excite."

From Bolton's old monastic Tower.—P.81.

It is to be regretted that at the present day Bolton Abbey wants this
ornament: but the Poem, according to the imagination of the Poet, is
composed in Queen Elizabeth's time. "Formerly," says Dr Whitaker,
"over the Transept was a tower. This is proved not only from the   125
mention of bells at the Dissolution, when they could have had no other
place, but from the pointed roof of the choir, which must have termi-
nated westward, in some building of superior height to the ridge."

A rural Chapel, neatly drest.—P.82.

"The Nave of the Church having been reserved at the Dissolution,
for the use of the Saxon Cure, is still a parochial Chapel; and, at this 130
day, is as well kept as the neatest English Cathedral."

Who sate in the shade of the Prior's Oak.—P.82.

"At a small distance from the great gateway stood the Prior's Oak,
which was felled about the year 1720, and sold for 70l. According to
the price of wood at that time, it could scarcely have contained less
than 1400 feet of timber."   135

When Lady Aaliza mourn'd.—P.88.

The detail of this tradition may be found in Dr Whitaker's book, and
in the foregoing Poem, The Force of Prayer, &c.

121/122   *note to the Borderers quotation inserted:*
'Action is transitory—'
                    that
This and the five lines∧following were either read or recited by me, more than thirty years since,
                        ⌠t
to the late Mr Hazlit⌡ , who quoted some expressions in them (imperfectly remembered) in a
work of his published several years ago. *MS. 1832/36 (JC); adopted as rev 1836– with* Mr] Mr.
    135/136   *note to l. 187 del:* "From Rylstone she hath found her way" "At this time (viz. not long
after the Dissolution) "a white Doe, say the aged People of the neighborhood, long continued to
make a weekly pilgrimage from Rylstone over the fells to Bolton, and was constantly found in the
abbey church-yard during divine service, after the close of which she returned home as regularly
as the rest of the congregation." Rylstone was the property and residence of the Nortons, which
led one to connect their fate with this tradition. *MS. 1815*
    137   the foregoing Poem,] a Poem to be found in the Fourth Volume of this Collection, *1820*
a Poem in the Fourth volume of this collection *1827–1840 but* the Fourth volume] the Third
Volume *1832, then* Third *rev to* fifth *MS. 1832/36; adopted as* the Fifth Volume *1836–1840* a

Pass, pass who will, yon chantry door.—P.88.

"At the East end of the North aisle of Bolton Priory Church is a
chantry belonging to Bethmesly Hall, and a vault, where, according to
tradition, the Claphams" (who inherited this estate, by the female line   140
from the Mauliverers) "were interred upright." John de Clapham, of
whom this ferocious act is recorded, was a name of great note in his
time; "he was a vehement partisan of the House of Lancaster, in whom
the spirit of his chieftains, the Cliffords, seemed to survive."

Who loved the Shepherd Lord to meet.—P.89.

In the second volume of Poems published by the author, will be   145
found one, entitled, "Song at the Feast of Brougham Castle, upon the
Restoration of Lord Clifford the Shepherd to the Estates and Honours
of his Ancestors." To that Poem is annexed an account of this person-
age, chiefly extracted from Burn's and Nicholson's History of Cum-
berland and Westmoreland. It gives me pleasure to add these further   150
particulars concerning him from Dr Whitaker, who says, "he retired to
the solitude of Barden, where he seems to have enlarged the tower out
of a common keeper's lodge, and where he found a retreat equally
favourable to taste, to instruction, and to devotion. The narrow limits
of his residence shew that he had learned to despise the pomp of   155
greatness, and that a small train of servants could suffice him, who had
lived to the age of thirty a servant himself. I think this nobleman
resided here almost entirely when in Yorkshire, for all his charters
which I have seen are dated at Barden.

"His early habits, and the want of those artificial measures of time   160
which even shepherds now possess, had given him a turn for observing
the motions of the heavenly bodies, and, having purchased such an
apparatus as could then be procured, he amused and informed him-
self by those pursuits, with the aid of the Canons of Bolton, some of
whom are said to have been well versed in what was then known of the   165
science.

"I suspect this nobleman to have been sometimes occupied in a more
visionary pursuit, and probably in the same company.

"For, from the family evidences, I have met with two MSS. on the
subject of Alchemy, which, from the character, spelling, &c., may al-   170
most certainly be referred to the reign of Henry the Seventh. If these
were originally deposited with the MSS. of the Cliffords, it might have

---

Poem of this Collection *1845–*   foregoing *and* The Force of Prayer &c. *inserted by* WW MS.
1815
　142   name] man *1832–*   his] this *1832*
　144   his *rev from the MS. 1815*
　145   the second] this *1845*   Poems published by the author] these Poems *1820–1840,*
1846– Poems *1845*

been for the use of this nobleman. If they were brought from Bolton at
the Dissolution, they must have been the work of those Canons whom
he almost exclusively conversed with.   175

"In these peaceful employments Lord Clifford spent the whole
reign of Henry the Seventh, and the first years of his son. But in the
year 1513, when almost sixty years old, he was appointed to a principal
command over the army which fought at Flodden, and shewed that
the military genius of the family had neither been chilled in him by   180
age, nor extinguished by habits of peace.

"He survived the battle of Flodden ten years, and died April 23d,
1523, aged about 70. I shall endeavour to appropriate to him a tomb,
vault, and chantry, in the choir of the church of Bolton, as I should be
sorry to believe that he was deposited when dead at a distance from the 185
place which in his life-time he loved so well.

"By his last will he appointed his body to be interred at Shap if he
died in Westmoreland; or at Bolton if he died in Yorkshire."

With respect to the Canons of Bolton, Dr Whitaker shews from MSS.
that not only alchemy but astronomy was a favourite pursuit with   190
them.

Ye Watchmen upon Brancepeth Towers.—P.100.

Brancepeth Castle stands near the river Were, a few miles from the
city of Durham. It formerly belonged to the Nevilles, Earls of West-
moreland. See Dr Percy's account.

Of mitred Thurston, what a Host
He conquered!—P. 107.

See the Historians for the account of this memorable battle, usually   195
denominated the Battle of the Standard.

In that other day of Neville's Cross.—P.108.

"In the night before the battle of Durham was strucken and begun,
the 17th day of October, *anno* 1346, there did appear to John Fosser,
then Prior of the abbey of Durham, commanding him to take the holy
Corporax-cloth, wherewith St Cuthbert did cover the chalice when he   200
used to say mass, and to put the same holy relique like to a banner-
cloth upon the point of a spear, and the next morning to go and repair

---

191/192   Towers] Tower *MS. 1815*   Ye . . . Towers. *rev to*
        'Now joy to you who from the towers
        Of Brancepeth look in doubt and fear,'— *MS. 1832/36; adopted as rev 1836– but* Of]
'Of *1836* fear,'—] fear,' *1836–*
195–196   *entered by WW in space MS. 1815*
199   Durham,] Durham, a Vision, *1832–*

to a place on the west side of the city of Durham, called the Red Hills, where the Maid's Bower wont to be, and there to remain and abide till the end of the battle. To which vision, the Prior obeying, and taking 205 the same for a revelation of God's grace and mercy by the mediation of holy St Cuthbert, did accordingly the next morning, with the monks of the said abbey, repair to the said Red Hills, and there most devoutly humbling and prostrating themselves in prayer for the victory in the said battle: (a great multitude of the Scots running and pressing by 210 them, with intention to have spoiled them, yet had no power to commit any violence under such holy persons, so occupied in prayer, being protected and defended by the mighty Providence of Almighty God, and by the mediation of Holy St Cuthbert, and the presence of the holy relique.) And, after many conflicts and warlike exploits there had 215 and done between the English men and the King of Scots and his company, the said battle ended, and the victory was obtained, to the great overthrow and confusion of the Scots, their enemies: And then the said Prior and monks, accompanied with Ralph Lord Nevil, and John Nevil his son, and the Lord Percy, and many other nobles of 220 England, returned home and went to the abbey church, there joining in hearty prayer and thanksgiving to God and holy St Cuthbert for the victory atchieved that day."

This battle was afterwards called the Battle of Neville's Cross from the following circumstance:— 225

"On the west side of the city of Durham, where two roads pass each other, a most notable, famous, and goodly cross of stone-work was erected, and set up to the honour of God for the victory there obtained in the field of battle, and known by the name of Nevil's Cross, and built at the sole cost of the Lord Ralph Nevil, one of the most excellent and 230 chief persons in the said battle." The Relique of St Cuthbert afterwards became of great importance in military events. For soon after this battle, says the same author, "The prior caused a goodly and sumptuous banner to be made, (which is then described at great length,) and in the midst of the same banner-cloth was the said holy 235 relique and corporax-cloth enclosed, &c. &c. and so sumptuously finished, and absolutely perfected, this banner was dedicated to holy St Cuthbert, of intent and purpose, that for the future it should be carried to any battle, as occasion should serve; and was never carried and shewed at any battle but by the especial grace of God Almighty, and 240 the mediation of holy St Cuthbert, It brought home victory; which

---

208   and there most *over illeg eras MS. 1815*
224   This] The *1850*
234   banner *over* to be *eras MS. 1815*

banner-cloth, after the dissolution of the abbey, fell into the possession of Dean WHITTINGHAM, whose wife was called KATHARINE, being a French woman, (as is most credibly reported by eyewitnesses,) did most injuriously burn the same in her fire, to the open contempt and   245
disgrace of all ancient and goodly reliques."—Extracted from a book entitled, "Durham Cathedral, as it stood before the Dissolution of the Monastery." It appears, from the old metrical History, that the above-mentioned banner was carried by the Earl of Surry to Flodden Field.

> An Edifice of warlike frame
> Stands single (Norton Tower its name.)—P. 121.

It is so called to this day, and is thus described by Dr Whitaker.   250
"Rylstone Fell yet exhibits a monument of the old warfare between the Nortons and Cliffords. On a point of very high ground, commanding an immense prospect, and protected by two deep ravines, are the remains of a square tower, expressly said by Dodsworth to have been built by Richard Norton. The walls are of strong grout-work, about   255
four feet thick. It seems to have been three stories high. Breaches have been industriously made in all the sides, almost to the ground, to render it untenable.

"But Norton Tower was probably a sort of pleasure-house in summer, as there are, adjoining to it, several large mounds, (two of them   260
are pretty entire,) of which no other account can be given than that they were butts for large companies of archers.

"The place is savagely wild, and admirably adapted to the uses of a watch-tower."

> —despoil and desolation
> O'er Rylstone's fair domain have blown.—P. 135.

"After the attainder of Richard Norton, his estates were forfeited to   265
the crown, where they remained till the 2d or 3d of James; they were then granted to Francis Earl of Cumberland." From an accurate survey made at that time, several particulars have been extracted by Dr W. It appears that the mansion-house was then in decay. Immediately adjoining is a close, called the Vivery, so called undoubtedly from the   270
French Vivier, or modern Latin Viverium; for there are near the house large remains of a pleasure-ground, such as were introduced in the earlier part of Elizabeth's time, with topiary works, fish-ponds, an

---

243   wife was called] wife, called *1832*–
253   an *rev to* and *del to* an *MS. 1815 (WW)*
261   other *inserted MS. 1815*
273   an] and *1850*

island, &c. The whole township was ranged by an hundred and thirty
red deer, the property of the Lord, which, together with the wood,   275
had, after the attainder of Mr. Norton, been committed to Sir Stephen
Tempest. The wood, it seems, had been abandoned to depredations,
before which time it appears that the neighbourhood must have exhib-
ited a forest-like and sylvan scene. In this survey, among the old ten-
ants, is mentioned one Richard Kitchen, butler to Mr Norton, who   280
rose in rebellion with his master, and was executed at Ripon."

In the deep fork of Amerdale.—P. 140.
"At the extremity of the parish of Burnsal, the valley of Wharf forks
off into two great branches, one of which retains the name of Wharf-
dale to the source of the river; the other is usually called Littondale,
but more anciently and properly Amerdale. Dern-brook, which runs   285
along an obscure valley from the N.W. is derived from a Teutonic
word, signifying concealment."—Dr WHITAKER.

When the Bells of Rylstone played
Their Sabbath music—"𝕲𝖔𝖉 𝖚𝖘 𝖆𝖞𝖉𝖊."—P. 142.
On one of the bells of Rylstone church, which seems coeval with the
building of the tower, is this cypher, 𝕵. 𝕹. for John Norton, and the
motto, "𝕲𝖔𝖉 𝖚𝖘 𝖆𝖞𝖉𝖊."   290

The grassy rock-encircled Pound.—P. 143.
Which is thus described by Dr Whitaker:—"On the plain summit of
the hill are the foundations of a strong wall, stretching from the S.W.
to the N.E. corner of the tower, and to the edge of a very deep glen.
From this glen, a ditch, several hundred yards long, runs south to
another deep and rugged ravine. On the N. and W. where the banks   295
are very steep, no wall or mound is discoverable, paling being the only
fence that would stand on such ground.
    From the Minstrelsy of the Scottish Border, it appears that such
pounds for deer, sheep, &c. were far from being uncommon in the
south of Scotland. The principle of them was something like that of a   300
wire mouse-trap. On the declivity of a steep hill, the bottom and sides
of which were fenced so as to be impassable, a wall was constructed
nearly level with the surface on the outside, yet so high within that
without wings it was impossible to escape in the opposite direction.
Care was probably taken that these enclosures should contain better   305

---

287   —Dr. Whitaker *added MS. 1815*
297   would] could *1820–*
301   wire *rev from* common *MS. 1815*

feed than the neighbouring parks or forests; and whoever is acquainted with the habits of these sequacious animals, will easily conceive, that if the leader was once tempted to descend into the snare, an herd would follow.

I cannot conclude without recommending to the notice of all lovers   310
of beautiful scenery—Bolton Abbey and its neighbourhood. This enchanting spot belongs to the Duke of Devonshire; and the superintendance of it has for some years been entrusted to the Rev. William Carr, who has most skilfully opened out its features; and in whatever he has added, has done justice to the place by working with an invisible hand   315
of art in the very spirit of nature.

THE END.

---

308   an] a *1845–*
310–316   *added by* WW MS. *1815*
312   superintendance *rev from* management MS. *1815* superintendence *1827–*
313   been entrusted *inserted MS. 1815*   William *rev from* Mr. MS. *1815*
314–315   in whatever he has added *rev from* in all *inserted MS. 1815*
317   *omitted 1820–*

Nonverbal Variants

38   church] Church *MS. 1815*
39   feel:] feel; *MS. 1815*
40   'tis] tis *MS. 1815*   sun-rise]
      sunrise *1832–*   zeal,] zeal; *MS.*
      1832/36–
41   prime,] prime *1832*
45   For,] For *MS. 1815, MS. 1815/20*
      WD, 1820–   priest] Priest *MS.*
      1815 priest, *MS. 1815/20 WD,*
      1820–   tranquilly] tranquilly,
      MS. 1815/20 WD, 1820–
46   liturgy] Liturgy *MS. 1815*
52   gateway,] Gateway *MS. 1815*
53   bound,] bound *MS. 1815*
54   church-yard] Church-yard *MS.*
      1815   ground;] ground, *MS.*
      1815 ground— *MS. 1832/36–*
57   —Comes] Comes *MS. 1815, eras to*
      Comes *MS. 1832/36–*
61   lily] lilly *MS. 1815*
62   moon] Moon *MS. 1815*
63   driven,] driven *1832–*
64   heaven] Heaven *MS. 1815*
65   ship] Ship *MS. 1815*
67   ship] Ship *MS. 1815*
68   ocean] Ocean, *MS. 1815*
69   graves] graves, *1827–*
70   church-yard] Church-yard *MS.*
      1815
71   living . . . cares,] living, . . . cares;
      1827–
72   multitude] multitudes *with* s *eras*
      MS. 1815 multitude, *1827–*
      prayers,] prayers; *1827–*
74   delight!] delight. *MS. 1815*
76   go;] go: *1832–*
79   Spirit,] Spirit *1836–*
83   state,] state *1836–*
95   cell] cell, *1845–*
96   framed *rev to* framed; *MS. 1815*
101 flower] Flower *MS. 1815*
104 show;] shew; *MS. 1815*
105 re-appearing] reappearing *1845–*
106 blessedness,] blessedness.— *MS.*
      1815
109 votary's] Votary's *MS. 1815*
110 perform,] perform *MS. 1815*
113 shrine,] shrine *MS. 1815*
114 divine? *rev from* divine, *MS. 1815*
116 worshipped,] worshipped *MS.*
      1815   Man] man *MS. 1815*
119 concealing,] concealing,— *MS.*
      1815
120 healing,—] healing? *MS. 1832/36–*
121 altar . . . cross] Altar . . . Cross *MS.*
      1815   rent,] rent,— *with dash*
      eras MS. 1815

123 bare,] bare *MS. 1815*
124 wild-rose] wild rose *1820–1832*
126 chamber's] Chamber's *MS. 1815*
127 warrior] Warrior *MS.*
      1815   stone] stone, *MS. 1815/20*
      WD, 1820–
128 weeds] weeds, *1820–*   alone;]
      alone *1827–1832*
129 warrior] Warrior *MS. 1815*
130 side,] side,— *MS. 1815*
132 breast:] breast; *1836–*
133 sight,] sight *1836–*
134 creature might:] Creature might;
      MS. 1815
135 care,] care *MS. 1815*
136 elsewhere.] elsewhere: *MS. 1815*
137 —But] But *MS. 1815*
138 moves,] moves— *MS. 1815/20 WD,*
      1820–
145 died,] died. *1820*
146 vessel's] Vessel's *MS. 1815*
149 going,] going *MS. 1815*
151 river] River *MS. 1815*   flowing;]
      flowing— *MS. 1815/20 WD, 1820–*
      1832
153 pass,] pass,— *MS. 1815*
157 people] People *MS. 1815*
158 chear] cheer *1827–1832*
159 song; *rev from* song! *MS. 1815*
160 temple] Temple *MS.*
      1815   throng—] throng; *MS.*
      1815 throng, *MS. 1832/36–*
161 abroad—] abroad,— *MS. 1815*
      abroad, *MS. 1832/36–*
163 some,] some— *1836–*   band]
      band, *1827–1832*
165 children—] children *rev to*
      Children— *with dash eras MS. 1815*
166 mothers] Mothers *MS.*
      1815   hung,] hung— *1836–*
167 paid,] paid *1836–*
168 spot,] spot *MS. 1815*
173 divide:] divide; *MS. 1815*
179 near;] near, *MS. 1815*
181 harm;"—] harm"— *MS.*
      1815   Boy,] Boy *MS. 1815*
183 smiled] smiled, *1832–*
184 shame-faced] shamefaced *MS.*
      1815
188 sabbath-day] Sabbath-day *MS. 1815*
      sabbath day *1845–*
189 be,] be *MS. 1815*
191 keep,] keep *1827–1836*
192 sabbath] Sabbath *MS. 1815*
195 Creature—] Creature, *MS.*
      1832/36 (pencil and ink)–
196 her—] her, *MS. 1832/36 (pencil and*

ink)—   yea] yea, *1832–*
bright—] bright; *1827–*
197 seems?—] seems? *1827–*
199 himself— . . . doubts—]
himself, . . . doubts,— MS. *1832/36*
(pencil and ink)–
200 will:] will. *MS. 1815*
201 he] he *rev to* He MS. *1815*
(WW)   standers-by] standers-by
rev to Standers-by MS. *1815 (WW)*
209 enquiring] inquiring *1827–*
211 'spite] spite *1827–*   truth,] truth
MS. *1815* Truth *1836–*
213 belong,] belong; MS. *1815*
214 undeceived,] undeceived MS. *1815*
216 here,] here. *1832* here, *restored* MS.
1832/36 (in pencil)–
217 *line left out, then inserted MS.*
1815   fear,] fear,) MS. *1815*
218 strong, *rev from* strong; MS. *1815*
220 Sire,] Sire— *1836–*
221 (Who] Who *1836–*
222 convent-bread,] Convent bread,
MS. *1815* convent bread, *1832*
convent-bread *1836–*
225 wars)] wars— *1836–*
226 Old] old MS. *1815*   Man—]
Man, MS. *1832/36 (pencil and ink)–*
227 spectacle—] spectacle, MS. *1832/36*
(pencil and ink)–
229 Aäliza] Aaliza MS. *1815*
230 despair,] despair *1836–*
233 Egremound] Egermound *rev to*
Egremound MS. *1815 (WW)*
234 affliction,] affliction— MS.
1832/36–
235 place,] place— MS. *1832/36–*
236 structure] Structure MS. *1815*
237 up—] up, MS. *1832/36 (pencil and*
ink)–
238 work,—] work; MS. *1832/36 (pencil*
and ink) work;— *1836–*
243 bright,—] bright; *1827–*
244 o'er] oer MS. *1815*
245 chantry] Chantry MS. *1815*
246 in the *with* the *over illeg eras* MS.
1815 (WW)
247 griesly *rev from* grisly MS. *1815*
(WW)
249 There] There, MS. *1815, 1827–*
251 son   sire] Son   Sire MS *1815*
252 Esquire,—] Esquire, *1827–*
253 man] Man MS. *1815*   dread,]
dread *1836–*
254 Red;—] Red; *1827–*
255 church,] Church, MS. *1815* church
1845–

256 porch] Porch MS. *1815*
260 intent:—] intent: *1836–*
265 ancestry] Ancestry MS. *1815*
267 scholar] Scholar MS. *1815*
268 native vale] Native vale *rev to* native
Vale MS. *1815*
269 conceit: *rev from* conceit, MS. *1815*
271 Shepherd Lord] Shepherd-lord
MS. *1832/36 (pencil and ink)–*
272 solitary;] solitary: *1827–*
274 Nature's *rev from* nature's MS. *1815*
277 she] She MS. *1815; rev to* She MS.
1832/36 (pencil and ink)–
278 oftentimes] often-times MS. *1815*
280 lady] Lady MS. *1815*   fair,] fair;
1827–
281 shewed] showed *1827–*
284 shepherd] Shepherd MS. *1815,*
1827–1836   grey,] grey; MS.
1832/36 (pencil and ink)–
287 Flodden field] Flodden-field *1836–*
292 delight,] delight,— MS. *1815*
293 *no italics* MS. *1815*
294 state;] state: MS. *1815*
295 elevate,—] elevate, MS. *1815*
297 quietness.] quietness; MS. *1815*
298 friends] Friends MS. *1815*
299 fraternity] Fraternity MS. *1815*
300 church] Church MS. *1815*
302 sky;—] sky; *1827–*
303 Or . . . cells] Or, . . . cells, *1827–*
305 fire:] fire; MS. *1832/36–*
306 fled—] fled, MS. *1832/36–*
308 dead!] dead; *1820*
309 Scholar!] Scholar, *1827–*   so,]
so; *rev from* so, MS. *1815*
312/313 *line space and indentation omitted*
1845, 1850
314 vision] Vision MS. *1815*
315 people . . . ring,] People . . . ring
MS. *1815*
317 Yca,] Yea MS. *1815*
323 vanish,] vanish *1832–*
324 gone.] gone! *rev to* gone.— MS.
1815
331 harp] Harp MS. *1815, 1836–*
cease,—] cease— *1827–*
332 angel wings] angel-wings *1832*
334 thee,] thee— *1836–*
336 chaunt] chant *1827–*
END OF CANTO FIRST. *omitted* MS.
1815, 1820–

title Second Canto MS. *1815* CANTO
SECOND. *del* MS. *1815/20* WD, *re-*
stored 1820–
338 obeyed:] obeyed; *1827–*

339 shade,] shade *1832*–
341 song] song *rev to* Song *MS. 1815*
343 friend] Friend *MS. 1815, 1827*–
    sight,] sight *MS. 1815*
344 light,—] light; *1827*–
345 companion] Companion *MS. 1815*
349 vermeil *rev from* vermil *MS. 1815*
    (WW)
350 unblessed] unblest *1827*
357 Sacred] sacred *MS. 1815, MS.*
    1832/36 (in pencil)–
360 company] Company *MS. 1815*
362 sovereign] Sovereign *MS. 1815,*
    1827–
363 crown] Crown *MS. 1815*
364 virgin] Virgin *MS. 1815*
367 vassalage] Vassalage *MS. 1815*
368 right,— *rev from* right; *MS. 1815*
    right, *1827*–
369 earls] Earls *MS. 1815, 1827*–
375 Banner,] Banner *1850*
376 exprest,] exprest *MS. 1815, 1827*–
377 life,] life *1827*–
379 call] Call *MS. 1815, 1836*–
380 Rylstone Hall] Rylstone-hall *1836*–
381 came,—] came; *MS. 1832/36 (pencil*
    and ink)–
386 name;] name: *1827*–
387 queen] Queen *MS. 1815, 1827*–
    1845
389 humanity.] humanity.— *1836*–
390 'Tis] 'Tis *rev to*—'Tis *MS.*
    1815   scorn,—] scorn; *MS.*
    1832/36 (pencil and ink)–
391 son] Son *MS. 1815*
392 lordship . . . land] Lordship . . .
    Land *MS. 1815*
393 knees—] knees; *MS. 1832/36 (pen-*
    cil and ink)–
394 hand,—] hand, *MS. 1832/36 (pencil*
    and ink)–
395 men] Men *MS. 1815*
397 brethren's] Brethren's *MS. 1815*
399 hall] Hall *MS. 1815*
401 fall,] fall— *MS. 1832/36*–
402 dear,—] dear; *MS. 1832/36 (pencil*
    and ink) dear, *1836*–
403 banner] Banner *MS. 1815*
406 staff . . . say:] Staff . . . say; *MS.*
    1815
407 bear'st *rev from* bearest *MS.*
    1815   father's] Father's *MS.*
    1815
408 ensign] Ensign *MS. 1815*
409 same:] same; *MS. 1815*
411 seven *rev to* Seven *MS.*
    1815   thou,] thou *MS. 1815*

413 sons] Sons *MS. 1815*
414 band] Band *MS. 1815*
418 tenantry] Tenantry *MS. 1815*
419 ride;] ride,— *MS. 1832/36*–
420 —A *rev from* A *MS. 1815* A *MS.*
    1832/36–
421 hall] Hall *MS. 1815*
423 phantasm,] phantasm *MS. 1815*
424 Shook—tottered—] Shook,
    tottered, *MS. 1832/36*–   sight,]
    sight; *1827*–
425 night.] night! *1827*–
427 postern-gate] Postern-gate *MS.*
    1815
428 length,] length *1820*
432 long] loug *1832, corr. MS.*
    1832/36–
433 chear,] cheer, *1827*–
437 unknowingly,—] unknowingly, *MS.*
    1832/36–
439 heart agony] heart-agony *1836*–
442 reviewed:] reviewed; *MS. 1815*
444 Man] man *MS. 1832/36*–
445 tree] Tree *MS. 1815*
446 hide,] hide *MS. 1815*
448 Heaven . . . pair] heaven . . . Pair
    MS. 1815
450 yew,—] yew— *MS. 1832/36*
452 feeling:] feeling; *1827–1832, re-*
    stored to feeling: *MS. 1832/36*–
453 chuse] choose *1827–1832*
455 son] Son *MS. 1815*
456 to-day] to day, *rev to* to day." *MS.*
    1815
458 said,] said— *MS. 1832/36*–
459 —"Gone] "Gone *MS. 1832/36*–
461 comfort *rev from* comfort, *MS.*
    1815
466 misled,] misled; *1827*–
468 lord] Lord *MS. 1815*
470 Percy,—] Percy; *MS. 1832/36*–
    force] force, *MS. 1815/20 WD,*
    1820–1827
471 stronger] stronger, *MS. 1815/20*
    WD–
472 to-day] to day *MS. 1815*
477 proved;] proved: *1832*–
486 He] he *MS. 1815*
487 flower] Flower *MS. 1815*
489 father's] Father's *MS. 1815*
493 prayed;] prayed, *1827–1832*
499 Then] "Then *MS. 1815*   each,]
    each *MS. 1832/36*–
501 heaven,—] heaven, *1827–1832*
    heaven— *MS. 1832/36*–
506 man's] Man's *MS. 1815, 1836*–
509 easier] easier, *1827*–

511 their's] theirs *1827–*
514 body] Body *MS. 1815*
517 occasions . . . wait,] occasions, . . . wait,— *MS. 1815*
519 Bare] "Bare *MS. 1815* hand."— *rev from* hand;" *MS. 1815*
520 Therewith *rev to* —Therewith *then to* Therewith *MS. 1815*   lance] lance, *1827–*
521 trance,] trance; *MS. 1832/36–*
522 it—] it, *MS. 1832/36–*
527 Man;—] Man; *MS. 1832/36* man; *1836–*
531 —O] "O *1831, 1834*
533 well;—] well; *MS. 1815* well: *MS. 1832/36–*
535 thee] thee, *MS. 1832/36–* woman] Woman *MS. 1815*   weak;] weak: *MS. 1832/36–*
541 abyss:] abyss; *rev to* abyss: *MS. 1815* abyss. *1836–*
543 upon.] upon: *MS. 1832/36–*
550 ours,—] ours— *1836–*
551 bowers;] bowers, *1827–*
552 hall,] Hall, *MS. 1815* hall— *1836–*
554 Horse] horse *MS. 1832/36 (pencil and ink)–*
556 Hawk] hawk *MS. 1832/36 (pencil and ink)–*   perch,—] perch— *1820–1827, 1832, 1834* perch; *MS. 1832/36–*   Hound] hound *MS. 1832/36 (pencil and ink)–*
558 away,] away— *MS. 1832/36–*
560 Creature!"] Creature"! *MS. 1815*   saying] saying, *1832, 1836–*
563 Creature] creature *MS. 1832/36 (pencil and ink)–*
567 came,—] came; *MS. 1832/36–*
569 Rylstone Hall] Rylstone-hall *1836–*
571 heaven's] Heaven's *1832, 1834*
574 faith—] faith; *MS. 1832/36–*
575 led] led, *1827–*
576 O *rev from* o *MS. 1815*
577 way—] way; *MS. 1832/36–*
579 read—] read; *MS. 1832/36–*
581 zeal,] zeal *1832; comma restored MS. 1832/36–*
583 Forbearance,] Forbearance *1827–* self-sacrifice—] self-sacrifice; *MS. 1832/36–*
585 preared—] prepared; *MS. 1832/36–*
590 soul] Soul *1827–*
593 more:] more; *1832, 1836–*
594 Yew-tree] yew-tree *MS. 1832/36 (pencil and ink)–*

595 Mansion's] mansion's *MS. 1832/36 (pencil and ink)–*
598 armed] armèd *1827–* END OF CANTO SECOND *omitted MS. 1815, 1820–*
title Third Canto *MS. 1815* CANTO THIRD. *1820–*
599 chear] cheer *1827–1832*
600 Towers *rev from* towers *MS. 1815*
602 hours! *rev from* hours, *MS. 1815*
603 Masters] masters *1832; capital restored MS. 1832/36 (pencil and ink)–*
604 Band] band *MS. 1832/36 (pencil and ink)–*
605 Watchmen] watchmen *1836–*
606 descry] descry, *MS. 1832/36–*
607 armed] armèd *1832–*
609 Pair] pair *MS. 1832/36 (pencil and ink)–*
610 Plain—] Plain,— *MS. 1815* plain— *MS. 1832/36 (pencil and ink)–*
613 you:—] you: *MS. 1832/36 (pencil and ink)–*
614 us:—] us: *MS. 1832/36 (pencil and ink)–*   Swale,] Swale *rev to* Swale,— *MS. 1815*
615 horse . . . harness] Horse . . . Harness *1832; restored to* horse . . . harness *MS. 1832/36 (pencil and ink)–*
617 mine,] mine *MS. 1815*
619 incline] incline, *1827–*
621 all"—] all—" *MS. 1815*   here,] here— *MS. 1832/36–*
623 birth,] birth *MS. 1815*
625 side] side, *1827–*
626 eight] Eight *1832–*   pride!] pride; *MS. 1815*
627 ripe—with] ripe. With *MS. 1832/36–*
628 People] people *1820–*
629 Fowl . . . Feeder's] fowl . . . feeder's *MS. 1832/36–*
637 self-defence] self defence *1836*
640 right!" *rev from* right" *MS. 1815*
643 said,] said; *MS. 1832/36–*   The *rev from* the *MS. 1815*   minds] Minds *1820–*
657 hope,] hope; *MS. 1832/36 (pencil)–*
658 Altars,—] Altars— *MS. 1832/36–*
660 old] Old *rev from* old *MS. 1815*
661 must] must, *MS. 1815*
665 folds— *rev from* folds," *MS. 1815*
667 be,—] be; *MS. 1832/36–*
669 died!] died *1850*

677 Listeners] listeners *1845–*
678 die"—] die." *MS. 1832/36–*
680 said,] said; *MS. 1832/36–*
683 secretly."—] secretly." *1832–*
684 it,"] it!" *1827–*
685 thoughtful *with last two letters over eras MS. 1815*   ensued.] ensued: *MS. 1832/36, 1836, 1850* ensued *1845*
687 multitude,] multitude *1845–*
693 Durham,] Durham *MS. 1815*
694 Towers] towers *1845–*   shout!] shout *rev to* shout! *MS. 1832/36*
699 Rills] rills *1836–*
700 forked] forkèd *1832–*   Hills.—] Hills— *1820–1832* hills— *1836–*
701 hundred] Hundred *1832*
706 Chivalry] chivalry *MS. 1832/36 (pencil and ink)–*
707 —Not *rev from* Not *MS. 1815*
711 fealty;] fealty, *1827–*
714 Burgher, Yeoman . . . Esquire] burger, yeoman . . . esquire *MS. 1832/36–*
715 Priest . . . Priest's] priest . . . priest's *MS. 1832/36–*
720 Mass . . . Prayer] mass . . . prayer *MS. 1832/36 (pencil and ink)–*
721 Bible] bible *MS. 1832/36 (pencil and ink)–*
722 free,] free. *MS. 1815* free *1845–*
723 "They] 'They *1836–*   Host] host *MS. 1832/36 (pencil and ink)–*
724 see;"] see;' *1836–*
725 choicest] Choicest *1845–*
728 lance—] lance, *1827–*
736 Triumphantly] triumphantly *1836–*
740 Sire, *rev from* Sire; *MS. 1815* Sire; *MS. 1832/36–*
742 Man] man *MS. 1832/36 (pencil and ink)–*
743 day:] day. *1827–*
746 stature *rev from* Stature *MS. 1815*
750 state,—] state; *MS. 1832/36–*
751 venerate,—] venerate; *MS. 1832/36–*
752 strong,] strong; *MS. 1832/36–*
753 thick-spread] thick spread *1832–*
754 morion *over partial eras MS. 1815*
755 hunter's *rev from* hunter *MS. 1815*
761 girdle *over partial eras MS. 1815*
762 Who . . . thousands] Who, . . . thousands, *1845–*   Friend] friend *MS. 1832/36–*
766 Shepherds] shepherds *MS. 1832/36 (pencil and ink)–*
767 Mariners] mariners *1836–*
773 —Bold] Bold *MS. 1832/36–*

776 fixed,] fixed *1836–*   hour.] hour, *1820* hour: *1827–*
777 sometimes,] sometimes *1845–*
778 lies,—] lies; *1827–1832* lies *1836–*
780 bask,] bask,— *MS. 1815*
787 sight] sight, *MS. 1815/20 WD, 1820–*
792 Royal *rev from* royal *MS. 1815*
793 Rising of the North;] Rɪsɪɴɢ ᴏꜰ ᴛʜᴇ Nᴏʀᴛʜ; *1827–*
795 And] And, *1827–*   led!] led!— *MS. 1832/36–*
798 gazed;] gazed, *1836–*
799 opprest] oppressed *MS. 1815*
803 *double quotation marks converted to single MS. 1832/36–*
805 Hold *rev from* hold *MS. 1815*
809 them—] them *MS. 1815, MS. 1832/36 (pencil and ink)–* them; *1827–1832*
816 spake,—] spake;— *MS. 1832/36–*
817 field!] field!— *MS. 1832/36–*
818 heaven] heaven, *1836–*
821 Thurston,] Thurston— *MS. 1832/36–*
822 Saw *rev from* saw *MS. 1815*   Plain, *rev from* Plain *MS. 1815* Plain *1836–*
823 *parens added MS. 1815*
824 proved?— *rev from* proved, *MS. 1815*   battle] Battle *MS. 1815*
825 Standard] Standard, *MS. 1832/36–* sacred] Sacred *1820– but* sacred *pencil alt MS. 1832/36*   wain,] Wain *1827–*
828 Ensigns *rev from* ensigns *MS. 1815* ensigns *1832*
829 victory!] victory!— *MS. 1832/36–*
830 Name] name *1836–*
831 Westmoreland] Westmorland *MS. 1815*
836 Relic *rev from* relic *MS. 1815*
843 chastise;] chastise: *MS. 1832/36–*
844 we] we, *1832–*   old] Old *rev from* old *MS. 1815*
845 uphold."—] uphold." *MS. 1832/36* uphold: *1836–*
846 confounded,] confounded *then comma added in pencil MS. 1815*
847 given—] given *MS. 1815* given, *MS. 1832/36–*   sounded;] sounded: *MS. 1832/36–*
852 hope] Hope *MS. 1815*
857 stem,"] stem" *MS. 1815* stem;" *1820–1832* stem—" *MS. 1832/1836–*
859 spake, . . . quell] spake— . . . quell, *MS. 1832/36–*

862 Father] father *1832–*
867 more;] more: *1832–*
878 wept,—] wept; MS. *1832/36–*
882 Jesu's *rev from* Jesus MS. *1815*
883 tears:—] tears: MS. *1832/36–*
884 far,] far *1836–*
887 Parent, *rev from* Parent MS. *1815*
888 laid, *rev from* laid MS. *1815* laid:
　　MS. *1832/36–*
890 docile,] docile MS. *1815*
891 back— *rev from* back, MS. *1815*
892 woe!— *rev from* woe. MS. *1815*
　　woe! *1836–*
892/893　*line space 1836–*
894 chear] cheer *1827–1832*
895 rear:] rear, MS. *1832/36–*
899 oppose,"] oppose" MS. *1815*
900 Foes; *rev from* Foes, MS. *1815*
903 unblamed;] unblamed:— *1827–
　　1832*
905 high,] high; MS. *1815*
906 brow;] brow: *1832*
908 injury,—] *rev from* injury, MS. *1815*
　　injury— *1827–1832*
909 bear, *rev from* bear MS. *1815*
913 Men] men *1832*　　lead,] lead MS.
　　1815
916 sacrifice?] sacrifice?— MS.
　　1832/36–
918 shelter, *rev from* shelter MS. *1815*
920 rest; *rev from* rest MS. *1815*
930 prayer?] prayer MS. *1832/36–*
931 raised,] raised MS. *1815*
934 allay,] allay; *1836*
936 Brothers *rev from* Brothers' MS.
　　1815　　love—] love; MS. *1815*
937 withdrew;] withdrew, MS. *1815*
939 e'er *rev from* ever MS. *1815*
　　END OF CANTO THIRD *omitted MS.*
　　1815, 1820–

title　Fourth Canto MS. *1815* CANTO
　　FOURTH. *1820–*
940 down,] down MS. *1815*
944 Tees;—] Tees— *rev from* Tees MS.
　　1815
945 And,] And *1827–*
947 valley] Valley MS. *1815*
952 smoke, *rev from* smoke MS.
　　1815　　wreaths] wreathes MS.
　　1815
953 hushed;— *rev from* hushed MS.
　　1815
954 Grey-hounds] greyhounds MS.
　　1832/36–
955 Peacock] peacock MS. *1832/36–*
　　ash-tree] ash tree *1845–*

959 day-light; *rev from* day-light MS.
　　1815 daylight; *1827–*
960 still,] still *1827–1834*　　bower]
　　bower, *1832*
962 Hall-clock] hall-clock MS. *1832/36–*
　　moonshine] moonshine *1827–*
963/964　*line space 1836–*
964 *indented 1836–*　　—Ah!] Ah!
　　1836–
965 sway? *rev to* sway; MS. *1815*
967 day; *rev from* day MS. *1815*
968 surface— *rev from* surface, MS.
　　1815 surface, MS. *1815/20* WD,
　　1820–
969 play—] play, MS. *1815/20* WD,
　　1820–
971 light] light, *1831, 1834*
973 seen:— *rev from* seen MS.
　　1815　　and,] and *1832–*
974 Doe:] Doe— *1836–*
978 yew-tree *over partial eras, illeg,* MS.
　　1815　　shade;— *rev from* shade
　　MS. *1815* shade, *1836–*
979 Creature, *rev from* Creature MS.
　　1815
981 now,] now— *1845–*
983 lawns,] lawns *1827–*
988 array,—] array, *1845–*
990 wide] wide, *1832*
991 boughs *rev from* boughs boughs
　　MS. *1815*
992 lie; *rev from* lie MS. *1815*
994 That,] That MS. *1815*
995 Range—] Range, MS. *1815,* MS.
　　1815/20 WD, *1820* Range *1827–*
　　wind—] wind. MS. *1815* wind, MS.
　　1815/20 WD, *1820–*
1003 snow,] snow— *1836–*
1005 glade,] glade,— MS. *1815* glade
　　MS. *1832/36–*
1006 screen;] screen— MS. *1832/36–*
1007 relic! which, *rev from* relic which
　　MS. *1815*
1008 Shepherd] shepherd MS. *1832/36–*
1009 eye. *rev from* eye MS. *1815*
1010 —Nor] Nor MS. *1832/36–*　　she]
　　She MS. *1832/36–*
1011 Doe!] Doe. MS. *1815* Doe MS.
　　1832/36–
1012 *line begins flush left, then marked for
　　indentation* MS *1815*
1013 Erewhile,] Erewhile *1827–1832*
1015 Emily; *rev from* Emily MS. *1815*
1017 gain,— *rev from* gain— MS.
　　1815
1018 play; *rev from* play MS. *1815*
1020 gainsaid.] gainsaid *rev to*
　　gainsaid.— MS. *1815*

1021 breeze!] breeze *rev to* breeze, MS.
       1815 (punct in pencil)
1024 stealing;—] stealing. MS. *1815*
       stealing; *1820*
1026 woodbine] woodbine, *1827–*
1027 overheard,] overheard; *1827–1832*
1030 Alcove] alcove MS. *1832/36–*
1031 pendant] pendent *1832–*
1033 fondly anxious] fondly-anxious
       1827–
1036 —Yes,] Yes *rev to* —Yes MS. *1815*
       Yes, MS. *1832/36 (pencil and ink)–*
       soothed:— *rev from* soothed MS.
       1815 soothed: MS. *1832/36 (pencil*
       and ink)–   faint—] faint, MS.
       1832/36–
1038 bless'd] blest MS. *1815*   her;—]
       her— MS. *1832/36–*
1040 Child, *rev from* Child MS. *1815*
1041 prattler] Prattler MS.
       1815
1043 *comma over eras* MS. *1815*
1044 faith] Faith MS. *1815*
1045 Vision, *rev from* Vision MS. *1815*
       vision, *1820–1832 restored to*
       Vision, MS. *1832/36–*
1046 influence! *rev from* influence MS.
       1815 influence; *1845–*
1047 oh! . . . above, *rev from* oh . . .
       above MS. *1815*
1048 love, *rev from* love MS. *1815*
1049 eyes, *rev from* eyes MS. *1815*
1050 Ghosts] ghosts MS. *1832/36–*
1051 fear; *rev from* fear MS. *1815*
1053 Vouchsafed—] Vouchsafed, *1827–*
1056 voice, . . . say, *rev from* voice . . . say
       MS. *1815*
1057 "That . . . away!" *rev from* That . . .
       away MS. *1815* 'That . . . away!' "
       1827–1832
1060 issues.— *rev from* issues— MS.
       1815 issues. MS. *1832/36 (pencil*
       and ink)–   She *rev from* she MS.
       1815   go; *rev from* go MS. *1815*
       go! *1845–*
1061 war, *rev from* war MS. *1815*
1062 Father's] father's *1832 restored to*
       Father's MS. *1832/36 (pencil and*
       ink)–   knees;—ah, no! *rev from*
       knees—ah no. MS. *1815*
1063 bar, *rev from* bar MS. *1815*
1064 laid; *rev from* laid MS. *1815*
1065 charge— *rev from* charge MS.
       1815   obeyed! *rev from* obeyed
       MS. *1815* obeyed— MS. *1832/36–*
1066 debate, *rev from* debate MS. *1815*
1067 that; *rev from* that MS. *1815*
1069 fate: *rev from* fate. MS. *1815*

1070 *line italicized* MS. *1815/20 WD,*
       1820–   wait; *rev from* wait MS.
       1815
1072b–1073 and . . . pure. *converted to*
       capitals, MS. *1815/20 WD, 1820–*
1074 *indented, then marked* no para *and*
       dash inserted MS. *1815*   cheared]
       cheered *1827–1832*
1076 —And] And MS. *1815* —But
       1827–1832
1081 "An *rev from* An MS.
       1815   Man's] man's MS.
       1832/36–   take; *rev from* take:
       MS. *1815* take: MS. *1832/36–*
1082 day!] day; MS. *1815*
1084 way." *rev from* way? MS. *1815* way.
       1832, restored to way." MS.
       1832/36–
1087 friendship;— *rev from* friendship—
       MS. *1815*   him— *rev from* him,
       MS. *1815*
1092 *no italics* MS. *1815*
1093 You] *You (italicized)* MS. *1815*
1094 hope . . . Will *rev from* Hope . . .
       will MS. *1815*   Divine] divine
       1827–
1095 "Hope," *rev from* "Hope, MS. *1815*
       "Hope" *1820*
1096 "Must *rev from* Must MS.
       1815   end.—] end. MS. *1815*
1097 wilds] Wilds *1836–*
1098 Men:] Men. MS. *1815* men: *1820–*
1099 underground] under ground *1820–*
       1820–
1100 grave, *rev from* grave MS. *1815*
1101 rave; *rev from* rave MS. *1815* rave:
       1836–
1102 Tweed,] Tweed MS. *1815*
1104 *not indented* MS. *1815*   —"Ah]
       "Ah MS. *1832/36 (pencil and ink)–*
       not!" *rev from* not" MS. *1815*
1105 exhort,— *rev from* exhort MS. *1815*
       exhort, MS. *1832/36–*
1107 yon,] yon *1820*
1108 befalls;— *rev from* befalls— MS.
       1815 befals; *1836–*
1109 done;— . . . ask!" *rev from*
       done, . . . ask" MS. *1815*
1111 Sire, . . . age,] Sire . . . age MS.
       1815
1115 save:] save. *1836–*
1117 field.] field; MS. *1836–*
1119 Towers,— *rev from* Towers: MS.
       1815
1121 flight!" *rev from* flight" MS. *1815*
1122 change,] change. *1832*
1126 Moon *rev from* moon MS. *1815*
1127 mid-heaven] mid heaven MS. *1815*

1130   Castle] castle *1832–*
1131   Vault] vault *MS. 1832/36 (pencil
       and ink)–*
1132   Sons] sons *1832–*   laid! *rev from*
       laid *MS. 1815*
1133   issue—! *rev from* issue *MS.
       1815*   He *rev from* he *MS. 1815*
       he *1832–*
1134   yield, *rev from* yield *MS. 1815*
1136   dismayed, *rev from* dismayed *MS.
       1815*
1137   aid; *rev from* aid *MS. 1815*
1139   he] *he (italicized) MS. 1832/36–*
1140   sick;— *rev from* sick— *MS. 1815*
1142   Wall, *rev from* wall *MS. 1815* wall,
       1836–
1143   night, *rev from* night *MS. 1815*
       night,— *1849*   planted!" *rev
       from* planted" *MS. 1815* planted!
       1820–1827
1144   done:— *rev from* done,— *MS. 1815*
       done— *1832* done: *MS. 1832/36–*
       his] [?]is *rev to* His *then to* his *MS.
       1815 (WW)*   all;—] all; *MS.
       1832/36–*
1145   undaunted;] undaunted *1827–
       1832, 1845–* undaunted, *1836*
1146   follow—] follow;— *1827–*
1147   court—] court;— *MS. 1832/36–*
       'Tis *rev from* 'tis *MS. 1815*
1149–1150   *written as one line, then divided
       MS. 1815 (WW)*
1150   deed *rev to* deed, *MS. 1815*
1151   foes! *rev from* foes: *MS. 1815*
1153   band; *rev from* band! *MS. 1815*
1155   stand;— *rev from* stand *MS. 1815*
1158   Standard!" *rev from* standard" *MS.
       1815*
1159   walls; *rev from* walls *MS. 1815*
1160   Standard falls!— *rev from* standard
       falls— *MS. 1815*
1162   fled— ... detained;] fled; ...
       detained: *MS. 1832/36–*
1164   West] west *MS. 1832/36–*
       END OF CANTO FOURTH. *omitted MS.
       1815, 1820*

title   Fifth Canto *MS. 1815* Canto Fifth.
       1820–
1166   ground,] ground *1832–*
1167   Fell,] Fell *1845–*
1169   Foresters *rev from* Forresters *MS.
       1815* foresters *MS. 1832/36–*
       Shepherds] shepherds *MS.
       1832/36–*
1170   Edifice] edifice *MS. 1832/36–*

1171   (Norton] —Norton *MS. 1832/36–*
       name,)] name) *MS. 1815* name);
       1827–1832 name—; *MS. 1832/36*
       name *1836–*
1174   stream,] stream *1845–*
1176   ascent,] ascent— *MS. 1832/36–*
1178   Pennygent] Pennygent, *MS. 1815*
1179   wet,] wet— *MS. 1832/36–*
1192   *no identation 1827*   his Child *over
       illeg eras MS. 1815*
1194   'Tis] Tis *MS. 1815*   tale,— *rev
       from* tale, *MS. 1815* tale, *1827–*
1200   eye,—] eye, *MS. 1815*
1203   *not indented 1820–*   she had] she
       had *1820–*
1207   Brother's] brother's *1827–*
1209   Brother's] brother's *1827–*
1210   cheared] cheered *1827–*
1214   O'erburdened] O'erburthened
       1827–1832
1217   (That] That *MS. 1832/36–*
1219   friendship,] friendship; *MS.
       1832/36–*   Hunters] hunters
       1836–
1220   Warriors] warriors *1836–*   day)]
       day; *MS. 1832/36–*
1222   sought:] sought, *MS. 1832/36–*
1225   see.] see, *rev to* see;— *MS. 1815*
1226   turned;] turned. *MS. 1815*
1228   Brother] brother *1845–*
       spared,] spared; *1836–*
1229   dared.] *punct defective 1827* dared;
       1832–
1232   heaven's] Heaven's *1832–*
1235   duty] duty, *1827–*
1238   "I] I *MS. 1832/36–*
1239   tied!] tied; *1832–*
1241   But, ... shame, *rev from* But ...
       shame *MS. 1815* But ... shame—
       MS. 1832/36–
1242   triumph, *rev from* triumph *MS.
       1815*   pride.] pride, *1832* pride;
       MS. 1832/36–
1243   "Lo] 'Lo *1820* 'Lo, *1827–*
       comes,"] comes,' *1820–*
1244   "A] 'A *1820–*
1245   'Tis] Tis *MS. 1815*
1245–1255   *opening quotes omitted 1820–*
1246   Piety] piety; *1836–*
1247   he] he, *MS. 1832/36–*
1252   unanimity—] unanimity. *MS.
       1832/36–*
1255   indignity!"] indignity.' *1820–*
1256   "And *rev from* And *MS. 1815;* re-
       stored *to* And *MS. 1832/36–*
1257   Maid!] Maid— *1820* Maid, *1827–*
1259   distress] distress, *1820–*
1261   reverend] reverent *1820–*

1262   love,] love; *1820–*
1263   fate,] fate *MS. 1815*
1266   strong-hold] strong hold *MS. 1815*
1267   "Your *rev from* Your *MS. 1815,*
        restored to Your *MS. 1832/36–*
1269   returned—] returned: *MS.*
        1832/36–
1271   said,] said— *MS. 1832/36–*
        "We] 'We *1820–*   stop,] stop
        MS. 1815
1272–1274   *opening quotation marks omitted*
        1820–1832
1273   'Tis] Tis *MS. 1815*
1274   ear."] ear.' *1820–1832*
1277   "Might] "'Might *1827–1832* 'Might
        1836–   enterprize] enterprise
        1827–
1278–1295   *opening quotation marks omitted*
        1820–
1281   Altars] altars *MS. 1832/36–*
1285   aye. *rev from* aye; *MS. 1815*
1286   then,] then— *MS. 1832/36–*
1288   truth] Truth *1832–*
1289   youth; *rev from* youth, *MS. 1815*
1290   arrayed;] arrayed, *MS. 1815*
        arrayed— *MS. 1832/36–*
1293   rest:] rest; *MS. 1815*
1296   "A] "'A *1827–1832* A *MS.*
        1832/36–
1297   chear] cheer *1827–*
1297–1301   *opening quotation marks omitted*
        1820–
1302   "Hear then,"] "'Hear then,' *1827–*
        1832 Hear then,' *MS. 1832/36–*
        "while] 'while *1827–*   impart,
        rev from impart *MS. 1815*
1303–1328   *opening quotation marks omitted*
        1820–
1304   —"The] —The *1820–1832* The
        MS. 1832/36–   regain;] regain,
        MS. 1815
1307   consign?—] consign? *MS. 1815*
1309   shrine,— *rev from* shrine; *MS. 1815*
        shrine; *MS. 1832/36–*
1311   Mid] 'Mid *1827–*   Sanctities]
        sanctities *MS. 1832/36–*
1313   displayed;] displayed, *MS. 1815*
1315   name,] name *MS. 1815*
1318   Brood, *rev from* Brood *MS. 1815,*
        restored to Brood *1832*
1320   Thee, . . . Son!] Thee . . . Son; *MS.*
        1815
1322   unshed,—] unshed, *MS. 1815*
        unshed;— *MS. 1832/36–*
1323   known] known, *1827–*
1325   blest!"] blest!' *1827, 1836–*
1326   "Then *rev from* Then *MS. 1815*

1327   "If] 'If *1820–1832*   be."] be.'
        1827–1832
1328   "Immediately *rev from* Immediately
        MS. 1815
1331   Prisoners] prisoners *1845–*
        fate. *rev from* fate *MS. 1815*
1334   rose—] rose,— *MS. 1815*
1337   forth.] forth: *1827–1832*
1339   Banner] Banner, *1832*
1343   punishment;] punishment: *MS.*
        1832/36–
1345   ordained: *rev from* ordained. *MS.*
        1815, restored to ordained. *1827–*
1349   Soldier's] soldier's *MS. 1832/36–*
1350   People] people *1832–*
1354   breath,] breath; *MS. 1832/36–*
1355   death!] death!— *MS. 1832/36–*
1357   insult, *rev from* insult *MS. 1815*
1359   spectators] Spectators *MS. 1815*
1363   passed *rev from* past *MS.*
        1815   Him *rev from* him *MS.*
        1815
1371   Old] old *MS. 1815*
1373   Yet,] Yet *MS. 1815*
1376   place."] place. *1832*
1379   took.—] took. *1836–*
        END OF CANTO FIFTH. *omitted MS.*
        1815, 1820–

title   Sixth Canto *MS. 1815* Canto Sixth.
        1820–
1380   —Joyful *rev from* joyful *MS. 1815*
        (WW)   chear] cheer *1827–1832*
1381   parental] Parental *MS. 1815*
1383   City:— *rev from* City *MS. 1815*
        City: *1832*
1384   fled—] fled, *MS. 1832/36* fled,—
        1836–   flight] flight, *MS.*
        1832/36–
1385   Minster-bell; *rev to* Minster-bell:
        MS. 1815, restored to Minster-bell:
        MS. 1832/36–
1386   That] —That *MS. 1815*
1387   Marmaduke, *rev from* Marmaduke
        MS. 1815
1388   Ambrose] Ambrose— *MS. 1815*
1389   Flower! *rev from* Flower, *MS. 1815*
1391   Thoughts] thoughts *rev to*
        —Thoughts *MS. 1815* (WW)
1393   Dove; *rev from* Dove, *MS. 1815*
        dove; *MS. 1832/36–*
1394   Messenger,] messenger, *MS.*
        1832/36 messenger *1836–*
1395   Angel-guest] Angel guest *MS. 1815*
        angel-guest *MS. 1832/36*
1399   sight,] sight; *MS. 1832/36*

1400 And] And, MS. *1832/36*   cross]
      'cross MS. *1815*   flight, *rev from*
      flight MS. *1815*
1401 leads,] leads MS. *1815*
1402 on;— *rev from* on MS. *1815*
1403 sorrow] sorrow, *1836–*
      Villages;] Villages, *1832–*
1406 remorse, *rev from* remorse; MS.
      1815 remorse. *1827–*
1410 along,— *rev from* along, MS. *1815*
      along— MS. *1832/36–*
1411 Banner] banner *1820–1832*
1412 felt,] felt— MS. *1832/36–*
1413 betrayed: *rev from* betrayed MS.
      1815
1415 Oh *rev from* Oh! MS. *1815*   end]
      end? *1836, 1846*
1417 —Can *rev from* can MS. *1815*
1418 Instrument] instrument *1820–*
      woe, *rev from* woe. MS. *1815*
1421 No, ... Men] No; ... men MS.
      1832/36–
1423 Here *rev from* "Here MS.
      1815   it,— ... how,] it;— ...
      how? MS. *1832/36–*
1424 The *rev from* "The MS. *1815*
1425 Again ... see? *rev from* "Again ...
      see?" MS. *1815*
1426 maintain] maintain, *1836–*
1427 rest; *rev from* rest, MS. *1815*
1428 gain; *rev from* gain, MS. *1815*
1431 burden—] burthen; *rev to*
      burthen,— MS. *1815*
      thought] thought, MS. *1815/20*
      WD, *1820–*
1433 Man] man *1820–*   wrong: *rev
      from* wrong, MS. *1815* wrong.
      1827–
1434 how,] how— MS. *1832/36–*
1435 all-disposing *rev from* all-desposing
      MS. *1815* all disposing *1820*
1436 shewn,] shown, *1832* shown— MS.
      1832/36–
1437 Banner] banner MS. *1815, 1820–
      1832*
1439 own?] own; *1827–1832*
1440 prevent] prevent, *1832*
1441 wish] wish, *1827–1832*
1443 prophecy *rev from* prophesy MS.
      1815
1445 shade: *rev from* shade. MS. *1815*
1447 hour. *rev from* hour, MS. *1815*
1449 —and *rev from* and MS. *1815*
1455 Pursued;—and *rev from* Pursued,
      and MS. *1815*
1457 rise. *rev from* rise, MS. *1815*
1459 hark! *rev from* hark— MS. *1815*

1460 Horsemen] horsemen *1820–*
1461 heard] heard, MS. *1815/20* WD,
      1820–
1462 Band: *rev from* Band, MS. *1815*
1465 Death] death *1845–*   drunk *rev
      from* drank MS. *1815*
1468 disappeared; *rev from* disappeared,
      MS. *1815*
1469 Standers-by] standers-by *1832–*
1472 censure,— *rev from* censure, MS.
      1815, restored to censure, *1820–*
1473 Men] men *1820–*
1479 sight.] sight, MS. *1815*
1480 proof,] proof." MS. *1832/36–*
1482 *He rev from* He MS. *1815*   aloof!
      rev from aloof,— MS. *1815*
1483 —to *rev from* to MS.
      1815   Land;— *rev from* Land—
      MS. *1815* land;— *1836–*
1484 Traitor *rev from* traitor MS. *1815*
1485 cowardly!"] cowardly!"— *1827–
      1832*
1487 "Though *rev from* Though MS.
      1815
1489 yon] yon, *1827–1832*
1493 towards] tow'rds *1827–1832, re-
      stored to* towards MS. *1832/36–*
1494 'vantage] vantage *1845,
      1850*   shewed] showed *1832–*
1497 —nor ... now; *rev from* nor ..
      now, MS. *1815*
1499 —and *rev from* and MS. *1815*
1500–1535 *for readings of MS. 1832/36,
      rev in stages toward 1836, see tran-
      scriptions and photos, pp. 374–379.*
1500 round:— *rev from* round,— MS.
      1815 round *1836* round; MS.
      1836/45, 1840–
1501 held; *rev from* held, MS. *1815*
1502 straight] straight, *1827–
      1832*   impelled] impelled, *1827–
      1832*
1505 same:—instinctively] same—
      instinctively *rev to* same. —
      Instinctively— MS. *1815* (WW)
1507 advance; *rev from* advance, MS.
      1815
1508 But,] But *1836–*
1510 stroke:— *rev from* stroke— MS.
      1815   oh,] oh *1832*
1511 fell: *rev from* fell; MS. *1815*
1519 Country] country, *1836–*   near;
      rev from near. MS. *1815*
1522 Forester *rev from* Forrester MS.
      1815
1526 troubled— *rev from* troubled, MS.
      1815

1527 recognized] recognised *1832*
pallid *rev from* palid MS. *1815*
1528 ran,] ran *1836–*
1529 People] people *1836–*
1533 bear! *rev from* bear, MS. *1815*
1534 Forester *rev from* Forrester MS.
1815   express'd, *rev from*
expressed, *restored to* expressed,
1820 expressed; *1827–1832*
1539 make; *rev from* make, MS. *1815*
1545 they,— *rev from* they, MS. *1815*
1546 Blood; *rev from* Blood, MS. *1815*
blood; *1836–*
1550 Body . . . bier] body . . . bier; MS.
1832/36 (JC)–
1551 chear] cheer *1827–1832*
1557 she,— *rev from* she, MS. *1815*
1558 went *rev from* went, MS. *1815*, re-
stored to went *1827–*
1561 Vale] vale MS. *1832/36–*
1562 Funeral] funeral MS. *1832/36–*
Knot *rev from* Knott MS. *1815* knot
1832–
1564 Bird] bird MS. *1832/36–*
1568 truth! *rev from* truth. MS. *1815*
END OF CANTO SIXTH *omitted 1815,
1820–*

title   Seventh Canto MS. *1815* CANTO
SEVENTH. *1820–*
1569 Harp] harp *1836–*
1578 beat, *rev from* beat MS. *1815* beat—
1836–
1582 rock— . . . dale—] rock, . . . dale,
MS. *1832/36 (pencil)–*
1583 Sea—] Sea, MS. *1832/36 (pencil)–*
desart—] desert— *1827–1832*
desert, *1836–*
1587 blown; *rev from* blown, MS. *1815*
1589 weeds,] weeds; *1832–*
1592 unknown:] unknown. *1827–*
1597 And . . . agreeing] And, . . .
agreeing, MS. *1832/36–*
1600 placed:] placed; MS. *1815* placed.
1836–
1606 Tree *rev from* tree MS. *1815 (WW)*,
restored to tree MS. *1832/36–*
stood; *rev from* stood, MS. *1815*
stood: *1832–1836, restored to* stood,
1845–
1607 boughs,] boughs MS. *1815, 1836*
1608 Bird's *rev from* Birds MS. *1815*
Birds' *1827* bird's MS. *1832/36–*
carolling] caroling MS. *1815*
1609 Virgin] virgin *1836–*   her, . . .
Queen, *rev from* her . . . Queen MS.
1815

1614 change, *rev from* change MS. *1815*
1615 holy, *rev from* holy MS. *1815*
1616 rigorous, *rev from* rigorous MS.
1815
1617 authority, *rev from* authority MS.
1815
1618 awfulness, . . . face,— *rev from*
awfulness . . . face, MS. *1815*
1620 o'ershadow] oe'ershadow *rev to*
overshadow MS. *1815*
1622 utterly] utterly, MS. *1832/36*
gleams] gleams, *1836–*
1623 delight] delight, *1827–*
1624 bright: *rev from* bright, MS. *1815*
1625 mien;—] mien:— *1832–*   dress]
dress, MS. *1815*
1626 vest,] vest *1832–*   woollen]
woolen MS. *1815*
1627 undyed] undied MS. *1815*
1628 —fashioned] fashioned MS. *1815*
1631 star; *rev from* star, MS. *1815*
1634 Ship] ship MS. *1832/36–*
random] Random *1820*
1638 Roof] roof *1836–*
1640 borne,] borne MS. *1815*
1641 forlorn: *rev from* forlorn MS. *1815*
1642 fast, *rev from* fast MS. *1815*
1645 love; *rev from* love, MS. *1815*
1648 so—] so, MS. *1815*
1649 Oak, *rev from* oak, MS. *1815* oak
MS. *1832/36–*
1651 saved—] saved, MS. *1815*
1653 Flower] flower MS. *1832/36–*
1659 Deer] deer MS. *1832/36–*
1660 And, *rev from* And MS. *1815*
1661 Deer] deer MS. *1832/36*
1662 One] One, *1836–*
1664 Emily,] Emily; MS. *1832/36–*
1666 Creature] creature MS. *1832/36–*
silver-bright] silver bright MS.
1815
1667 stayed; *rev from* staid— MS. *1815*
1668 made; *rev from* made, MS. *1815*
1670 her— *rev from* her, MS. *1815*, re-
stored to her, MS. *1832/36–*
near,] near *1832* near— MS.
1832/36–
1671 again;—but, *rev from* again—but
MS. *1815*
1676 benignity, *rev from* benignity MS.
1815
1677 memory. *rev from* memory: MS.
1815, memory; *1827–1832*
1679 years!] years!— *1836–*
1681 subdued,] subdued MS. *1815*
1683 grace] grace, *1832–*
1685 Pair!] Pair *1836–*

1686 heaven, heaven's] Heaven,
Heaven's *1832–*   care!] care
1820 care, *1827–*

1687 greeting,— *rev from* greeting, *MS.*
1815, restored to greeting, *1832*
greeting; *MS. 1832/36–*

1688 meeting. *rev from* meeting; *MS.*
1815

1690 forego] forego, *1832*

1691 Peer] peer *MS. 1832/36 (pencil and*
ink)–

1694 Chronicler] chronicler *MS.*
1832/36 (pencil and ink)–

1697 face,] face; *MS. 1832/36–*

1699 re-union] re-union, *MS. 1815*

1700 communion] communion, *MS.*
1815, MS. 1815/20 WD, 1820–

1701 weather,] weather *MS. 1815*

1703 when, *rev from* when *MS.*
1815   ere] 'ere *MS.*
1815   evening-dew] evening
dew *MS. 1815* evening-dew, *1827*
evening dew, *1832–*

1706 Dwelling-place] dwelling-place *MS.*
1832/36 (pencil and ink)–

1711 Hut . . . Trees] hut . . . trees *MS.*
1832/36 (pencil and ink)–

1712 Brook] brook *MS. 1832/36 (pencil*
and ink)–

1715 pain,] pain *MS. 1832/36–*

1718 bear;— *rev from* bear; *MS. 1815*

1719 But . . . round] But, . . . round,
MS. 1815/20 WD, 1820–

1720 trouble-haunted *rev from* trouble
haunted *MS. 1815 (WW)*
ground.] ground; *1845–*

1724 Vale] vale *MS. 1832/36–*

1725 Cottage— *rev from* Cottage *MS.*
1815 cottage, *MS. 1832/36 (pencil*
and ink)–

1728 before.— *rev from* before— *MS.*
1815, restored to before— *1820*
before. *1827–*

1731 strengthening *rev from*
strength'ning *MS. 1815*

1732 cheared] cheered *1827–*

1734 deed,] deed— *MS. 1832/36–*

1736 eyes!] eyes; *MS. 1832/36–*

1737 Reason] reason *MS. 1832/36–*

1740 desire,] desire; *1836–*

1741 voice] voice, *1827*

1744 over-deeply] over deeply *MS. 1815*

1749 rouzing] rousing *1827–*

1751 browzing] browsing *1832–*

1756 They . . . Pair] They, . . . pair, *MS.*
1832/36–

1760 high,] high *MS. 1832/36–*

1762 —What *rev from* What *MS. 1815*

1766 They . . . side] they, . . . side, *1827–*

1767 Shepherd's] shepherd's *MS.*
1832/36–   playing; *so MS.*
1832/36, with semicolon reinforced in
pencil but playing, *1836–*

1771 came,— *rev from* came *MS. 1815*
came; *1827–*

1772 And, . . . groves, *rev from* And . . .
groves *MS. 1815*

1774 undistrest *rev from* undistressed
MS. 1815

1776 spring-day *rev from* spring day *MS.*
1815

1780 Bells] bells *MS. 1832/36 (pencil and*
ink)–

1781 Sabbath] sabbath *1836–*   double
quotation marks added MS. 1815, rev
to single MS. 1832/36–   𝔞𝔶𝔡𝔢 *rev*
from aid *MS. 1815*

1783 legend,] legend *1832–*

1784 Bells] bells *MS. 1832/36 (pencil and*
ink)–

1785 Grandsire's] Gransire's *1820*

1787 Childhood] childhood *MS. 1832/36*
(pencil and ink)–   same,] same;
1836–

1791 Bells] bells *MS. 1832/36–*

1793 "𝔊𝔬𝔡] '𝔊𝔬𝔡 *MS. 1832/36–*   𝔞𝔶𝔡𝔢"!
rev from aid"! *MS. 1815* 𝔞𝔶𝔡𝔢;" *1827–*
1832 𝔞𝔶𝔡𝔢;' *MS. 1832/36–*

1794 Hills] hills *MS. 1832/36–*

1796 she] She *MS. 1815, 1827–1832, re-*
stored to she *MS. 1832/36–*

1799 wide.] wide; *1827–1832* wide,
1836–

1800 stilled,— *rev from* stilled; *MS. 1815*

1802 prophecy *rev from* prophesy *MS.*
1815

1804 failed,— *rev from* failed; *MS. 1815,*
restored to failed; *1827–*

1807 left,—] left; *1827–*

1811 him, . . . one] him— . . . one,
1832–

1813 soul's *rev from* souls *MS. 1815*

1817 spot!] spot; *1836–*

1819 manifold— *rev from* manifold. *MS.*
1815

1822 -encircled *rev from* -encercled *MS.*
1815

1824 Thrall,] Thrall *1832–*

1825 (A] A *MS. 1815*   foam,)] foam,
MS. 1815 foam) *1832–*

1827 home,] home; *MS. 1832/36–*

1828 Boy] boy *MS. 1832/36–*

1831 go: *rev from* go; *MS. 1815, restored*
to go; *1836–*

1843 Companion *rev from* companion
      MS. 1815
1846 recognition!] recognition; *MS.*
      1815
1847 countenance;—] countenance—
      MS. 1815 countenance; *1820–*
1857 When, *rev from* When *MS.*
      1815   solitude, *with comma eras,*
      then restored MS. 1815
1859 And, *rev from* And *MS.*
      1815   dreams, *rev from* dreams
      MS. 1815
1862 dead,— *rev from* dead, *MS.*
      1815
1863 Earth] earth *MS. 1832/36 (pencil*
      and ink)–
1869 blessed] blessèd *MS. 1832/36–*
1870 tow'rds *rev from* towards *MS. 1815,*
      restored to towards *MS. 1832/36–*
1874 Friend,— *rev from* Friend, *MS.*
      1815 Friend; *MS. 1832/36 (pencil*
      and ink)–
1875 stopped;—] stopped; *MS. 1832/36*
      (pencil and ink)–
1876 supplied— *rev from* supplied; *MS.*
      1815 supplied: *MS. 1832/36 (pencil*
      and ink)–
1877 bore,] bore *MS. 1815*
1878 cares:] cares; *MS. 1815*
1879 more,] more; *rev to* more,— *MS.*
      1815
1882 Peasants] peasants *MS. 1832/36–*
      prayers] Prayers *MS. 1815*
1883 length,] length *MS. 1815*
1885 soul, *rev from* soul *MS. 1815*
1886 Family *rev from* family *MS. 1815,*
      restored to family *1820–*
1889 side. *rev from* side *MS. 1815*
1890 sunset!— *rev from* sunset *MS. 1815*
      sunset! *1832–*
1891 Survives— *rev from* Survives, *MS.*
      1815 day;] day— *1832–*
1895 Partakes . . . degree] Partakes, . . .
      degree, *1827–*   heaven's]
      Heaven's *1832–*
1898 chear] cheer *1827–*
1899 dear: *rev from* dear *MS. 1815*
1900 most— *rev from* most *MS. 1815*
1901 Church-yard] church-yard *1836–*
1902 Ghost] ghost *MS. 1832/36—*
1903 Sabbath] sabbath *1836–*
1904 People . . . Bells] people . . . bells
      MS. 1832/36 (pencil and ink)–
1907 Sabbath-day] sabbath-day *1836–*
1911 fret-work *rev from* fretwork *MS.*
      1815
1913 vault,] vault; *MS. 1832/36–*
1915 Dim-gleaming *rev from* Dim
      gleaming *MS. 1815*

1916 brave; *rev from* brave, *MS. 1815*
      brave: *MS. 1832/36–*
1919 Visitant] visitant *1845–*   seen.
      rev from seen! *MS. 1815*
1922 Spectacle *rev from* spectacle *MS.*
      1815, restored to spectacle *MS.*
      1832/36 (pencil and ink)–
1924 methinks, *rev from* methinks *MS.*
      1815
1927 say,] say— *MS. 1832/36–*
1929 Prime!" *rev from* Prime." *MS. 1815*
      END OF THE WHITE DOE. *omitted MS.*
      1815, 1820–

The Force of Prayer
title 4 PRIORY] Priory, *MS. 1815*
       5 TRADITION] Tradition. *MS.*
          1815
       2 Tale,] Tale; *MS. 1815*
       7 ENDLESS SORROW] Endless
          sorrow *MS. 1815*
       9 words,] words *MS. 1815*
      16 doe; *rev from* doe *MS. 1815*
      24 shall—] shall *MS. 1815*
      46 to-morrow] tomorrow *MS. 1815*
      48 her's] hers *MS. 1815*
      54 "Let *rev from* Let *MS. 1815*
      55 field] Field *MS. 1815*
      59 Matins *rev from* matins *MS. 1815*
      60 Even-song *rev by eras from* Even
          song *MS. 1815*

Notes
variations in the form of quotations from the
text and changes in page references and line ref-
erences required by changes in pagination are not
recorded, nor are reductions of double quotes to
single in MS. 1832/36
       1 *not indented 1832*
       2 Collection,] Collection *MS.*
          1815   entitled] entitled, *1827–*
       3 follows:] follows:— *1832–*
     3–4 "About . . . time," . . . "a]
          'About . . . time,' . . . 'a *1836–*
       4 Dissolution *rev from* dissolution *MS.*
          1815
     4–5 Doe, . . . long] Doe,' . . . 'long
          1836–   people] People *MS.*
          1815
       6 Bolton,] Bolton; *MS. 1815*
       8 congregation."] congregation.'
          1836–   DR] DR. *1820–*
       9 WHITAKER'S] WHITAKER'S *1827–*
          1840
      11 Insurrection,] Insurrection; *1827–*
          tradition] Tradition *MS. 1815*
      12 [Ballad] Ballad. *1820–*
      31 Tower] tower *MS. 1815*
      38 When,] When *MS. 1815*

44 banner] Banner MS. *1815*
47 Camden,)] Camden), MS. *1815*
49 Bible,] Bible MS. *1815*
64 Though] Tho' MS. *1815*
65–66 George Bowes, . . . army,] Geo.
  Bowes . . . army MS. *1815*

ballad

6 leddie:] ladie: MS. *1815*
22 subtiltie:] subtiltie; MS. *1815*
35 Maister] maister MS. *1815*
50 goodlye *rev from* goodly MS.
  1815   companie *rev to*
  companye MS. *1815*
54 seem'st] seemst MS. *1815*
57 counselle's *rev from* counsell's
  MS. *1815*
74 brave,] brave; MS. *1815*
83 years, *eras to* years MS. *1815*
103 Dogs *rev from* dogs MS. *1815*
106 faire;] faire: MS. *1815*
107 Crosse,] crosse MS. *1815*
118 anone,] anone MS. *1815*
119 ere] e're MS. *1815*
121 news] newes MS. *1815*
130 harneis *rev from* harness MS.
  1815
132 countrie.] countrie MS. *1815*
134 The Erle] Th'erle MS. *1815*
136 wiss] wiss, MS. *1815*
140 Halfe Moone] halfe moone
  MS. *1815*   hye *rev from* hi
  MS. *1815*

76 "Bolton Priory,"] 'Bolton Priory,'
  1836–   Dr] Dr. *1820–*   the]
  The *1827–*
77 Deanry] Deanery *1820–*
  "stands] stands *1820–1832* 'stands
  1836–
81 "Opposite] 'Opposite *1836–*
  Church,] Church MS. *1815*
85 process,] process *1827–*
88 beyond,] beyond MS. *1815*
90 "But] 'But *1836–*
91 landscape] landscape, *1836–*
94 &c.] &c, MS. *1815*, *1845*
96 forward] forward, *1827–*
98 Barden Fell *rev from* Bardden fell
  MS. *1815*
100 "About] 'About *1836–*   Valley]
  valley *1820–*
103 "This] This *1836–1840* This *rev to*
  'This MS. *1836/45*, *1845–*
104 River *rev from* river MS. *1815 rev to*
  river MS. *1832/36–*
111 "The] 'The *1836–*
112 formed,] formed *1832–*
113 side,] side *1836–*   rock-basons]
  rock-basins *1827–*
119 "The] 'The *1836–*

121 excite."] excite. MS. *1815* excite.'
  1836–
124 "Formerly,"] 'Formerly,' *1836–*
  Dr] Dr. *1820–*
125 "over] 'over *1836–*   Transept
  rev from transept MS. *1815*
128 ridge."] ridge.' *1836–*
129 "The] 'The *1836–*
131 Cathedral."] Cathedral.' *1836–*
  1845 Cathedral *1850*
132 "At] 'At *1836–*
135 timber."] timber.' *1836–*
136 Dr] Dr. *1820–*
137 The] "The *1827–*   Prayer, &c.]
  Prayer," &c. *1827–1840, 1846*
  Prayer." *1845, 1850*
138 "At] 'At *1836–1845, 1850* At
  1846   Church] Church, *1832–*
140 Claphams"] Claphams' *1836–*
  line] line, *1836–*
141 Mauliverers] Mauleverers *1832–*
  "were] 'were *1836–*   upright."]
  upright.' *1836–*
143 time;] time: *1827–*   "he] 'he
  1836–   House] house *1836–*
144 Cliffords,] Cliffords *1820*
  survive."] survive.' *1836–*
144/145 Shepherd Lord *rev to*
  Shepherd-lord MS. *1836/45*
145 volume] Volume *1827–*   author]
  Author MS. *1815*
146 one,] one *1836–*
147 Restoration] restoration MS.
  1815   Clifford] Clifford, MS.
  1815, 1836–   Shepherd]
  Shepherd, MS. *1815, 1836–*
148 personage] Personage MS. *1815*
149 Burn's] Burns *1845–*
151 him] him, *1832–*   Dr] Dr. MS.
  1815, 1820–   says, "he retired]
  says he 'retired *1836–*
152 tower] Tower MS. *1815*
153 keeper's] Keeper's MS. *1815*
154 favourable] favorable MS. *1815*
155 shew] show *1832–*
156 him,] him MS. *1815*
157 nobleman] Nobleman MS. *1815*
160 "His] 'His *1836–*
161 shepherds] Shepherds MS. *1815*
162 bodies,] bodies; *1832–*
167 "I] 'I *1836*
169 "For] For MS. *1815* 'For *1836–*
  MSS.] M.S.S. MS. *1815* MSS.,
  1850
170 Alchemy] alchemy MS. *1815*
171 Seventh] seventh MS. *1815*
172 MSS.] M.SS. MS. *1815*
173 nobleman] Nobleman MS.
  1815

176   "In] 'In *1836–*
177   Seventh] seventh *MS. 1815*   son]
      Son *MS. 1815*
179   army] Army *MS. 1815*   shewed]
      showed *1832–*
180   family] Family *MS. 1815*
182   "He] 'He *1836–*   23d] 23rd
      1836–
183   70.] 70– *MS. 1815*
185   deposited] deposited, *1827–*
      dead] dead, *1820–*
186   life-time] lifetime *1827–*
187   "By] 'By *1836–*   will] Will *MS.
      1815*   Shap] Shap, *1827–*
188   Westmoreland] Westmorland *MS.
      1815*   Bolton] Bolton, *1827–*
      Yorkshire."] Yorkshire.' *1836–*
189   Dr] Dr. *1820–*   shews] shows
      1832–
191/192   Ye . . . Towers.] "Ye . . .
      Towers." *1827–1832*
193   city] City *MS. 1815*   Durham. It]
      Durham; it *MS. 1815*
194   Dr] Dr. *MS. 1815, 1820–*
      account.] account *MS. 1815*
194/195   Of . . . conquered!] "Of . . .
      conquered!" *1827–1832* 'Of . . .
      conquered!' *1836–*
      Thurston, what] Thurston! what
      MS. 1815 Thurston—what *MS.
      1832/36–*
195   See] see *MS. 1815*
196   Standard.] Standard *1845*
197   "In] 'In *1836–*
198   *anno*] Anno *MS. 1815*
199   abbey] Abbey *MS. 1815*
200   Corporax-cloth *rev from* Corpora
      cloth *MS. 1815*   St] St. *MS.
      1815, 1820–*
201   relique] Relique *MS. 1815*
      banner-cloth] Banner-cloth *MS.
      1815*
203   west] West *MS. 1815*   city] City
      MS. 1815
205   vision] Vision *MS. 1815*
206   God's] God s *1840, 1846*
      mercy] mercy, *1832–*
207   holy] Holy *1836–*   St] St. *MS.
      1815, 1820–*   monks] Monks
      MS. 1815
210   battle] Battle *MS. 1815*
214   St] St. *MS. 1815, 1820–*
215   relique.)] Relique.) *MS. 1815*
      relique). *1836–*
217   company] Company *MS. 1815*
      battle] Battle *MS. 1815*
219   monks,] Monks, *MS. 1815* monks
      1832–

220   son] Son *MS. 1815*   nobles]
      Nobles *MS. 1815*
221   abbey church] Abbey Church *MS.
      1815*
222   holy] Holy *MS. 1815, 1836–*   St]
      St. *MS. 1815, 1820–*
223   atchieved *rev to* achieved *MS.
      1832/36–*   day."] day.' *1836–*
224   battle] Battle *MS. 1815*
226   "On] 'On *1836–*   west] West
      MS. 1815   city] City *MS. 1815*
227   cross] Cross *MS. 1815*
228   erected,] erected *1832–*
229   field of battle] Field of Battle *MS.
      1815*   Nevil's *rev from* Neville's
      MS. 1815
231   battle."] Battle." *MS. 1815* battle.'
      1836–   St] St. *MS. 1815, 1820–*
233   battle] Battle *MS. 1815*   "The]
      'The *1836–*   prior] Prior *MS.
      1815*
234   made,] made," *1832* made,' *1836–*
      and] "and *1832* 'and *1836–*
      banner-cloth] Banner-cloth *MS.
      1815*
235   length,)] length) *MS. 1815*
236   relique] Relique *MS. 1815*
      corporax-cloth] Corporax-cloth
      MS. 1815   &c. and] &c., and
      1836–
237   banner] Banner *MS. 1815*   holy]
      Holy *1836–*   St] St. *MS. 1815,
      1820–*
238   purpose,] purpose *1832–*
239   battle] Battle *MS. 1815*
240   shewed] showed *1836–*   battle]
      Battle *MS. 1815*
241   holy] Holy *1836–*   St] St. *1820–*
242   banner-cloth] Banner-cloth *MS.
      1815*   dissolution] Dissolution
      MS. 1815   abbey] Abbey *MS.
      1815*
244   eye-witnesses] Eye-witnesses *MS.
      1815*
245   fire] Fire *MS. 1815*
246   reliques."] Reliques." *MS. 1815*
      reliques.' *1836–*
249   banner] Banner *MS. 1815*
      Surry] Surrey *1827–*
250   Dr] Dr. *MS. 1815, 1820–*
      Whitaker.] Whitaker:— *1832*
251   "Rylstone] 'Rylstone *1836–*
254   tower] Tower *MS. 1815*
255   -work,] work *MS. 1815*
259   "But] 'But *1836–*   pleasure-
      house] Pleasure-house *MS. 1815*
260   mounds,] mounds *MS. 1815*
261   entire,] entire *MS. 1815*

263   "The] 'The *1836–*
264   watch-tower."] watch-tower.' *1836–*
       1840 watch tower.' *1845–*
265   "After] 'After *1836–*   Norton,]
       Norton *MS. 1815*   estates]
       Estates *MS. 1815*
266   crown *rev to* Crown *MS. 1815*
       2d or 3d] 2d or 3rd *MS. 1815* 2nd
       or 3nd *1836–*
267   Cumberland."] Cumberland.'
       1836–   survey] Survey *MS. 1815*
268   time,] time *MS. 1815*   Dr] Dr.
       MS. 1815, 1820–
269   the *rev to* 'the *MS. 1832/36–*
       mansion-house] Mansion-house
       MS. 1815
270   close *rev to* Close *MS. 1815*
       Vivery,] Vivery; *MS. 1815*
       called] called, *1832–*
       undoubtedly] undoubtedly, *1832–*
271   Viverium;] Viverium: *MS. 1815*
       Vivarium *1832–*
273   fish-ponds *over partial eras MS.*
       1815
275   which,] which *MS. 1815*
276   Mr] Mr. *MS. 1815, 1820–*
279   survey,] survey *1845–*   tenants]
       Tenants *MS. 1815*
280   butler] Butler *MS. 1815*   Mr]
       Mr. *1820–*
281   master] Master *MS. 1815*
       Ripon." *rev to* Ripon.' *MS.*
       1832/36–
282   "At] 'At *1836–*   parish of
       Burnsal,] Parish of Burnsal *MS.*
       1815
283   Wharfdale] Wharfdale, *1832–*
284   Littondale,] Littondale; *MS. 1815*
285   properly] properly, *1832–*
       Dern-brook] Dernbrook *1845,*
       1850
286   N.W.] N.W., *1832–*
287   concealment."] concealment.'
       1836–   —Dr] Dr. *MS. 1815*
       —Dr. *1820–*
287/288   *black-letter phrase in single quotes*
       1827– with exclamation point included
       1832–

288   bells] Bells *MS. 1815*   church]
       Church *1850*
289   tower] Tower *MS. 1815*   *black-*
       letter initials enclosed in single quotes
       MS. 1832/36–
290   *black-letter phrase enclosed in single*
       quotes 1836–   ayde] ayd *MS. 1815*
291   Dr] Dr. *1820–*   Whitaker:—]
       Whitaker *MS. 1815*   "On] 'On
       1836–
292   wall,] wall *1827–*
293   tower] Tower *MS. 1815*
294   glen, . . . long,] glen . . . long *MS.*
       1815
298   From] "From *1827–1832* 'From
       1836–   Border,] Border *MS.*
       1815
299   pounds] Pounds *MS. 1815*   &c.]
       &c, *MS. 1815*
300   south] South *MS. 1815*
302   fenced] fenced, *MS. 1815*
303   within] within, *1820–*
306   parks] Parks *MS. 1815*   forests]
       Forests *MS. 1815*
307–308   animals, . . . conceive, . . .
       snare,] animals . . . conceive . . .
       snare *MS. 1815*
309   follow.] follow." *1820–1832* follow.'
       1836–
310   recommending] recommending,
       1845–1846   notice] Notice *MS.*
       1815   lovers] Lovers *MS. 1815*
311   scenery— *rev from* scenery, *MS.*
       1815 scenery, *1845–*   Abbey *rev*
       from abbey *MS. 1815*
312   enchanting *begun* Enc *then eras MS.*
       1815   spot] Spot *MS. 1815*
313   Rev.] Revd *MS. 1815*
314   skilfully *rev from* skillfully *MS.*
       1815   and] and, *1827–*
315   added,] added *1850*   place]
       place, *1832–*
316   hand of art] Hand of Art *MS.*
       1815   spirit of nature] Spirit of
       Nature *MS. 1815*

Transcriptions with Photographic Reproductions

Prose "Advertizement": DC MS. 61
Epistle Dedicatory: "In trellis'd shed"
  DC MS. 80
  MS. 1815, at King's College, Cambridge
The White Doe of Rylstone
  Fair-Copy Verse Passages: DC MSS. 61 and 62
  Verse Drafts: DC MS. 61
  Selected Revisions in MS. 1832/36, at Wellesley College

Prose "Advertizement"
DC MS. 61

DC MS. 61 is a small homemade notebook bound in a wrapper of parchment cut from a legal document, like the wrappers of *The Waggoner*, MSS. 1 and 5 (see *Benjamin the Waggoner*, ed. Paul F. Betz [Ithaca, 1981], p. 135). The notebook now contains 37 whole leaves and at least seven stubs, bound in six gatherings, successively of eight, four, two, eight, six or eight, eight, and eight leaves. The number and relation of several stubs in the fifth gathering have been obscured by modern restoration of the manuscript, but the adjacent text shows that five successive leaves have been lost between the third and last whole leaves of the gathering. Other stubs represent the last two leaves of the first gathering and the first and last leaves of the last gathering. Leaves measure 10.4 by 16.5–16.9 centimeters, and the paper is the coarse cream wove paper watermarked 1801 which was in use during the first half of 1805 for *The Prelude*, MS. Z (DC MS. 49), and during the summer of 1806 for *Home at Grasmere*, MS. B (see *Home at Grasmere*, ed. Beth Darlington [Ithaca, 1977], pp. 12 and 270). A revision slip stitched to the recto of the last leaf of the second gathering appears to be cut from the same paper.

The first gathering contains fair copy, on rectos and versos, of "Part 1st" of *The White Doe* in Mary's hand, with revisions by William. The remainder of the notebook contains the conclusion of the first part and text that runs through much of "Part Third," fair-copied on rectos only, mostly by Dorothy and William; versos contain drafts (mostly in William's hand) toward revision of Cantos IV and VII, drafts toward the prose "Advertizement," and fair copy with revisions of *The Force of Prayer*. The first gathering, which is the only portion of the manuscript in which fair copy is entered on both rectos and versos, was apparently separate at one time, and may represent an earlier version of the text.

The notebook probably contains work recorded sometime between 2 December 1807, when Dorothy wrote Catherine Clarkson that her brother had composed "above 500 lines of a new poem," and 3 January 1808, when she told Lady Beaumont that he had written "over 1200."

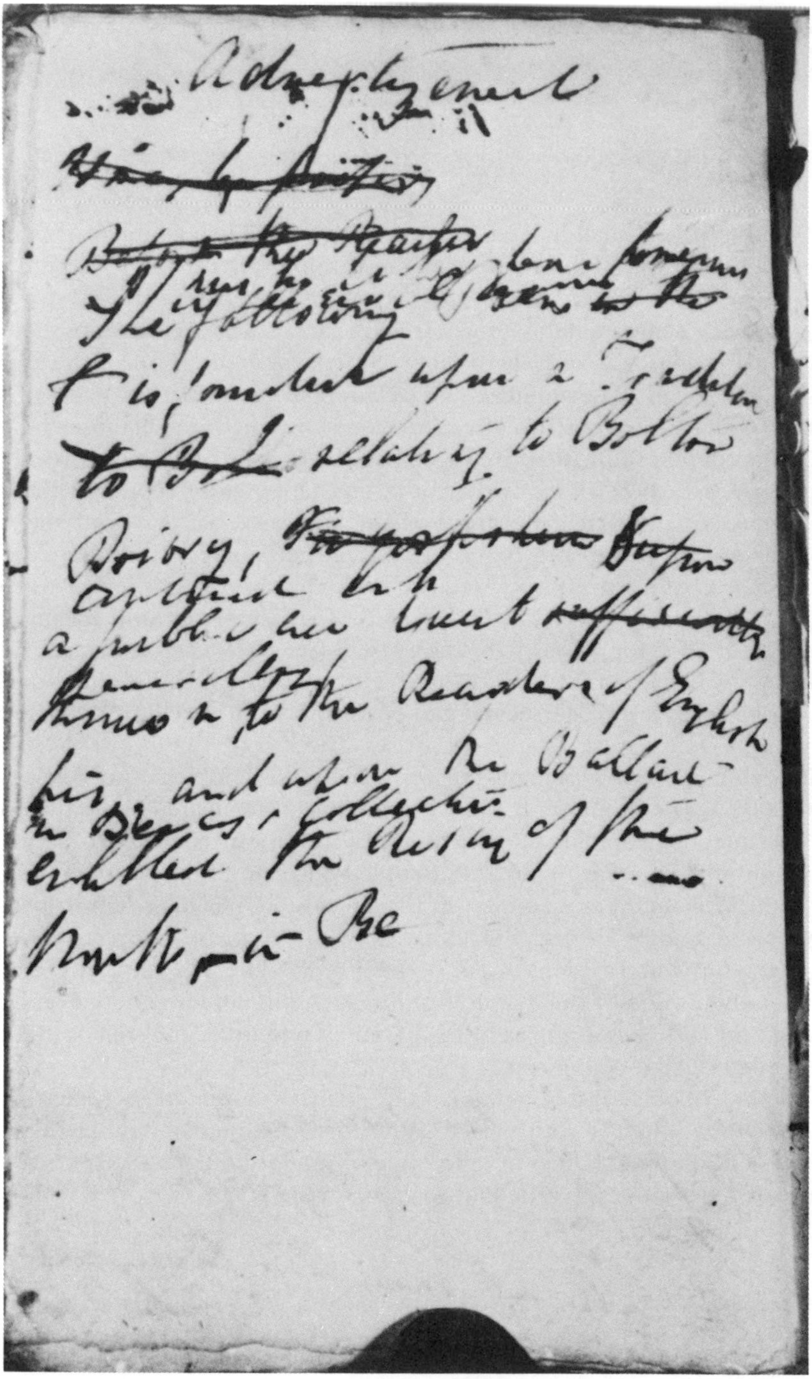

[24ᵛ]

Advertizement

~~It may be proper~~
~~Before the Reader~~ ⎰ peruses
           here ⎱ [?]
    It may be [?]
      [?] [?several reasons]
The following Poem ~~in the~~
[-?-] is founded upon a Tradition
~~To Bolto~~ relating to Bolton
Priory, ~~[In Yorkshire]~~, ~~& upon~~
    antient [?aut]
a publisher [?trust] ~~sufficiently~~
    generally
known to the Readers of English
his. and upon the Ballad
    in Percys Collection
entitled the Rising of the
North,—in—Be

Following leaf 24 are three (or five) stubs (the number is rendered uncertain by modern restoration of the notebook). WW's numbering of surrounding text shows that five leaves have been removed; their rectos would have contained 78 lines of fair copy.

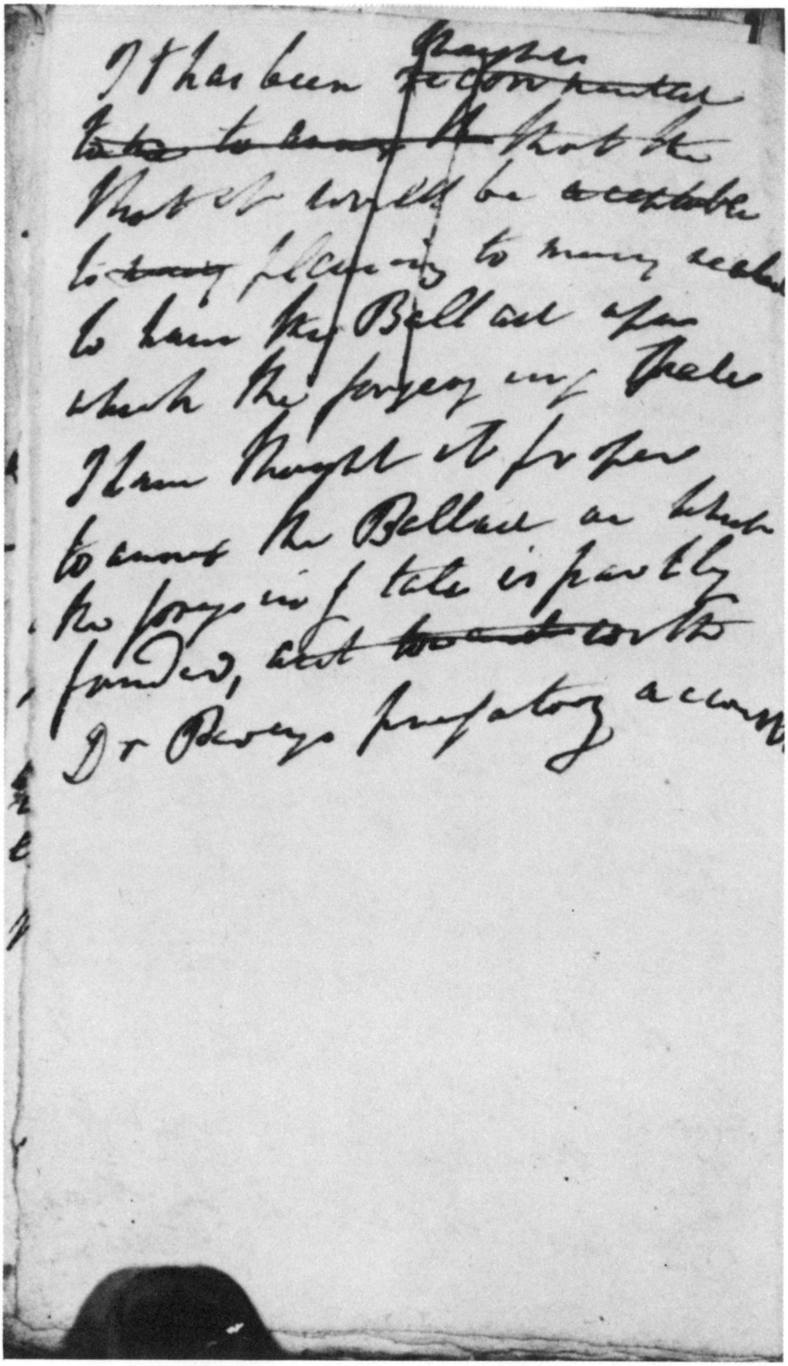
It has been suggested
that the
that it would be acceptable
pleasing to many readers
to have the Ballad upon
which the foregoing tale
I have thought it proper
to annex the Ballad on which
the foregoing tale is partly
founded, and with
Dr Percy's prefatory account

[30ᵛ]

           thought
It has been ~~recommended~~
~~to me to annex th that the~~
that it would be ~~aceptable~~
to ~~many~~ pleasing to many readers
to have the Ballad upon
               { T
which the forgeog ing {[?]ale

I have thought it proper
to annex the Ballad on which
the forgoing tale is partly
founded, ~~and tow end w~~ith
Dr Percys prefatory account.

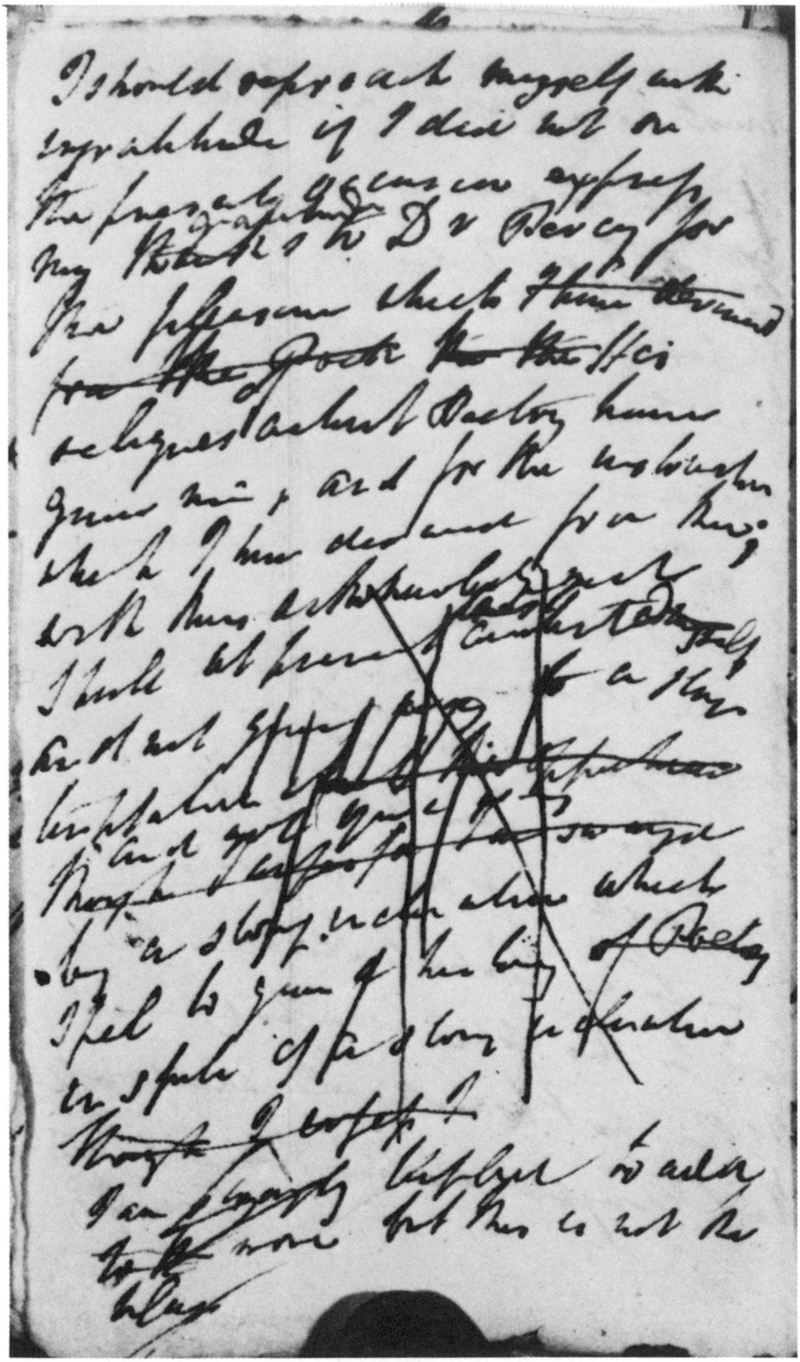

[31ᵛ]

I should reproach myself with
ingratitude if I did not on
the present occasion express
          gratitude
my ~~thanks~~ to Dr Percy for
the pleasure which ~~I have derived~~
~~from the Poetr the the~~ His
          of
reliques ~~antint~~ Poetry have
                              ʾ⎫
given me.⎦ and for the instruction
                              :⎫
which I have derived from them,⎦
with this acknowledgment
          [?] rest   ⎧ed
Shall   at present content⎩   ~~myself~~
and not give way to a strong
temptation ~~which this opportuni~~
          and not give way
~~though I confess for I am swayd~~
by a strong inclination which
I feel to give a history ~~of Poetry~~
in spite of a strong inclination
~~though I confess I~~
I am strongly tempted to add
~~to th~~ more but this is not the
place

[32ᵛ]

~~Happenin~~
Happening in the course of last
summer to be on a visit to some
Friends in Yorkshire I was by
them conducted to Bolton Priory
⎰A
or ⎱abbey as it is generally called;
The ~~delicious Vale in which it~~
  and from the impression of that
is ~~situated, the~~
                    I owe ~~to the~~
  day the foregoing owes its birth
The beautiful Ruin the delicious
  and its accompanying history & tradition
Vale which it adorns the River
which flows by it, ~~the lawn, woods~~
The chasm of the Strid ~~with its~~
                    s ⎱ B ⎰arden
accompanying tradition[?]⎰ & th⎱
        the [?favorites]
Tower ~~& the memory~~ of Lord
Clifford the Shepherd whose
~~interes~~ History had interested
me from my earliest childhood,
upon all those objects I looked
        high   t⎱
with that delight which in⎰ is
natural to man ~~to express~~
in ~~Verse~~ when I look back

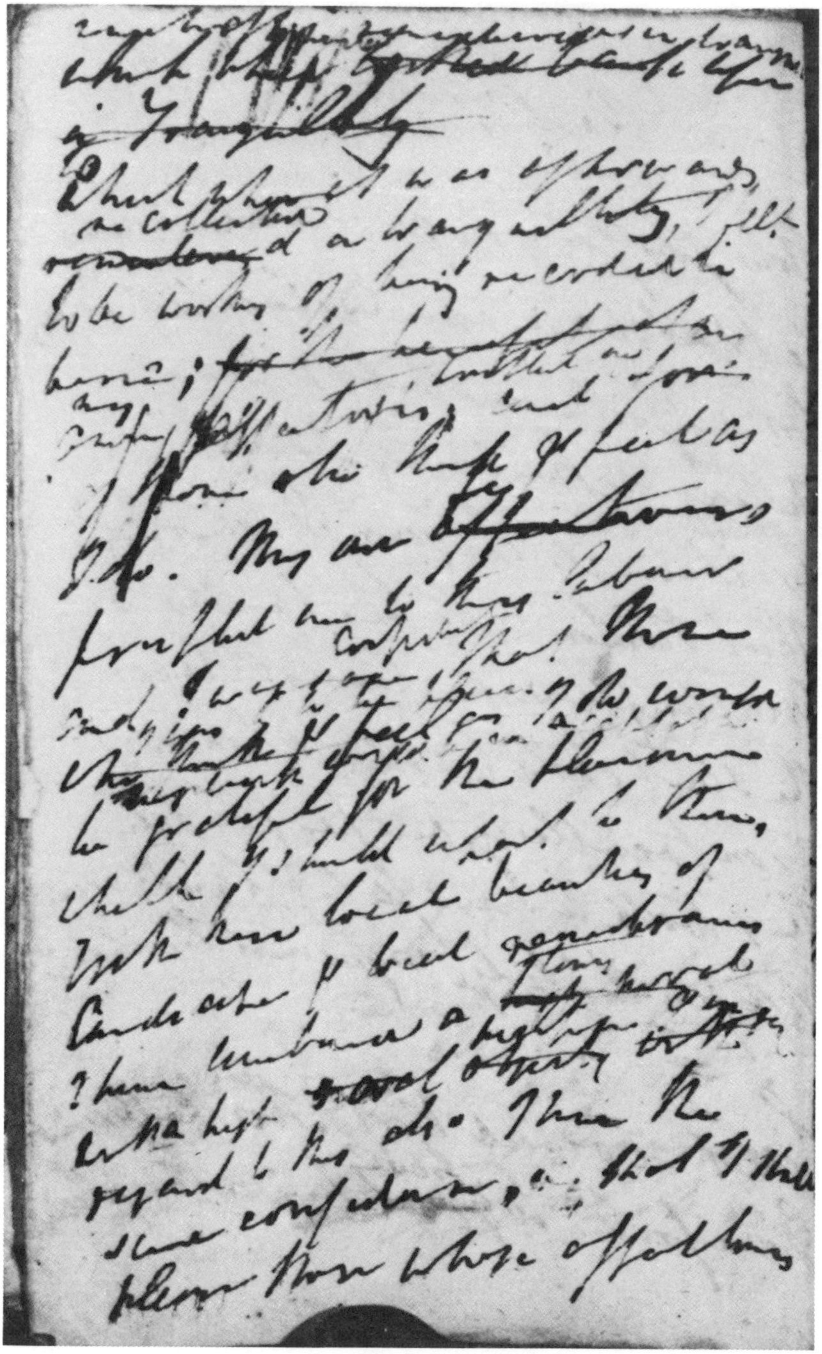

[33^v]

such affections remembered in tranquil
which when ~~looked back~~ upon
~~in Tranquillity~~
   to
which when it was afterwards
  recollected
~~remembered~~ in tranquillity, I felt
to be worthy of being recorded in
Verse; ~~for the benefit of~~ my
   my   prompted me
own affections; and ~~for~~
of those who think & feel as
           fe
I do. My own ~~affect~~ions
prompted me to this labour
       confident
and I was ~~sure~~ that those
   I was to be please
~~who think & feel as I~~ do would
  my work would be acceptable
be grateful for the pleasure
which I should impart to them,
with new local beauties of
landscape & local remembrances
           strong
I have mentioned a ~~high moral~~
       purpose & in [?reg]
with a high ~~moral object with~~
regard to this also I have the
same confidence, as that I shall
please those whose affections

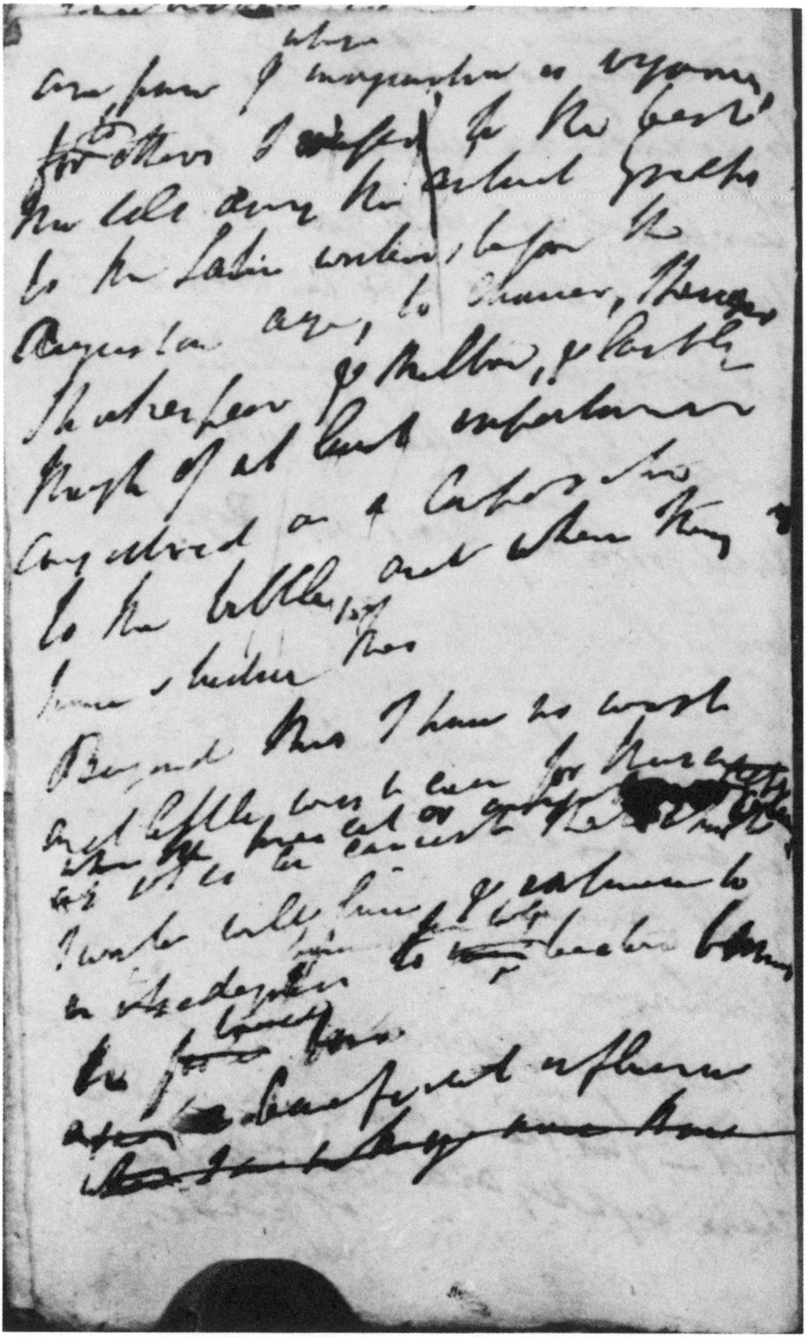

[34ᵛ]

           whose
are pure & imagination is vigourous
     to   { refer
for others I { [?] to the best
models among the antient Greeks
to the Latin writers before the
                  s }
Augustan age, to Chaucer, Spenc } er
Shakespear & Milton, & lastly
though of at least importance
considered as a Composition
to the bibble, and when they
        [?]
have studied thes
Beyond this I have no wish
and little wish even for that except
   when the present or accompany [?]
as with an earnest that what
I write will live & continue to
     a [?   ?   ] [?help]
an [?   ] to [?]ᴧbestow blessing
    [?]
to foster bene
exert a beneficient influence
when I am nothing more than

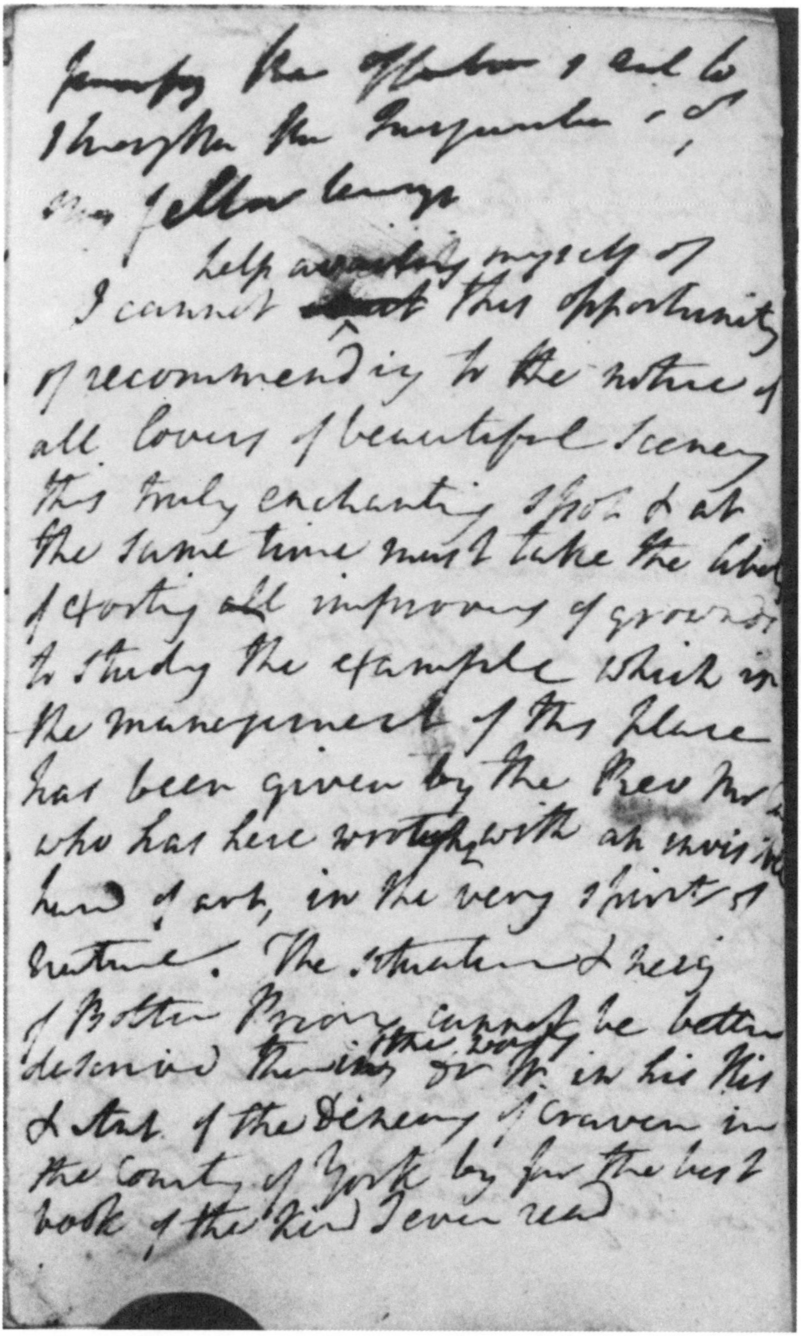

[35ᵛ]

purify the affections and to
strengthen the Imaginations of
my fellow beings

help {availing} myself of
   [?]
I cannot ~~omit~~ this opportunity
             ^
of recommending to the notice of
all lovers of beautiful Scenery
this truly enchanting spot & at
the same time must take the liberty
of exorting ~~all~~ improvers of grounds
to study the example which in
the management of this place
                b
has been given t}y the Rev Mr Carr
           {ught
who has here wro{te with an invisible
hand of art, in the very spirit of
nature. The situation & neig
of Bolton Priory cannot be better
               in\ the words
described than by} Dr W. in his His
& Ant of the Denery of Craven in
the County of York by far the best
book of the kind I ever read

The hand not WW's is MW's.

[36ᵛ]

        For though an anapestic verse
           twelve
of ~~eleven~~ syllables, with its ~~ac[?c]~~
four long and accompany eight
short syllables does in fact
          to pronounce
take up more time than a
trochaeic Verse of seven, with
its four, and accompanying three
short syllables, nevertheless the
      or hurry
rapidity given to the ~~movement~~ of
      additional s ⎱
verse by the ~~dactylic~~   o⎰hort
syllables, ~~reduces it to the feeling~~
     causes
~~produce gives bir~~th to a delusion
which reduces the two Verses
  however different as to number
as to the feeling of time within
the same limits

however different the Verses
may be as to number of syllables
reduces

As to the style after what has
been said in the preface to the
Lyrical Ballads I have nothing
to add. The only Readers so
whom I wish to please are
those whose affections are
represented chim of the affections
of men in action,

[37ᵛ]

As to the style after what has
been said in the preface to the
Lyrical Ballads I have nothing
to add. The only Readers
⎰　h
whom I wis⎰[?hed] to please are
those whose affections are
representative of the affections
　　　　　[?pure]
of human nature, ~~clear health[?y]~~
& ~~independent,~~

Epistle Dedicatory: "In trellis'd shed"
DC MS. 80

DC MS. 80, described in Jared Curtis's edition of *Poems, in Two Volumes* for this series (Ithaca, 1983), p. xxiii, is a red leather-bound notebook used mainly for drafting and copying of poems to be published in 1815. The earliest surviving copy of the dedicatory poem to Mary is written in Wordsworth's hand on leaves 4ᵛ–6ʳ. Line numbers in the left margins are keyed to those of the published text.

The lines at the bottom of 6ʳ, shown in the photograph, are from a version of the opening of *Artegal and Elidure,* published in 1820.

Epistle dedicatory

Three years of wedded life were as a day
Whose cordial answers to the heart's desire,
If in some bower, with ~~flowering~~ glistening trees, gay
Or happy by the blazing winter fire,
Did we together read in Spenser's lay,
How ~~howsoever~~ thus sad of soul, in soul other,
The gentle Una, born of heavenly birth,
To seek her knight went wandering o'er the
                                    earth.

Ah, then, Beloved, blessing was the smart
And the tear precious in compassion shed
For her, who, pierced by sorrow thrilling dart
Did meekly bear the pang unmerited
Made us that Emblem of her own by heart
The milkwhite Lamb which in a line she led
And faithful, loyal in her innocence,
& the brave lion slain in her defence.

Often could we hear as of a faery shell
Attuned to words with sacred wisdom fraught
For fancy forged such ... miracle
And all its tender inspiration caught
Around the green bower and in our rustic Cell
... larger ... things were taught

[4ᵛ]

Epistle dedicatory

3   When years of wedded life were as a day
4   Whose current answers to the hearts desire,
                   clustering   y⎫
1   Oft in some bower, with ~~opening~~ ∧roses, gai⎭
2   Or haply by the blazing winter fire,
5   Did we together read in Spenser's lay,
6   How ~~heavenly~~ Una sad of soul, in sad attire,
7   The gentle Una, born of heavenly birth,
8   To seek her knight went wandering oer the
                                                 earth.

9   Ah, then, Beloved, pleasing was the smart
             t ⎱
10   And the p⎰ear precious in compassion shed
11   For Her, who, pierced by sorrows thrilling dart
12   Did meekly bear the pang unmerited
13   Meek as that Emblem of her lowly heart.
14   The milkwhite Lamb which in a line she led
15   And faithful, loyal in her innocence,
     Like
16   ~~As~~ the brave Lion slain in her defence.

17   Notes could we hear as of a faery shell
18   Attuned to words with sacred wisdom fraught
19   Free fancy prized each specious miracle
20   And all its finer inspiration caught
21   Mid the green bower, and in our rustic Cell;
22   Till we by lamentable change were taught
     That bliss with

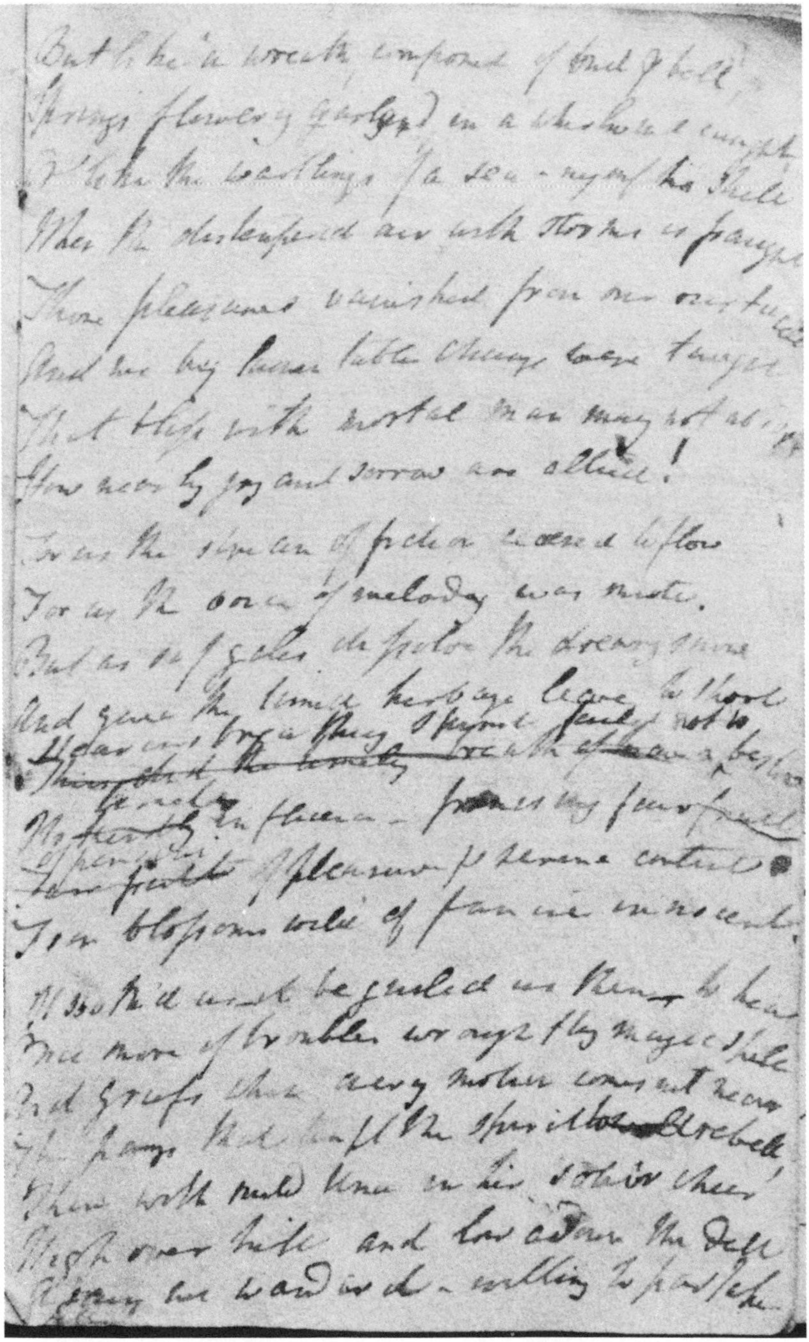

[5^r]

But like ^a wreath, composed of bud & bell,

{and
Spring's flowery   garl⸤[?], in a whirlwind caught,
Or like the warblings of a sea-nymph's shell
When the distempered air with storms is fraught
Those pleasures vanished from our rustic cell

22   And we by lamentable change were taught
23   That bliss with mortal man may not abide.
24   How nearly joy and sorrow are allied!

25   For as the stream of fiction ceaesed to flow
26   For us the voice of melody was mute.
27   But as sof gales dissolve the dreary snow
28   And give the timid herbage leave to shoot
        Heavens breathing Spirit failed not to
29   ~~Thus did the timely breath of heaven~~ ∧bestow
            timely
30   Its ~~kindly~~ influence — promising fair fruit
        Of pensive
31   ~~Fair fruit~~ of pleasure & serene content
32   For blossoms wild of fancies innocent.

                                    —}
33   It sooth'd us — it beguiled us then, } to hear
34   Once more of troubles wrought by magic spell
35   And griefs whose aery motion comes not near
36   The pangs that tempt the spirit to ~~well~~ rebell,
37   Then with mild Una in her sober cheer
38   High over hill and low adown the dell
39   Again we wanderd — willing to partake
        All

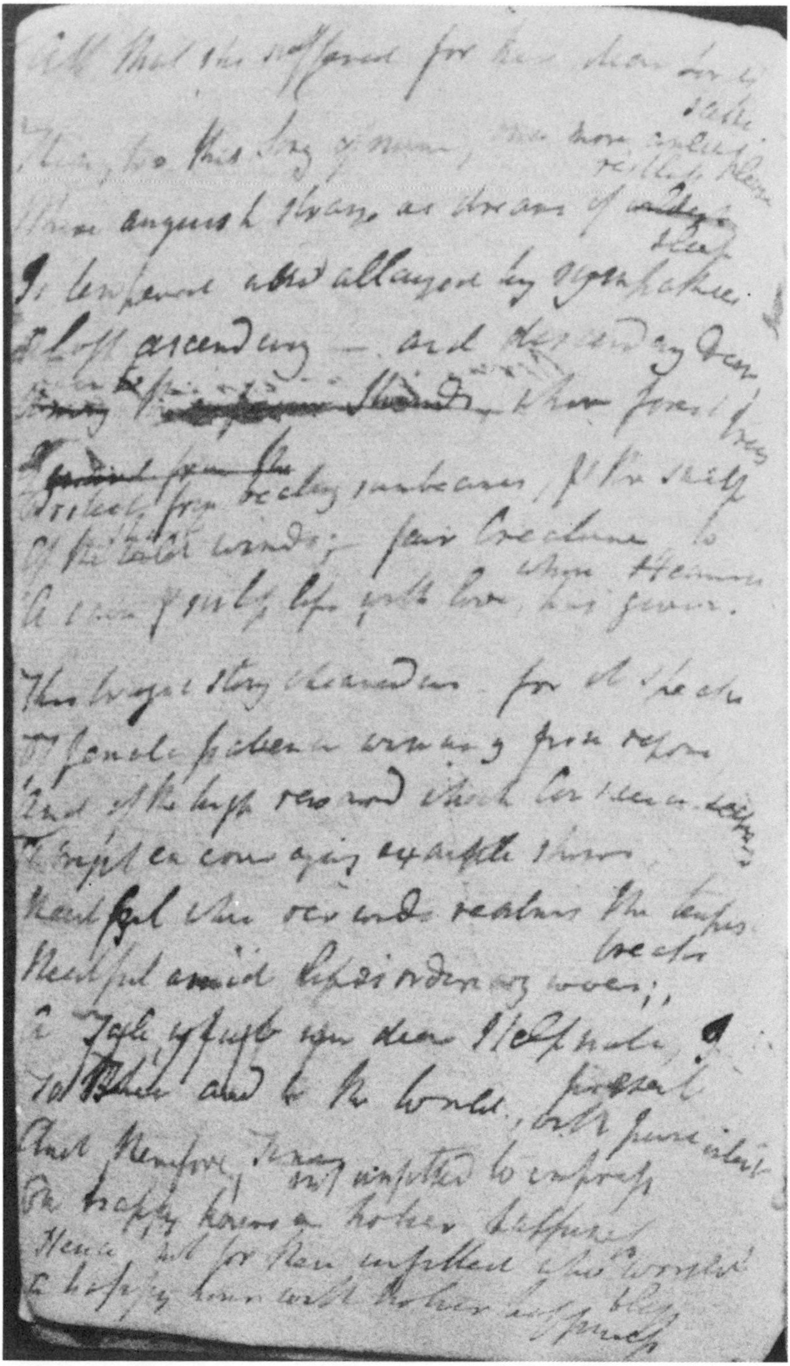

[5ᵛ]

40   All that she suffered for her dear Lord's
                        sake.

41   Then, too this Song of mine, once more could
                        please
              restless
42   Where anguish strange as dreams of ~~wildest~~
                        sleep
          ⌠nd
43   Is tempered al⌊[?] allayed by sympathies
44   Aloft ascending — and descending deep,
      Even to
45   ~~Among~~ the ~~inferior Kinds,~~ whom forest trees
    ~~Guard from the~~
46   Protect from beating sunbeams, & the sweep
        sharp
47   Of the ~~wild~~ winds;— fair Creature, to
                 whom Heaven
48   A calm & sinless life, with love, has given.

49   This tragic story cheared us — for it speaks
50   Of female patience winning firm repose,
51   And of the high reward which Conscience seeks
                ⌠mple
52   A bright, encouraging exal⌊[?] shows,
       ⌠ful
53   Needl⌊[?] when oer wide realms the tempest
                      breaks
54   Needful amid life's ordinary woes;,
    A Tale, which now dear Helpmate, I
                 present
      ⌠Thee
    To ⌊th and to the World, with pure intent
          [?Times]
    And, therefore,   not unfitted to impress
    On happy hours a holier happiness
55   Hence, not for them unfitted who would
                    bless
56   A happy hour with holier happiness

[6ʳ]

                                  erringly
57   *He* serves the Muses ~~ingloriously~~ and ill
                 se aim is
58   Who ~~aims at~~ pleasures light & fugitive:
                      power
59   Oh that my ~~mind~~ were equal to
                                fulfill
                 The comprehensive
60   M~~ore worthy the~~, mandate which
                           they give!
             suffering of our earnest will:
       ~~But, on this product of a simple ∧skill~~
61   Vain aspiration of an earnest will!
       ~~As Thou has smiled, Beloved, it may live;~~
62   Yet in this moral Strain a power may live
       ~~And other unto others such delight~~
                         impart
63   Beloved Wife such pleasure tͦ
64   As it has yielded to thy tender hea
         The

Epistle Dedicatory: "In trellis'd shed"
MS. 1815, at King's College, Cambridge

MS. 1815 is the printer's copy of *The White Doe*, chiefly in the hand of Mary Wordsworth with revisions by William Wordsworth. It was prepared and sent to the printer in small hand-sewn packets of six to eight leaves. There are three types of paper in the manuscript: two leader and two trailer leaves bear the countermark "W / 1812" (probably Whatman paper, inserted when the manuscript was bound in leather after publication); the poetic text (folios 4 to 58) is written on paper bearing an ornamental "P" above the date "1810"; and the notes (folios 59–85) appear on a mixture of the Whatman paper and paper bearing the countermark "GOLDING & SNELGROVE / 1806." It is all laid paper with chain lines running horizontally at intervals of 2.6 centimeters in the Whatman paper, 2.7 centimeters in the "P /1810" paper, and 2.4 centimeters in the GOLDING paper. The outside measurements are about 20 by 15.9 centimeters.

The manuscript was paginated by Mary Wordsworth, from 1 to 97 (the end of *The White Doe*); *The Force of Prayer* is unpaginated, and the pagination of the notes begins again with "1" but the sequence deteriorates as a result of Wordsworth's having added the ballad and its note (moved forward from its first entry as a note to l. 187) to the first general note.

Preserved with the manuscript is half of a single sheet of proof of the 1815 printing. The full sheet must have measured approximately 50.1 by 45.8 centimeters before it was cut into smaller segments. Three surviving pieces, torn and folded to fit into the manuscript when bound, make up most of 3 and 4 of the K gathering. The proof was posted to Wordsworth as a "single sheet" by the printer, James Ballantyne of Edinburgh, who wrote out on a blank portion of K3 a version of the text for a note on the ballad. On other blank portions of K3 and K4 Wordsworth transcribed the poem beginning "In trellis'd shed" and above it he wrote: "The following is to be prefixed to the Poem." The sheet bears two postmark dates: April 8 and April 14.

Line numbers in the left margins of the transcription of "In trellis'd shed" correspond to those of the published text, in which the poem is dated April 20, 1815.

The following is to be prefixed to the Poem.

In trellis'd shed with clustering roses gay,
And oft beside our blazing winter fire,
Where years of wedded life were as a day,
Whose current answers to the heart's desire,

Did we together read in Spenser's lay
How Una, sad of soul—in sad attire,
The gentle Una, born of heavenly birth,
To seek her Knight went wandering over
                                        the earth.

Her hopes we shared, and
                      pleasing was the smart
The tear precious in compassion shed
For one, who, pierced by sorrow's thrilling dart,
Did meekly bear the pang unmerited;
Meek as that emblem of her lowly heart
The milk-white Lamb which in a line she led,
And faithful, loyal in her innocence,
Like the brave Lion slain in her defence.

While notes were heard
                    as of a faery shell
Attuned to words with sacred wisdom
Free Fancy prized each specious miracle,
And all its fairer inspiration caught,
Till in the bosom of our
                    rustic Cell,
We by a lamentable change were taught

[MS. 1815, 1ʳ, col. 1]

To M—W—

In trellis'd shed with clustering roses gay,
      ,⎰Mary!
And ⎱∧oft beside our blazing ~~winter~~ fire,

1 When years of wedded life were as a day
2 Whose current answers to the heart's desire,
      ~~mid~~
3 ~~Oft, in some bower with clustering roses gay,~~
4 ~~Or haply by the blazing winter fire,~~
                  ⎰r
5 Did we togethe⎱re read in Spenser's Lay
6 How Una, sad of soul—in sad attire,
7 The gentle Una, born of heavenly birth,
8 To seek her Knight went wandering oer
                              the earth:

      Her hopes we shared,—and
                  e⎱
9 ~~Ah! then, Bl⎰oved~~∧pleasing was the smart,
      ⎰T   was
10 ~~And~~ ⎱the tear∧precious in compassion shed
            one,
11 For ~~Her~~∧ , who, pierced by sorrow's thrilling dart,
12 Did meekly bear the pang unmerited;
13 Meek as that emblem of her lowly heart
14 The milk-white Lamb which in a line she led,—
15 And faithful, loyal in her innocence,
16 Like the brave Lion slain in her defence.

      While [?] notes were heard
   ⎰ ~~While notes were~~ ⎱   ⎰d
17 ⎱[?Notes did we] ~~hear~~⎰ as of a faery shell
18 Attuned to words with sacred wisdom fraught,
19 Free Fancy prized each specious miracle,
20 And all its finer inspiration caught,
      'Till in the bosom of our ~~rustic~~
                  ⎰b   ⎰'
21 ~~Mid~~∧ ~~the green~~ ⎱Bower, ~~or in our~~ rustic Cell⎱
      ⎰W   a
22 ~~'Till~~ ⎱we by∧lamentable change have taught

That bliss with mortal Man may not abide —
How nearly joy and sorrow are allied!

For us the stream of fiction ceased to flow,
For us the voice of melody was mute.
—But, as soft gales dissolve the dreary snow
And give the timid herbage leave to shoot,
Heaven's breathing influence failed not to bestow
A timely promise of unlooked-for fruit,
The fruit of pleasure and serene content
From blossoms wild of fancies innocent.

It soothed us—it beguiled us—then, to hear
Once more of troubles wrought by magic spell;
And griefs whose aery motion comes not near
The pangs that tempt the spirit to rebel;
Then, with mild Una in her sober cheer
High over hill and low adown the dell
Again we wandered, willing to partake
All that she suffered for her dear Lord's sake.

Then, too, this song of mine once more could please
Where, anguish, strange as dreams of restless sleep,
Is tempered and allayed by sympathies
Aloft ascending, and descending deep,

[MS. 1815, 1ʳ, col. 2]

                           taught

23   That "bliss with mortal Man may not abide"{ :—
24   How nearly joy and sorrow are allied!—

25   For us the stream of fiction ceased to flow,
26   For us the voice of melody was mute.
27   —But, as soft gales dissolve the dreary snow
28   And give the timid herbage leave to shoot,
                     influence
29   Heaven's breathing ~~Spirit~~ failed not to bestow
            { mise
        A timely pro{[?duce] of unlooked-for fruit,
30   ~~Its kindly influence, promising fair fruit,~~
        Fair
31   ~~The~~ ∧fruit of pleasure and serene content
32   From blossoms wild of fancies innocent.

33   It soothed us—it beguiled us—then, to hear
              troubles
34   Once more of ~~pleasures~~ wrought by magic spell;
35   And griefs whose aery motion comes not near
                   {s   {;
36   The pangs that tempt the {spirit to rebel{
37   Then, with mild Una in her sober chear
38   High over hill and low adown the dell
39   Again we wandered, willing to partake
40   All that she suffered for her dear
                            Lord's sake.

41   Then, too, this Song <u>of mine</u> once more could please,
         {re
42   Whe{n, anguish, strange as dreams of
                          restless sleep,
       tempered
43   Is ~~softened~~ and allayed by sympathies
44   Aloft ascending, and descending deep,

WHITE DOE OF RYLSTONE.

[MS. 1815, 2ʳ]

descending deep

         {T
45 Even to the inferior Kinds; whom forest {trees
46 Protect from beating sunbeams, and the sweep
        {;—
47 Of the sharp winds{ fair Creatures!—to whom Heaven
           {th
48 A calm and sinless life, with love, ha{s given.
49 This tragic Story cheared us; for it speaks
           {;
50 Of female patience winning firm repose{ /
          s}c
51 And of the recompense which conc{ ˄ience seeks
          {;
52 A bright, encouraging example shows{ /
53 Needful when oer wide realms the tempest breaks,
54 Needful amid life's ~~ordin~~[?] ordinary woes;—
55 Hence, not for them unfitted who would bless
56 A happy hour with holier happiness.

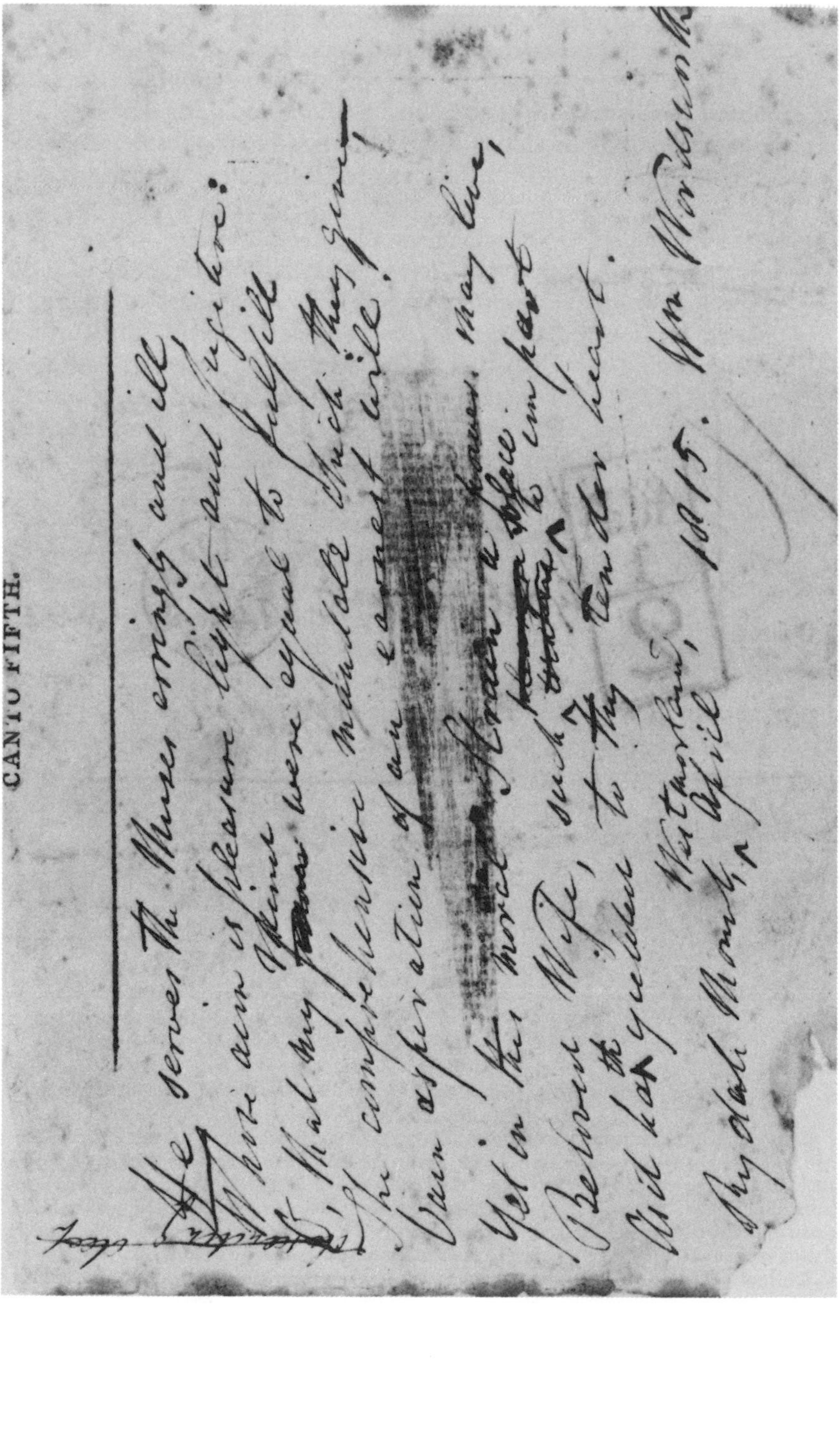

[MS. 1815, 3ʳ]

descending deep

57 He serves the Muses erringly and ill,
58 Whose aim is pleasure light and fugitive:
                Mind
59 O, that my power were equal to fulfill
60 The comprehensive mandate which they give⌉,
61 Vain aspiration of our earnest will!
62 Yet in this moral Strain a power may live,
                    pleasure solace
63 Beloved Wife, such∧[?virtue]∧to impart
                th
                ∧
64 As it ha⌉s yielded to thy tender heart.
            Westmorland,
    Rydale Mount,∧April   1815.   Wᵐ Wordsworth

The White Doe of Rylstone
Fair-Copy Verse Passages: DC MSS. 61 and 62

The following transcriptions and *apparatus criticus* of DC MSS. 61 and 62 present the portions of fair copy of *The White Doe* that survive from the period of composition preceding Coleridge's criticisms in 1808 and Wordsworth's subsequent withdrawal of the poem from the publisher (see Introduction, pp. 31–37).

MS. 61 is described above (p. 185). MS. 62 consists of remnants of what was pretty clearly the manuscript sent to Coleridge in the spring of 1808 for publication by Longman; the manuscript was later taken apart and its pages were scrambled, discarded, and in part rejoined as Wordsworth used blank versos for work on *Vaudracour and Julia* in 1819, preparatory to MS. C of *The Prelude*. On the rectos of the twenty whole leaves and four stubs that survive of the original manuscript, Mary entered fair copy of *The White Doe,* and she numbered the surviving rectos of the restitched portion of the manuscript (in their present order of binding) 67–69, 56, 25–26, 28–36, 36 (misnumbered). William's hand appears on the verso of the second page 36 and page 41. Two bifolia—an unstitched gathering of four which stab holes show to have once been part of the main manuscript—were left separate when the other leaves were restitched; Mary's numbering of these recto pages was 40 to 43. Two gatherings of four survive within the restitched portion; they are formed by the leaves numbered 28 to 31 and 34 to the second 36. The leaves numbered 25 and 26 are a bifolium, and the leaves numbered 32, 33, 56, and 69 have stub conjugates.

Leaves measure approximately 15.9 by 20.3 centimeters. Paper is white and laid, with chain lines approximately 2.4 centimeters apart; it is watermarked with a Britannia, seated, within a crowned oval medallion and countermarked GOLDING / & / SNELGROVE / 1806.

After Coleridge penciled some notes on page 43 and the facing verso of the original manuscript, revised fair copy was entered on that verso, on the verso of page 41 (facing p. 42), and the verso of 43, and these three versos were numbered with the numbers of the pages facing them—42, 43, and 44. The supplementary pages 42, 43, and 44 are editorially foliated 42a, 43a, and 44a.

About half of the fair copy of *The White Doe* in MS. 62 follows the point at which the earlier stage of work, in MS. 61, breaks off. Where the contents of the two manuscripts overlap, the readings of MS. 62 are reported in an *apparatus criticus* to the transcription of MS. 61; the rest of MS. 62 is presented in full transcription. To help the reader follow the early form of the poem as it survives in these two manuscripts, line numbers are provided in the left margins, running sequentially through the text in both manuscripts. The numbers run without interruption in MS. 61 from 1 to 419; the poet's own marginal tally allows confident assignment of numbers in the same sequence to succeeding pieces of text: 482–497 in MS. 62, 498–733 in MS. 61, 800–888 in MS. 62. Numbers thus derived from Wordsworth's count are printed in italics. The concluding fragments in MS. 62 follow a gap of undeterminable length, so these large-type lines simply carry within brackets the numbers of the corresponding lines in the final text of the first edition (1815). Elsewhere the pertinent 1815 line numbers, also in brackets, are entered at the upper right of each page of transcription. Lines from the post-Coleridge work in this manuscript, entered when the manuscript was still being kept neat as possible printer's copy, appear on pages 42a, 43a, and 44a; they are unnumbered and in small type, but again the pertinent 1815 numbers are carried in brackets at the upper right.

The *apparatus criticus* records all variants in the text of MS. 62 from the numbered base text of MS. 61 where the two texts overlap except for single-letter miswritings in MS. 62 corrected by the copyist and for the exchange of "and" for the ampersand and vice versa.

Part 1ˢᵗ

The °ld morning bells from Bolton f—
~~From Bolton~~ old monastie
~~Are speaking with~~ ~~into watery~~ hour
~~The bells sung load with~~
The sun is bright the fields are gay

With people in their best array
                          hood
Of stole & doublet ~~hose~~ & scarf

Along the banks of the crystal Wha

Through the vale retired & lowly

Trooping to that Summer holy

And up among the m inlands see

What sprinklings of blithe company

Of Lasses & of Shepperd-grooms

That down the steep hills force their way

Like cattle through the budded brooms

Path or no path what care they

Part 1ˢᵗ   *1*

    al
1   *The ~~morning bells from~~ Bolton tower*
    From Boltons old monastic
            Tower
2   *~~Are speaking with a voice of power~~*
    The Bells ring loud with glad
              some [?power]
3   *The sun is bright the fields are gay*
4   *With people in their best array*
           hood
5   *Of stole & doublet, ~~hose~~ & scarf*
6   *Along the banks of the crystal Wharf*
          the
        {the   {lowly
7   *Through* {a   *vale retired &* {holy
        {at
8   *Trooping to th*\e *summons holy*
9   *And up among the moorlands see*
10   *What sprinklings of blithe company*
11   *Of Lasses & of Shepperd-grooms*
12   *That down the steep hills force their way*
13   *Like Cattle through the budded brooms*
14   *Path or no path what care they*

The copyist is MW, through 6ᵛ.

And thus in joyous mood they hie
To Bolton's mould'ring Priory

What would they there? full fifty
                        till its noble
That Pile with ~~hundred of its~~ Peers
~~That sunbeams Pile unroll'd so~~
Too harshly hath been doom'd to taste
The bitterness of wrong & waste
Its courts are ravaged but the Tower
Is standing with a voice of power
That ancient voice ~~that~~ wont to call
To mass or some high Festival
And in the ~~Prior~~ head
Remaineth one protected part
A rural chapel neatly drest
In covert like a little nest

2

15 *And thus in joyous mood they hie*
16 *To Bolton's mould'ring Priory*

17 *What would they there? full fifty years*
        all its stately
18 *That Pile with* ~~hundred of~~ *its Peers*
        That sumptuous Pile with all its [? Peers]
19 *Too harsly hath been doom'd to taste*
20 *The bitterness of wrong & waste*
                    the
21 *Its courts are ravaged but* ~~its~~ *Tower*
22 *Is standing with a voice of power*
                w⎱ ⎰ich
23 *That ancient voice t* ⎰h⎱*at wont to call*
24 *To mass or some high festival*
                    ⎰ F
        shatter'd ⎱[?f]abrics
                    l
25 *And in the* ~~Ruins mould'ring~~ *heart*
26 *Remaineth one protceted part*
27 *A rural chapel neatly drest*
28 *In Covert like a little nest*

And thither young and old repair
This Sabbath-day for praise & prayer

First the Church-yard fills—anon
Look again and ~~they~~ all are gone
The cluster round the Porch & the folk
That sate in the shade of the Prior Oak
~~And scarcely have~~
~~All like these~~ have disappeared
~~one~~
~~And~~ the prelusive hymn is heard
With one consent the People rejoice
Filling the Church with a lofty voice
~~For all~~ ~~~~~~~~~~~~~~~~~~~~~~~~~~~~~~
~~~~~~~~ who are there join
In great ~~~~~~~~—golden times
~~~~~~ moment ends
~~Now have they ceased~~ their fervent dirge
And all is hush'd without & within
For though the Priest with calmer glee

3

29   *And thither young and old repair—*
30   *This Sabbath-day for praise & prayer*

31   *Fast the Church-yard fills—anon*
              they
32   *Look again and*ˬ*all are gone*
33   *The cluster round the Porch & the folk*
34   *That sate in the shade of the Priors Oak*
              ⌠But
              ⌡And scarcely have
35   *A̶l̶l̶ ̶l̶i̶k̶e̶ ̶F̶a̶r̶i̶e̶s̶ have disappeared*
              Ere
36   *A̶n̶d̶ the prelusive hymn is heard*
37   *With one consent the People rejoice*
38   *Filling the Church with a lofty voice*
              They sing a service which they feel
              For tis the sunrise now of Zeal
39   *F̶o̶r̶ ̶p̶i̶e̶t̶y̶ ̶w̶a̶s̶ ̶i̶n̶ ̶i̶t̶s̶ ̶p̶r̶i̶m̶e̶*
              And Faith and hope are thier prime
40   *In great Eliza's golden time*

              A
              O̶n̶e̶ moment ends
41   *N̶o̶w̶ ̶h̶a̶v̶e̶ ̶t̶h̶e̶y̶ ̶c̶e̶a̶s̶e̶d̶ their fervent din*
42   *And all is hush'd without & within*
43   *For though the Priest with calmer glee*

4

Begins the holy Liturgy

You cannot hear his voice—'tis drown'd

In the neighbouring Rivers sound.

When, soft! the dusky trees between

And down the path through the open green

Where is no living thing to be seen

And through the gate which is the bound

Of the Church-yards private ground

And right across the verdant sod

Towards the very house of God

Comes gliding in with lovely gleam

Comes gliding in serene & slow

Soft and silent as a dream

A solitary Doe

                 4
44   *Begins the holy liturgy*
45   *You cannot hear his voice—'tis drown'd*
46   *In the neighbouring Rivers sound*
47   *When, soft! the dusky trees between*
48   *And down the path through the open green*
49   *Where is no living thing to be seen*
50   *And through the gate which is the bound*
51   *Of the Church-yards private ground*
52   *And right across the verdant sod*
53   *Towards the very house of God*
54   *Comes gliding in with lovely gleam*
55   *Comes gliding in serene & slow*
56   *Soft and silent as a dream*

57   *A {ˢSolitary Doe*

White she is as lilly of June

And beauteous as the silver moon

When out of sight the clouds are driven

And she is left alone in heaven

Or like a Ship, some gentle day

In sunshine sailing far away

A glittering Ship that hath the plain

Of Ocean for her own domain

Lie silent in your graves ye dead

Lie quiet in your church-yard bed

Ye living tend your holy cares

Ye multitude pursue your prayers

And blame not me if my heart & sight

Be occupied with one delight

58	*White she is a* ⟨*s*⟩ ⟨*l* *Lilly of June*⟩ ⁵
59	*And beauteous as the silver moon*
60	*When out of sight the clouds are driv'n*
61	*And she is left alone in heaven*
62	*Or like a Ship, some gentle day*
63	*In sunshine sal*⟨*i*⟩*ling far away*
64	*A glittering Ship that hath the plain*
65	*Of Ocean for her own domain*
66	*Lie silent in your graves ye dead*
67	*Lie quiet in your Church-yard bed*
68	*Ye living tend your holy cares*
69	*Ye multitude pursue your prayers*
70	*And blame not me if* ⟨*my* [?*your*]⟩ *heart & sight*
71	*Are occupied with one delight*

Tis a work for Sabbath hours
If I with this bright creature go
Whether she be of forest bowers
Of the bowers of earth below
Or a Spirit for one day giv'n
A gift of grace from purest heaven
What harmonious pensive changes
Wait upon her as she ranges
Round and through this Pile of state
Overthrown and desolate
Now a step or two her way
Is through space of open day
Where the enamoured sunny light
Brightens her that was so bright
Now doth a delicate shadow fall

> 6
> 72 *Tis a work for Sabbath hours*
> 73 *If I with this bright creature go*
> 74 *Whether she be of forest bowers*
> 75 *Of the bowers of earth below*
> 76 *Or a Spirit for one day giv'n*
> 77 *A gift of grace from purest heaven*
> 78   *What harmonious pensive changes*
> 79 *Wait upon her as she ranges*
> 80 *Round and through this Pile of state*
> 81 *Overthrown and desolate*
> 82 *Now a step or two her way*
>
> 83 *Is through space of o{[?]en day*
> 84 *Where the enamoured sunny light*
> 85 *Brightens her that was so bright*
> 86 *Now doth a delicate shadow fall*

7

Falls upon her like a breath
From some lofty arch or wall
As she passes underneath

Now some gloomy nook partakes
Of the glory that she makes

High-ribb'd Vault of stone, or cell

With perfect cunning frani'd as well

Of stone & Ivy & the spread

Of the elder's bushy head

Some jealous & forbidding cell

That doth the living stars repel

And where no Flower hath leave to

The presence of this Milk-white Doe

Fills many a damp obscure recess

With radiance of a saintly shew

7

87   *Falls upon her like a breath*
88   *From some lofty arch or wall*
89   *As she passes underneath*
90   *Now some gloomy nook partakes*
91   *Of the glory that she makes*
92   *High-ribb'd va⎰u⎰llt o[?r]⎰f⎱ stone, or cell*
93   *With perfect cunning fram'd as well*
94   *Of stone & Ivy & the spread*
95   *Of the elder's bushy head*
96   *Some jealous & forbidding cell*
97   *That doth the living stars repel*
98   *And where no Flower hath leave to dwell*

99   *The presence of this Milk-white Doe*
100   *Fills many a damp obscure res⎰c⎱ess*
101   *With radiance of a saintly shew*

---

88   Apparently omitted by mistake, then crowded in.

And re-appearing, she no less

To the open day gives blessedness

But say amongst these holy places

Which thus assiduously she paces

Comes she with a Votary's task

Rite to perform or boon to ask

Fair Pilgrim! harbours she a sense

Of sorrow or of reverence

Are she be grieved for guine or sh

Crush'd as if by wrath divine

by what

What survives of house where God

Was worshipp'd or where Planab

Of magnificence undone

Or the gentler work begun.

8

102	*And re-appearing, she no less*
103	*To the open day gives blessedness*
104	*But say amongst these holy places*
105	*Which thus assiduously she paces*
106	*Comes she with a Votary's task*
107	*Rite to perform or boon to ask*

                                    !⎫
108   *Fair Pilgrim* ⎰ *harbours she a sense*
109   *Of sorrow or of reverence*

              n ⎫
110   *Ca[?]*⎰ *she be grieved for quire or shrine*
            Cr⎫
111   *[?]*⎰*ush'd as if by wrath divine*
                For what
112   *W̶h̶a̶t̶* ∧*survives of house where God*
113   *Was worshipp'd or where Man abode*
              l ⎫
114   *O[?f]*⎰*d magnificence undone*
                    w ⎫
115   *Or the gentler [?l]*⎰*ork begun*

9

By nature softening & concealing.
And busy with the hand of healing
The altar whence the cross was rent
Now rich with mossy ornament
The dormitory's length laid bare
Where the wild-rose blossoms fair
And sapling ash whose place of birth
Is that lordly chamber hearth
There low now he lurketh but proud will he
When the North wind shall rock him afar
                                    spread by the
He sees a Warrior carv'd in stone
Among the thick weeds stretch'd alone
A Warrior with his shield of pride
Leaving humbly to his side
And hands in resignation press'd

9

116 *By nature softening & concealing*

     a
117 *And busy with ~~the~~ hand of healing*
118 *The altar whence the cross was rent*
119 *Now rich with mossy ornament*
120 *The dormitory's lenght laid bare*
121 *Where the wild-rose blossom's fair*
122 *And sapling ash whose place of birth*
123 *Is that lordly chamber hearth*
124 *There low now he lurketh but proud will he*
                be
125 *When the North wind shall rock him a far-*
             spreading tree
126 *She sees a Warrior carv'd in stone*
127 *Among the thick weeds stretch'd alone*
128 *A warrior with his shield of pride*
129 *Cleaving humbly to his side*
130 *And hands in resignation press'd*

Palm to palm on his ~~soft~~ tranquil breast

Methinks she passeth by the sight

As a common creature might

If she be doom'd to inward care

Or service it must lie elsewhere

But here are ~~are~~ eyes serenely bright

And on she moves with pace so lightly

Nor spares to stoop her head ~~to taste~~ and

The dewy turf with flowers bestrewn

And in this way she fares, till at last

~~Beside~~ the ridge of a grassy grave

In quietness she lays her down

Gently as a weary wave

Sinks when the summer breeze hath

died

11

tranquil

131   *Palm to palm on his ~~open~~ breast*
132   *Methinks she passeth by the sight*
133   *As a common Creature might*
134   *If she be doom'd to inward care*
135   *Or service it must lie elsewhere*

        {are
136   *But hers {—her eyes serenely bright*

                      { pace how light }
137   *And on she moves with {[?paces light]}*

                          and
138   *Nor spares to stoop her head ~~to~~ taste*

                      o}
139   *The dewy turf with flowers bestre}wn*
140   *And in this way she fares, till at last*

            d }
141   *Beside the ri[?g]}ge of a grassy grave*
142   *In quietness she lays her down*
143   *Gently as a weary wave*
144   *Sinks when the summer breeze hath*
                              died

MW's page number should have been "10"; from here on, through 13ᵛ, her numbers overshoot by one.

12

Against an anchor'd Vessel's side
Even so without distress doth she
Lie down in peace & lovingly

This day is warm quiet in its going
As its tranquil measures bound
Is the River in its flowing,
Can there be a softer sound?

So the balmy minutes pass
While this radiant creature lies
Couched upon the sacred grass
Pensively with downcast eyes

When now again the people rear
A voice of praise with awful cheer
It is the last the parting song
And from the Temple forth they throng

12

145   *Against an anchor'd Vessel's side*
146   *Even so without distress doth she*

                              i ⎫
147   *Lie down in peace & love*⎬*ngly*

                    e   placid
148   *This day is ~~quiet~~ in its going*
                    as
149   *To ~~its~~ tranquil measures bound*
150   *As the River in its flowing,*
                    ⎰*e*
151   *Can thei*⎱*r be a softer sound?*
152   *So the balmy minutes pass*
153   *While this radiant Creature lies*
154   *Couched upon the sacred grass*
155   *Pensively with downcast eyes*
156   *When now again the people rear*
                              ⎰*C*
157   *A voice of praise with awful*⎱*chear*
158   *It is the last the parting song*
159   *And from the Temple forth they throng*

---

151   In revision the "i" was made to serve as an "r"; thus "their" became "there."

13.

And quickly spread themselves abroad

Each pursues in search of

But some a variegated band

Of middle-aged & old & young

And little children by the hand

                    Green boughs
Upon their leading brothers hung

Turn with ~~serious~~ gladly paid

Towards the spot where full in view

The ~~famous~~ Doe of Whitest hue

Her sabbath couch hath made

It was a solitary mound

Which two spears length of level

Did from all other graves divide

As if in some respect of pride

13

160 *And quickly spread themselves abroad*
        ⎰While
161 ⎱*Each each pursues his several road*
162 *But some a variegated band*
163 *Of middle-aged & old & young*
164 *And little children by the hand*
               ~~Grandsires~~
165 *Upon their leading ~~Mothers~~ hung*
          obeisance
166 *Turn with ~~devotion~~ gladly paid*
167 *Towards the spot where full in view*
        ~~Peerless~~ lovely
168 *The ~~famous~~ Doe of whitest hue*
169 *Her Sabbath couch hath made*

170   *It was a solitary mound*
171 *Which two spears length of level ground*
172 *Did from all other graves divide*
173 *As if in some respect of pride*

---

161 MW left a gap for a line that WW wrote in.

Two stubs follow, with no interruption in the text. Scraps of writing visible on the stubs indicate that MW's transcription ran through at least three more pages before being cut out and supplanted by DW's.

14

Or sorrow that retains her mood,
Still shy of human brotherhood
Or guilt that humbly would express
A penitential loneliness.

"Look there she is, my Child, draw
                                near
She fears not, wherefore should we fear?
She means no harm" but still the Boy
To whom the words were softly said
Hung back, & smiled, & blushed with joy
A shame-facid blushing glowing red
The thing he dreamt of was fulfilled
He look'd again, & his heart was still,
Again the Mother whisper'd low,
                         have   anew
"Now have you   seen the
From Rilstone she hath found her way
Over the hills this sabbath day
Her work, whate'er it be, is done
And she will depart when we are
                                    gone

174   *Or sorrow that retains her mood,*
175   *Still shy of human brotherhood*
176   *Or guilt that humbly would express*
177   *A penitential loneliness.*

178   *"Look there she is, my Child, draw*
                                       near,
179   *She fears not, wherefore should we fear?*
180   *She means no harm" but still the Boy*
181   *To whom the words were softly said*
182   *Hung back, & smiled, & blush'd with joy*
183   *A shame-fac'd blush of glowing red,*
184   *The thing he dreamt of was fulfill'd*
185   *He look'd again, & his heart was still'd.*
186   *Again the Mother whisper'd low,*
                                  famous
                     have   ｆfamous
187   *"Now ~~have~~ you⋀seen the* ⎰*milk white Doe*
                                  ⋀
188   *From Rillestone she hath found her way*
189   *Over the hills this sabbath day*
190   *Her work, whate'er it be, is done*
191   *And she will depart when we are*
                                       gone

Using rectos only, DW carried transcription on through the remainder of MS. 61.

16

Thus doth she keep from year to year
Her sabbath morning, foul or fair,
This knows the blissful Boy full well
This knows the Country far & near
But, Matron, there is more to tell
For certes, if I rightly trace
The characters of every face

A thousand earnest thoughts are here
An ample creed of love and fear
Repose of heart, and truth that sees
A world of fond remembrances

And likewise here are fancies strong
That do the gentle Creature wrong
That loaded staff supported she
Who in his youth hath —————
Full cradled —— old tales ——
That Old Mans mind, I guess, hath been
                                           turn'd
To days far off, hath mounted high
To Albemarle & Romilly

When Lady Aaliza mourn'd
Her Son, & felt in her despair

192 *Thus doth she keep from year to year*

193 *Her sabbath morning, foul or fair,*⸣
　　a paragraph
194 ∧*This knows the blissful Boy full well*
195 *This knows the Country far & near*
196 *But, Matron!, there is more to tell*
197 *For, certes, if I rightly trace*
198 *The characters of every face*
199 *A thousand earnest thoughts are here*
200 　　*An ample creed of love and fear*
201 *Repose of heart, and truth that sees*
　　　　　　　　d ⸣
202 *A world of fon[?]*⸥ *remembrances*
203 *And likewise here are fancies strong*
204 *That do the gentle Creature wrong.*
　　　　　　That bearded staff-supported Sire
　　　　　Who in his youth hath often fed
　　　　　Full chearily on Convent bread
　　　　　And heard old tales by the kitchen fire
205 *That Old Man's mind, I guess, hath*
　　　　　　　　　　　　　turn'd
206 *To days far off, hath mounted high*
207 *To Albemarle & Romilly*
208 *When Lady Aaliza mourn'd*
209 *Her Son, & felt in her despair*

---

200 Apparently omitted by mistake, then crowded in.
204/205 WW crowded his lines into the space between two paragraphs.

18

The pang of unavailing prayer,
Her Son in Wharf's abysses drown'd,
The noble Boy of Egremound:
From which affliction when God's grace
At length had in her heart found
                      place
A pious Structure fair to see
Rose up, this stately Priory,
The Lady's work, but now laid low
To the grief of her soul that doth
                come & go
In the beautiful Form of her walk
                      -white Doe-

Pass, ~~ye~~ he who will the Chauntry door
And thro' the chink in the practured floor
Look down, & see a grisly sight,
A Vault where the Bodies are inned up
                    right
There face by face, & hand by hand
The Clapham's & Mauleverers stand,
And in his place among Son & Sire

210   *The pang of unavailing prayer,*
211   *Her Son in Wharf's abysses drown'd,*
212   *The noble Boy of Egremound.*
213   *From which affliction when God's grace*
214   *At length had in her heart found*
                                   place
215   *A pious Structure fair to see*
216   *Rose up, this stately Priory,*
217   *The Lady's work, but now laid low*
218   *To the grief of her soul that doth*
                              come & go
219   *In the beautiful Form of this milk-*
                              -white Doe.

               he
220   *Pass, ~~ye~~ who will, the Chauntry door*
221   *And thro' the chink in the fractured floor*
222   *Look down, & see a grisly sight,*
223   *A Vault where the Bodies are buried up=*
                              =right
224   *These face by face, & hand by hand*
225   *The claphams & Mauleverers stand,*
226   *And in his place among Son & Sire*

To John de Clapham, that fierce Esquire
A valiant Man, & a name of dread
In the unhappy Wars of the White & Red,
Who dragg'd Earl Pembroke from
                                    Banbury Church
And smote off his head on the stones of the Porch.
Look down & thro' the pavements see
A glimpse of this dismal Family
Look down among them if you dare
The white Doe oft is peeping there
And for no good — A Dame of blood
Thinks thus, that Dame with the
                                    haughtly air
Who hath a Page her book to hold
And wears a Frontlet edged with gold

A   by birth and she

Loves not the   q   of Bellingsley

That slender Youth, a Scholar
                                    pale
From Oxford come to his vacation

227   *Is John de Clapham, that fierce Esquire,*
228   *A valiant Man, & a name of dread*
229   *In the ruthless Wars of the White & Red,*
230   *Who dragg'd Earl Pembroke from*
                                Banbury Church
231   *And smote off his head on the stones of the Porch.*
          ⌈& thro' the pavement see
232   *Look down ⌊among them if you dare*
233   *A glimpse of this dismal Family*
234   *Look down among them if you dare*
235   *The white Doe oft is peeping there*
236   *And for no good—A Dame of blood*
237   *Thinks thus, that Dame with the*
                                haughty air

A   by birth and she
Loves not the Hall of Bethmesley.

That slender Youth, a Scholar pale
From Oxford come to his native Vale
           a⌉
He [?]⌊lso hath his own conceit
It is, thinks he, the gracious Fairy

                                          ⌈hold
238   *Who hath a Page her book to ⌊bear*
239   *And wears a Frontlet edged with gold*
240   *A   by birth and she*
241   *Loves not the ̶[̶?̶]̶ of Bethmesley*

242   *That slender Youth a Scholar p̶a̶l̶*
                                pale
243   *From Oxford come to his native Va*

The revision attached by the stitched-on slip was written before transcription resumed on 13ʳ. The photograph shows the stitch-on in place.

241–242   Deletions by erasure.

He also hath his own conceit.
It is, thinks he, the gracious Fairy
Who loved the Shepherd Lord to meet
In his wanderings solitary
And taught him signs, & shew'd him
                                        sights
In Craven's dens, on Cumbria's Heights
When under cloud of fear he lay,
A Shepherd clad in homely grey,
Nor left him at his later day
And hence when he with spear
                              and shield
Rode full of years to Flodden field
His eye could see the hidden spring
And how the current was to flow,
The fatal end of Scotland's King,
And all that hopeless overthrow
But not in wars did he delight
This Clifford wish'd for worthier
                                    might

244   *He also hath his own conceit*
245   *It is, thinks he, the gracious Fairy*
246   *Who loved the Shepherd Lord to meet*
247   *In his wanderings solitary*
248   *And taught him signs, & shew'd him*
                        sights
                 {D
249   *In Craven's* {*dens, on Cumbria's Heights*
250   *When under cloud of fear he lay,*
251   *A Shepherd clad in homely grey,*
252   *Nor left him at his later day*
253   *And hence when he with spear*
                 and shield
254   *Rode full of years to Flodden Field*
255   *His eye could see the hidden springs*
256   *And how the current was to flow,*
257   *The fatal end of Scotland's King,*
258   *And all that hopeless overthrow.*
259   *But not in wars did he delight*
260   *This Clifford wish'd for worthier*
                        might

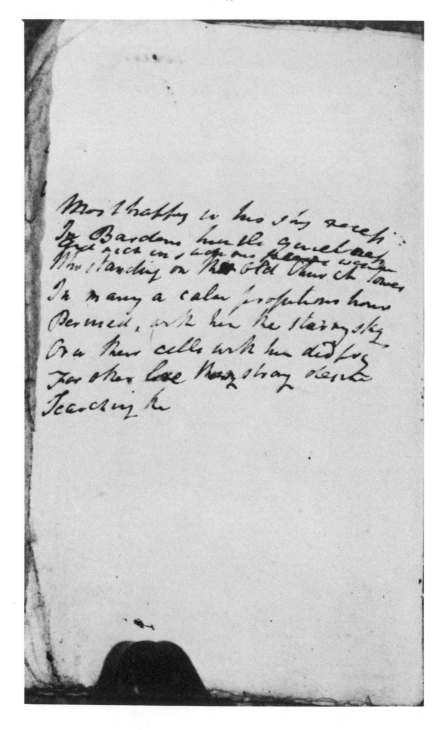

Most happy to his smiling reach

The Bardens have the genial each

[illegible]

Now standing on the old church tower

In many a calm propitious hour

Bermind, with him the starry sky

Or a these cells with him did [illegible]

For other love they stray desire

Searching he

Most happy in his shy recess
In Bardens humble quietness
    And rich in studious friends was he
                 {e
Who standing on th{is Old Church Tower
In many a calm propitious hour
Perused, with him the starry sky
Or in their cells with him did pry
            {[?]
For other lore th{eir strong desire
Searching the

These lines revise text on the facing recto, 14ʳ.

Nor in broad pomp or courtly state

From his own thoughts did elevate

~~But happy in his forest Bower~~

The ^choiceless o^ ~~lady of Border~~ ~~Love~~

And ^choice^ ~~many~~ studious friends had he

^In^ Bolton's dear Fraternity

~~Who standing on his old Churchyard Tower~~
~~Who may at each that fallons hours~~
~~Who read with him the starry sky~~

~~Or did for other knowledge pry~~

~~In mutual help & strong desire~~

Searching the earth with cheering ^fire^

But they & their good works are fled

And all is now disquieted,

And peace is none for living or
^dead.^

Ah! pensive Scholar, think not so

But look again at that radi-
:ant Doe

261   *Nor in broad pomp or courtly state*
262   *Him his own thoughts did elevate,*
263   *~~Most happy in his private Bower,~~*
            choice o
264   *The ~~humble lodge of Barden~~ Tower.*
            choice of
265   *And ~~many~~ ⋀studious Friends had he*
            In
        ⌠ ~~Of~~
266   ⌡*In Bolton's dear Fraternity*
                        ⌠on
        Who standing ⌡in this old Church Tower
        In many a calm propitious hour
267   *Who read with him the starry sky,*
268   *~~Or did for other knowledge pry~~*
269   *~~In mutual help & strong desire~~*
                                    ⌠c
270   *Searching the earth with chemy*⌡*'d*
                                    fire
            ey⌉
271   *But this*⌡ *& their good works are fled*
272   *And all is now disquieted,*
273   *And peace is none for living or*
                                    dead.

274   *Ah! pensive Scholar, think not so*
275   *But look again at the radi=*
                        =ant Doe

263–270 Revised on the facing verso, 13ᵛ.

What quiet watch she seems to keep
Alone beside that grassy heap:

Why mention other thoughts unmeet
For a vision that is so sweet
While stand the people in a ring,
Gazing, doubting, questioning,
~~Yes many over come in shelter~~
~~of so called as any clear & bright~~
~~but doth it unto some impart~~
Which yet do unto some impart
An undisturb'd repose of heart

~~While ~~~~~~~~~~~~~~~~~~~~~~~~~~~~~
~~'love over the through high sight~~
And all the Assembly own a law
Of orderly respect & awe
To a superior Presence due

But

276   *What quiet watch she seems to keep*
277   *Alone beside that grassy heap.*

278   *Why mention other thoughts unmeet*
279   *For a vision that is so sweet*
280   *While stand the people in a ring,*
281   *Gazing, doubting, questioning,*
                Yea many over come in spite
                Of recollections clear & bright
282   *~~Yet doth it unto some impart~~*
                Which yet do unto some impart
283   *An undisturb'd repose of heart*
284   *~~While recollections clear & bright~~*
285   *~~Consecrate the tranquil sight~~*
286   *And all the Assembly own a law*
287   *Of orderly respect & awe*
288   *To a superior Presence due.*
        ~~But~~

288/   Deletion by erasure.

But now they dwindle to a few
These also vanish one by one
And, last, the Doe herself is gone
.

Harp sound the truth upon thy
                            strings
For a Spirit with angel wings
Is near us, & a Spirits' hand;
A Voice is with thee, a command
To chaunt in strains of heavenly
                        glory
A tale of tears, a mortal story.

The Harp in lowliness obey'd
And first we sang of the green
                        wood shade
And a solitary Maid,
Beginning where the Song must
                        end

289   *But now they dwindle to a few*
290   *These also vanish one by one*
291   *And, last, the Doe herself is gone.*

292   *Harp sound the truth upon thy*
                            strings
293   *For a Spirit with angel wings*
294   *Is near us, & a Spirit's hand;*
295   *A Voice is with thee, a command*
296   *To chaunt in strains of heavenly*
                            glory

        ⎧*t*
297   *A* ⎨*Tale of tears, a mortal story.*

298   *The Harp in lowliness obey'd,*

                   g ⎤
299   *And first we san[?]*⎦ *of the green=*
                        =wod shade
300   *And a solitary Maid,*
301   *Beginning where the Song must*
                        end

---

298 By entering a line number, "20," at the top of 18ʳ, WW converted DW's line space here into the beginning of Part II.

With her & with her sylvan Friend
The Friend who stood before her sight,
Her only unextinguish'd light,
Her last upholder, in a dearth
Of love upon a hopeless earth.

For She it was, the Maid who
   Meekly with foreboding wrought
In vermile colours & in gold,
An unbless'd work, which stand=
   Her Father did with joy behold,
Exulting in the imagery,
   A Banner, one that did fulfil
Too perfectly his headstrong will
For on this Banner had her hand
Embroider'd (such was the comma

302   *With her & with her sylvan Friend,*
303   *The Friend who stood before her sight,*
304   *Her only unextinguish'd light,*
305   *Her last upholder, in a dearth*
306   *Of love upon a hopeless earth.*

307   ⌈For She it was,⌉
       ⌊*She was it, even*⌋ *this Maid who*
                  wrought
308   *Meekly, with foreboding thought*
309   *In vermile Colours & in gold,*
310   *An unbless'd work, which stand=*
                  =ing by,
311   *Her Father did with joy behold,*
312   *Exulting in the imagery,*
313   *A Banner, one thad⌋ did fulfil*
314   *Too perfectly his headstrong will*
315   *For on this Banner had her hand*
316   *Embroider'd (such was the command)*

The sacred Cross, & pictured there
The five dear wounds our Lord did bear,
Full soon to be uplifted high,
And float in rueful company.

'Twas ~~tost~~ the time when England's
                                    Queen
Ten years had reign'd, a sovereign
Nor yet the restless   dread,
~~~~ 'd upon her virgin head
But ~~~~ now the early-wakened
~~~~   North
Was ripe to send her thousands forth,
A potent Vassalage, to fight
In Percy's & in Neville's right,
Two Earls fast leagued in discon-
                                    :tent
Who gave their wishes open vent,

317 20 *The sacred Cross, & figured there*
318   *The five dear wounds our Lord did bear*
319   *Full soon to be uplifted high,*
320   *And float in rueful company.*

              It was
321   *~~'Twas now~~ the time when England's*
                                  Queen
322   *Ten years had reign'd, a̶s̶ Sovereign*
                                  dread,
              Nor yet the restless
323   *~~Yet oftentimes the~~ Crown had been*
324   *Disturb'd upon her virgin head*
              But ~~now~~ now the inly-working
325   *~~And once again the~~   North*
326   *Was ripe to send her thousands forth,*
327   *A potent Vassalage, to fight*
328   *In Percy's & in Neville's right,*
329   *Two Earls fast leagued in discon=*
                                  =tent—
330   *Who gave their wishes open vent,*

And boldly urged a general plea
The rites of ancient piety,
To be by force of arms renewed,
Glad prospect for the multitude
And that same Banner on whose
                                    breast
The blameless Lady had express'd
40 Memorials chosen to give life
And sunshine to the dangerous strife
This Banner, waiting for the Call
Stood quietly in Rilstone Hall.

It came, and Francis Norton wm̄
O Father! rise not in this fray
The hairs are white upon your head
Dear Father hear me when I say
Tis for you too late a day

331   *And boldly urged a general plea*
332   *The rites of ancient piety,*
333   *To be by force of arms renewed,*
334   *Glad prospect for the multitude*
335   *And that same Banner on whose*
                                            breast
336   *The blameless Lady had express'd*
337 40 *Memorials chosen to give life*
                            a
338   *And sunshine to* ~~the~~ ∧ *dangerous strife,*
339   *This Banner, waiting for the Call*
340   *Stood quietly in Rillestone Hall.*

341   *It came, and Francis Norton said*
342   *O Father! rise not in this fray*
343   The hairs *are white upon your head*
344   Dear Father hear me when I say
345   It is for you too late a day

Bethink you of your own good name?
Just and gracious Queen Maria,
Pure religion, and the claim
Of peace on ours humanity
    That tenders your scorn

I am your Son your eldest born
But not for Lordship or for land
Thy Father do I clasp your knees,
The banner touch not, stay your hand
This multitudes of men disband
And live at home in blessful ease
For these my Brethrens sake forme
And most of all for Emily   60

Loud noise was in the crowded Hall
And scarcely could the Father hear
That name which had a dying
                    fall,

346   Bethink you of your own good name!
347   A just and gracious Queen have we,
348   A pure religion, and the claim
349   Of peace on our humanity
350   Tis meet that I endure your scorn
351   I am your Son your eldest born
                    L⎫
352   But not for l⎰ordship or for land
353   My Father do I clasp your knees
354   The banner touch not, stay your hand
355   This multitude of men disband
356   And live at home in blissful ease
357   For these my Brethren's sake for me
                                    60
358   And most of all for Emily

359   *Loud noise was in the crowded Hall*
360   *And scarcely could the Father hear*
361   *That name which had a dying*
                        fall,

---

350   WW left a space for the line, and later wrote it in.

The name it ~~was~~ of his Daughter dear
And on the Banner which stood near
He glanced a look of holy pride
And his wet eyes were glorified.
Then seiz'd the Staff; & thus did
"Thou, Richard, bear'st thy Father's
Keep thou this Ensign till the day
When I of thee ~~demand~~ the same
Thy place be on my better
And serven as true as Thou I
Will cleave to this good cause
~~He spake~~." & eight brave sons
All follow'd him, a gallant
when Sire & sons appear'd
A Shout, a ~~lofty~~ shout was rear'd
With din of arms & minstrelsy
&c

only
362   *The name* ~~it was~~ *of his*∧*Daughter dear*
363   *And on the Banner which stood near*
364   *He glanced a look of holy pride,*
365   *And his wet eyes were glorified.*
366   *Then seiz'd the Staff; & thus did*
                         say
367   *"Thou, Richard, bear'st thy Father's*
                         name,
368   *Keep thou this Ensign till the day*
               require
369   *When I of thee* ~~demand~~ *the same*
370   *Thy place be on my better*
               hand
371   *And seven as true as Thou I*
                see
372   *Will cleave to this good cause*
                & me
       ⌈He spake⌉
373   ⌊*Come ye*⌋*," & eight brave Sons*
                  straitway
374   *All follow'd him, a gallant Band,*
      F⌉
375   ~~And~~ *f*⌋*orth, when Sire & Sons appear'd*
      gratulating
376   *A* ~~shout, a lofty~~ *shout was rear'd*
377   *With din of arms & minstrelsy*
                80

---

375 Deletion by erasure.

From all his warlike tenantry.
~~At stood about which'd & deferd~~
~~And all the sele intirely replied~~
~~those~~ ~~to which for He~~ replied
~~all~~ ~~with hw to hide~~
A skirt to which the hills replied

But Francis in the vacant Hall
Stood silent under dreary weight,
A phantasm in which rooof & wall
Fell round him like a Dream of
                                    night.

And dreaming, walking, desolate,
He found his way to a postern gate
And when he walked at length his
                                    eye
Was on the calm & silent sky
With air about him. breathing sweet
And verdant grass beneath his
                                    feet
Nor did he fail ere long to hear

378 *From all his warlike tenantry.*
   ~~A shout which welcom'd & defied~~
   ~~And all the antient hills replied~~
   horse
380 *~~A shout to which the Hills replied~~*
     ho hors'd & harness'd
   All ~~ready arm'd~~ₐ with him to ride
   A shout to which the hills replied

381 *But Francis in the vacant Hall*
382 *Stood silent under dreary weight,*
383 *A phantasm in which roof & wall*
384 *Fell round him like a dream of*
          night.
385 *And dreaming, walking, desolate,*
386 *He found his way to a postern gate*
387 *And when he waked, at length his*
          eye
388 *Was on the calm & silent sky*
389 *With air about him breathing sweet*
390 *And verdant grass beneath his*
          feet
391 *Nor did he fail ere long to hear*

378/380 WW's two lines fill a one-line space left by DW; DW's l. 380 was apparently deleted at the time of WW's entry. Later (probably in post-London revision) WW deleted his own lines, 378/380, and entered replacements at 380/381; one of the new lines is reentered on 21ᵛ, facing (see transcription of 21ᵛ in "Verse Drafts," p. 367, below).

A sound of military chear,
Faint, but it reach'd that shelter
                              shot,
He heard, & it disturb'd him not

There stood he leaning on a lance
Which he had grasp'd unknow:
                              :ingly,
100 Had blindly grasp'd in this strong
                              trance
That dinness of heart-agony.
There stood he, cleansed from the
                              despair
And sorrow of this fruitless prayer
The past he calmly hath review'd
But where will be the fortitude
Of this brave Man when ~~~~~~~
                    he shall see
That Form beneath the spreading
                              tree
And know that it is Emily

392   *A sound of military chear,*
393   *Faint, but it reach'd that shelter'd*
                        spot,
394   *He heard, & it disturb'd him not*

395   *There stood he leaning on a lance*
396   *Which he had grasp'd unknow=*
                        =ingly,
397 100 *Had blindly grasp'd in that strong*
                        trance,
398   *That dimness of heart-agony.*
399   *There stood he, cleansed from the*
                        despair
400   *And sorrow of ~~this~~ fruitless prayer*
401   *The past he calmly hath review'd*
402   *But where will be the fortitude*
403   *Of this brave Man when ~~his eye~~*
                    he shall see
404   *That Form beneath the spreading*
                        Tree
405   *And know that it is Emily*

Oh! hide them from each other, hide,
Kind Heaven! this Pair severely
                              tried.

                                    in view
He saw the Maid where full
She sate beneath the spreading
                              yew
And thitherward he turn'd straight
                                   :way
And, greeting her, did promly say
"Might ever Son command a Sire
This act were justified today
Gone are they—They have their
                              'desire
And I with thee one hour will
                              stay
To give thee comfort if I may"

He paused her silence to partake
And long it was before he spake
Then all at once his thoughts
                    2. 113 turn'd round

406   *Oh! hide them from each other, hide,*
407   *Kind Heavens! this Pair severely*
                                            tried.

408   *He saw the Maid where full*
                                in view
409   *She sate beneath the spreading*
                                    yew
410   *And thitherward he turn'd strait=*
                                    =way
411   *And, greeting her, did firmly say*
412   *"Might ever Son command a Sire*
413   *This act were justified today*
414   *Gone are they—they have their*
                                    desire
415   *And I with thee one hour will*
                                    stay
416   *To give thee comfort if I may".*

417 120 *He paused her silence to partake*
418   *And long it was before he spake*
419   *Then all at once his thoughts*
                                turn'd round

---

407   Deletion by erasure.
Following leaf 24 five leaves are missing. The lines probably contained on the last of the missing leaves are included in MS. 62; see p. 25 of the transcription of MS. 62, below, p. 319, where the line numbers at the left run on sequentially.

Hawk forget his perch the Hound
Be parted from his ancient ground
Blast will sweep us all away,
One desolation, one decay
And even this creature" which word
He pointed to a lovely Doe,   saying
A few steps distant, feeding, stray=
Fair Creature, & more white than snow   ing
Even she will to her peaceful woods
Return, & to her murmuring flood
And be in heart & soul the same
She was before she hither came
Ere she had learn'd to love us all
Herself beloved in Rilstone Hall
But thou, my Sister, doom'd to be
The last leaf which by Heaven's
                                      decree

498   *The Hawk forget his perch the Hound*
499   *Be parted from his ancient ground,*
500   *The Blast will sweep us all away,*
501   *One desolation, one decay*
502   *And even this Creature" which word*
                                 saying,
503   *He pointed to a lovely Doe,*
504   *A few steps distant, feeding stray=*
                                 ing,
505   *Fair Creature, & more white than snow*
506   *Even she will to her peaceful woods*
507   *Return, & to her murmuring floods*
508   *And be in heart & soul the same*
509   *She was before she hither came*
510   *Ere she had learn'd to love us all,*
511   *Herself beloved in Rilleston Hall*
512   *But thou, my Sister, doom'd to be*
513   *The last leaf which by Heaven*
                                 decree

---

505 *p. 26 begins*   snow!"
507 floods,
509 came,
510 learnt
511 Rylstone Hall.
512 —But
513 Heaven's

498–504   These lines are duplicated at the foot of p. 25, MS. 62; see p. 319, below.

Must hang upon a blasted tree
If not in vain we have breathed the
break
Together, of a purer faith
If hand in hand we have been led
And thou, O happy thought this day!
Not seldom foremost in the way
If on one thought our minds have fed
And we have in one meaning read
If when at home our private weal
Hath suffered from the shock of zeal
Together we have learnt to prize
Forbearance & self-sacrifice
If we like Combatants have fared
And for this issue been prepared
If thou art beautiful, and youth
And thought endue thee with all
truth

514   *Must hang upon a blasted tree*

    f ⎫
515   *In* ⎭ *not in vain we have breathed the*
                              breath

516   *Together, of a purer faith*

517   *If hand in hand we have been led*
                          220

518   *And thou, O happy thought this day!*

519   *Not seldom foremost in the way*
    on ⎫ *on*
520   *If in* ⎭ *one thought our* minds have fed

521   And we have in one meaning red

522   If when at home our private weal

523   Hath Suffered from the shock of Zeal

524   Together we have learn'd to prize

525   Forbearance & self-sacrifice
            ⎰C
526   If we like ⎱combatants have fared

527   And for this issue been prepared

528   If thou art beautiful, and youth

529   And thought endue thee with all
                          truth

---

514   tree,
515   If
516   Together . . . faith—
518   thou (O . . . day!)
519   way—
520   on one   fed,
521   read—
522   If,
523   suffered . . . zeal,
525   Forbearance, . . . self sacrifice—
526   Combatants   fared,
527   prepared—
528   *p. 26 ends and the following leaf, with ll. 529–540, is missing*

Be strong, be worthy of the grace
Of God and fill thy destined place
A Soul by force of sorrows high
Uplifted to the purest sky
Of undisturb'd humanity.

He ended, or She heard no more
He led her from the Eightree shade
And at the Mansion's silent door
He stopp'd the consecrated Maid   246
And down the Valley he pursued
Alone the armed multitude,   249

Alone the armed multitude

530   Be strong, be worthy of the grace
531   Of God and fill thy destined place

                ⌠s
532   A ⌡Soul by force of sorrows high
533   Uplifted to the purest sky
534   Of undisturb'd humanity.

535   He ended, or She heard no more
536   He led her from the Eughtree shade

                ⌠m
537   And at the ⌡Mansion's silent door
                                        240
538   He kiss'd the consecrated Maid
539   And down the Valley he pursued
540   Alone the armed multitudes

                        ⎧50⎫
                        ⎩ 4⎭
                    242⌡

        Alone the armed multitude

---

540   WW's revision of his line count may relate to revision of text on leaves 25–29, removed.

Part Third

Now joy for you ye sudden cheer
Ye watchmen upon Brancepeth Towers
Loking forth in doubt & fear
Telling melancholy hours
Proclaim it let your Masters hear
That Norton with his band is near
Marching down the banks of Weir
The stout Earls heard & at ouzel
From trembling and perplexity   free
They took to theirs fa test band force
With general pledge conferned the choice

Scarce recovered Norton tho the Pair
Gone forth to ~~~~~ his in the place

Part Third
541   Now Joy for you & sudden chear
542   Ye Watchmen upon Brancepeth Towers
543   Looking forth in doubt & fear
544   Telling melancholy hours
545   Proclaim it let your Masters hear
546   That Norton with his band is near
547   Marching down the banks of Weir
     {E
548   The stout {earls heard & at once set
           free
549   From tremblings and perplexity
550   They took to their fate & hand & voice
551   With final pledge confirm'd the choice.

       to }
552   Said revered Norton the} the Pair
      hail
553   Gone forth to ~~greet~~ him on the plain

Part Third] Third Canto *at beginning of p. 28*
541   *indented*   joy
    {s,
542   Tower{!
543   fear,
544   hours!
545   it,
547–551   *deleted, then marked* In in in *(WW)*
547   Banks of Were!
548   It was proclaimed, and the Earls, set free
549   perplexity,
    T}
550   They took] ~~They~~ U}   fate;
551   confirmed
552   *indented*   revered] fearless   to
553   hail   Plain,

...ng meeting noble Lords, looke faire
bring with me a goodly leven
Their hearts are with you: Hill & Dale
Have help'd us & the we cross'd of Swale
And horse and has hep followed — see
The best part of their Yeomanry!
Stand forth, my Sons! These eight are
mine 20
Whom to this service I commend
Which way soe'er our fate incline
These will be faithful to the end
They are my all — (voice fail'd him here)
My all save one a Daughter dear
Whom I have left the mildest birth
The meekest Child on this blessed earth
I had — but there are by my side
these eight, and this is a day
                                of pride,

554 This meeting, noble Lords, looks fair
555 I bring with me a goodly train.
556 Their hearts are with you: Hill & Dale
557 Have help'd us: Ure we cross'd & Swale
558 And horse and harness followed—see

              {Y
559 The best part of their {yeomanry!

                  {e
560 Stand forth, my Sons! these {Eight are
                        mine 20
561 Whom to this service I commend
562 Which way-soe'er our fate incline
563 These will be faithful to the end
564 They are my all—(voice faild him here)
565 My all save one a Daughter dear
566 Whom I have left the mildest birth
567 The meekest Child on this blessed earth.
568 I had—but these are by my side
569 These eight, and this is a day
                of pride,

---

554 Lords! . . . fair,
555 train;
556 *p. 28 ends*
557 crossed   *pencil dash overwritten with pencil comma following* crossed   *pencil dash follow-*
ing swale
558 Horse   Harness *entered above line in pencil*
559 Yeomanry!
560 *l. no. 20 penciled in margin*   forth my Sons!—   eight
561 commend;
562 way soe'er
563 end;
564 all"—voice railed him here,
565 "My . . . one, . . . dear!
566 left,
569 pride;

he time is ripe — with festive din
Lo! how the people are flocking in
Like hungry fowls to the Feeder's hand
heir snow lies heavy upon the land.

e spake bare truth for far & near
from
every side came noisy swarms
f peasants in their homely gear
And, mix'd with these, to Brancepeth
came
brave Gentry of estate & name
bad Captains known for work in
arms
And pray'd the Earls in self-defence
48
To rise, & prove their innocence
"Rise, noble Earls, put forth your
might
For holy Church, & the People's
right

570   The time is ripe—with ~~eager~~ festive din
571   Lo! how the people are flocking in
572   Like hungry fowl to the Feeder's hand
573   When snow lies heavy upon the land.

574   He spake bare truth for far & near
575   ~~On~~ ^from^ every side came noisy swarms
576   *Of peasants in their homely gear*
577   *And, mix'd with thi⎰se,⎱m to Brancepeth*
                                          came
578   *Grave Gentry of estate & name*
579   *And Captains known for worth in*
                                          arms
580   *And pray'd the Earls in self-defence*
                                          40
581   *To rise, & prove their innocence*
582   *"Rise, noble Earls, put forth your*
                                          might,
583   *For holy Church, & the People's*
                                          right

---

570   festive
571   People . . . in,
572   Fowl
573   upon] on *rev to* upon   land."

574   *indented as para*   truth,⎱;⎰ *with semicolon in pencil*
575   From
576   Peasants . . . gear;
577   mixed   these, *inserted with caret*
578   name,
579   arms,
579/580   *p. 29 ends, p. 30 begins*
580   40 *penciled in margin*   prayed
581   innocence.—
582   might
583   right!"

---

576   DW resumes transcription.

The Norton fix'd, at this demand,
His eye upon Northumberland,
And said, "the minds of men will owe
No loyal rest while England's crown
Remains without an heir, the bant
Of strife, & factions desperate
Who, paying deadly hate in kind
Through all things else, in this can
A mutual hope, a common mind,
And plot & pant to overwhelm
All ancient honour in the realm,
Brave Earls, to whom heroic very
Our noblest blood is given in trust
To you an injured State complains

Th
584 *The Norton fix'd, at this demand,*
585 *His eye upon Northumberland,*
586 *And said, "the minds of men will own*
587 *No loyal rest while England's crown*
588 *Remains without an heir, the bait*
589 *Of strife, & factions desperate*
590 *Who, paying deadly hate in kind*
591 *Through all things else, in this can*
                                    find
592 *A mutual hope, a common mind,*
593 *And plot & pant to overwhelm*
594 *All ancient honour in the realm,*
595 *Brave Earls, to whose heroic veins*
596 *Our noblest blood is given in trust,*
597 *To you an injured State complains*

---

584   *indented*   fixed,
586   "The . . . Men
587   Crown
588   Heir,
589   strife . . . desperate;
590   Who, *with comma in pencil*   kind,
593   plot, & pant,
594   realm. *with period in pencil*

        —⎫   !⎫
595   ⎭Brave Earls;⎭
597   an injured *rev by eras to* a suffering   complains,

583/584   Deletion by erasure.

And ye must raise her from the
                                        dust
With thoughts how dear: of boldest
                                        scope
Ph you we look, our two fold Hope
                                        60.
Not only for redress of wrongs
In what to high or low belongs
Or to a Crown without an Heir
That hangs to drop we know not
                                        where
But for our Altars, for the prize
In Heaven, of life that never dies
For the old & holy Church we mourn
And must in joy to her return
Behold—"and from the Son, whose then
Was on his right: from that guar=
                                =dian hand
He took the Banner & unfurld
The precious fold. "behold" said he
The ranson of a sinful world'

598	And ye must raise her from the
	dust.
599	With thoughts how dear! of boldest
	scope
	⎧On
600	⎩To you we look, our twofold Hope,
	60
601	Not only for redress of wrongs
602	In what to high or low belongs
603	Or to a Crown without an Heir
604	That hangs to drop we know not
	where
605	But for our Altars, for the prize
606	In Heaven, of life that never dies
607	For the old & holy Church we mourn
608	And must in joy to her return
609	Behold"—and from the Son, whose stand
610	Was on his right: from that guar=
	=dian hand
611	He took the Banner & unfurl'd
612	The precious folds, "behold" said he,
613	The ransom of a sinful world

---

598 dust;. *with period in pencil*
599 thoughts how dear! of boldest *rev by eras to* wishes of still bolder
600 On   our two fold *rev by eras to* with dearest   hope,
600/601 *p. 30 ends, p. 31 begins*
601–604 *deleted*
605 But *rev by eras to* Even   Altars,—
606 dies;
607 Old . . . mourn,
608 return.
609 Behold!—" and   the *rev by eras to* his   Son
610 right,   that
611 Banner, and unfurled
612 folds,—"behold,"   he," *with quotation mark added in pencil*
613 "The *with quotation mark added in pencil*   world,

Let this your preservation be
The wounds of hands, & feet & side
And the   Cross on which
                    Jesus died
This being (from an antient hearth   76
These Emblems wrought in pledge of
                              love
By hands of no egnoble birth
A Maid so whom the blessed Dove
            80
Vouchsaf'd in gentleness & pride
Which she the holy work pursued.
        the standards
Uplift, [uplift it]   [listeners]   was the cry
From all the [   ] that stood
                                  round
Plant it, by this we live or die"
The Norton ceas'd not [   ] that sound
But said, the prayer which
                      ye have heard
                              head
Much-injur'd Earls by these prossess'd
[   ]
[   ]

614   *Let this your preservation be*
615   *The wounds of hands, & feet & side*
                { C
616   *And the*   { *cross on which*
               Jesus died
                 76
617   This bring I from an antient hearth
618   These Emblems wrought in pledge of
                         love
619   By hands of no ignoble birth
     { M
620   A { maid oer whom the blessed Dove
                   80
621   Voutchsaf'd in gentleness to brood
622   Which She the holy work pursued.
          { S
       the { standard
623   Uplift, ~~uplift it~~ was the cry
              Listeners
            { listeners
624   From all the { ~~people~~∧ that stood
                   round
625   Plant it, by this we live or die"
626   The Norton ceas'd not for that sound
627   But said, the prayer which
                 ye have heard
628   Much-injur'd Earls by these preferr'd
629   ~~Is offer'd to the saints on high~~
630   ~~By tens of thousands, secretly~~

---

614   be,
615   hands . . . side,
616   sacred Cross . . . died!

      − }
617   } This   ancient hearth,

618   Emblems *rev by eras to* Records
619   birth,
620   Maid
621   Vouchsafed
622   Which] While   she
622/623   *p. 31 ends, p. 32 begins*
623   "Uplift the Standard!"
624   *80 penciled in margin*   Listeners . . . round,
625   "Plant it,— *with dash in pencil*   die"—
626   sound,
627   "The . . . heard,
628   Much injured Earls! . . . preferred
629–630   Is offered to the Saints, the sigh
           Of tens of thousands, secretly".—

629–630   These lines were probably deleted when they were reentered at the top of 40ʳ.

proffered to the Saints, the sighs
of tens of thousands, secretly
uplift it. 'erued once more the band
And then a thoughtful pause ensued
Whilst it said Northumberland
Whereat from all the multitude
Who saw the Banner raised on high
Disclosed its dread emblazonry
With tumult & indignant rout
A voice of utter breaking out
The transport was ... wisdom ...
That ... transport ...
to the voice
And Durham, the time-honour'd Durham
nd the Towers of St Cuthbert did hear
the ... are 100
stirred by the shout.

Now was the North in arms: they shine
In warlike twin from Tweed to Tyne
Of Percy ...: and Nevill ...
His followers gathering in
from Tees

Is offered to the Saints, the sigh

⎧tens
Of ⎩tho of thousands, secretly

631   Uplift it! cried once more the band
632   And then a thoughtful pause ensued

⎧said
633   Uplift it ⎩cried Northumberland

                    t ⎱
634   Whereat from all the multid⎰ude
635   Who saw the Banner rias'd on high

      In ⎱ In⎱
636   [?With]⎰ ⎰ all its dread emblazonry,
637   With tumult & indignant rout

              most
638   A voice of utter∧ joy brake out

      The transport was roll'd down the River of Weir
639   ~~The sound & the transport were give'n~~
                          ~~to the Weir~~
640   And Durham, the time-honour'd Durham,
                             did hear

                          100

                       are
641   And the Towers of St Cuthbert ~~were~~∧
                    stirrd by the shout.

642   Now was the North in arms: they shine
643   In warlike trim from Tweed to Tyne

        voice
      In   train
644   At Percy ~~call~~: Ann Nevill sees

      ⎧His
645   ⎩The Followers gathering in
                   from Tees

---

631   "Uplift it" . . . Band,
632   ensued.
633   "Uplift it"! said Northumberland—
634   Whereat, . . . multitude,
635   rias'd] reared
636   In
638   uttermost . . . out:

                                   ⎧ere
639   The transport was rolled down the river of W⎩eir ,
640   time-honoured Durham! did hear,
641   The . . . St. . . . . were stirred . . . shout!
642   *indented*   arms:—
642/643   *p. 32 ends, p. 33 begins*
643   Tyne,
644   100 *penciled in margin*   At Percys voice: and Neville sees
645   His . . . Tees,

Leaf 39 has been removed. Traces of writing on the stub ("[?U] / A") may be the beginnings of ll. 631–632, and the leaf may have held a version of the lines that begin on 40ʳ. On 38ᵛ, which now faces 40ʳ, MW entered a portion of l. 623: "Uplift it cried once."

From

And from
On Rubys everlace by Pile

Not loth the sleepy lance to weild
And greet the old patronel
They heard the summons & few the sun
~~~~~~~~~~~~~~~~ eight degree
Unbound by pledge of fealty
Appeared with free & open hate
Of as well as in chase oh Jo late
Stout Burgh & Yes may & Eager
And the Romish Preist in proscies
That these is as as a zealous band
Proceeding

From
———
And from

         slopes that smile
        {*P*
On Rabys everlasting {*pile*

Not loth the sleepy lance to wield
And greet the old paternal
             shield
They heard the summons & furthermore
   ~~With him came multitu~~
~~Came multitudes of~~ each degree
    Foot & horsemen of ea
Unbound by pledge of fealty
Appeared with free & open hate
Of novelties in church & state
Knight Burger Yeoman & Esquire
And the Romish Priest in priests
               attire
 And⎫ ⎰these
That ⎭ ⎱ this in arms a zealous band
Proceeding

The upper set of lines, in MW's hand, is an incomplete alternate for the lines that face them on 41ʳ; the dashlike stroke signifies retention of l. 647 there. The lower set of lines revises ll. 653–659 on 41ʳ; the revision between the fifth and sixth base lines is in MW's hand.

646 From Wear & all the r⌉ittle rills
       1⌉
647 Concealed among the forked hills
648 Seven hundred Knights retainers
         all
      [?Leighs]
649 Of Nevill at their Masters call
     to⌉   that vast
650 Had sate to [?]⌋gether in ~~Raby~~ Hall
    S⌉
651 T⌋uch strenght the Nevills held
        of yore
652 Nor wanted at this time rich Store
        .⌉
653 Of well appointed chivalry⌋
654 And numbers came of each degree
655 Unbound by pledge of fealty
656 Appeared with free and open hate
657 Of novelties in church & state

658 ~~And thus a well appointed band~~
659 Proceeding under joint command
    To ~~D~~
    ~~From~~⌉
660 ~~To D⌋ Brancepeth Castle~~ forth they fare
   To Durham first their course they bear
661 And in St Cuthberts antient seat
      ⌠tore
662 Sung mass and ⌊[?] the book of pray'r
663 And trod the Bible beneath their
        feet

---

646 Were, little Rills
647 Hills.—
648 Knights, Retainers
649 Neville, . . . Master's
650 Had sate together in Raby Hall!
651 Such strength that Earldom held of yore;
653–659 Of well appointed Chivalry.—
    Not loth the sleepy Lance to wield,
    And greet the old paternal Shield,
    They heard the summons;—and, furthermore,
    Came Foot and Horsemen of each degree,
    Unbound by pledge of fealty;
    Appeared, with free and open hate
    Of novelties in Church and State;
    Knight, Burgher, Yeoman, and Esquire;
    And the Romish Priest, in Priest's attire.
    And thus, in arms, a zealous Band
[p. 34] Proceeding under joint command, *with* 120 *penciled opposite final line in margin of*
facing stub
660 To Durham first their course they bear;
661 Cuthbert's ancient Seat
662 Sung Mass,—and tore the Book of Prayer—
663 feet.

Then a marching forced
southward southward
They muster'd their host at Wetherby
Full thirteen thousand fair to see
The choicest warriors of the North
But none for undisputed worth
Like those eight sons who in a row
Stood by their Sire on Clifford-moor
All armed, in beauty flourishing
To guard the Standard which he bore
They guarding him he round them threw
While for them he held his dear heart's
                              boast,
Gods proof of love unmerited
A light of glory dim'nied with dread
Such mixture as his countenance bred
Yet still the glory uppermost.
Rare sight to embolden & inspire
Beyond was the field of songs &c

                                    southward smooht & free
664   Thence marching ~~forward~~
665   They muster'd their Host at Weather
                                    by
666   Full thirteen thousand fair to see—
667   *The choicest Warriors of the North*
                    { for
668   But none {[?] undisputed worth
669   Like those eight sons who in a ring
670   Stood by their Sire on Clifford-moor
                    flour ⎫
671   All arm'd, in beauty [?cher]⎰ishing
                        220
672   To guard the Standard which he
                                    bore
673   They guarding him he round them shed
674   While firm he held his dear hearts
                                    boast,
675   Gods proof of love unmerited,
676   A light of glory dimm'd with dread
677   Such mixture as his Countenance bred
                        u ⎫
678   Yet still the glory m⎰ppermost.
679   Rare sight to embolden & inspire
        Pr⎫   s⎫
680   [?]⎰oud was the field of Son⎰ & Sire

---

664 *indented*   Thence marching southward smooth and free,
665 "They mustered . . . Wetherby,
666 sixteen Thousand . . . see;"
667 *in base text with* North!
668 for
669 Sons; . . . ring,
669/670 Each with a lance‾ₐerect and tall,
              A falchion, and a buckler small, *dash and caret in pencil*
670 Clifford-moor,
671 In youthful beauty flourishing,
672 bore,
673–678 —With feet that firmly pressed the ground
                    { and g ⎱irt
              They stood, {with feet⎰ their Father round;
              Such was his choice;—no Steed will he
    [p. 35] Henceforth bestride,—triumphantly
              He stood upon the verdant sod,
                            the
              Trusting himself to ₐ earth, and God.
679 inspire!
                    {;—
680 Proud . . . Sons and Sire{, *with punct rev in pencil*

---

667 Entered by MW in a space left by WW.
671/672 The line number is in pencil.

Of him the most; and sooth to say
No shape of man in all the array
So grac'd the sunshine of that day
The monumental pomp of age
Was with this goodly Personage
A stature undepress'd in size
Unbent; which rather seem'd to rise,
In open victory oer the weight
Of seventy years, to higher height;
Magnific limbs of withered state,
A face to fear and venerate
Eyes dark & strong, and on his head
A crown of silver hair thick spread
Curl'd to his stod ...
The Who sees him. Many see, and one
With unparticipated gaze
Who, mong these thousands 'Tween
                                    with none
And treads in solitary way

681   Of him the most: and sooth to say
682   No shape of man in all tharray
683   So gracd the sunshine of that day
684   The monumental pomp of age
685   Was with this goodly personage
686   A stature undepressd in size
687   Unbent, which rather seemed to rise,
688   In open victory oer the weight
689   Of seventy years, to higher height.
690   Magnific limbs of withered state,
691   A face to fear and venerate
692   Eyes dark & strong and on his head
693   A crown of silver hair thick-spread

                                    advancing
        And so he stood, ~~uplifting~~ ∧high
        The   banners floating pageantry
                        { o
694   Wh⌊[?] sees him? many see, and one
695   With unparticipated gaze
696   Who 'mong these thousands Friend
                                    hath none
697   And treads in solitary ways

---

681   most; and, . . . say,
682   Man   theŕ array *with del by eras*
683   graced . . . day:
685   Personage;
686   A Stature undepressed in size,
688   o'er
689   height;
690   witherd state,— *with dash in pencil*
691   venerate,— *with dash in pencil*
692   strong,
693   Rich locks of silver hair, thick-spread,
                        { o }
693/694 Which a Brown Mori⌊[?]⌋n half-concealed,
         Light as a Hunter's of the field;
[p. 36] And thus, with girdle round his waist,
         Whereon the Banner-staff might rest:
                        {,
         At need, he stood⌊ advancing high *with comma in pencil*
         The glittering, floating Pageantry.
694   *indented*   Who . . . him?— . . . One
695   gaze;
696   Thousands . . . none,
697   ways.

He, climbing wheresoe'er he might
Hath watch'd the banner from afar
As Shepherds watch a lonely star
Or Mariners the distant light
That guides them on a stormy night
And to yon Plot of rising ground
From earliest dawn hath he
This day there stakes his   been borne
With breast unmailed, unweaponed   far off stand
Nor doth his faithful eye forego
The pause   is with his
To   duty is with his
Which way the tide is doom'd to flow
A knowledge which he soon shall earn
   ane Amos
— To London, London let   hill
This   the universal cry
     here the Chieftains
But what avails the bold intent
A royal army is gone forth

[MS. 61, 44ʳ]   [764–772; 785–792]

698	He, climbing wheresoeer he might
699	Hath watch'd the banner from afar
700	As Shepherds watch a lonely star
701	Or m⌋ariners the distant light M⌉
702	That guides them on a stormy night
703	And to yon Plot of rising ground
704	From earliest ⌊Dawn hath he ⌈d
	been bound
705	~~This day⌉~~ t ⌉ ⌈far off ~~Far off~~⌋ there [?st]⌋akes his ⌊distant This day far off stand
706	With breast unmailed, unweapon'd hand,

---

698 He, following wheresoe'er he might,
699 watched ... Banner ... afar, *with comma in pencil*
700 ⌊distant Star,   ⌈lonely
701 Mariners
702 night.
703–705   And now upon a chosen plot
          Of rising ground, yon heathy spot!
          He takes this day his far-off stand,
706 unweaponed hand.

He, climbing wheresoeer he might
Hath watch'd the banner from afar
As Shepherds watch a lonely star
Or Mariners the distant light
That guides them on a stormy night
And to yon Pilot-tree in ground
From earliest dawn hath he
This day~~ there stakes his ~~been born~~ far off I stand
With breast unmailed, unweaponed too
Nor doth his faithful eye forego
The ~~peace~~ ~~glory is with him~~ ~~pursue~~
Tear ~~by~~ ~~to a hope~~ to learn
Which way the tide is doom'd to flow
A knowledge which he soon shall earn
~~To London~~ Anne Cmon London let ~~thy~~ hill
~~Ihis~~ the universal cry
~~And~~ ~~the~~ were the Chieftains be
But what avails the bold intent
A royal army is gone forth

[MS. 61, 44ʳ, continued]

707   Nor doth his faithful eye forego

708   The pageant glancing to & ⎰fro
                           ⎱for
          hope is with him thence
709   For ~~by this help he ho~~pes to learn
710   Which way the tide is doom'd to flow
711   A knowledge which he soon shall earn.

                   ⎰us
712   —— ~~To London, London let~~ ⎱~~me~~ hie
713   ~~This was the universal cry~~
          To London
714   ~~And thither~~ were the Chieftains bent
715   *But what avails the bold intent*
716   *A royal army is gone forth*

707–711   —Bold is his aspect; but his eye
               Is pregnant with anxiety,

                  ⎰,   ⎰,
               While⎱ like a Tutelary Power⎱ *commas in pencil*

                             ⎰,
               He there stands fixed⎱ from hour to hour. *comma in pencil*
               Yet sometimes, in more humble guise,
[p. 36a]   Stretched out upon the ground he lies,
               As if it were his only task
               Like Herdsman in the sun to bask,
               Or by his Mantle's help to find
               A shelter from the nipping wind;
               And thus with short oblivion blest
               His weary Spirits gather rest.
               Again he lifts his eyes; and lo!
               The pageant glancing to and fro;
               And hope is wakened by the sight
               That he thence may learn, ere fall of night,
               Which way the tide is doomed to flow.
712–713 *omitted*
714 *indented*   To London . . . bent;
715 intent?
      ⎰A
716 ⎱army

---

712 MW resumes transcription.

To quell the rising in the north
They march with Dudley at their head
And hitherward from York are led
Gay twenty thousand men be raised
To speedily & brought so near
The Earls upon each other gazed
And Neville was oppress'd with fear.
For tho' he bore a valiant name
His heart was of a timid frame
And bolder if both had been yet
Against so many might not stay.

        Word for retreat was giv'n — we yield
"Said Norton," then bow unfought
Ev'n these proceedings of mine would ten
(Half to himself & half to then
Ye shatterd would slew or quell a force
Sir times their number mand & horse

[MS. 61, 45ʳ]   [793–803; 815–817; 857–860]

717   *To quell the rising in the North*
718   *They march with Dudley at their head*
719   *And hitherward from York are led*
720   *Can thirty thousand Men be raised*
                   Thus suddenly
721   *~~So speedily~~ & brought so near*
722   *The Earls upon each other gazed*
723   *And Neville was oppress'd with fear*
                   a ⎫
724   *For tho' he bore a vali[?e]⎰nt name*
725   *His heart was of a timid frame*
726   *And bold if both had been yet*
                                    they
727   *Against so many might not stay.*

       70
728   Word for retreat was givn—we yield
                   an⎫
729   "Said Norton," then [?]⎰ unfought field
730   Evn these poor eight of mine would stem
731   (Half to himself & half to them
732   He spake) would stem or quell a force
733   Ten times their number man & horse

---

717   in] of   North;
718   head,
                         ten
719–720 And, in ~~three~~ day's space, will to York be led!
                   such a mighty host
             Can ~~thirty thousand Men~~ be raised
                   three   ten
with all revs and del lines in pencil, as well as seven *written in margin*
721   Thus suddenly, . . . near?
722   gazed;
723   oppressed with fear;
724   For, though . . . valiant Name,
             ;⎫
725   frame,⎰
726   been,   *p. 36a ends; on the verso WW wrote out, then canceled, the lines that follow in the 1815*
text:

       And therefore will retreat to seize
                                            ⎰;
       A strong Hold on the banks of Tees⎱
                                      ⎰,
       There wait a favorable hour⎱
       Untill Lord Dacre with his power
                   Naworth
       From ~~Irthing~~ comes; and Howard's aid
       Be with them openly displayed. *with added punct in pencil*

727/728 The line number is in pencil.
    Following this leaf the notebook contains only a single stub, on which the only surviving text is some illegible penciling at the top of the verso. The large area of the recto (1.2 by 2.3 centimeters wide) is blank, so that fair copy of *The White Doe* resembling that on the previous leaves could not have stood there. Possibly some draft was present: a version of l. 865 (of the 1815 text) was entered on 45ᵛ (facing) before *The Force of Prayer* was entered there.
    The line numbers at the left continue sequentially on p. 40 of MS. 62.

25

Acknowledging a grace in this,
A comfort in the dark abyss;
But look not for me when I am gone,
And be no farther wrought upon.
Farewell all wishes, all debate,
All prayers for this cause or for that!
Weep, if that aid thee; but depend
Upon no help of outward Friend;
Espouse thy doom at once, and cleave
To fortitude without reprieve.
For we must fall, both we and ours,
This Mansion and these pleasant bowers,
Walks, pools and arbours, homestead, Hall,
Our fate is theirs, will reach them all
The young horse must forsake his manger,
And learn to glory in a stranger;
The hawk forget his perch, the Hound
Be parted from his ancient grounds
The blast will sweep us all away,
One desolation, one decay!
And even this creature!" which word saying
He pointed to a lovely Doe,
A few steps distant, feeding, straying,

25

482	Acknowledging a grace in this,
	:⎱
483	A comfort in the dark abyss;⎰
484	But look not for me when I am gone,
485	And be no farther wrought upon.
486	Farewell all wishes, all debate,
487	All prayers for this cause or for that!
488	Weep, if that aid thee; but depend
489	Upon no help of outward Friend;
490	Espouse thy doom at once, and cleave
491	To fortitude without reprieve.
492	For we must fall, both we and ours,
493	This Mansion and these pleasant bowers,
494	Walks, pools and arbours, homestead, Hall,
495	Our fate is theirs, will reach them all;
496	The young Horse must forsake his manger,
497	And learn to glory in a Stranger;
498	The Hawk forget his perch, the Hound
499	Be parted from his ancient ground:
500	The blast will sweep us all away,
501	One desolation, one decay!
502	And even this Creature"!" which word saying
503	He pointed to a lovely Doe,
504	A few steps distant, feeding, straying,

The copyist throughout MS. 62 is MW.

The line numbers at the left carry on sequentially from p. 30ʳ of MS. 61, where versions of ll. 498–504 appear.

483   Punctuation altered in pencil.

40

She steeped, but not for Jesu's sake,
This Cross in tears—by her, and One
Unworthier far, we are undone—
Her Brother was it who assailed
Her tender spirit and prevailed:
& While thus he brooded, music sweet
Was played to chear them in retreat;
But Norton lingered in the rear:
Thought followed thought, and, ere the last
Of that unhappy train was past,
Before him Francis did appear.

     "Now when 'tis not your aim to oppose"
Said he, "in open field your Foes,
Now that from this decisive day
Your multitude must melt away,
An unarmed Man may come unblamed
To ask a grace, that was not claimed
Long as your hopes were high; he now
May hither bring a fearless brow,
When his discountenance can do
No injury, may come for you.
Though in your cause no part I bear

40

800	*She steeped, but not for Jesu's sake;*
801	*This Cross in tears:—by her, and One*
802	*Unworthier far, we are undone—*
803	*Her Brother was it who assailed*
804	*Her tender Spirit and prevailed.*
805	*While thus he brooded, music sweet*
806	*Was played to chear them in retreat;*
807	*But Norton lingered in the rear:*

—⎫
808   *Thought followed thought ,⎭ and, ere the last*
809   *Of that unhappy train was past,*
810   *Before him Francis did appear.*

811   *"Now when 'tis not your aim to oppose"*
812   *Said he, "in open field your Foes,*
813   *Now that from this decisive day*
814   *Your multitudes must melt away,*
815   *An unarmed Man may come unblamed;*
816   *To ask a grace, that was not claimed*

⎧;
817   *Long as your hopes were high⎩, he now*
818   *May hither bring a fearless brow,*
819   *When his discountenance can do*

to
820 280 *No injury, may come for you.*
821   *Though in your cause no part I bear*

John Carter contributed the penciled title at the top of the page; the line number is in a modern hand.

805   The circled X in the margin indicates inclusion of drafting on the facing verso, now missing.

814   Deletion by erasure.

817, 820   Revisions in pencil. The line number in the margin, which is also in pencil, indicates that WW had reached the latter half of Canto III.

41

Your indignation I can share,
Am grieved this backward march to see,
How careless and disorderly!
I scorn your Chieftains, Men who lead
And yet want courage at their need;
Then, look at them with open eyes!
Deserve they further sacrifice?
My Father! I would help to find
A place of ~~tatty~~ Shelter ~~till~~ the rage,
~~Of cruel men your shelter held~~!
Be Brother now to Brother joined!
Admit me in the equipage
Of your misfortunes, that at least,
Whatever fate remains behind,
I may bear witness in my breast
To your nobility of mind"!

            "Thou Enemy, my bane and blight!
Oh! bold to fight the Coward's fight
Against all good "— but why declare,
At length, the issue of this prayer?
Or how, from his depression raised
The Father on his Son had gazed;

41

822	*Your indignation I can share;*
823	*Am grieved this backward march to see,*
824	*How careless and disorderly!*
825	*I scorn your Chieftains, Men who lead*
826	*And yet want courage at their need;*
827	*Then, look at them with open eyes!*
828	*Deserve they further sacrifice?*
829	*My Father! I would help to find*

shelter till

from

830	*A place of ~~safety till~~ } the rage*

~~Of cruel men, some shelter hind!~~

833	*Be Brother now to Brother joined!*
834	*Admit me in the equipage*
835	*Of your misfortunes, that at least,*
836	*Whatever fate remains behind,*
837	*I may bear witness in my breast*
838	*To your nobility of mind"!*

839	*"Thou Enemy, my bane and blight!*
840 300	*Oh! bold to fight the Coward's fight*
841	*Against all good"—but why declare,*
842	*At length, the issue of this prayer?*
843	*Or how, from his depression raised*
844	*The Father on his Son had gazed;*

830/833 The asterisk indicates inclusion of revision lines on the facing verso (p. 40ᵛ), included in the penciled line numbering at l. 840:

831 Of cruel men do like the wind

832 Exhaust itself and sink to rest

Be Brother &c

All soft and lulling is heard
of streams inaudible by day
The garden pool's dark surface – strewn
By the moss & Insects in their play
Breaks into triangles small & bright
A thousand thousand rings of light
That shape themselves and disappear
almost as soon as seen – and lo

Fourth Canto

From cloudless ether looking down
The Moon this tranquil evening sees
A camp and a beleaguered Town
And castle like a stately crown
On the steep rocks of Wharfe's Tees
And southward far with moors between
Hill tops and floods and forests green
The bright moon sees that valley small

A venerable image yields

42   sound
                A soft and lulling is heard   Ah who would think that
Of streams inaudible by day   sadness here
The garden pool's dark surface—stirred   Had any ⎫
By the night Insects in their play   [?   ?] ⎬ sway or pain or fear?
        Di ⎱
Breaks into [?]⎰mples small & bright
A thousand thousand rings of light
That shape themselves and disappear
Almost as soon as seen—and Lo
Not distant far the milkwhite Doe

        Fourth Canto
        ————————

From cloudless ether looking down
The Moon this tranquil evening sees
A Camp and a beleaguered Town
And Castle like a stately Crown
On the steep rocks of winding Tees
And southward far with moors between
                floods
Hill tops and ~~streams~~, and forests green
The bright Moon sees that Valley small
                ~~venerable Hall~~
Where Rylstone's ~~old sequestered~~ Hall   A venerable image
    With its grey roof an image yields   yields
        ⎰(
Stands ⎱ *as might seem from all distress*
        ~~Embowerd [?in] [?] an image yields~~
)⎱
~~Removed~~ ⎰ ~~in rural quietness~~
    of quiet to the neighbouring fields
While from one pillared chimney breathes
The silver smoke and mounts in wreathes
    ~~Yes—who would~~
        ~~But list the Dog, the household Guard~~
~~Repeats a faint uneasy howl~~
~~And from the distant crags are heard~~
~~The houtings of the riotous Owl~~

MW's fair copy of Canto IV, continued on 43a and 44a, represents a first level of revision, carried out while the manuscript was still being kept neat for use as printer's copy. At the top of the page WW's added lines represent a second level of revision, toward the version of 1815.

42.

Suffice it, that the son gave way,
Nor strove that passion to allay,
Nor did he turn aside to prove
His Brothers' wisdom or their love;
But calmly from the spot withdrew,
The like endeavours to renew,
Should e'er a kindlier time ensue,

937

End of the 3 Canto
turn to Corr. Leaves

Not otherwise than he had said,
At from the Royal power they fled
That followed close on their dismay,
Did this rash levy day by day
Dissolve,—while Neville's brow betrayed
A sadness visible to all;
For promise fails of Norfolk's aid,
Nor can Lord Dacre rise the call
For him too hazardous was made.
Yet still in arms a few are left,
Though of their Chieftains now bereft;
And Norton to the last is true,
And for the cheering of this few
The Banner is by him displayed;
But what can they who give them aid?

42.

845   *Suffice it, that the Son gave way,*
846   *Nor strove that passion to allay;*
847   *Nor did he turn aside to prove*
848   *His Brothers' wisdom or their love;*
849   *But calmly from the spot withdrew,*
850   *The like endeavours to renew,*
851   *Should e'er a kindlier time ensue.*
                    _____ *end of the 3 Canto*
                                   turn to loose leaves
852   *Not otherwise than he had said,*
853   *As from the Royal power they fled*
                          t⌉ ⌠eir
854   *That followed close on* ⌡h⌊is *dismay,*
855   *Did this rash levy day by day*
           is⌉   ;⌉
856   *De* ⌡solve,⌡ *—while Neville's brow betrayed*
857   *A sadness visible to all;*
858   *For promise fails of Norfolk's aid,*
859   *Nor can Lord Dacre rise, the call*
860 320 *For him too suddenly was made.*
861   *Yet still in arms a few are left,*
862   *Though of their Chieftains now bereft;*
863   *And Norton to the last is true,*
864   *And, for the chearing of this few,*
865   *The Banner is by him displayed;*
866   *But what can save, who give them aid?*

---

860   WW's line number, in pencil, was entered before this portion of Canto III was broken off and Canto IV begun, first on the facing verso (p. 42a), then, at a later stage of revision, on loose leaves that have not survived.

43 The courts are hushed

~~All over it still~~ for kindly sleep
The greyhounds to their kennels creep
The Peacock in the broad ash tree
Aloft is roosted for the night
He who in proud prosperite

Of colours manifold and bright
Walked round affronting the day-light
And higher still above the bower
Where he is perch'd from yon lone Tower
The Hall-clock in the clear moonshine
With glittering finger points at nine

~~Ask by the house-tree and fair~~
~~· · · · · ·~~
If Emily called forth to seek
She trace she cannot find within
By restlessness or blank despair
Impelled she wanders here and there
And if no comfort she may win
As twice has seen the cool night air
Breathes freshly on her feverish cheek

She through the garden takes her way
Where round a tree soft shadows play
And lift and lift the willows hoary
That screen a small secluded Pile
Right in the centre of an isle
Her Father's secret Oratory

*If who could
from else*

43
> The courts are hush'd
> ~~All else is still~~ for timely sleep
> The Greyhounds to their kennels creep
> The Peacock in the broad ash tree
> Aloft is roosted for the night
>> Ravenswood or Moor in Northumberland
> He who in proud prosperity
>> Cumberland or Westmoreland is intended
>> { lours
> Of col [?ulors] manifold and bright
> Walked round affronting the day-light
> And higher still above the bower
> Where he is perch'd, from yon lone Tower
> The Hall-clock in the clear moonshine
> With glittering finger points at nine   & Who could
> ~~Not by the hour serene and fair~~   turn back
> ~~Not by the freshness of the air~~
> Is Emily called forth to seek
> The place she cannot find within
> By restlessness or blank despair
> Impelled she wanders here and there
> And if no comfort she may win
> No truce yet still the cool night air
> Breathes freshly on her feverish cheek
>
>> She through the Garden takes her way
> Where round a Pool soft breezes play
> And lift, and lift the willows hoary
> That screen a small secluded Pile
> Right in the centre of an isle
> Her Father's secret Oratory

STC's prose note for the facing recto, l. 870, was entered, in pencil, before MW's fair-copy
revision lines, as can be seen from the slant and spacing of her lines.

Though hope doth yet with some remain
The Scottish Border thus to gain.
And wandering in this wretched plight
Through   wood, at fall of night,
In little knots, or Man by Man,
They seek for shelter where they can;
The Nortons who had chanced to espy
A Forest-lodge in a lonely glade,
Deserted now and half-decayed,
Turn to that shattered canopy
Their toil-worn steps, and together there
May sleep in covert from the air.

            Yet One is left with unclosed eyes,
And, forced by anxious thought to rise,
Beside the door walks to and fro;
And yet Another, and the best,
Is near them in this time of rest,
A guard of whom they do not know,
'Tis Francis.—much he longs to entreat
(For he hath cause of dread this night)
That they would urge their weary feet
To yet a further, further flight,

[MS. 62, p. 43]

43

867	*Though hope doth yet with some remain*
868	*The Scottish Border thus to gain.*
869	*And wandering in this wretched plight*
870	*Through wood, at fall of night,*
871	*In little knots, or Man by Man,*
872	*They seek for shelter where they can;*
873	*The Nortons who had chanced to espy*
874	*A Forest-lodge in a lonely glade,*
875	*Deserted now and half-decayed,*
876	*Turn to that shattered canopy*
877	*Their toil-worn steps, and together there*
878	*May sleep in covert from the air.*
879	*Yet One is left with unclosed eyes,*
880 340	*And, forced by anxious thought to rise,*
881	*Beside the door walks to and fro;*
882	*And yet Another, and the best,*
883	*Is near them/ in this time of rest,*
884	*A guard of whom they do not know,*
885	*'Tis Francis!—much he longs to entreat/*
886	*(For he hath cause of dread this night)*
887	*That they would urge their weary feet*
888	*To yet a further, further flight,*

---

870   The gap was filled in pencil by STC, and his characteristic mark in the margin points to his penciled note on the facing verso (p. 43a).

880   WW's line number is in pencil.

883, 885   Deletion by erasure.

There stands the Holy-water Stone
From which he crossed his wrinkled brow
Entering here to pray alone
And offer up his private vows
There to with reverential dread
The Banner was deposited
And thence did come that fatal morn
When forth in triumph it was borne.

She takes her seat with varying pace
Driven by her thoughts from place to place
all now are stript to rest
Empty the courts and hushed but coly

The same fair creature which was near
stealings in carpuilley

Within Francis
stirred to the Maid
His last word in the yew-tree shade
The same fair creatures who hath found

Nor the water fills

So this way
their into forbidden ground
Where now within this spacious plot
For pleasure made a goodly spot
With lawns and beds of flowers and shades
Of trellis work in long arcades

44

There stands the Holy-water Stone
From which he crossed his wrinkled brows
Entering here to pray alone
And offer up his private vows
There to with reverential dread
The Banner was deposited
And thence did come that fatal morn
When forth in triumph it was borne.
     She takes no heed with varying pace
Driven by her thoughts from place to place
    All now are slunk to rest
~~*Pale sad companionless   but lo!*~~
    Empty the Courts and hushed but lo!
Not distant far the Milk-white Doe
              nigh
The same fair Creature which was ~~*near*~~
    Feeding in tranquillity,
~~*When Francis from his Sister dear*~~
    When Francis
~~*Departing uttered*~~ *to the Maid*
His last words in the yew tree shade
           who hath found
The same fair Creature ~~*she no more*~~
~~*Delights the Forest to explore*~~
~~*Nor the waste Hills but rather loves*~~
~~*Small sheltered Crofts and household Groves*~~
~~*And hath unwonted entrance found*~~
   Her way
~~*This night*~~ *into forbidden ground*
Where now within this spacious plot
For pleasure made a goodly Spot
With lawns and beds of Flowers and Shades
Of trellice work in long Arcades

The line number in the bottom corner is a modern editor's.

56

These things, which thus had in the sight
And hearing past of him who stood
With Emily on the Watch Tower height
In Rylstone's woeful neighbourhood,
He told; and oftentimes with voice
Of power to encourage or rejoice;
For deepest sorrows that aspire
Go high, no transport ever higher.
"Yet, yet in this affliction," said
The old Man to the silent Maid;"
"Yet, Lady! heaven is good—the night
Shews yet a Star which is most bright,
Your Brother lives—he lives—is come
Perhaps already to his home;
Then let us leave this dreary place."
She yielded, and with gentle pace,
Though without one uplifted look,
To Rylstone Hall her way she took.

                                                          56

[1362]   *These things, which thus had in the sight*
[1363]   *And hearing past of him who stood*
[1364]   *With Emily on the Watch Tower height,*
[1365]   *In Rylstone's woeful neighbourhood,*
[1366]   *He told; and oftentimes with voice*
                              r ⎫
[1367]   *Of power to encourage on⎰ rejoice;*
[1368]   *For deepest sorrows that aspire*
[1369]   *Go high, no transport ever higher.*
[1370]   *"Yet, yet in this affliction, "said*
[1371]   *The old Man to the silent Maid,"*
[1372]   *"Yet, Lady! heaven is good—the night*
[1373]   *Shews yet a Star which is most bright,*
[1374]   *Your Brother lives—he lives—is come*
[1375]   *Perhaps already to his home;*
[1376]   *Then let us leave this dreary place."*
                                  ⎰ a
[1377]   *She yielded; and with gentle p⎩ece,*
[1378]   *Though without one uplifted look,*
[1379]   *To Rylstone Hall her way she took.—*
                    ————

The short line drawn beneath the text indicates that the original Canto IV ended here, corresponding to the end of Canto V in 1815. Drafting in the margins is overflow from *Vaudracour and Julia*.

The unbended walks, and Pools are Neg

1370 The walks and pools Neglect hath sown   67
With weeds, the bowers are overthrown,
Or have given way to slow mutation;
While in their ancient habitation
The Norton name hath been unknown:
The lordly Mansion of its pride
Is stripped; the ravage hath spread wide
Through park and field, a perishing
That mocks the gladness of the Spring!
And with this silent gloom agreeing
There is a joyless human Being,
Of aspect such as if the waste
Were under her dominion placed;
Upon a primrose bank, her throne
Of quietness, she sits alone;
There seated may this Maid be seen,
Among the ruins of a wood,
Erewhile a covert bright and green
And where full many a brave tree stood,
That used to spread its boughs, and ring
With the sweet Birds carrolling.
Behold her like a Virgin Queen
Neglecting in imperial state

The untended walks and Pools are sown
[1588]   *The walks and pools Neglect hath sown*   *67*
[1589]   *With weeds, the bowers are overthrown,*
[1590]   *Or have given way to slow mutation,*
[1591]   *While in their ancient habitation*
[1592]   *The Norton name hath been unknown:*
[1593]   *The lordly Mansion of its pride*   20
[1594]   *Is stripped; the ravage hath spread wide*
[1595]   *Through park and field, a perishing*
[1596]   *That mocks the gladness of the Spring!*
[1597]   *And with this silent gloom agreeing*
[1598]   *There is a joyless human Being,*
[1599]   *Of aspect such as if the waste*
[1600]   *Were under her dominion placed;*
[1601]   *Upon a primrose bank, her throne*
[1602]   *Of quietness, She sits alone;*
                                      is ⎱
[1603]   *There seated may the* ⎰ *Maid be seen,*
[1604]   *Among the ruins of a wood,*
[1605]   *Erewhile a Covert bright and green*
[1606]   *And where full many a brave tree stood,*
[1607]   *That used to spread its boughs, and ring*
[1608]   *With the sweet Birds carrolling.*
[1609]   *Behold her like a Virgin Queen*
[1610]   *Neglecting in imperial state*

1593   Since WW's penciled line numbers run by cantos, the "20" here shows that the original final canto (Canto VI) began on p. 66, now missing.

1597–1600   The space shows that only two lines originally lay where four are now entered; they may have been ll. 1608–1609, below, which are crossed out by a vertical pencil stroke.

68

These outward images of *[illegible]*;
And carrying inward a serene
And perfect sway, through many a *[illegible]*
Of chance and change that hath been *[illegible]*
To the subjection of a holy
Though stern and vigorous melancholy
The like authority, with grace
Of awfulness, is in her face,
There hath she fixed it; yet it seems
To overshadow by no native right
That face, which cannot lose the gleams,
Lose utterly the tender gleams
Of gentleness and meek delight,
And loving kindness ever bright.
Such is her sovereign mien—her dress,
(A vest, with woollen cincture tied,
A hood of mountain-wool undyed)
Is homely; and doth more express
A wandering Pilgrim's humbleness.

    And she hath wandered, long and far,
Beneath the light of *[illegible]* stars;

68

[1611]   *These outward images of fate,*
[1612]   *And carrying inward a serene*
[1613]   *And perfect sway, through many a thought*
                 ⎧an⎫
[1614]   *Of ch⎨oi⎬ce and change that hath been brought*
[1615]   *To the subjection of a holy   40*
[1616]   *Though stern and rigorous melancholy!*
[1617]   *The like authority, with grace*
[1618]   *Of awfulness, is in her face,*
[1619]   *There hath she fixed it; yet it seems*
[1620]   *To ~~oeershadow~~ by no native right   by*
[1621]   *That face, which cannot lose the gleams,*
[1622]   *Lose utterly the tender gleams*
[1623]   *Of gentleness and meek delight,*
[1624]   *And loving kindness ever bright.*

                                     ⎧;
[1625]   *Such is her sovereign mien⎨,— her dress,*
                 ⎧(
[1626]   ⎨*A Vest, with woolen cincture tied,*
                                           ⎧y⎧)⎫
[1627]   *A Hood of mountain wool und⎨i⎨ed,⎬*
                       fashioned to
[1628]   *Is homely; ~~and doth~~ more express*
                                   ⎧s
[1629]   *A wandering Pilgrim⎨ [—?—] humbleness*

[1630]   *And she hath wandered, long and far,*
[1631]   *Beneath the light of sun and star,*

1615   The line number is in pencil.
1620   The "by" in the margin is in pencil.
1628   Deletion in pencil, revised reading in ink.
The lines in the margin, inscribed vertically, are further overflow from *Vaudracour and Julia.*

69

Hath roamed in trouble and in grief,
Driven forward like a withered leaf;
Yea like a Ship, at random blown
To distant places and unknown.
But now she dares to seek a Haven
Among her native wilds of Craven;
Hath seen again her Father's Roof,
And put her fortitude to proof;
The mighty sorrow hath been borne
And she is thoroughly forlorn:
Her soul doth in itself stand fast
Sustained by memory of the past,
And strength of Reason; held above
The infirmities of mortal love,
Undaunted, lofty, calm, and stable,
And ~~wilfully~~ impenetrable.

       And so, beneath a mouldered Tree,
A self-surviving ~~branchless~~ leafless Oak,
By unregarded age from stroke
Of ravage saved, sate Emily.
There did she rest, with head reclined,
Herself most like a stately Flower,
(Such have I seen) whom chance of birth

                                                          69

[1632]   *Hath roamed in trouble and in grief,*
[1633]   *Driven forward like a withered leaf;*
                                   bl ⎤
[1634]   *Yea like a Ship, at random thr⎦own*
[1635]   *To distant places and unknown.*   60
[1636]   *But now she dares to seek a Haven*
[1637]   *Among her native wilds of Craven;*
                             R ⎤
[1638]   *Hath seen again her Father's r⎦oof,*
[1639]   *And put her fortitude to proof;*
[1640]   *The mighty sorrow hath been borne*
[1641]   *And she is thoroughly forlorn:*
[1642]   *Her soul doth in itself stand fast*
[1643]   *Sustained by memory of the past*
                       R ⎤
[1644]   *And strength of r⎦eason; held above*
[1645]   *The infirmities of mortal love,*
[1646]   *Undaunted lofty, calm, and stable,*
                    awfully
[1647]   *And ~~wilfully~~ impenetrable.*

[1648]   *And so, beneath a mouldered Tree,*
                    leaf
[1649]   *A self-surviving ~~branchless~~ Oak,*
[1650]   *By unregarded age from stroke*
[1651]   *Of ravage saved, sate Emily.*
[1652]   *There did she rest, with head reclined,*
[1653]   *Herself most like a stately Flower,*
[1654]   *(Such have I seen) whom chance of birth*

1635   The line number is in pencil.
1647   Deletion in pencil, revised reading in ink.

The White Doe of Rylstone
Verse Drafts: DC MS. 61

The following transcriptions contain drafts (mostly in Wordsworth's hand) toward revision of Cantos IV and VII. They appear on versos only of MS. 61, described above (p. 185). Approximate line numbers of the 1815 text appear in brackets at the upper right.

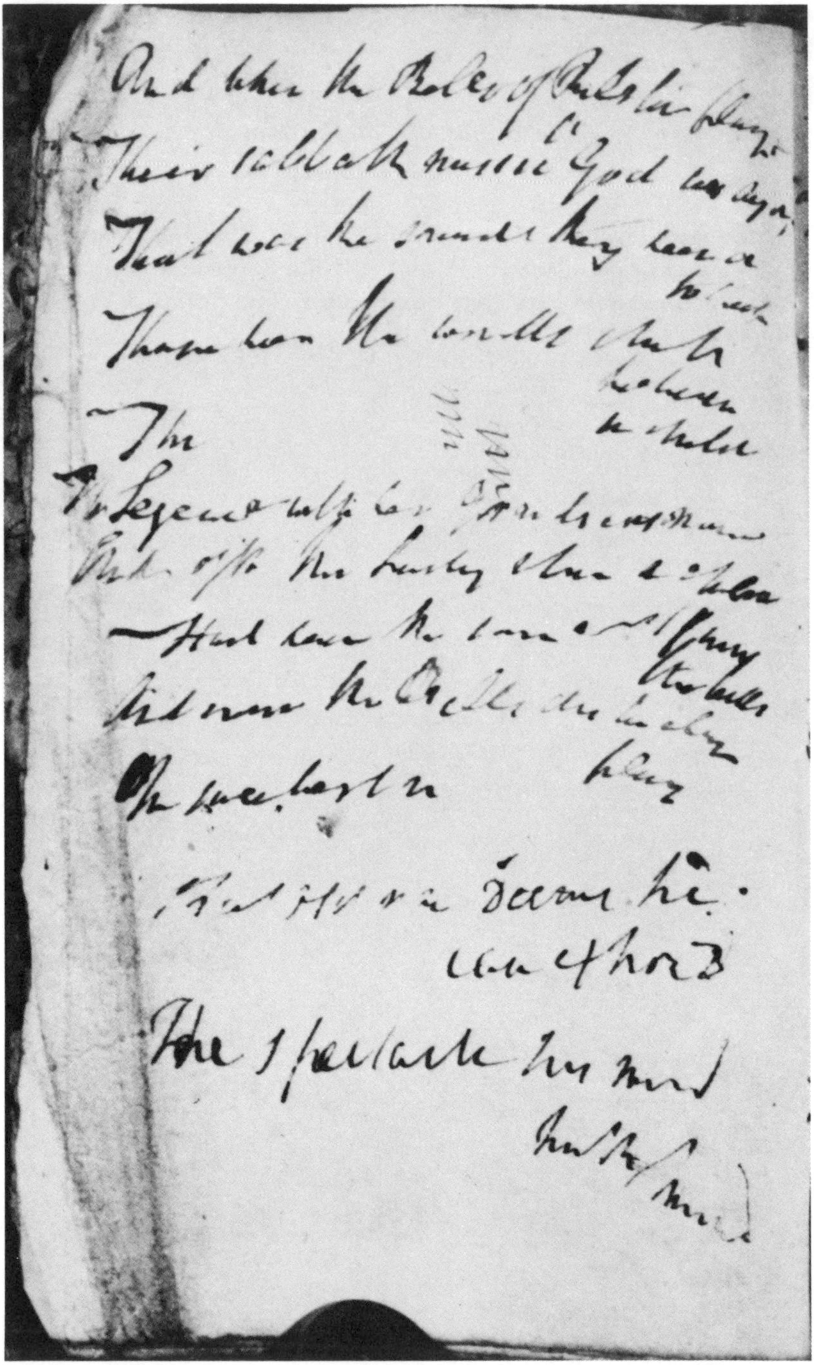

And when the Bells of Rilston playd
Their sabbath music "God us ayd,—
That was the sounds they heard
                                    to speak
Those were the words which
                [?She when]
                a child

The
The Legend with her Grandsires name
And ofth the Lady when a child
—Had heard the sounds & now
                            the bells
And now the Bells distinctly
                        play
The sweetest m

    That old man deems he
        ⌠he   can expound
    T⌡o spectacle his mind
                        hath found

Drafting further developed on 10ᵛ and 11ᵛ.

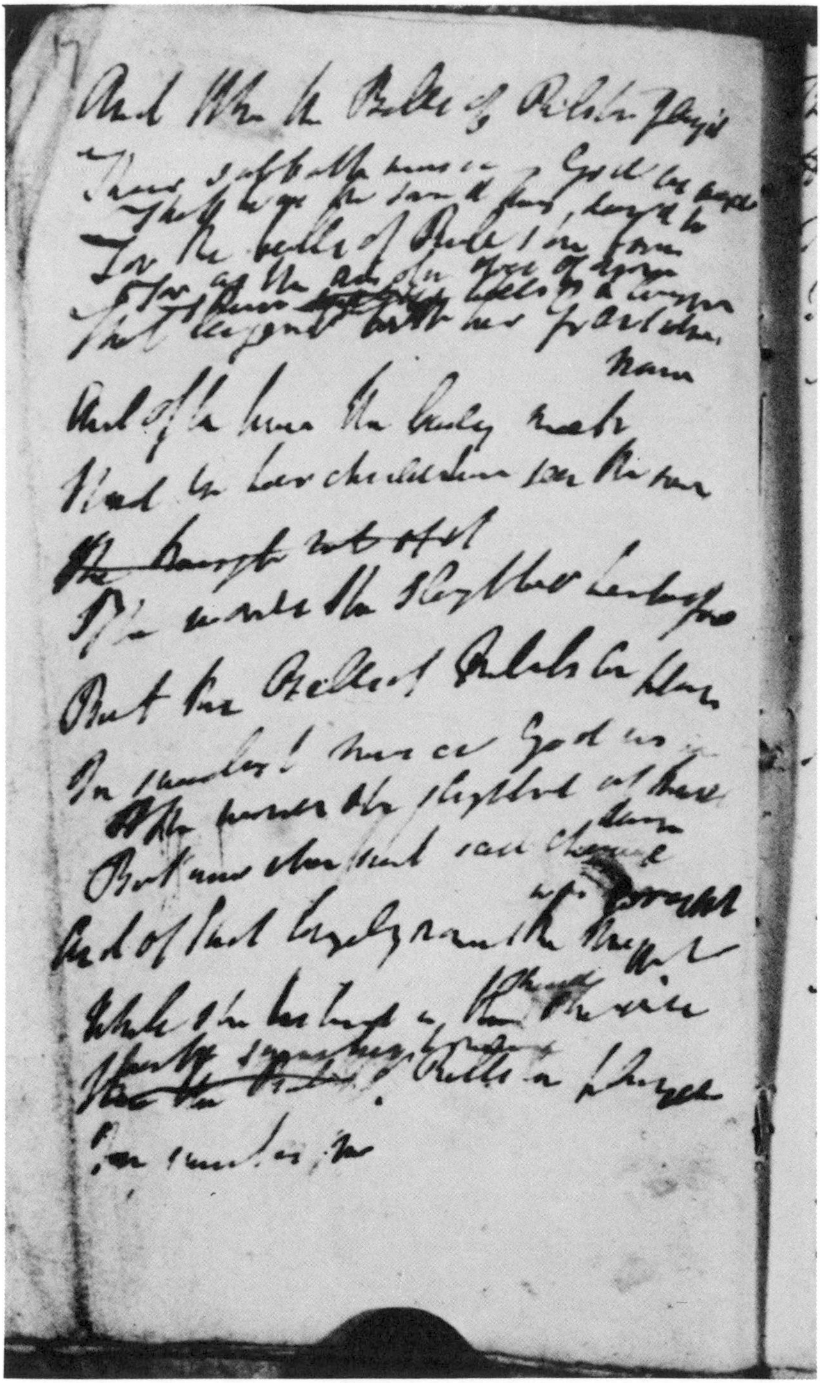

And When the Bells of Rilston play'd
Their sabbath music—God us ayd
   That was the sound they seem'd to
For the bells of Rileston bore
    For as the custom was of yore
      These [?holy] bells a legend
             ⌠bore
   That legend which ⌡with her Grandsires
                    name
And oftn times the lady meek
Had in her child [?time] seen the same
~~She though not of it~~
The words She slighted hertofore
But the Bells of Rililston play
In sweetest music God us ai
    ⌠The   ⌠at
    ⌡[?] words she slighted at th⌡[?]
               day
   But now when such sad change
             was wroght
And of that lonely name she thought
         [?shade]
While she listend in the [?shaded]
    With sweetest music
~~[?When] the Bells~~ of Rillston playd
In sweeter m

A further development of 9ᵛ, leading to the fullest version on 11ᵛ.

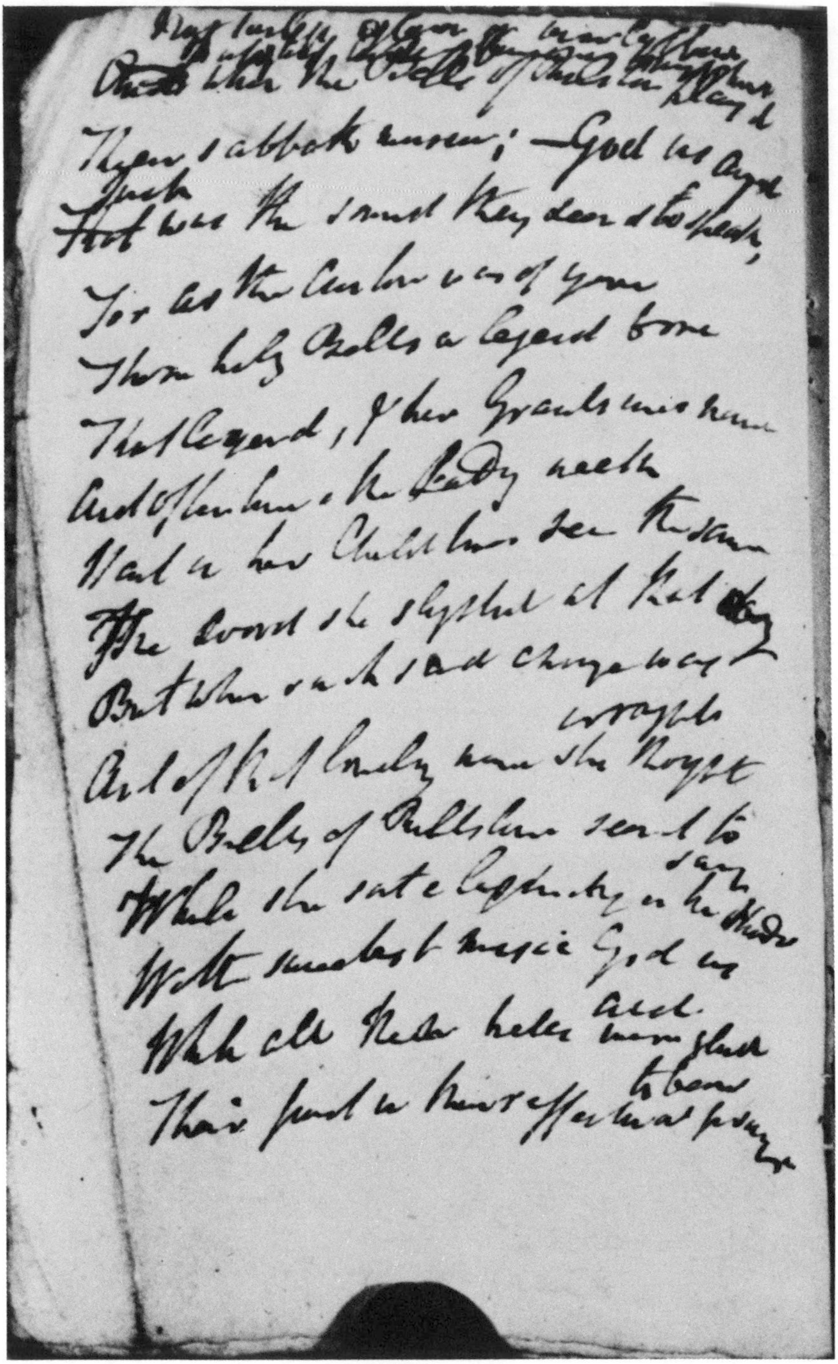

Not sunless gloom or unenlightened
    But often tender fancies brightened
~~And~~ when the Bells of Rilston play'd
Their sabbath music:—God us ayd
  Such
~~That~~ was the sound they seemd to speak,
For as the Custom was of yore
These holy Bells a legend bore
That legend, & her Grandsires name
And oftentimes the Lady meek
Had in her Childtime seen the same
T⎫   w⎫   ⎰day
F⎰he [?s]⎰ord she slightd at that ⎱ [?]
But when such sad change was
                    wrought
And of that lonely name she thought
The Bells of Rillstone seemd to
                    say
W⎫   ⎰ listening
T⎰hile she sate ⎱[?legend] in the shade
With sweetest music God us
                    aid
        ⎰ ir
While all the⎱[?se] hills were glad
                    to bear
Their part in their effectual prayer

The most finished of the three versions on 9v, 10v, and 11v.

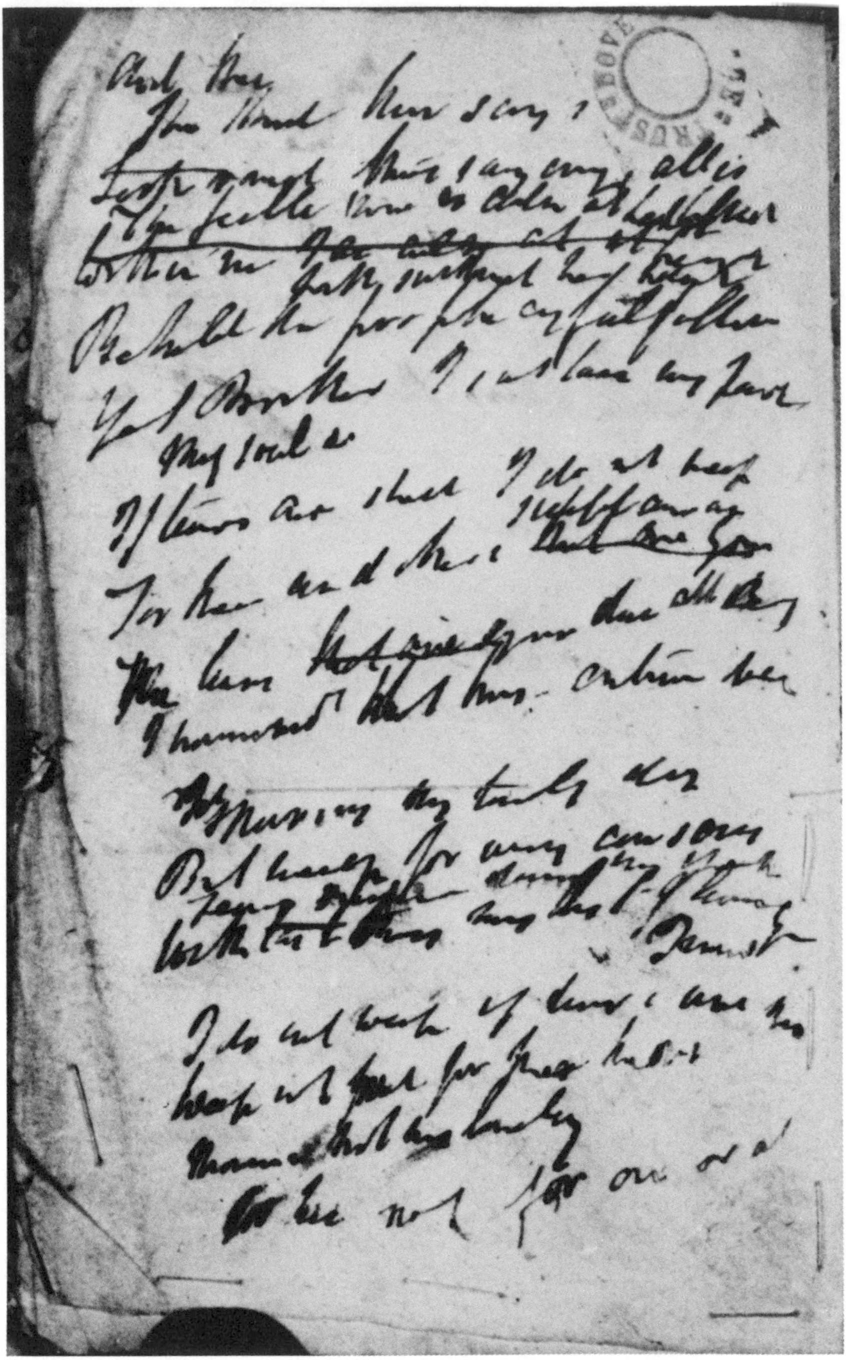

And th[?en]
  She Heard him say i
~~Look r~~ound thus saying all is
                stilled
  The feeble [?Now] is calm at heart
~~Within me I am calm at at~~ heart
       hath subdued her heart
Behold the prophecy fulfilled
Yet Brother I sustain my part,
  My soul s
If tears are shed I do not weep
          swept away
For thee and others ~~that are gone~~
⌠The   ⌠lay
⌡[?] tears ~~that are y~~our due all ⌡[?]
       what⌡
I [?mourned] [?that]⌡ this crture may

   ⌠[?Yet]
   ⌡[?]
    [?Mourning my lonely day]
But [?weeep] for very company
       ⌠[?run]
 [?Tears] ⌡[?] [?down my cheek]
With ~~last~~ [?this] my last & living
             Friend

I do not weep if tears are [?shed]
     ⌠ for
Weep not ⌡[?that] for [?their heart]
Mourn not my lady
[?for her] not for one or al

Related to drafting on 14ᵛ.

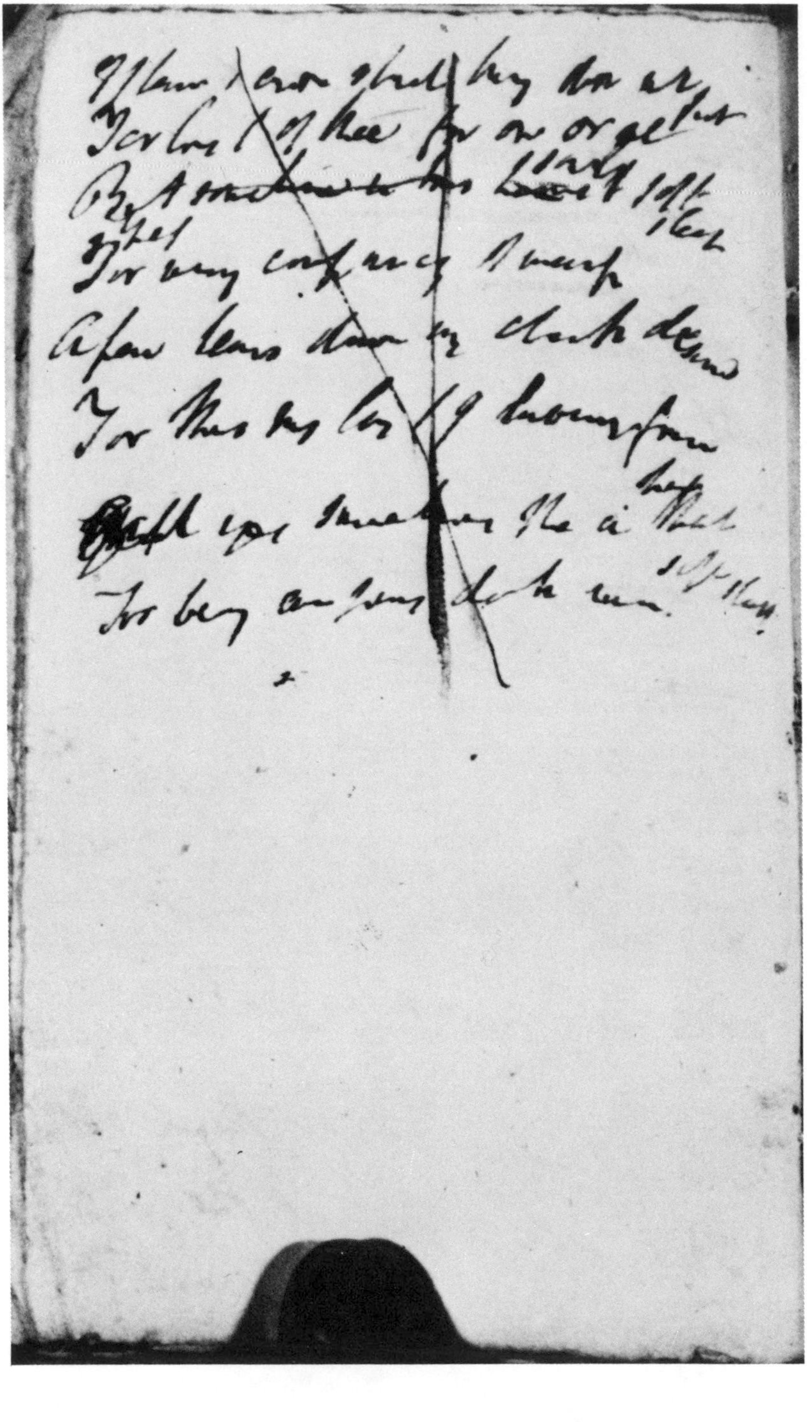

If tears are shed they do not
              fall
For lost of thee for one or al
          souls
But ~~sometimes in [?my heaviest]~~ soft
              sleep
  Yet
For very company I weep
A few tears down my cheek descend
For this my last & living friend
 { But   her
 {[?Yet] yet sometimes She in that
            soft sleep
For very company doth seem

Related to drafting on 12ᵛ.

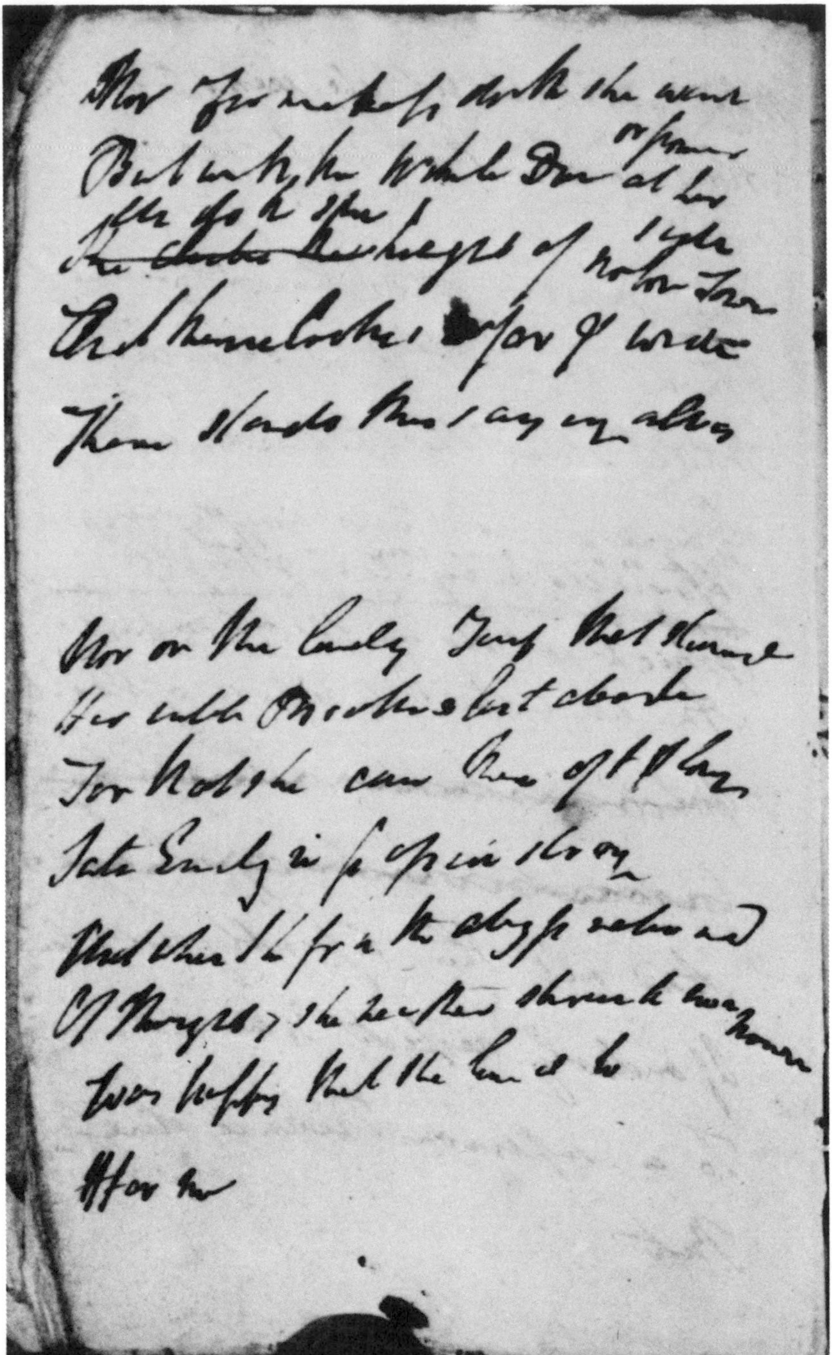

Nor Firmness doth she want
                      or power
But with her White Doe at her
                            side
     Up doth she
~~She climbs the~~ height of Norton Tower
A⎫
T⎰nd thence looks [?] far & wide
Then stands thus saying [?alone]

Nor on the lonely Turf that showed
Her noble Brothers last abode
For that she came there oft & long
Sate Emily in passion strong
And when She from th abyss returnd
Of thought, she neither shrunk nor mourn
Was happy that she livd to
Her m

And whether with the clouds they
Some ——— of —— regard to day
——— known a her kneel to pray
To kneel on any ——— prair
But ——— ——— ———

——— ———
The —— ———

——— Emily ——— in
The lonely Doe ———
———
Her ——— ——— in

[16ᵛ]

And hither hath she clomb this
                              day
      —[?trib]
Some ~~look of~~ kind regard to
                          g⎫
                           ⎬[?give]
Fair Service in her kind to pay
To steal away some pain
But how can Emily take he

Alas her pains [?one] [?   ]
                        [?]
She may bound   or [?prort] or
                              feed

How can Emily [?take he]
The lovely Doe may bound or feed
                among [?   ]
              ⎰upon yon
    Repose ⎱~~or play~~ tombs or play
    How [?kneeling] Emily Em

Further developed on 17ᵛ, 18ᵛ, 19ᵛ, and 20ᵛ.

[17ᵛ]

What {a
     {[?]nxious moments have been
                          counted
Here, or on lofty Simon-seat
{Or
{And somestimes, too, the White doe
                          mountetet
Following her with [?doubtfull] feet
At distance following for through
                          fear
The willing Creature came not near
And Hither had she clomb this day
Some look of kind regard to [?give]
But still neglected & [? rejecte]
    All its [? ? ? ?]
       And [? ? ? ? ? ?]
                             {eed
~~The lovely doe~~ may bound or f{l
       B[?] lovely Doe [? ?]
Repose upon the turf or play
How [?can] Emily [?would] take no
                          heed
      {he
But s{a at length is wholly
                 check
Or hath yield d to neglect
    I see not
~~She follows~~ not this rueful day
    Bu }
[?Tha]t feeds lesewhere [?her] & well she

Further drafts toward the most finished version, on 20ᵛ.

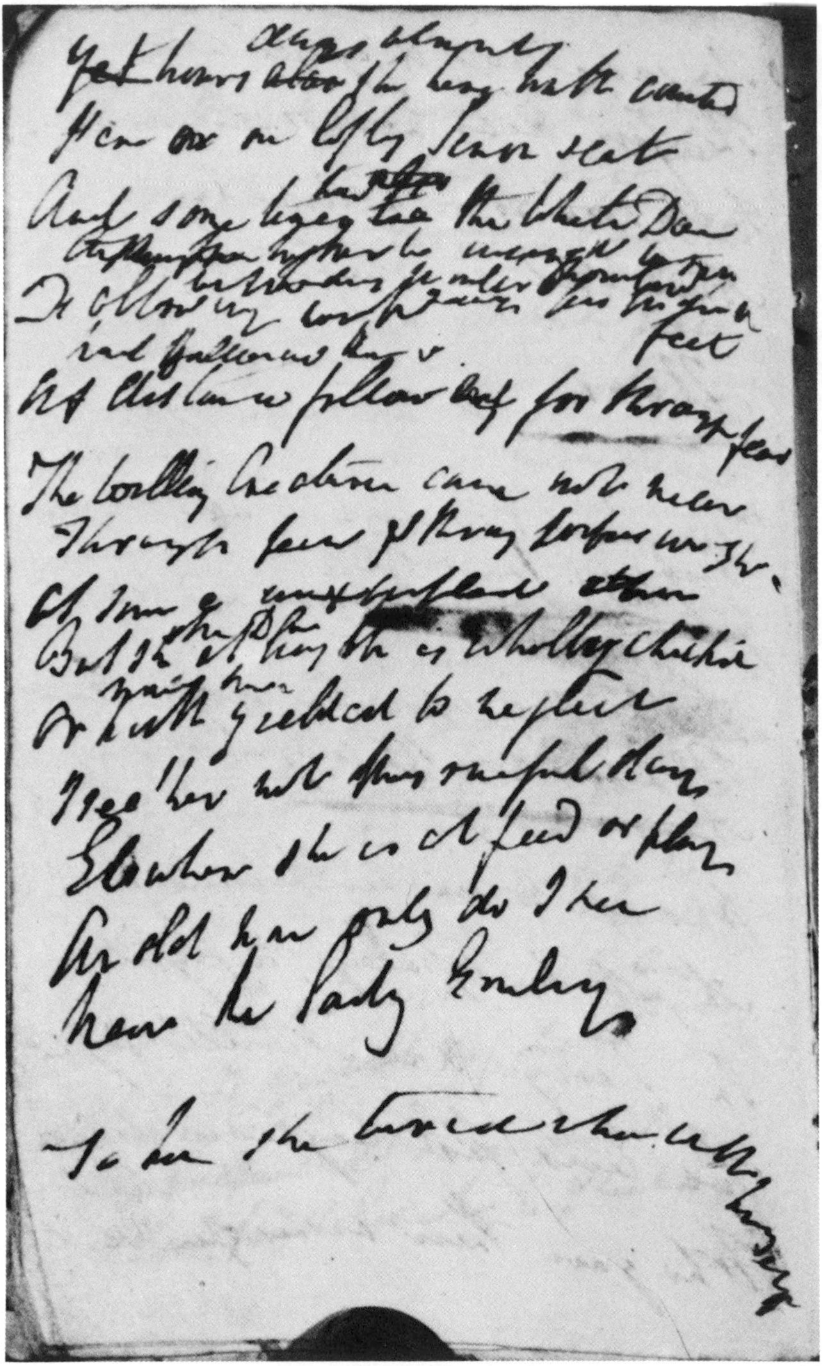

[18v]

days almost
~~Yet~~ hours ~~alas~~ she here hath counted
{or
Here {on on lofty Simon seat
had ~~also~~
And sometimes ~~too~~ the White Doe
{[?Though] mounted
A{nd th hitherto unused to roam
[?heavy] wanderd
with [?] [?hesitating]
Following with feet
had followed [?her] w
{ed
At distance follow{ing for through fear
The willing Creature came not near
Through fear & thrug [?honfusion strge]
c}
At some unexampled t}hange
the Doe
But she at length is wholly check'd
may have
Or hath yielded to neglect
I see her not this rueful day
Elswhere she is at feed or play
An old man only do I see
Near the Lady Emliy

To him she turnd who with his eye

Further drafts toward the most finished version, on 20v.

wander

Unmoved to follow fair for here
Yes! with her Lady thro' the Claw
of distance

But love or solace sped the horse
The Lady Eleanor looks now gone
And the Doe is wholly cheerful

There stopp'd her think it was
losst that this unwonted Spring
satisfied
                            wherein she supplies
she to to heck would return her love
And the delight to if my
Nor fell her to run a law

[19ᵛ]

          wander
Unused to ~~follow~~ far from home
Yet with the Lady there she clomb
At distant

But love or notice found she none
The ~~lady~~ natural looks were gone
And the Doe is wholly checkd

         '⎞
There stopp ⎰d her thirst was
                satisfied
With what this innocent spring
               supplied
  A sanction inwardly she
            bore
She to to that world return d no
              more
⎰And⎞
⎱ A ⎰
  Th⎰ the delights of human kind
        [?]
     [?their] [?]
⎰Nor   ⎰or
⎱[?] felt the ⎱[?] huma [?]

   The first half of this leaf contains further drafts toward the most finished version, on 20ᵛ; the drafting on the second half is related to drafts on 22ᵛ. In the seventh line the added comma is in pencil.

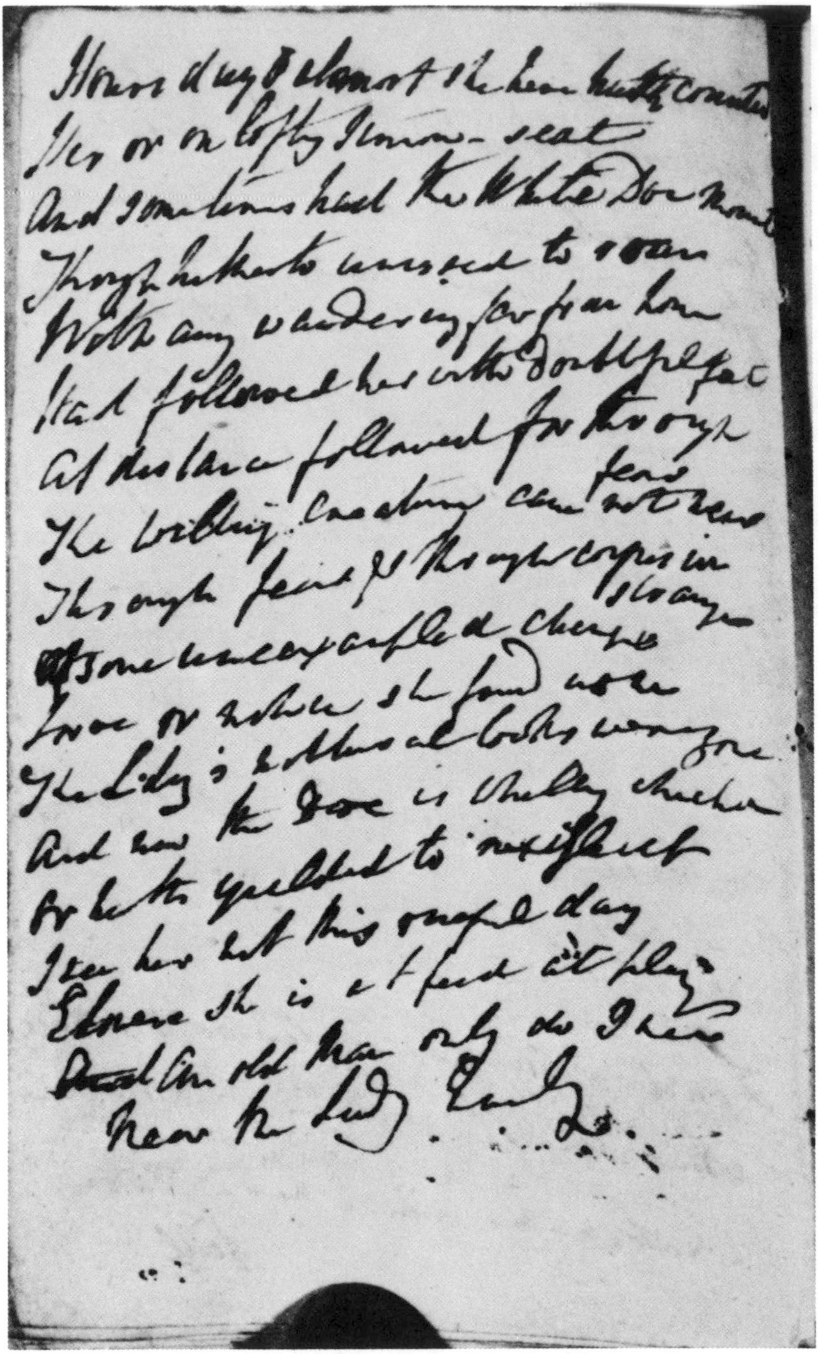
Hours a day & almost the [illegible] counted
Her or on lofty Stone-seat
And sometimes had the White Doe near
Though hitherto unused to roam
With any wanderings far from home
Had followed her with doubtful feet
At distance followed for through
The willing creature came not near
fear
Through fear & through caprice in
strange
Of some unaccountable change
Love or whatever she found none
The Lady's [illegible] all both were gone
And now the Doe is [illegible]
Or better yielded to neglect
I see her not this [illegible] day
Elsewhere she is at feed at play
~~[illegible]~~ An old Man only do I see
Near the Lady [illegible] . . . . . .

[20ᵛ]

⌠th
Hours days almost she here ha⌡d counted
Her or on lofty Simon-seat
And sometimes had the White Doe mounted
Though hitherto unused to roam
With any wandering far from home
Had followed her with doubtful feet
At distance followed for through
                              fear
The willing creature came not near
Through fear & through confusion
                                    strange
⌠At
⌡[?] some uneexampled change
Lovoe or notice she found none
The Lady's nattural looks were gone
              D⌡
And now the d⌡oe is wholly checkd
Or hath yielded to [?negglect]
I see her not this rueful day
Elswere she is at feed at play
~~And~~ An old Man only do I see
    Near the Lady Emily

The most finished version of drafts on 16ᵛ, 17ᵛ, 18ᵛ, and 19ᵛ.

```
                        viewless
        Such as [ ? ] invisible Spirits
        Power which the viewless Spirits

        All hors'd & harness'd with him
                                    to ride

                        ⎧ by
                        ⎨ with    with ⎧ P      ⎧ —
        A mortal song we sing but       ⎨ powers ⎨ ,
                                        bowr
            are given us
        Assisted from celestial bowers
            Falls [?on us] invisib
            [?]           [ ? ]
        Are by the [?orien oren] Spirit shed
            The same
        By whom we were first visited
                    ⎧ V
        Whose ⎨ voice we heard, whose hand
                                    & wigns
                        the conscious
        Seemd like a breeze to touch his
                                    strings
                in   apart in
        When left in solitude erewhile
                w left alone
        We stood [?beside] the
                        ⎧ h
        In presence of this ⎨ [?]oary pile

        When left in solitude erewhile
        We stood before this Ruined Pile
        And quitting unsubstantial dreams
```

Drafting continues on 22ᵛ and 23ᵛ. The third line visible in the photograph is related to revision on the facing recto; see transcription of 22ʳ, p. 279, above.

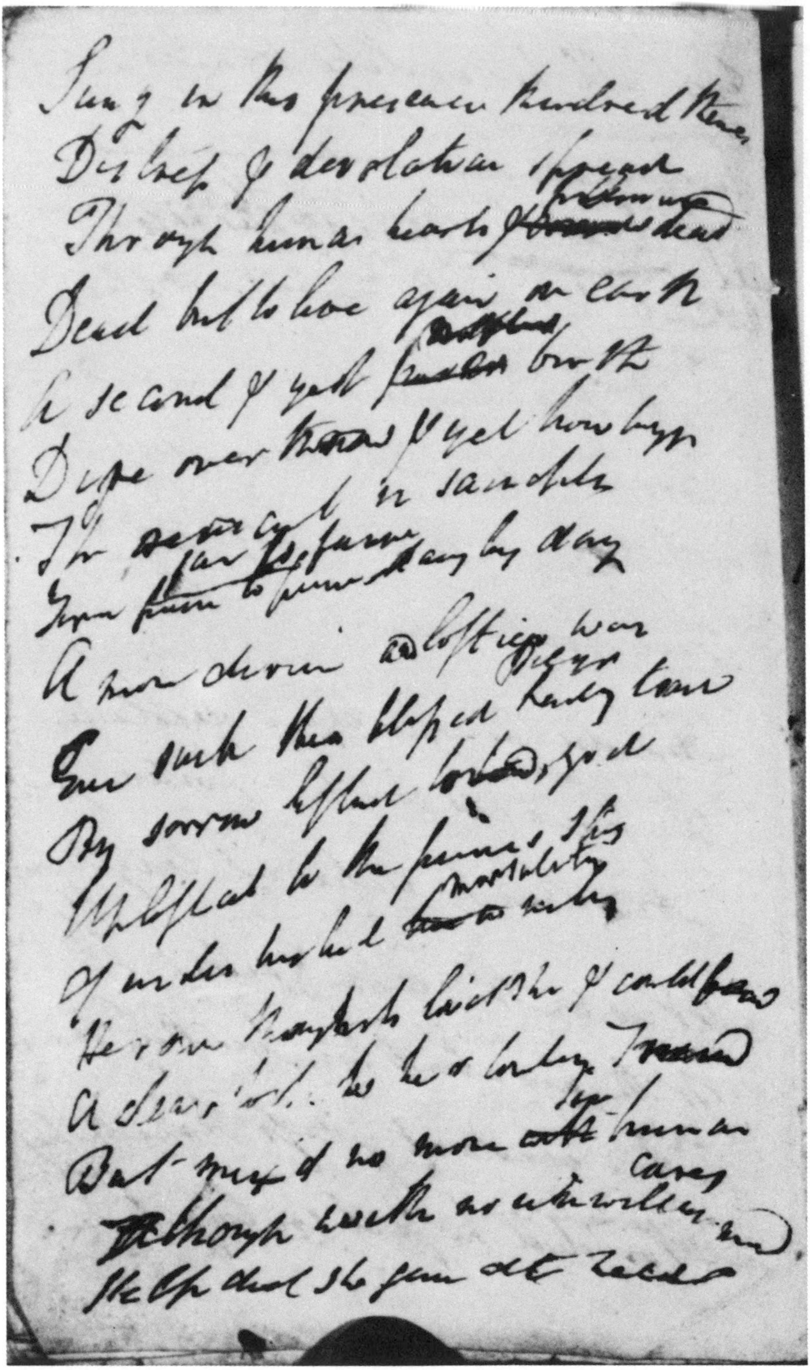

Sung in this presence kindred themes
Distress & desolation spread
                              pleasure
Through human hearts & ~~sorrow~~ dead
Dead but to live again on earth
                    ⎰ nobler
                    ⎱[?   ]
                         ⎰ er
A second & yet ~~pur[?]~~ birth
     ⎰   re   ⎰ throw
Di⎰[?rge] over ⎱[?them] & yet how high
   reas ⎱
The as ⎰cent in sanctity
              fair to faire
From ~~pure to~~ purer—day by day
                    ⎰nd
A more divine a⎱   loftier way
                         Pilgr
Even such this blessed Lady trod
                    ⎰ towards ⎰
By sorrow lifted ⎱[?to] [?her]⎱ god
Uplifted to the pures sky
                    mortality
Of undisturbed ~~human~~ity
              ⎡ hsts ⎤
         ⎰oug⎱h
Her own th⎱[?] ing lov'd she & could bend
A dear look to her lowley Friend
                         in
But mix'd no more ~~with~~ human
                              cares
A⎰
T⎱lthough w with no unwilling mind
Help did she give at need

Drafting continued from 21ᵛ and continuing on 23ᵛ. Some of it relates to drafting on the second half of 19ᵛ.

The Wharfdale Peasants in her hour
At length thus sorrowfully, sorrowfully teach
To cast she was self free & deer
Thy soul quellux Emily
Thou of the blasted family
Drove to the Heaven & for a shroud
— In R Aston Churchyard her mortal
was buried by her brother's side

Roof glow giving ray start of the day
In news a gleam of twilight gray

The Wharfdale Peasants in their
                              prayers
At length thus faintly faintly tied
To earth She was set free & died
                  E⎤
Thy Soul exalted F⎦mily
                  F⎤
Maid of the blasted E⎦amily
R⎤
[?]⎦ose to the Heaven from which
                              it came.
—In Rilston Church her mortal
                              frame
                       ⎧ M
Was burried by her ⎨ [——?——]
                       ⎩
                  Mother's sid

⎧What
⎨[?And] glowing sunset & a ray
Survives a gleam of twilight
                              grey

Drafting continued from 21ᵛ and 22ᵛ.

The White Doe of Rylstone
Selected Revisions in MS. 1832/36
at Wellesley College

The following transcriptions contain revisions written into one page of a copy of *Poetical Works* (1832) used in preparation of the 1836 edition of *Poetical Works,* now in the English Poetry Collection, Wellesley College Library. The revisions that appear in roman type are in Wordsworth's hand; those in italic type are in the hand of Dora Wordsworth or John Carter. The entire page was covered by a paste-over, itself mostly covered by a second paste-over. Both are lifted for the transcriptions, in which the 1832 printed text is rendered in boldface type. The two pasted-down revision slips are numbered editorially according to the pages to which they were attached, with the suffixes "P1" and "P2" added to the base page numbers. Line numbers of the 1832 text appear in brackets at the upper right.

106　　　　　THE WHITE DOE　　　CA

Their motions, turning round and round,
His ~~w~~ hand the Banner held;
And ~~night, by savage zeal impelled,~~
~~Forth rushed a Pikeman, as if he,~~
~~Not without harsh indignity,~~
~~Would seize the same: — instinctively~~
~~To smite the Offender,~~ — with his lance
Did Francis from the brake advance;
But, from behind, a treacherous wound
Unfeeling, brought him to the ground,
A mortal stroke :— oh grief to tell !
Thus, thus, the noble Francis fell;
There did he lie of breath forsaken;
The Banner from his grasp was taken,
A ultingly away;
An ody was left on the ground where it lay

Two days, as many nights, ~~he slept~~
Alone, unnoticed, ~~and unwept;~~
For at that time distress and fear
Possessed the Country far and near;
The third day, One, who chanced to pass,
Beheld him stretched upon the grass.
~~A gentle Forester was he,~~
~~And of the Norton Tenantry ;~~
And he had heard that by a Train
Of Horsemen Francis had been slain
Much was he troubled — for the Man
~~Hath recognised his pallid face ;~~
And to the nearest Huts he ran,
And called the People to the place.
 How desolate is Rylstone-hall !
 was the instant thought of all;
And if the lonely Lady there

106

       Their motions, turning round and round:—⌉

          [?]
While his ∧~~His~~ weaker hand the Banner held;

             a
      ~~And straight, by savage zeal impelled,~~

~~To seize it~~ [?] the apparent [?aim]

      ~~Forth rushed a Pikeman, as if he,~~

~~To seize it,~~   ~~Forth from the throng a [?Pikeman]~~

      ~~Not without harsh indignity,~~

~~With scornful threats~~

      ~~Would seize the same:—instinctively—~~

~~Urged to repel the indignity~~

      ~~To~~ smite the Offender—with his lance

   And

      Did Francis from the brake advance;

      But, from behind, a treacherous wound

   That instant

      ~~Unfeeling~~, brought him to the ground,

      A mortal stroke:—oh grief to tell!

   And as

      ~~Thus, thus,~~ the noble Francis fell:

   And life poured out her crimson f[?]

      There did he lie of breath forsaken;

   It mingled with the pictured blood

      The Banner from his grasp was taken,

   As He whose side was pierced upon

      And borne exultingly away;

      And the Body was left on the ground where it lay.

                unwept
      Two days, as many nights, ~~he slept~~

                    an
      Alone, unnoticed, ~~and unwept;~~ Francis

      For at that time distress and fear

      Possessed the Country far and near;

      The third day, One, who chanced to pass,

      Beheld him stretched upon the grass.

      ~~A gentle Forester was he,~~

      ~~And of the Norton Tenantry;~~

      And he had heard that by a Train

      Of Horsemen Francis had been slain.

      Much was he troubled—for the Man

      Hath recognised his pallid face;

      And to the nearest Huts he ran,

      And called the People to the place.

      —How desolate is Rylstone-hall!

   This

      ~~Such~~ was the instant thought of all;

      And if the lonely Lady there

      Sho[   ]

100 The Assailants, turning round and round
But from behind with treacherous wound
A Spearman brought him to the ground;
~~...~~
~~...~~
~~...~~
~~...~~
~~...~~
More deeply tinged the embroidered show
If his whole side was pierced upon the Rood.
The horsemen slipped & bore away
The Standard; and where Francis lay
There was he left alone, unwept,
And for two days unnoticed slept.
For ~~...~~ that time ~~bewildering~~ fear
Possessed the country, far and near;
But, on the third day, passing by
One of the Norton Tenantry
Espied the uncovered corse; the Man
Shrunk as he recognized the face,
And to the nearest homesteads ran
And called the People to the place.
How desolate is Rylstone-Hall!
This was the instant thought of all;
And if the lonely Lady there
Squid be, to her they cannot bear
The weight of anguish and despair.

106

The Assailants, turning round and round;
But from behind {with/a} *treacherous wound*
A Spearman brought him to the ground
~~*Grasping the Banner Francis fell*~~
~~*To rise no more; and there, as low*~~
~~*He lay on earth, O grief to tell,*~~
~~*The gushing current of life blood*~~
~~*With* }
~~*[?]*~~ *}* ~~*[?penetrative] overflow*~~
More deeply tinged the em{b/l}*proidered sh*{o/l}*ew*
Of His whose side was pierced upon the Rood.

The Horsemen s{ei/lie}*zed & bore away*

The Standard,{;/}* and where Francis lay*
There was he left alone, unwept,
And for two days unnoticed slept.
                    bewildering
For at that time ~~*distress and*~~ *fear*
   [?Bewildering]
Possessed the Country, far and near;
But, on the third day, passing by
One of the Norton Tenantry
Espied the uncovered Corse; the Man
Shrunk as he recognized the face,
And to the nearest homesteads ran
And called the People to the place.
—}
}Now desolate is Rylstone-{h/l}*Hall!*
This was the instant thought of all;
And if the lonely Lady there
Should be; to her they cannot bear
This weight of anguish and despair.

The first 10 lines were revised by WW, the rest by Dora; she erased "[?Bewildering]" where she first entered it, apparently by mistake, below the 16th line.

[1509–1515]

to the ground.
The guardian lance, as Francis fell,
Dropped from him; but his other hand
The Banner clenched; till, from out the Band,
One, the most eager for the prize,

Rushed in; and⎰ while, O grief to tell!
(A glimmering sense still left) with eyes
Unclosed the noble Francis lay—
Seized it, as hunters seize their prey,
But not before the warm life blood
Had tinged with searching overflow,
More deeply

The hand is John Carter's.

Transcriptions: Parallel Texts

The Force of Prayer: Dorothy Wordsworth's Letter
to Jane Marshall, 18 October 1807, facing

DC MS. 61

Dorothy Wordsworth to Jane Marshall, 18 October 1807, facing DC MS. 61

The earliest surviving version of *The Force of Prayer* is a fair copy transcribed by Dorothy Wordsworth in a letter to Jane Marshall dated 18 October 1807 (see *MY*, I, 167–169). The letter is a single untrimmed folio sheet of white wove paper, folded to make a bifolium measuring 33.2 to 33.5 centimeters high by 41.2 to 41.5 centimeters wide, watermarked 1801. The paper is the same as that used for DC MS. 61 (see the headnote to the transcription of the prose "Advertizement," p. 185, above. The only other early version of the poem is in William Wordsworth's hand, entered on what now comprises the last four versos of DC MS. 61 after the rectos had been used for *The White Doe;* this version dates from sometime between the date of Dorothy's letter and the spring of 1808. It is arrayed in transcription, below, facing a transcription of the text in the letter.

Dorothy gave the poem no title, calling it only "a short one . . . on the story of young Romelli and the Strid," and offered it in lieu of *The White Doe,* which William was "now writing." The false starts and revisions in MS. 61 show William drafting a title there. Convincing evidence of priority lies in a line (l. 30) where Dorothy twice revised her transcript of a word, and finally settled on the version that appears in the base text of MS. 61 and in the published versions of 1815.

Both of the 1815 printings of the poem, the first in the two-volume collection of *Poems* (where it appeared among "Poems of Sentiment and Reflection") and the second, about a month later, at the end of *The White Doe* volume, are closer to the text in MS. 61 than to the text in Dorothy's letter of 1808. All variant readings in the printed texts through 1850 are shown in Carl Ketcham's edition of *Shorter Poems: 1807–1820,* in this series (although an unauthorized version in the *Courier,* which Wordsworth declared "printed with vile incorrectness" [*MY*, II, 239] has been ignored).

Editorial line numbers in the left margins of the MS. 61 text correspond to those assigned to the text in Dorothy Wordsworth's letter; bracketed numbers at the upper right correspond to the lines in the version printed with *The White Doe* in 1815.

1   *"What is good for a bootless bene?"*
2   *The Lady answer'd, "Endless sorrow"*
3   *Her words are plain; but the Falconer's words*
4   *Are a path that is dark to travel thorough.*

5   *These words I bring from the Banks of Wharf,*
6   *Dark words to front an ancient tale:*

                                                    spring
7   *And their meaning is, Whence can comfort* ~~sprung~~
8   *When prayer is of no avail?*   ∧

9   *"What is good for a bootless bene?"*
10 *The Falconer to the Lady said,*
11 *And she made answer as ye have heard,*
12 *For she knew that her Son was dead.*

13 *She knew it from the Falconer's words,*
14 *And from the look of the Falconer's eye,*
15 *And from the love that was in her heart*
16 *For her youthful Romelli*

17 *Young Romelli to the Woods is gone,*
18 *And who doth on his steps attend?*
19 *He hath a Greyhound in a leash,*

                ⎰f
20 *A chosen* ⎱Forest *Friend.*

The force of Prayer
or the foun
<u>What is good for a bootless bene</u>

The force of prayer, ~~or the~~
F⎫   or the
f⎬ounding of Bolton ~~Abbey~~
                          Priory
a Tradition.

1	<u>What is good for a bootless Bene?</u>
2	The Lady answer'd, <u>Endless sorrow.</u>
3	Her words are clear; but the
	Falconer's words
4	Are a path which is dark to
	travel thorough.
	Dark
5	~~These~~ words I bring from the
	banks of Wharf,
6	Dark words! to front an antient Tale,—
7	And their meaning is, whence can
	comfort spring
	⎰n
8	Whe⎱re prayer is of no avail.
9	<u>What is good for a bootless Bene?</u>
10	The Falconer to the Lady said;

	⎰sorrow
	<u>Endless</u> ⎱[?]
11	And She made answer, ~~as Ye have~~
	~~heard,~~
12	For she knew that her Son was dead.
13	She knew it from the Falconer's
	words,
14	And from the look of the Falconer's
	eye,
15	And from the love which was
	in her heart
16	For her youthful Romilly.
17	Young Romilly to the woods is
	gone,
18	And who doth on his steps attend?
19	He hath a Greyhound in a leash,
20	A chosen, forrest Friend.

21   And they have reach'd that famous Chasm
22   Where he who dares may stride
23   Across the River Wharf, pent in
24   With rocks on either side.

[2ʳ]   [25–52]

25   And that striding place is call'd the <u>Strid</u>,
26   A name which it took of yore;
27   A thousand years hath it borne that name,
28   And shall a thousand more.

29   And thither is young Romelli come;
              ~~shall~~
30   And what ~~should~~ now forbid
              may
31   That He, perhaps for the hundredth time,
32   Shall bound across the Strid?

33   He sprang in glee; for what cared he
                                  ⸨r
34   That the River was strong, & the ⸨Rocks were steep?
35   But the Grey-hound in the Leash hung back,
36   And check'd him in his leap.

37   The Boy is in the arms of Wharf,
38   And strangled with a merciless force;
39   For never more was young Romelli seen
40   Till he was a lifeless corse.

41   Now is their stillness in the Vale
42   And long unspeaking sorrow,
43   Wharf has buried fonder hopes
44   Than e'er were drown'd in Yarrow.†

†alluding to a Ballad of Logan—

---

22   The commas, added later, are in pencil.

21   And the Pair have reached
                    that famous chasm,,

22   Where he⌉ who dares⌉ may stride
23   Across the River Wharf, pent in
24   With rocks on either side.

[MS. 61, 44ᵛ]   [25–36]

25   This Striding-place is called,
                    The Strid,
26   A name which it took of yore;
27   A thousand years hath it borne
                    that name,
28   And shall a thousand more.

29   And hither is young Romilly come,
30   And what may now forbid
31   That He, perhaps for the 100th
                            time,
32   Shall bound across The Strid.

33   He sprang in glee; for what
                    cared he
34   That the River was strong and
                    the rocks were
                            steep?
35   But the Greyhound in the
                    leash hung back
36   And check'd him in his leap.

[MS. 61, 45ᵛ]   [37–50]

37   The Boy is in the arms of Wharf,
38   And strangled with a merciless
                    force,
39   For never more was young Romilly
                            seen
                    ⌠C
40   Till he was a lifeless ⌡corse.——

41   Now is there stillness in the Vale,
42   And long unspeaking sorrow:
43   Wharf hath buried fonder hopes
44   Than ere were drown'd in Yarrow.

45   *If for a Lover the Lady wept*
46   *A comfort she might borrow*

        {*d*
47   *From* ⎰*Death, and from the passion of death;*
48   *Old Wharf might heal her sorrow.*

49   *She weeps not for the Wedding-day*
50   *That was to be tomorrow* *
51   *Her hope was a farther-looking hope,*
52   *And her's is a Mother's sorrow.*

[2ᵛ]   [53–72]

53   *Oh! was he not a comely tree?*
54   *And proudly did his branches wave,*

                  {*t*
55   *And the Root of this delightful* ⎰*Tree*
56   *Is in her Husband's grave.*

57   *Long, long in darkness did she sit,*
58   *And her first word was, "Let there be*
59   *At Bolton, in the Fields of Wharf*
60   *A stately Priory.*

    A̶
61   *And the stately Priory was rear'd,*
62   *And Wharf, as he moved along,*

     M ⎱
63   *To* [?]*atins join'd a mournful voice,*
64   *Nor fail'd at Even-song.*

65   *And the Lady pray'd in heaviness*
66   *That wish'd not for relief;*
67   *But slowly did her succour come,*
68   *And a patience to her grief.*

69   *Oh! there is never sorrow of heart*
70   *That shall lack a timely end*
71   *If but to God we turn, & ask*
72   *Of him to be our Friend.*

    —From the same Ballad—

---

61 Deletion by erasure.

45   If for a Lover the Lady wept
46   A solace she might borrow
47   From death, and from the
                        passion of death,
48   Old Wharf might heal her sorrow.

49   She weeps not for the Wedding-day
50   That was to be to morrow;

50/   The MS. 61 text breaks off here.